Sermons On The Second Readings

Series III

Cycle C

Richard Gribble, CSC
Steven E. Albertin
April Yamasaki
Charles L. Aaron Jr.
Scott Suskovic

CSS Publishing Company, Inc., Lima, Ohio

SERMONS ON THE SECOND READINGS, SERIES III, CYCLE C

Copyright © 2009 by
CSS Publishing Company, Inc.
Lima, Ohio

All rights reserved. No part of this publication may be reproduced in any manner whatsoever without the prior permission of the publisher, except in the case of brief quotations embodied in critical articles and reviews. Inquiries should be addressed to: Permissions, CSS Publishing Company, Inc., 517 South Main Street, Lima, Ohio 45804.

Some scripture quotations are from the New Revised Standard Version of the Bible, copyright 1989 by the Division of Christian Education of the National Council of the Churches of Christ in the USA. Used by permission.

Some scripture quotations are from the Holy Bible, New Living Translation, copyright © 1996. Used by permission of Tyndale House Publishers, Inc., Wheaton, Illinois 60189. All rights reserved.

Some scripture quotations are from the Revised Standard Version of the Bible, copyrighted 1946, 1952 ©, 1971, 1973, by the Division of Christian Education of the National Council of the Churches of Christ in the USA. Used by permission.

For more information about CSS Publishing Company resources, visit our website at www.csspub.com or email us at custserv@csspub.com or call (800) 241-4056.

Cover design by Barbara Spencer

ISSN: 1937-1454

ISBN-13: 978-0-7880-2620-1
ISBN-10: 0-7880-2620-8   PRINTED IN USA

Table Of Contents

**Sermons For Sundays
In Advent, Christmas, And Epiphany**
Gifts Of Thanksgiving
by Richard Gribble, CSC

Preface	15
Advent 1 Thanksgiving Means Giving 1 Thessalonians 3:9-13	19
Advent 2 Jesus — The Leader Of Our Team Philippians 1:3-11	25
Advent 3 Rejoicing Brings Peace Philippians 4:4-7	29
Advent 4 Obedience: Our Gift To Jesus Hebrews 10:5-10	35
Christmas Eve/Christmas Day Leading Others To Jesus Titus 2:11-14	41
Christmas 1 Learning The Recipe For Love Colossians 3:12-17	47

Christmas 2   53
    The Hidden Gifts Of Christ
    Ephesians 1:3-14

The Epiphany Of Our Lord   59
    Ambassadors Of The Lord
    Ephesians 3:1-12

The Baptism Of Our Lord
Epiphany 1
Ordinary Time 1   65
    Responsibility Comes With Privilege
    Acts 8:14-17

Epiphany 2
Ordinary Time 2   71
    Strength Through Diversity
    1 Corinthians 12:1-11

Epiphany 3
Ordinary Time 3   77
    Teammates In Building The Kingdom
    1 Corinthians 12:12-31a

Epiphany 4
Ordinary Time 4   83
    Love — The Basic Christian Call
    1 Corinthians 13:1-13

Epiphany 5
Ordinary Time 5   89
    The Great Sacrifice Of Love
    1 Corinthians 15:1-11

Epiphany 6   95
Ordinary Time 6
    Raised To New Life Today
    1 Corinthians 15:12-20

Epiphany 7   101
Ordinary Time 7
    Formula For Eternal Life
    1 Corinthians 15:35-38, 42-50

Epiphany 8   107
Ordinary Time 8
    Christ: The Victor Over Death
    1 Corinthians 15:51-58

Epiphany 9   113
Ordinary Time 9
    Don't Compromise Your Beliefs
    Galatians 1:1-12

The Transfiguration Of Our Lord   119
(Last Sunday After Epiphany)
    Transformed To Christ
    2 Corinthians 3:12—4:2

**Sermons For Sundays
In Lent And Easter**
But!
by Steven E. Albertin

Preface   127

Ash Wednesday   129
    Show Me Your Credentials
    2 Corinthians 5:20b—6:10

Lent 1   135
    Did God Really Say...?
    Romans 10:8b-13

Lent 2 — 143
    Enemies Of The Cross
    Philippians 3:17—4:1

Lent 3 — 151
    Passing The Test
    1 Corinthians 10:1-13

Lent 4 — 159
    A New Point Of View
    2 Corinthians 5:16-21

Lent 5 — 167
    Running The Race
    Philippians 3:4b-14

Passion/Palm Sunday — 175
    A Bloody Cheer!
    Philippians 2:5-11

Maundy Thursday — 181
    Meal Of Death
    1 Corinthians 11:23-26

Good Friday — 187
    A Bloody Sacrifice
    Hebrews 10:16-25

Easter Day — 191
    But…!
    1 Corinthians 15:19-26

Easter 2 — 197
    Cracking The Code
    Revelation 1:4-8

Easter 3 — 205
    The iPod Vs. The Larynx
    Revelation 5:11-14

Easter 4 215
    The Blood Of The Lamb And The Voice
        Of The Shepherd
    Revelation 7:9-17

Easter 5 221
    Heaven On Earth
    Revelation 21:1-6

Easter 6 227
    A Glimpse Of Glory
    Revelation 21:10, 22—22:5

The Ascension Of Our Lord 237
    It's A Good Thing He's Gone!
    Ephesians 1:15-23

Easter 7 243
    All In God's Time
    Revelation 22:12-14, 16-17, 20-21

**Sermons For Sundays
After Pentecost (First Third)**
Led By The Spirit
by April Yamasaki

Preface 253

The Day Of Pentecost 255
    Getting The Big Picture
    Romans 8:14-17

The Holy Trinity 261
    God's Chain Reaction
    Romans 5:1-5

Proper 4 267
Pentecost 2
Ordinary Time 9
    An Uncomplicated Gospel
    Galatians 1:1-12

Proper 5 273
Pentecost 3
Ordinary Time 10
    But When God ...
    Galatians 1:11-24

Proper 6 279
Pentecost 4
Ordinary Time 11
    Living With Integrity
    Galatians 2:15-21

Proper 7 285
Pentecost 5
Ordinary Time 12
    Thicker Than Blood
    Galatians 3:23-29

Proper 8 291
Pentecost 6
Ordinary Time 13
    Freedom Calling
    Galatians 5:1, 13-25

Proper 9 297
Pentecost 7
Ordinary Time 14
    On Not Giving Up
    Galatians 6:(1-6) 7-16

Proper 10　　　　　　　　　　　　　　　　　　303
Pentecost 8
Ordinary Time 15
　For All The Saints
　Colossians 1:1-14

Proper 11　　　　　　　　　　　　　　　　　　309
Pentecost 9
Ordinary Time 16
　Sing Praise
　Colossians 1:15-28

Sermons For Sundays
After Pentecost (Middle Third)
Faith, Hope, And Love: From Paul And After Paul
by Charles L. Aaron Jr.

Proper 12　　　　　　　　　　　　　　　　　　317
Pentecost 10
Ordinary Time 17
　When God Adds Insult To Injury
　Colossians 2:6-15

Proper 13　　　　　　　　　　　　　　　　　　325
Pentecost 11
Ordinary Time 18
　Killing What Is Already Dead
　Colossians 3:1-11

Proper 14　　　　　　　　　　　　　　　　　　331
Pentecost 12
Ordinary Time 19
　The Assurance Of Things Hoped For
　Hebrews 11:1-3, 8-16

Proper 15   337
Pentecost 13
Ordinary Time 20
    Running With Perseverance
    Hebrews 11:29—12:2

Proper 16   343
Pentecost 14
Ordinary Time 21
    God As A Consuming Fire
    Hebrews 12:18-29

Proper 17   349
Pentecost 15
Ordinary Time 22
    The Unchanging Christ In A Changing World
    Hebrews 13:1-8, 15-16

Proper 18   355
Pentecost 16
Ordinary Time 23
    From Slave To Brother
    Philemon 1-21

Proper 19   361
Pentecost 17
Ordinary Time 24
    The Utmost Patience For The Foremost Sinner
    1 Timothy 1:12-17

Proper 20   367
Pentecost 18
Ordinary Time 25
    A Peaceful Life In An Unpeaceful World
    1 Timothy 2:1-7

Proper 21 371
Pentecost 19
Ordinary Time 26
   How Rich Is Rich?
   1 Timothy 6:6-19

Proper 22 377
Pentecost 20
Ordinary Time 27
   Guarding The Treasure
   2 Timothy 1:1-14

Sermons For Sundays After Pentecost (Last Third)
A New Resolve
by Scott Suskovic

Proper 23 385
Pentecost 21
Ordinary Time 28
   Living In Chains
   2 Timothy 2:8-15

Proper 24 391
Pentecost 22
Ordinary Time 29
   The Word Alone
   2 Timothy 3:14—4:5

Proper 25 397
Pentecost 23
Ordinary Time 30
   Endurance
   2 Timothy 4:6-8, 16-18

Reformation Day 403
   Saint And Sinner
   Romans 3:19-28

All Saints   **409**
    The Final Word
    Ephesians 1:11-23

Proper 26   **415**
Pentecost 24
Ordinary Time 31
    Worthy Of Your Call
    2 Thessalonians 1:1-4, 11-12

Proper 27   **419**
Pentecost 25
Ordinary Time 32
    Sarah
    2 Thessalonians 2:1-5, 13-17

Proper 28   **425**
Pentecost 26
Ordinary Time 33
    No Work, No Food!
    2 Thessalonians 3:6-13

Christ The King   **429**
Proper 29
    This Is A King?
    Colossians 1:11-20

Thanksgiving Day   **435**
    A New Resolve
    Philippians 4:4-9

Lectionary Preaching After Pentecost   **441**

US/Canadian Lectionary Comparison   **443**

About The Authors   **445**

Sermons On The Second Readings

For Sundays In Advent, Christmas, And Epiphany

Gifts Of Thanksgiving

Richard Gribble, CSC

Preface

Giving and receiving gifts are activities in which we all participate. Gifts come in all shapes and sizes and are given for many reasons and on various occasions. Some gifts are very large, others are very small; yet their significance has nothing to do with their size. We give gifts to people on special occasions — birthdays, anniversaries, graduations, special achievements in life, and special holidays, such as Christmas. The reasons we give gifts vary, as well. Sometimes we want to celebrate milestones in our lives. Annually we celebrate with our friends on the day of their birth and their anniversary of commitment through marriage. We recognize major accomplishments in school, business, our work in the civic community, the military, or the church. We give gifts to demonstrate our love, care, and affection for special people in our lives. In such cases there is no need for a special occasion; the catalyst is the love that binds us to other individuals.

As we give gifts to each other, God has never ceased giving gifts to us. Each of us has received the gift of varied and multiple strengths. These manifest themselves through physical talents, the opportunities we enjoy in life, and the time necessary to properly utilize these great gifts in the promotion and building of God's kingdom in our world. All of us have been given certain material possessions. Some enjoy a great abundance of the fruits of the earth; some, unfortunately, have very little. Most of us, at least in the United States, find ourselves somewhere in the middle. God has given us a certain amount of power and prestige. We may hold it in our place of work, civic community where we live, the church we attend, or in the family of which we are members. Again, for some, power and prestige are significant, for others minimal, and for most, sufficient for their needs.

The Advent and Christmas seasons are a time for us to prepare and celebrate the Incarnation. God's greatest gift to the world, Jesus Christ, chose to come among us as a human being in order to set us free from all that binds us and keeps us prisoners. During this holy season we make many preparations to give gifts. In our society, however, we recall that it is our custom, when celebrating a birthday, to give gifts to the one whose anniversary or birth we remember. Therefore, as we prepare for and celebrate Christ's birth, we must ask ourselves, "What are we prepared to give to the newborn king of the Jews?" We all know that Christ wants and needs nothing of a material nature from us. There is nothing we could possibly conceive that God does not already possess. There is one thing, however, that the Lord desires and deserves from us. The best possible gift we can present to Christ is our fealty, commitment, and persistence in the Christian life. In other words, the greatest gift we can give to Christ is ourselves, seeking to be the best possible person we can. In short, Jesus wants our gift of thanksgiving. We are to give thanks to God for our lives and all that we have been given. We must live our lives in an attitude of thanksgiving to God.

The sermons in this volume speak of our thanksgiving to God. How is our thanksgiving to God manifest? Obviously, there is no one answer, but the second lesson scripture readings during these holy seasons provide us some insight. First, we learn that we must be giving people, to others and to God. Scripture teaches us that we must rejoice in God's presence and be obedient to God. Our call to be disciples and lead others to the Lord is an integral part of giving thanks to God. We also learn of our need to work with others in building the kingdom of God in our world. Overall, it is our thanksgiving to God through love, the element that binds all wonderful qualities together, that always must be evident in our lives.

The sermons in this book reflect my personal thanksgiving to God. How one expresses thanks is unique to the individual. My hope is that these reflections might resonate in some way, spark an idea or two in others, or serve as a catalyst to inspire the reader into asking, "What is my gift to the newborn king of the Jews?" God has and will continue to shower upon us varied and multiple gifts.

Now, especially during these holy seasons of Advent and Christmas, it is incumbent upon us to consider our response. Hopefully these reflections will assist the reader not only to ponder, but to respond in love to God, whose great love gave us the Incarnation, and to Jesus whose life, death, and resurrection brought us the possibility of eternal life.

— Richard Gribble, CSC

Advent 1
1 Thessalonians 3:9-13

Thanksgiving Means Giving

When Billy Walsh was a youngster, his family lived near Mrs. Smithson. A widow eighty years of age, Mrs. Smithson was in constant pain and crippled by rheumatoid arthritis that ravaged her body. Living alone she could only walk a few steps at a time with the help of her cane. Every week when Billy's mom went to the market, she took her son, who would always deliver groceries to the old widow. The family car would pull up into Mrs. Smithson's driveway and the command would be heard, "Billy, here are Mrs. Smithson's groceries." That was all the instruction that was needed. Billy instantly responded, delivering the groceries with a sense of delight. Without fail Mrs. Smithson always gave Billy a quarter for his efforts.

The boy enjoyed the older woman, especially listening to her stories. She told him about her life, a beautiful, old church in the woods, horse and buggy rides on Sunday afternoons, and much about her family's farm that had no modern conveniences such as electricity or running water. After a short time together the older woman would give Billy his quarter, which he would half-heartedly refuse, knowing that she would insist that he keep it. Usually he walked across the street to Johnson's candy store and bought himself a treat.

One day in mid-December Billy was delivering the woman's groceries as usual, but the season's first significant snow was falling and the boy very much wanted to go out and play. He decided, therefore, to make his delivery and refuse to accept Mrs. Smithson's weekly offering of 25 cents. The snow beckoned him to go outside.

Thus, Billy delivered the groceries much faster than normal. The older woman took the items out of the bag and told Billy where each went in the cabinets. Normally he enjoyed this, but the snow was calling. Then, somewhat suddenly Billy began to realize how lonely Mrs. Smithson must have been. She had been a widow for nearly twenty years and she had no children. Her only living relative, who never came to visit, lived far away in Boston. Nobody even called her at Christmas. When the holiday drew near, the house had no tree, no presents, and no stockings. For her, Christmas was just another day on the calendar. Billy began to think, *Maybe the snow could wait a bit; it wasn't that important.*

Billy and Mrs. Smithson sat and talked about many things but especially past Christmas celebrations. The journey of reflection and memories must have been somewhat healing for the older woman. Then she said, "Well, Billy, I bet you want to go out and play in the snow." She reached into her purse, fumbling to find the proper coin. "No, Mrs. Smithson," he said, "I cannot take your money this time. I am sure you have more important uses for it."

But she replied, "What more important thing could I do with it than give some to a friend at Christmas time?" She placed a silver dollar in Billy's hand. He tried to give it back, but she would have none of that.

Billy hurried out the door and ran to Johnson's candy store. He wondered what he would buy — a comic book, a chocolate soda, or ice cream. Then he spotted a Christmas card with an old country church on the cover. It was just like the church Mrs. Smithson had described from her youth. Billy purchased the card and borrowed a pen to sign his name. "Is this for your girlfriend?" Mr. Johnson asked. Billy started to say, "No," but responded, "Well, yeah, I guess it is."

He walked across the street and rang the widow's doorbell. He handed her the card, saying, "Merry Christmas, Mrs. Smithson. Thank you for your kindness."

The older woman's hand began to tremble as she opened the card and read its contents. She began to cry. "Thank you very much," and then in almost a whisper, "Merry Christmas to you."

Several weeks later, one cold and blustery day, an ambulance arrived at Mrs. Smithson's home. Mrs. Walsh, Billy's mother, told her son that she had found Mrs. Smithson in bed; she had died peacefully in her sleep. On her nightstand was found, still illuminated by a light, a solitary Christmas card with an old country church on the cover.

This story, set during the Christmas season, provides a perfect entrée to the Advent period, which the church begins today. In essence the story is one of thanksgiving, the young boy's thanksgiving to the woman and her thanksgiving to him. Our second lesson, drawn from 1 Thessalonians, presents us with a message of thanksgiving, but one that is specific in giving thanks through giving.

Saint Paul wrote 1 Thessalonians, most probably the first letter of his corpus, approximately in the year 50 AD. He had founded the Christian community at Thessalonica during his second missionary journey (Acts 17:1-9). In the short passage we heard proclaimed, the apostle offers thanks to the Thessalonians. He is grateful for them and the faith they have demonstrated, but he wants to suggest certain ways that thanksgiving must be manifest.

First, Paul suggests that thanksgiving must be an act of presence; he believes we demonstrate thanks to each other by being physically present with one another. As a nation, we in the United States have just completed the celebration of our national day of Thanksgiving. Most people gathered with families and friends; we were present to each other. We intentionally sought to be with these people at this special time. Many people traveled great distances; one might say we went out of our way to be present to special people in our lives. We made these journeys joyfully because these are people we know and love; there was no great strain to be physically present with these people. We welcomed the opportunity.

However, Paul's concept of presence as an action of thanksgiving requires more of us. Being an excellent judge of human character, Paul realized that to be present to people we know, like, or perceive can be of advantage to us is not difficult at all. He realized the need, and so must we, to move beyond being present simply to those we like, but in an act of thanksgiving, to be present to those we know and possibly do not like. I suspect at the outset Billy was not too pleased to be present to Mrs. Smithson, as it would take him away from his friends. But he learned about the importance of being present, especially to those who needed him most. Equally importantly he discovered the peace and beauty that came to him through his act of thanksgiving. He found that he was serving not only the individual, but God who gives us the opportunity to be present and serve.

Being present can manifest itself in many different ways. We need to take up the challenge and be thankful by visiting a neighbor, a colleague at work, or a member of our church community who is sick, whether in the hospital or at home. Taking the time that we seemingly do not possess to be present with another and simply sit and listen is a great gift, almost a lost art in today's world. Many times all people need is simply a compassionate ear. We need to be present with the elderly, family members most assuredly, but also those we know in various ways. We need to be present for special events — birthdays, anniversaries, and weddings. But the everyday events, being present for meals, sporting events of children, and family time together is essential. Paul is asking the Thessalonians to be present to each other and thereby demonstrate thanksgiving. The same is true for us.

A second aspect of Saint Paul's concept of thanksgiving is mutual love. He writes, "May the Lord make you increase and abound in love for one another and for all, just as we abound in love for you" (1 Thessalonians 3:12). As the first season of the new liturgical year, Advent presents us the opportunity for new beginnings, to start afresh in demonstrating mutual love. If we are at odds with someone it is the perfect time to once again demonstrate the love to which all Christians are called. Jesus never held a grudge. In fact, we recall his words on the cross, "Father, forgive them for they do not know what they are doing" (Luke 23:34). Disagreements arise within families, coworkers, neighbors, and even within our church communions. Paul's words encourage us to "drop the hatchet" and move toward reconciliation and love. Still we must go further. We must reach across borders and boundaries that separate and drive people apart. Racial and ethnic divisions, national boundaries, and even religious denominations and teachings keep us from being the mutually loving people that is part of Paul's thanksgiving message to the Thessalonians.

Instead of division and strife we should offer love as the concept of belonging, unity, and harmony. A thanksgiving of mutual love requires us to be inclusive in all we do and say. Jesus continually crossed borders, both literally and figuratively, to demonstrate an inclusive ethic with all people. He visited lands and cities outside Israel, such as Tyre, Sidon, and the Gerasene Territory. He never shied away from lepers, cripples, the blind, or others with physical handicaps. On the contrary, he embraced these people, demonstrating an ethic of being inclusive.

Rather than being inclusive, too often people in contemporary life are exclusive. We choose our friends, opportunities, and associations with great care. Only certain people or possibilities that pass our personal litmus test show up on our radar screens. People are chosen based on their attributes, skills, and the possibilities they bring in our lives. Opportunities similarly are chosen if they will advance our personal or professional lives or serve us in an advantageous way. The thanksgiving effort of mutual love that Paul preaches to the Thessalonians is completely antithetical to such an exclusive way of thinking or acting.

Paul's third aspect of thanksgiving is proper conduct. He writes, "May he so strengthen your hearts in holiness that you may be blameless before our God and Father at the coming of our Lord Jesus Christ with all his saints" (1 Thessalonians 3:13). The new start that Advent brings challenges us to transform our lives of faith and make them more conformable to that of Christ. We should use this time to root out vices that ill-affect our health — smoking, overheating, excessive drinking, or laziness. It is a time to cast out hatred, jealousy, pride, and arrogance, those things that create violence in our lives, and replace them with justice, goodness, humility, kindness, and those things that generate peace. In short, we must root out actions that are inconsistent with our common Christian vocation to holiness. As a Christian hymn goes, "Let there be peace on earth and let it begin with me." We must find peace in our hearts by doing what is right. Right conduct leads directly to peace within our hearts.

There is a short little story that aptly illustrates this point. One day a young man answered a want ad for a farm hand. He told the owner about his previous experience, which was abundant, and his references were impeccable. He ended the interview in a rather odd way, however, by telling the owner that he could count on him, because he could sleep during the wind. The owner was confused but he could not argue with the man's credentials so he was given the job.

Late one night a fierce Midwest storm arose. It was two in the morning but the farmer arose, got dressed, and went outside to see what needed to be secured. First, he checked the barn, but the doors were closed, shutters were locked tight, and the animals were tethered and safe. He next checked the springhouse, the pump room, and storage shed, and all the trucks. Everything was secured. He ran from place to place thinking most assuredly that something must be out of order. Finally, the owner stuck his head in the bunkhouse and saw the farmhand fast asleep. He remembered the curious statement of the farmhand when he was interviewed, "I can sleep during the wind." The farmer smiled and thought to himself, "Yes, he is at peace and has done all things well. He can sleep during the wind."

As we begin a new liturgical year by lighting the first candle on the Advent wreath, Saint Paul encourages us to manifest an attitude of thanksgiving. While saying "thank you" in a physical sense is a start, we must go further. Paul tells the Thessalonians that he is grateful to them, but now they must demonstrate an ethic of thanksgiving of presence, mutual love, and right conduct to others. Similarly, we need to manifest thanksgiving in our lives. People need us to be present to them; they have the right to our love and respect. Society and God challenge us to reform our lives more along that of Jesus Christ. Let our Advent journey begin by being thankful. Our attitude can be so simply and succinctly stated, as articulated by Saint Ignatius of Loyola, "May all we do and say give greater glory and honor to God." Amen.

Advent 2
Philippians 1:3-11

Jesus – The Leader Of Our Team

One day a young girl came home from school in tears because she had only been given a small part in the school play, while her classmate and best friend had received the lead role. After drying the girl's eyes, her mother took off her watch, put it in her hand, and said, "What do you see?" The girl replied, "A gold band, the watch face, and two hands." Then the mother flipped the watch over, opened the back, and again asked her daughter, "Now, what do you see?" The little girl looked closely at all the internal watch mechanisms and saw many little wheels, springs, and other small pieces. The mother explained, "This watch would be useless without every part — even the tiny ones you can hardly see." The young girl always remembered her mother's lesson to realize that all must work together to make any operation function well.

The lesson the young girl learned from her mother is an important lesson for all of us who seek to follow Jesus, our leader in the faith. As the various components of the watch — some large, others small, some seemingly important, and others of lesser importance — must all work together for the watch to function, so too, must the Christian community work together as one, under the leadership of Christ, to further his message and to bring his peace to an oftentimes troubled world.

As with the second lesson last week from 1 Thessalonians, today's lesson is taken from the "thanksgiving" section of Paul's letter to the Philippians. Saint Paul speaks of the need to work as a team, headed by Christ, to bring Jesus' message to people of the region. He speaks generally of the mutuality of love and care that must reign in the community; he urges the people to remain pure and blameless in God's eyes. Yet, he goes much further, raising another highly significant concept, the idea of sharing through Jesus, the central figure of our faith. Paul is thankful because the Philippians hold him in their hearts as he does them. He longs for the community and wants to be an integral part of their life of faith. Yet, while this is important, he says it is secondary to sharing in God's grace. Paul wants the Philippians to be a community but only with Jesus as the hub, the central figure.

Clearly Paul, from his own conversion, understood the necessity of the centrality of Jesus in his life. When he heard Jesus' voice on the road, he knew the rest of his life would be centered on him. He had no idea at the time what this would mean and how much he would have to sacrifice, but he fully knew there was no way he could conduct his life without Jesus as his central guiding figure. Thus, for Paul, finding our way to life eternal is not only the goal, but Jesus is the way to achieve that lofty pinnacle.

The gospels, both the synoptic writers and John, affirm what Paul was telling the Philippians, namely the need to center our lives on Christ, his message, and his way of life. In the Sermon on the Mount, Jesus challenges his followers to follow the narrow, rougher, and less-traveled path, but the only one that leads to life,

> *Enter through the narrow gate; for the gate is wide and the road is easy that leads to destruction, and there are many who take it. For the gate is narrow and the road is hard that leads to life, and there are few who find it.*
> — Matthew 7:13-14

Saint John is unique among the gospel evangelists in the many titles he gives to Jesus. He describes Jesus as, "the way, the truth and the life," "the Bread of Life," the "door," and "gate." The powerful image of the vine and branches well illustrates the centrality of Jesus: "I am the vine, you are the branches. Those who abide in me and I in them bear much fruit, because apart from me you can do nothing" (John 15:5). Scripture clearly shows how Jesus is the central figure for our personal lives and our community of faith.

Too often, however, Jesus is forced to take a backseat to people and ideas that compete for our attention.

The need for a central figure in our lives of faith is made quite obvious when we see the absolute need for a unifying part, person, or ideal that serves to hold together things without unity. Take, for example, the hub at the center of a bicycle wheel. Each of the spokes of a wheel has importance, giving structure and strength, yet it is the hub that holds the spokes and thus the wheel together. Similarly, sports teams have many players but there is always a central figure or goal to hold a team together. Teams have managers and head coaches; they have goals such as the World Series in baseball, the Super Bowl in football, and the Stanley Cup in hockey. In families, while there are many members, it is the parents who stand at the hub and hold the family together, whether that is a nuclear or extended one.

As with other institutions of society, our churches also must seek unity and centrality. We have our pastors, bishops, and other central figures. These people are very important but only to the degree that they help lead us to the ultimate central figure who is Jesus Christ. The Bible is very clear about what Jesus asks of us and how he must be the central figure of our lives; yet we somehow believe we know more or better and seek another figure. When this happens we soon become lost.

The consequences that come to communities that refuse to have a centralizing ideal or person are quite obvious; they are manifest in varied ways in our world. If the spokes of a wheel do not have the hub there would be no central strength and the wheel would not function. In sports and even in families, when one desires to move out on one's own, breaking unity, disaster is not far off. In families this can be manifest through lack of discipline. It may be children who "do their own thing," parents who are unfaithful, or individuals who seek solace in things that lead nowhere — drugs, alcohol, and gambling. The list goes on and on.

In our churches we live in a fragile belief system or at least so it seems! Our churches have certain rules and regulations; there are certain ways of operating. Yet, individualism seems to have such a strong pull on our loyalties that we feel free to believe what we want and basically to do what we wish. Self-autonomy trumps the community. Such attitudes are present on all fronts. We can see it in individual parishes, local dioceses, and even our international communions. We have moved away from the centrality of Jesus, the door, the gate, the rough and narrow path, and have chosen to take alternate routes. But, as certain as the wheel does not function without the centrality of the hub, or the watch without all the parts working together, so too, our faith communities and our churches will not function well without our common focus on the centrality of Christ. The created world seeks unity; the parts of the watch must work together. Similarly God's greatest creation, the human race, must not only seek but find unity. We must work together to produce the desired result we seek.

A simple yet humorous story well illustrates our need for each other. A world-renowned organist was giving a performance at a local church using a huge, antique organ for his concert. It used a bellows for its pipes. The bellows was hand-pumped by a boy who was behind the screen, unseen by the audience. The first half of the concert, which featured the music of Johann Sebastian Bach, was well received by the audience. All in attendance were thrilled by the organist's ability at the keyboard of this beautiful instrument. After taking his bows and accepting the ovation of the audience, the famous musician walked triumphantly offstage by a side passageway. As he passed by, the boy who was pumping the bellows said, "We played well, didn't we, sir?" The famous musician rather haughtily replied, "And what do you mean by we? I was the one playing the music. I was the one whose ability was recognized by the audience."

After intermission, the organist returned to his seat at the impressive five-keyboard console and began to play. But nothing happened; not a sound was heard. Then the organist heard a youthful voice whisper from behind the screen, "Hey, mister, do you know what *we* means now?"

Let us, therefore, as individuals and a community of faith take Saint Paul's advice and follow the road to unity and find our life in Jesus our leader. Such obedience will place us on the train that leads to God and life eternal. Amen.

Advent 3
Philippians 4:4-7

Rejoicing Brings Peace

Mora Naba, a Mossi emperor in Burkina Faso, had conquered a powerful ethnic group in the south called the Kaesena. He extracted tribute from them once each year. One year, at tribute collecting time, the emperor made the mistake of sending his son, Nabiiga, a prince and his heir apparent. When the Kaesena saw Nabiiga with only a very small entourage of guardians, they overpowered the group and took the prince hostage.

His kingly robes were stripped from him, and he was forced to walk around in only a loincloth. The prisoner received only one meal per day and was forced out into the fields each morning to work. Normally, manual labor would be beneath the dignity of royalty, so the Kaesena made great sport of him. The women would pass by and belittle him. While he was working in the fields, the children would throw pebbles and stones at him.

But, to the great surprise of all those watching from day to day, the Mossi prince would work and sing. He sang cheerfully with a loud voice as he worked from sun up to sun down. At first his soft hands blistered and then bled as he was unaccustomed to using farm equipment. He lost significant weight, but he continued to be cheerful and to sing.

The elders of the Kaesena were much troubled by his singing and buoyant attitude. "How can he possibly sing," they would continually ask, "since we make him sleep on the ground and make sport of him each day? We give him very little food, and he is forced to labor from sun up to sun down. Our women and our children mock him, but he continues to sing!"

After a month of watching, they finally called him before a council. He stood in his loincloth straight and proud in their midst. The elder spokesperson for the Kaesena people asked the Mossi prince about his behavior: "Why do you sing?" Nabiiga answered, "It is true. You've taken away my fine clothes. You have made me work, you give me very little food to eat, and you make me sleep on the ground in a common hut. You have tried to take away all my pride and all my earthly possessions. You have brought great shame upon me. Now you ask me why, in spite of all this, I can sing. I can sing because you cannot take away my title and who I am. I am Moro Naba's first son. I am proud of that and will never react to your shameful behavior!"

The Kaesena people learned that they could not bring shame upon the Mossi prince because he was at peace and, therefore, could continue to sing. The peace that the prince felt inside was an active virtue manifest in his behavior; peace was not simply the absence of violence and war in his life. To become peacemakers, as the story suggests, we must proactively act and speak. As we light the third candle on the Advent wreath and know by the calendar, as well as Saint Paul's words, that Jesus is near, we must consider our response to the challenge to rejoice and, thereby, bring peace.

The Advent journey we have been traveling the last three weeks, a time of expectation and waiting, has concentrated on the second coming of Jesus and the ministry of John the Baptist. Today, however, we start to concentrate on the arrival of Jesus in time — the Incarnation. The Jews had waited many centuries since the prophecy of Isaiah, Jeremiah, Micah, and their predictions of a messiah. The Jews fully expected a great king who would restore the greatness of Israel as during the time of David. The Roman occupation of the land would end; the greatness of Israel would once again shine to all nations.

While we realize that the messiahship and kingdom that Jesus brought were far different from what the Jews expected, it is still a time of great rejoicing that the Lord is near. What Jesus brought is far more important than expectations of power and greatness, which dominated the thinking and hopes of the Jews. We must rejoice because we know, based on many factors, of the close proximity of

Jesus. First, the calendar tells us that December 25 is not far off. We cannot go very far in any mode of transportation without encountering some physical manifestation of Christmas — decorations, traffic at the malls, and billboards that announce sales. We hear Christmas carols on the radio, our mailboxes are filled with cards and other greetings from friends and family, and we are bombarded by commercials on television for all the latest things that various stories and retailers want us to buy for our friends and loved ones.

Scripture, too, informs us of the Lord's proximate arrival. Yes, we have the words of John the Baptist who speaks of the need to prepare for this great event. In today's second lesson Paul, writing to the Christian community at Philippi, suggests our preparation must include great rejoicing, because the Lord is near.

We all know how to rejoice with great fervor when things go right, and we are in control and on top of the situation. This is a rather natural reaction when our success is personal, that of one we know and love, or even that of an organization to which we have loyalty. We rejoice in our personal and family successes, the triumph of a friend over obstacles or disease. We rejoice when our favorite college or professional sports team wins the big game or even a championship.

Saint Paul tells us today that there is another element of rejoicing. He suggests we need to eliminate our propensity to worry and replace our anxiety with prayer and supplications to God. As a society we like to worry. In fact, we have a whole industry associated with it. When we worry we seek resolution through medications and various professionals. Certainly what medical science collectively has done for us with respect to our penchant to worry is laudable and generally helpful, but we worry far too much. Naturally we worry about our family: our children, our finances, our health, and our future. But, as we know, there are some people who prefer to worry; they do not seem content under any other mode of operation.

Paul suggests we must cast our cares on the Lord by substituting prayer and supplication to God instead of manifesting our worries and concerns. This sounds good, but we know it is not easy to accomplish. We want, like the Kaesena people, to find some answer to our concerns, to our lack of peace, but Paul suggests that if we trust God and let our prayer take the place of our worry, the elusive peace we ultimately seek will be ours. The author of the book of Proverbs was correct when he wrote: "Trust in the Lord with all your heart, and do not rely on your own insight" (Proverbs 3:5). Paul says that the peace of God, which surpasses all our understanding, will guard our hearts and minds. This peace is certainly a reality we all seek — to feel at peace and know that God will guard our hearts and minds to the attainment of this goal.

Scripture and tradition have provided Jesus with numerous titles, each of which resonates with certain people at different times. The image of Jesus as the good shepherd presents the Lord as the compassionate one who seeks out the lost, even going so far as to leave 99 perfectly good sheep to fend for themselves while he searches for us, the one who is lost. When Jesus describes himself as "the way, the truth, and the life," he helps us understand that he is the guide to all that we need, all that will sustain us. Jesus' description of himself as the vine and we as the branches, expressing our need to always remain connected to him, brings us both consolation and challenge. It is a challenge for we must follow and stay connected, but if we do, we have the promise that where Jesus resides we will one day be. The image of Jesus as the "Bread of Life" (John 6) helps us to know that he is our spiritual sustenance. We can always go to him with any and all needs.

Isaiah's image of the Messiah as the "Prince of Peace" (Isaiah 9:5), is especially relevant as we draw closer to Christmas. Our troubled world, with so much hatred, violence, and armed conflict, badly needs the peace that only Christ can bring. This peace must be active, however; it is never passive. Pope Paul VI put it so succinctly, "If you want peace, work for justice." Peace will only come when we actively seek it. Thus, we must cooperate with Jesus, the Prince of Peace, to assure that Christ's peace will be manifest in the world. The apostle suggests that the way we can bring peace is by being joyful people. Rejoicing truly can bring peace.

Rejoicing must become a way of life, not simply a momentary respite from our general worrisome and dour countenance. We cannot win every game; we don't always hit home runs. But, if we continue to play the game, if we never give up, we can rejoice that God is with us. As we draw closer to our Advent goal, as the signs, smells, and sounds of Christmas draw near, let us as Paul suggests, "Rejoice in the Lord always; again I will say, Rejoice" (v. 4a). Our spirit will bring us peace, and peace will bring us and our world one step closer to God and life eternal. Amen.

Advent 4
Hebrews 10:5-10

Obedience: Our Gift To Jesus

One day a man went to his son's bedroom and found him sitting on his bed with a whole stack of comic books around him. The father said to his son, "Matthew, where did you get the comic books?"

Matthew responded, "I took them out of the library."

"You took them out of the library? You mean you stole them from the library?"

The boy responded, "Yes."

The father called the library and said he was going to march his son immediately down with the comic books to apologize and to restore all he had stolen. After returning from the library he gave Matthew a stern lecture about stealing.

The following summer, the family took its vacation in a small community in Vermont where there was a general store. When they returned home after the summer, the father went into Matthew's room and again found a pile of comic books in his dresser drawer. Matthew this time admitted, "I stole them from the store in the summer."

This time the father took the comic books and started a fire in the fireplace. He threw the comic books into the flames and with each comic book they threw in, he reminded his son of the seventh commandment, "Thou shall not steal."

One year later, Matthew again stole some comic books and this time his father told Matthew he was going to have to spank him. He brought him into the study, put him over his knee, and spanked him quite soundly. While he did not want to hurt his son, he did want to teach him a significant lesson. After this session he sat down and wanted to talk with his son. It was obvious that Matthew did not want to shed a tear in front of his father. The father understood that and, so as not to ruin the boy's pride, said, "Matthew, I am going to leave you alone for a while, but I will be back in a few minutes."

The father then stepped out of the room and closed the door behind him. He himself began to cry and to do so in a manner that was quite obvious to his son behind the door. After a few minutes he regained his composure, went to the bathroom, washed his face, and then returned to his son's room to speak with him.

Years later, when Matthew was a teenager and he was with his mother driving back from a shopping trip, the two were reminiscing as parents and children often do. Matthew began to retell the story of when he was a youngster and often stole comic books. He said to his mother, "You know, after that incident with Dad, I never stole another thing."

His mother commented, "I suppose the reason was because your father spanked you."

"Oh, no," replied Matthew, "it was because when he stepped out of the room I could hear him crying."

Matthew's mother thought her son had learned a lesson in obedience from the punishment he received at the hands of his father, but she learned to her surprise that he learned this hard lesson in life through the pain he inflicted on his father. All the things Matthew could have done to bring his father joy — achievements such as straight A's in school, getting the winning basket or hit to bring a sports team a victory, or winning the local town's citizenship award — could not be measured against simply being obedient.

Obedience seems like such an easy task, yet in our contemporary world, which concentrates on self-promotion, being obedient is difficult. We learn the same lesson on this fourth Sunday of Advent. What Christ desires for a present on Christmas Day is not gold, frankincense, and myrrh, or any other material thing. What Jesus wants and can expect from us is our obedience — to be the best person we can possibly be.

The letter to the Hebrews, from which today's second lesson is drawn, has an interesting place in the New Testament corpus. Initially this letter was thought to be part of Saint Paul's writings, but scholars today almost universally agree that the apostle to the Gentiles did not pen this document. More likely a Jewish Christian with a Hellenistic background wrote the letter as a mini theological treatise for a broad audience of people. The language, form, and theology of the letter all testify to a non-Pauline authorship. The importance of the letter is, however, equally uncontested, especially its references to Christ's new covenant. Jesus, according to the letter to the Hebrews, is the capstone, the fulfillment of the Hebrew scripture, who came to complete the law and lead the Christian community in a new direction.

As we have heard proclaimed, the letter places strong emphasis on the rejection of sacrifices and offerings and the need to substitute in their place obedience to God's will. We learn an important lesson, similar to that which Matthew's father, somewhat accidentally, taught his son. The father thought Matthew would learn obedience as a result of the punishment he received for his failures to follow the older man's exhortation to refrain from stealing. But the boy learned the lesson more profoundly by how his action hurt his father.

Similarly, the author of Hebrews tells us that outward actions of sacrifice and cereal offerings, which were so common to the Israelites in the desert and offerings of priests in the temple, are not what God seeks. Surely to perform such acts in a prayerful spirit was good and well-intentioned, and they were not to be condemned or rejected. However, Jesus, the new Adam, desires a new sign of love, the obedience of his people.

> *Sacrifices and offerings you have not desired, but a body you have prepared for me; in burnt offerings and sin offerings you have taken no pleasure.... I have come to do your will, O God.* — Hebrews 10:5b-7a

We learn that Jesus' arrival, the great event we await, abolishes the first idea, namely that of sacrifice and offerings, and establishes a second, the idea of obedience. The perfect example is the obedience of Christ himself to the will of his Father by offering his own body. Jesus' sacrifice, in obedience to his Father's will, transformed the world, bringing us the possibility of salvation.

The Christmas season, upon whose doorstep we now rest, celebrates the Incarnation, God becoming human in Jesus Christ, our Lord and redeemer. In our society when we celebrate a birthday, it is customary to give a gift to the person so honored. We need to reflect and consider, therefore, what our gift will be to the newborn king of the Jews. In short, as stated earlier, Jesus is not interested in anything we can buy or make, but he is very interested in seeing us attain the fullness of our Christian call, to be the person God wants us to be. Today, the author of the letter to the Hebrews suggests the best possible gift we can give to Jesus is our obedience.

Society today creates many difficulties, roadblocks, and barriers that hinder us from being obedient people. As a society we stress the individual, self-accomplishment, individual awards, and honors. Competition is endemic to every facet of our society. At times we are all quite bullheaded; we want our way and no other. We believe that everybody else must change to accommodate our needs. We are not willing to move or change course.

A little story appropriately illustrates how we often behave and how such actions could be disastrous. A battleship had been at sea on maneuvers in heavy weather for several days. The visibility was poor with patchy fog, so the captain remained on the bridge keeping an eye on all activities. Shortly after dark, the lookout on the wing of the bridge reported, "Light, bearing on the starboard bow."

The captain called out, "Is it steady or moving astern?"

The lookout replied, "The light is steady, captain."

Realizing that the situation was a collision course, the captain shouted to the radio man, "Send a message, we are on a collision course. Advise you change course 20° to port."

Almost immediately a reply was received, "Advise that you change course 20° to port."

Angrily the captain ordered a second message: "I am the ship's captain. Change course 20° to port now!"

Again, a reply came, "I am seaman second class, but you better change course immediately."

By this time the captain was furious. He ordered, "Send this message: This is a battleship; change your course immediately."

Back in a flash came the reply: "This is a lighthouse!" The battleship changed course. If we are unwilling to change course in our lives we may find ourselves in extremis or experience a collision with dire ramifications.

Many people today see obedience as restrictive and problematic. We feel we sacrifice too much to be obedient. Yet, obedience is what gives us freedom. Can any of us imagine our society without the obedience of law? While the law seems to restrict our freedom, it actually provides a structure for our society. If we obey the law then we find freedom. Similarly following the rules or keeping the regimen of the team brings discipline, esprit de corps, and triumph in sports. While there are individual stars on the various school and professional sports teams, it is the team that wins or loses. Those who act and play like a team in obedience, generally find themselves on the victorious side of any contest.

Similarly obedience to God and meeting our responsibilities and duties brings the peace that only God can bring. The story of a holy monk and a decision he was forced to make illustrates my point. There was an old and holy monk who prayed many years for a vision from God to strengthen his faith, but it never came. He had almost given up hope when, one day, a vision appeared. The monk was overjoyed. Then, right in the middle of the vision, the monastery bell rang that meant that it was time to feed the poor who gathered daily at the monastery gate.

Coincidentally it was the old monk's turn to feed them. He realized that if he failed to show up with food, the poor would leave quietly, thinking the monastery had nothing to give them that day. The monk was torn between earthly duty and the heavenly vision. However, before the bell stopped tolling the monk had made his decision. With a heavy heart, he turned his back on the vision and went off to feed the poor.

Nearly an hour later, the old monk returned to his room. To his great surprise and joy when he opened the door he saw the vision of God was still there waiting for him. The monk dropped to his knees in thanksgiving. God said to him, "My son, had you not gone off to feed the poor, I would not have stayed."

As we light the fourth candle on the Advent wreath and make our final preparations for the celebration of Christmas, let us consider what we need to do to be more obedient — to the people and the ideas of our society, but most especially to Christ. Let us realize that what Jesus desires and deserves from us this Christmas is an attitude of obedience to his will. We can present him with no more significant gift. Let us not disappoint him. Amen.

Christmas Eve/Christmas Day
Titus 2:11-14

Leading Others To Jesus

It was the Christmas season and thus the time for the local elementary school to present its annual Christmas play. One little girl named Caitlin invited her parents to come to the performance. She told them, "Mom and Dad, please come to the play for I have the most important role in the entire production." Of course, Caitlin's parents were more than happy to accept their daughter's invitation to attend the event.

On the night of the performance the school auditorium was filled with family, friends, and other well-wishers who looked forward to the annual Christmas play. As the curtain was drawn back from the stage the audience initially beheld Joseph leading a donkey across the stage, with Mary astride. The narrator told the story of how Caesar Augustus had ordered a census of the whole world, and it was necessary for Joseph to travel with Mary, his pregnant wife, to Bethlehem to register. Upon their arrival the couple looked for a place to stay but could find no room in the local inn.

As the play continued, Caitlin's parents wondered where their daughter was. Based on what she had said, they were sure that she would have the role of Mary or one of the shepherds, but so far she had not been present on stage. Then the narrator spoke of the birth of Jesus and with this a brilliant star arose over the stable to mark the spot of Jesus' birth. Caitlin was carrying the star above her head. Wherever Mary went with Jesus in her arms, Caitlin followed behind; the star never left Jesus.

When the play concluded all in attendance and the participants gathered in the cafeteria for a celebration of cookies, cake, and beverages. Caitlin asked her parents, "Did you enjoy the play?"

Her parents responded, "We loved it; it was great!"

Her father continued, "Caitlin you told us that you had one of the leading roles but we noticed that you carried the star. We thought you might be Mary or possibly one of the shepherds or magi."

Caitlin responded, "I had the most important role. It was my task as the star to lead others to Jesus. There could not be any more important task and privilege in the entire world."

In many ways the average person might see Caitlin's role in the play as secondary, even of little importance. Yet, she insisted her role was not only essential, but the most significant, because she had responsibility of leading others to the Lord. As the world today welcomes the newborn king of the Jews, we must realize that while we bask in the glory of God made man, God chose to become human like us in all things but sin. We, as Christians, bear a significant responsibility. The Pauline author of the letter to Titus tells us that we must do our part by leading upstanding lives, to be an example, and thereby lead others to Christ. It is a responsibility we must not fail to engage, to be the best person our abilities will allow us to be.

The letter to Titus, along with 1 and 2 Timothy comprising the so-called Pastoral Epistles, form a unique part of the New Testament. Biblical experts are uncertain as to the authorship of these letters, but, as with the letter to the Hebrews, differences in language and theology lead many exegetes to doubt authentic Pauline authorship. However, the message of the letter to Titus, as we just heard proclaimed, is highly significant.

The central missive of the passage tells us that the grace of God has appeared bringing salvation to all people. We know that the Christmas story is central to God's plan of salvation history. From the time God called Abraham, through the formation of the Israelite people, the great exodus, the periods of the two kingdoms of Israel and Judah and the prophets, and even the infamous Babylonian exile, God continued to provide evidence to the fact that a plan was in progress to bring God's people the gift of eternal life. Jesus' arrival in history begins the process that leads to his salvific death and resurrection.

The Pauline author of Titus says that while we await the manifestation of God's glory, to be made present upon Jesus' return, we have several significant responsibilities. We are initially called to renewal and to cast out worldly passions. The message of Christ must have a significant bearing on our lives. We must demonstrate in our lives of faith that the message of Christ has made a difference. Worldly passions are an everyday enticement. The allure of the created world is strong. Since the attraction of the world is so strong and pervasive, we must overtly choose to take another route.

This new path requires us to be countercultural, to place value on things of God and faith over the materialism of the world. People will think us odd, even foolish in our rejection of what the majority of our first-world society considers indispensable, yet this is precisely what being countercultural means. We must be a sign in an alienated world of a value system that is contrary to that of the world. Such a stance will require courage because the rewards that are so readily apparent and tangible for those who choose the world are hidden and latent for the Christian who chooses to shun worldly ties. Yet, our faith teaches us of the necessity of holding fast. Saint Paul puts it powerfully and beautifully in 1 Corinthians 2:9: "No eye has seen, nor ear heard, nor the human heart conceived, what God has prepared for those who love him."

As Caitlin brought others to Christ through her role as the "star" in the play, so we must lead others by the example we set. Paul tells us in the present age, and thus for all ages, we are to live self-controlled, upright, and godly lives. In other words we must live lives consistent with our Christian vocation. We are to set an example that others would want to follow. If that life is consistent with Christ's message then we become a beacon of light, like the star, which draws others to Christ. We, like those who felt Caitlin's role was minimal, might think that setting an example is a rather passive and small role in God's plan, but nothing could be farther from the truth.

Jesus came into our world, as we celebrate today, to bring light, hope, and to show us how to lead our lives in a way that is pleasing to God. He came to fulfill and complete the law, initiated on Mount Sinai with Moses. Christ did his share, but the work was only initiated during his life. We, his followers, have the privilege and responsibility to continue his work in our world.

Jesus is the light who comes to dispel the darkness. We must carry the light in a proactive way. We must be willing to take some risks in providing the light to others. We cannot abdicate this serious responsibility nor think we are not qualified to be Christ's representatives in our world. We must avoid the hesitation and reticence that, if we are not careful, can creep into our lives.

A little story illustrates this challenge. Three wise men were encouraged to find and explore what many called the cave of wisdom and life. They made careful preparations for what would be a challenging and arduous journey. When they reached the cave, they noted a guard stood at the entrance. They were not permitted to enter the cave until they had spoken with the guard. He had only one question for them, and he demanded that they answer only after talking it over amongst themselves. He assured them they would have a good guide to lead them through the regions of the cave. His question was a simple one, "How far into the cave of wisdom and life do you wish to go?"

The three travelers discussed the matter and then returned to the guard saying that they only wanted to go a very short distance, only so far as to say that they had been there. The response of the guard manifested great disappointment as he summoned someone to lead the three seekers a short distance into the cave and then watched them set out again after a very short time.

The three travelers were hesitant and were not willing to risk in order to find wisdom and knowledge. I am sure that Jesus will be equally disappointed in us, as was the guard of the cave, if we refuse to move forward and to use the talent, time, energy, and opportunities we have been given to bring the Lord's message to the world.

The Advent season, a period of patient expectation, has ended and today we welcome Jesus, the light, the Prince of Peace, and our source of salvation. As we rejoice in the Incarnation and the great privileges initiated for us who bear the name of Christian, we must always be mindful that responsibility is an essential element of the Christian life. The letter to Titus today suggests our need to be countercultural, to move away from the teachings of the world's passions, materialism, and self-autonomy, which twenty-first-century America tells us is normative, and seek instead an attitude of community and greater simplicity of life.

Additionally, we are challenged to exercise self-control and to live upright lives according to the message that Jesus proclaimed. In other words, we are called to be good examples, to be the light of Christ to others. Our words, actions, and attitudes should bring people closer to Christ. It is an awesome and extremely important responsibility. As we celebrate the arrival of the light that no darkness can overcome, let us be the light to others. May the miracle of the Incarnation, God made man, transform our lives forever! Amen.

Christmas 1
Colossians 3:12-17

Learning The Recipe For Life

In ancient times, a king decided to find and honor the greatest person among his subjects. A man of wealth and property was singled out. Another was praised for his healing powers and a third for his wisdom and knowledge of the law. Still another was lauded for his business acumen. Many other successful people were brought to the palace, and it became evident that the task of choosing the greatest would be difficult.

Finally the last candidate stood before the king. This woman had white hair and her eyes shone with the light of knowledge, understanding, and love.

"Who is this?" asked the king. "What has she done?"

"You have seen and heard all the others," said the king's aide. "This one is their teacher!"

With this the people all applauded and the king came down from his throne to honor her as the greatest of his subjects.

Those at court learned that while worldly success might initially be perceived to be of greatest importance, the true formula for life is learning from others and teaching others to be successful. Contemporary society measures success by the number of things we possess, accolades and awards received, significant positions attained, or the amount of influence or power we wield. Yet, Jesus Christ, whom we follow and whose birth we continue to celebrate during this Christmas season, came among us as a poor man. He achieved few if any of the marks that today are labels for "success," yet more people follow him and his teaching today than any other religious leader. Why? Jesus was the teacher who taught us the formula for life.

Today we hear how Saint Paul, writing to the Colossians, gives the community a "recipe" for success, not in this world necessarily, but more importantly for eternal life, the goal to which his readers and all of us must daily strive.

In today's reading, Paul lays out in systematic order the qualities, virtues, and characteristics that when knitted together become a fabric, a garment that when worn and used properly becomes our garment that makes us followers of Jesus. First, he says we are God's chosen ones. From the beginning we have been given the privilege of being chosen by God. The message has been given to us; we have been entrusted with a special and magnificent gift. We then have a responsibility to clothe ourselves in this message and to bring it to others. Christ is our teacher and we must continue his work by teaching others, not only in words, but in our actions, attitudes, and in general the way we live our Christian call to holiness.

Because we have been chosen, Paul says we are seen as holy and beloved in God's sight. We are special to God; we are his children. To be seen as special in the eyes of the creator is certainly another great privilege. If God considers us holy, then we must respond and act accordingly. We must be holy people, demonstrating by our actions and our words that we desire to follow the pattern of Christ's life. Jesus clearly gave us a pattern for life, a way to live not only for ourselves but for others.

In order to live a life of holiness, patterned on the life of Jesus, Paul presents us with basic qualities that we must weave into the fabric of our own life. He says we must be people of compassion, kindness, humility, meekness, patience, and to bear with one another. Quite obviously, especially in our fast-paced and self-autonomous society, these are lofty and possibly utopian goals. Yet, if we seek to be holy and follow in the footsteps of Christ, we must do our best to not back away from the challenge that these virtues bring, but charge head on and do what is necessary to make these qualities part of our fabric of life.

Compassion and kindness are lofty goals. One of the basic qualities we seek in others is their ability to demonstrate kindness, but often we ourselves are anything but kind. Rather, we are often "at each other's throats," talking little of kindness or compassion, but rather seeking our own ends. Too often we view others as competitors; too much kindness or compassion toward them will place us at a disadvantage. To be kind and compassionate requires us to go beyond ourselves and our limited purview. We must seek to satisfy the needs of others. Kindness and compassion are not easy characteristics to exemplify; yet they are part and parcel of Paul's formula.

Today humility and meekness are often viewed as signs of weakness. Society tells us we must always appear strong, in control and command of any and all situations. Jesus' teaching in the gospel to sit at the low end of the table and wait to be called up higher (Luke 14:10) is inconsistent with today's message for success. We are always told to put our best foot forward. While we must maximize our potential and use God's gifts wisely to demonstrate to others our talent and potential, it should never be done at the expense of others. When applying for a job or entrance to college or other educational endeavors, our resume must be superior and stand out from others. Still, if we take the time and use our wisdom, this can be done in ways that demonstrate Christian humility. Meekness and humility are not weakness, but rather part of the fabric of holiness to which Paul, through his mentor Jesus Christ, calls us.

Patience is also an important virtue that is part of the formula for life. We have all heard the prayer, "O Lord, grant me patience and give it to me now!" Our society wants things instantly. We want instant gratification and success and the wealth and power that go with it. We want instant resolutions to problems, whether it is some type of significant business negotiation or simply the alleviation of personal pain through medication. We often say our internet connection is too slow and seldom think about the rapidity of our world and our day-by-day movement toward globalization. We do not like to wait for anything. We hate to be in lines, whether it is at the bank, the grocery store, or the queue to purchase something in the store.

Yet, if we think about it, many if not most of the great things in life actually take some time. We cannot rush the seasons; they come each year as the calendar dictates. You cannot rush your favorite recipe; great food takes time to prepare and, therefore, a certain sense of patience. Unless we receive a windfall, fortune, success, and prestige also take time. We do not build relationships overnight, but rather over a long period of time. Clearly, the important things in life are earned by some type of patient endurance.

Paul next asks us to bear with one another and to be forgiving. Too often we hold grudges and will not let the past go — past problems, hurts, or injuries, those we have initiated and those perpetrated against us. We use these events of the past as tools to "hammer" people today for the things of the past. Yet, holding onto a grudge and pain from the past actually holds us back; it slows us down. Past hurts are like a ball and chain shackled to our leg. Unless we cut the chain we will always be hindered in our ability to move forward.

Saint Paul says at the climax of the reading that we must envelop all of these virtues and qualities of his message in love, "which binds everything together in perfect harmony" (v. 14). Love is much more than *eros*, romantic love. It is also *fileo*, the love of brothers and sisters, and the greatest form of love, at least from the perspective of the Greeks, *agape*, the concept of service to others. We must bind our compassion, kindness, humility, meekness, and patience together in love through service to others. If we can do this in the peace of Christ, then the love Paul calls us to manifest will most assuredly reign in our hearts. Paul goes on to say that we have all been called to find this peace for it unites us as one body. We can never be a true community of faith if we do not live in harmony. Christ calls us to be one. As Jesus says in John's gospel, "That they may all be one. As you, Father, are in me and I am in you, may they also be in us, so that the world may believe that you have sent me" (John 17:21).

Paul also calls us to be grateful for all things. Our gratitude to God is obviously paramount and primary. We must demonstrate our gratitude and thanksgiving by leading lives that are consistent with his word and message. We are called to proclaim that thanksgiving in "psalms, hymns, and spiritual songs." Our whole life must be one of thanksgiving, however. We must give thanks for the many ways God blesses us — the people who help us along the path of life, for the opportunities that come our way, and for the talents we possess. We should also be grateful, believe it or not, for the weaknesses we possess and the failures in life as these can help us to learn invaluable lessons including adjusting our actions and thinking when necessary.

Paul in short exhorts the Colossians to learn from Christ, the master teacher and take on his persona. We, too, need to take Jesus seriously; we are called to learn the formula for eternal life, to be the Christ to others. A short prayer, first articulated by Saint Teresa of Avila, the Carmelite mystic and religious reformer of the sixteenth century, illustrates the challenge: Christ has no body on earth but yours — no hands, no feet, but yours. Yours are the eyes with which Christ looks with compassion for the world. Christ has no body on earth but yours.

Having a resume that will give us the desired job, entrance into a more well-respected college, or other life opportunity is fine, even necessary in our world. However, if we do not work equally as hard in learning and seeking the formula or resume for eternal life, then all worldly success will have little value. Jesus says it well, "For what will it profit them if they gain the whole world but forfeit their life?" (Matthew 16:26). Let us take this challenge seriously and learn from Jesus what we need to complete our resume for life. Our efforts will bring success and prosperity today, but more importantly, eternal life tomorrow. Amen.

Christmas 2
Ephesians 1:3-14

The Hidden Gifts Of Christ

One Christmas morning, Dennis, Nancy, and their young son, Eric, were traveling south from San Francisco to their home in Los Angeles. They had spent Christmas Eve with relatives in the Bay Area, but both parents had to work the next day, thus, it was necessary to travel on Christmas. About noon, Dennis and Nancy decided they were hungry so they stopped at a local diner for lunch. Naturally, because it was Christmas, the restaurant was nearly empty and Eric, their young son, was the only child in the restaurant.

As they entered the diner, Eric could be heard screaming with great glee, "Hithere," the two-word expression that he always thought was one. The little boy pounded his hands on the metal chair. He was excited and he wiggled and giggled with great joy. Then Nancy, his mother, saw the source of her son's merriment. On the other side of the restaurant sat a man in a tattered coat who was dirty, greasy, and wore baggy pants with his toes extending out from his worn-out shoes. He was smiling at Eric. "Hi there, little baby. Hi there, big boy. I see you." Dennis and Nancy exchanged looks and said without words, *"What are we to do with this poor devil?"*

Meanwhile, the meal they ordered came, but the man on the other side of the room continued to speak: "Do you know pattycake, little boy? Do you know peekaboo?" Eric continued to laugh and answered with his patented phrase, "Hithere." The whole scene was embarrassing to both Dennis and Nancy, so they decided to quickly pay the check and leave. They both implored heaven, *"Lord, let us get out of here before the man speaks to Eric again."*

However, Eric seemed to have other plans as he reached out both arms in a typical gesture of children that says, "Please, pick me up." Eric began to lunge toward the homeless man with his arms open wide.

The man asked Nancy, "Would you let me hold your baby?" There was no need to answer as Eric almost propelled himself into the man's arms. Suddenly an old and apparently homeless man and a very young baby, in a very real way, consummated their love. Eric laid his tiny head upon the man's ragged shoulder. The man's eyes closed and tears flowed down his cheeks. Both Nancy and Dennis were awestruck. "You take care of this baby," said the man to Nancy.

Somehow she managed to respond, "I will."

The man gave Eric back to his mother and said, "God bless you, ma'am. You have given me a great Christmas gift."

Nancy could say nothing more than a muttered, "Thanks." Now with Eric in her arms she and Dennis walked to the car both saying to God, *"Lord, forgive us, forgive us."*

Eric's mother was petrified and, I suspect most of us would be, too, if our infant child had an encounter with a homeless person. Society, unfortunately, has trained us when we perceive danger to remove ourselves from any encounter with those who stand on the fringes or margins of our society — the homeless, victims of AIDS, immigrants, even the elderly. We feel they have nothing to offer; how can something good come from those who are out of the mainstream? But, Nancy learned one of the great lessons of life and received a special revelation of the goodness of humanity, "through the back door," when she and her son gave a homeless man the only gift he wanted, someone who could give unconditional love.

Today, as the Christmas season continues, a time when society considers gifts given and received, we hear how Jesus, one born on the fringes, a poor and homeless child, brought gifts beyond all measure to our world. We, like the woman, only need to make the first step and Jesus will do the rest.

Saint Paul's thanksgiving to the Ephesians in today's lesson is a presentation of the many ways that Christ showered the Christian community, including those at Ephesus, with blessings, suggesting how this fledgling community might respond in faith. First, the Pauline author speaks of how we have been chosen by the Lord. Obviously, this reality began when God first called Abraham, asking him to move from his native land of Ur to what is now Israel, with the promise that if he was faithful he would become the father of a great nation as numerous as the stars in the sky. Throughout salvation history we know of God's faithfulness, even with the continual unfaithfulness of his people.

The Ephesians, and all of us by extension who have inherited the promise, are God's children by adoption. Made in the image and likeness of God, we were chosen by the creator for a special role in salvation history. What a privilege we have been given by God. But with the privilege comes responsibility in an equally challenging way. Children have significant responsibility to their parents. Thus, we, God's children, have the responsibility to hold up our end of the bargain. This means to be obedient, dutiful, and purposeful in our lives.

Another special blessing, a hidden gift from Jesus, is redemption. Jesus was given a mission by his Father. He was asked to initiate the kingdom of God, but this project continues to require our daily efforts. From our personal perspective, Jesus came to die in a salvific way for us. Jesus, the innocent lamb, was sacrificed for our redemption. The sin of the first Adam is now countered by the supreme obedience of the second. Since we have been ransomed by Jesus' sacrifice, we, as with our adoption as God's children, have a responsibility to repay. We must live as those who are ransomed; we must live in hope. Too often today, especially with the seemingly never-ending troubles, obstacles, and difficulties, the temptation to lose hope is great. But, as they say, "Hope springs eternal." Our status as redeemed people, ransomed at a great price, tells us that even in the darkest hour — personal health issues, financial collapse, divorce, or the death of a family member or friend — we must have the confidence, as the gospel says, to believe that Jesus is a light that no darkness can overcome.

The next special hidden gift of Christ to all of us is forgiveness of sins. The scriptures abound with stories about Jesus' desire to forgive sins. The story of the woman caught in adultery (John 8:1-11) presents the best example. There is no question the woman is guilty; Jesus and the woman never deny it. But Jesus' concentration is on forgiveness, not condemnation. He challenges the women's accusers to cast the first stone, but realizing their own sinfulness, they all drift away, one by one. Jesus then forgives the woman with the admonition, "Go your way, and from now on do not sin again" (John 8:11). The Lord's condemnation falls only on those who openly reject his message. On the other hand, any who sought reconciliation found it in Jesus. One of the few people we know, at least as far as scripture is concerned, who is with God now is the thief on the cross who asked Jesus to remember him. We recall Jesus words, "Truly I tell you, today you will be with me in paradise" (Luke 23:43).

The Pauline author says that Jesus has revealed to us another hidden gift, the mystery of his will. What is Christ's will? Paul tells us it is to gather all things in heaven and on earth under his headship. As a community of faith we form a team, but as with all teams, especially those in athletics, there is need for a leader or coach to guide the whole. For us, of course, the leader, the captain is Jesus. He is a central figure of our faith. As the hub of a wheel is essential to hold together the integrity of the whole unit, so the community of faith is nothing without Christ. Paul wants the Ephesians to know that he is only the messenger; he is not the captain. Jesus is the one who leads us. We, in turn, must be team players. While individual effort is essential in any team endeavor, it is the team that is most important. We must work together if we are to properly build the kingdom.

Another special hidden gift is our inheritance from Christ. This gift is nothing less than life. Following in the footsteps of Jesus, we will find the fullness of life today. Obviously, there is no guarantee that every day will go perfectly. From the fall of Adam, we live in a difficult, problematic, and sinful world. We are all participants in this reality. Yet, following Jesus will give us the fullness of life today. Guided by the light of Christ we will be able to maximize our potential to the fullness of the people we are called to be. More importantly, our inheritance will be, when God calls us home, eternal life. This is the most special of all gifts from Christ. Jesus has promised us we will hear his words: "Come, you that are blessed by my Father, inherit the kingdom prepared for you from the foundation of the world" (Matthew 25:34b).

Lastly, the Pauline author says that the community of faith of which we are members has been marked by the seal of the Holy Spirit. We cannot see the Spirit, but we know, after the first Pentecost, the Spirit entered the world, as Jesus had promised. The presence of the Spirit, sanctifying our world, unites the gifts of Christ and helps us, through our words and actions, to manifest those gifts to others.

The Christmas season is marked by a spirit of giving and receiving. While we spend lots of time and energy in crowded malls, preparing meals, and generally working to bring gifts and joy to others, the greatest gift we received this Christmas is Jesus himself. He brings with him all sorts of hidden gifts. As the homeless man and the little boy's mother each received hidden gifts at Christmas, so too Jesus showers us with gifts beyond our imagination. We have been chosen as God's adopted children. Jesus came to ransom us and to forgive our sins. God's plan to bring the world together in Christ has been revealed to us, and we have become inheritors of life, the fullness of life today and eternal life tomorrow. May we have the courage to respond to Christ's gifts, to maximize our potential and share our gifts, opportunities, and time with others in response to Christ. May the Christian spirit of giving allow us to give freely to others and thus respond to Christ, the giver of all good gifts. Amen.

The Epiphany Of Our Lord
Ephesians 3:1-12

Ambassadors Of The Lord

There is an ancient Christian story that speaks of a fourth wise man, Artaban, in his pursuit of the king of the Jews. As he journeyed with his friends, Caspar, Melchior, and Balthazar, he became separated from them. He never made it to Bethlehem. For many years he sought the Christ Child and in the process had many adventures and assisted many people, including dying beggars and frightened mothers, to whom he gave two of the three great jewels he had originally planned to give to Jesus. He even traveled to Egypt, hearing that Jesus and his parents had gone there, but was again frustrated in his quest. Now, after 33 years of searching he arrived in Jerusalem, hoping at last that he might find the child.

At Passover time, Artaban, now an old man, noted an unusual commotion and inquired about its cause. People answered him, "We are going to the place called Golgotha, just outside the walls of the city, to see two robbers and a man named Jesus of Nazareth, who are being crucified on crosses. The man Jesus calls himself the Son of God, and Pontius Pilate has sent him to be crucified because he claims to be the king of the Jews."

Artaban knew instinctively that this is the king he had been searching for his whole life. Thus, he rushed to the scene. On the way he encountered a young girl being sold into slavery. She saw his royal robes and fell at his feet pleading with him to rescue her. His heart was moved and he gave away the last jewel for her ransom. Just then, darkness fell over the land and the earth shook, and great stones fell into the streets. One of them fell upon Artaban, crushing his head.

As he lay dying in the arms of the girl he had just ransomed, he cried out in a weak voice, "Three and thirty years I looked for thee, Lord, but I have never seen thy face nor ministered to thee!" Then a voice came from heaven, strong and kind, which said, "Inasmuch as you did it to one of the least of my brothers or sisters, you did it to me." Artaban's face grew calm and peaceful. His long journey was ended. He had found his king!

This popular story, taken from the apocrypha of Christian tradition, powerfully presents the Epiphany message. The three magi of whom Saint Matthew speaks in his gospel brought their gifts of gold, frankincense, and myrrh, recognizing Jesus as priest, prophet, and king. Additionally, their presence in Bethlehem demonstrated how Christ was manifest to the nations. In a similar way, Artaban's adventure illustrated another essential idea — that Christ calls us to manifest his glory to all nations. Artaban's goodness and openness to all, even those he did not know, brought the face of Christ, namely the one he sought, to him. Additionally, those to whom he came, the poor and destitute, became Christ to him. Without realizing it, all his life he had been achieving his goal, to see the Christ Child. We, in turn, are challenged to be Christ to others; we must be ambassadors of the Lord.

Saint Paul clearly understood his role as an ambassador of Christ, but he had to learn the lesson "the hard way." The scriptures, both the Acts of the Apostles and the letter to the Galatians, tell us that Paul was a zealous persecutor of "the new way." He was present at and condoned the martyrdom of Stephen (Acts 7:54-60). But God had plans for Paul and directed him to his assigned task as the "apostle to the Gentiles" when he revealed his glory to him on the road to Damascus. Paul was the first and foremost of Christian missionaries. He, in a figurative sense, turned the world upside down by his preaching that this crucified man, Jesus, was Messiah and Lord. He was an especially hard working and dedicated ambassador of the Lord, completing three major missionary journeys around the Eastern Mediterranean world, forming Christian communities, instructing the faithful, and leaving a great legacy in his corpus of letters, which have become the basic foundation for Christian theology.

In today's reading, Paul writes to the Ephesians and reminds them of his special commission from God. As an ambassador of the Lord he has been sent to proclaim Jesus' message of inclusion. He says the mystery of the past, meaning the time before Christ, has now been revealed: "The Gentiles have become fellow heirs, members of the same body, and sharers in the promise in Christ Jesus through the gospel" (Ephesians 3:6). Paul goes on to say that his role as an ambassador means he is a servant of the gospel. While Paul calls himself "the very least of all the saints," due largely one might think from his earlier life, still God's grace was given so he could bring the good news of the boundless riches of Christ to all. Paul's task was to reveal the message of Christ that all were acceptable; no one was to be excluded.

Paul, however, is not simply informing the Ephesians of his role in God's plan; more importantly he is challenging that Christian community to fulfill its responsibility and, like Paul, be ambassadors of the Lord. He says that the church, in Ephesus and more generally God's people everywhere, are to carry forth the message, namely that all are acceptable to God.

Lastly, Paul exhorts his readers not to lose heart. He knows from his own experience that there will be difficult days; the road of being an ambassador of the Lord will not be easy. He says with Christ we can be bold and should have confidence. Thus, he tells his readers not to lose heart but rather to carry forward the mission and the message to others. Jesus' message is universal, thus Paul challenges the Ephesians to do their part, to shoulder the burden and bring Christ to the world.

We, members of the contemporary church, have the same responsibility given by Paul to the Ephesians. In today's world we often hear of people who serve as ambassadors. Most nations have ambassadors, men and women, who are sent to foreign lands to serve as representatives of the ideas, policies, and people of that nation. When heads of state need something from another nation they generally begin that quest by speaking with the ambassador, whose task it is to have the requisite knowledge and to follow the ideas and principles of the nation he or she represents.

Although he did not understand it, Artaban was a great ambassador of Christ. He *thought* he never met Jesus, but realized on death's door that he had been serving the Lord his whole adult life through his consistent, ever faithful, and diligent search for the Christ Child, a search which allowed him to serve many people. Artaban's experience tells us that, while being an ambassador is a necessary element to our common Christian vocation of holiness, we need not fulfill this responsibility in formal ways. In fact, few people will ever have the overt call, as did Saint Paul, to travel far and wide to foreign lands in an effort to bring Christ's message to the world. But this does not in any way negate or remove our responsibility. Being ambassadors of Christ is generally fulfilled in simple, yet profound ways. If we are to bring the message, then in essence we must bring the face of Christ to others as did Artaban.

Being the Christ to others is truly an awesome task. It is not the easy path, but then Jesus never promised that being his followers would be easy. Remember his great challenge:

> *If any want to become my followers, let them deny themselves and take up the cross and follow me. For those who want to save their life will lose it, and those who lose their life for my sake, and for the sake of the gospel, will save it.* — Mark 8:34b-35

We cannot shy away from this responsibility. There is too much riding on our failure if we do not accept our task to be ambassadors of the Lord. A little story captures our need to be responsible and the ramifications if we fail to answer the call:

One Friday night two rival high school football teams were playing their annual game. One team was, at least on paper, much better than the other. The players were bigger and faster, the team had a better record, and they had supreme confidence. The coach of the underdogs, realizing that he did not have the players to beat the other team, believed his one hope was Calhoun, the fastest halfback in the area.

Toward the end of the fourth quarter, the game was still close; the underdog team was only behind by four points. So the coach called a timeout and brought the team to the sidelines. He gave the players their last instructions. He said, "Men we can win this game, but our only chance is to give the ball to Calhoun." He instructed the quarterback to give the ball to Calhoun who could hopefully score a touchdown and win the game. On first down the quarterback gave the ball to another player who gained little. The coach didn't understand and sent in a player with the words, "Tell the quarterback — give the ball to Calhoun."

On second down the quarterback again gave the ball to another back resulting in no gain. The coach was becoming frustrated and again yelled out onto the field, "You know the plan; give the ball to Calhoun." On third down the quarterback tried a bootleg, but achieved little. Not understanding what was going on, the coach again sent in a player and told him, "We have one last chance; the play is to give the ball to Calhoun." On fourth down the quarterback went back to pass and was sacked. With that time ran out and the game was over.

The coach, frustrated beyond all belief, ran to the quarterback and asked him, "You knew the plan; why didn't you give the ball to Calhoun?"

The young quarterback answered, "Coach, each time we called the play, but Calhoun didn't want the ball." The message is clear; we must take our responsibility seriously. When God or others "call our number" we must take the ball and run with it.

How does one manifest being an ambassador of the Lord, being the Christ to others? First, we must be the person God calls us to be. If our vocation is marriage and family, then we should be the best spouse, parent, and worker we can be. If called to the single life, we might have more time to directly assist others and to be a more overt ambassador. Young people must fulfill their roles, assisting with family duties and chores, maximizing their efforts in the classroom, showing their peers the Christian way to resolve problems regardless of what contemporary society might suggest is the "quick fix" to what ails us personally or communally.

Being ambassadors is not a nine-to-five job. We must be Christians 24 hours a day seven days a week. A little story captures this challenge. One day a reporter was interviewing a well-respected man of the community. He asked him, "What do you do?"

The answer came back almost immediately, "I am a Christian."

"No," said the reporter, "you do not understand what I mean. What keeps you busy; what do you do every day?"

Again, the man responded, "I told you I am a Christian." Somewhat frustrated, the reporter for the third time asked, "No, sir, you do not understand my question. What do you do for a living; how do you occupy your time? What is your livelihood?"

The man once again answered, "I told you I am a Christian 24 hours a day seven days a week. But to pay the bills I own a furniture store."

Our role as ambassadors is part and parcel of our lives as Christians. Let us realize that like Artaban we may not *think* that our lives make a difference, but we are all players in God's magnificent plan of salvation history. Let us do our share to build the kingdom of God in our world. Let us be ambassadors of the Lord, today and to life eternal. Amen.

The Baptism Of Our Lord
Epiphany 1
Ordinary Time 1
Acts 8:14-17

Responsibility Comes With Privilege

Once upon a time there was a good king who ruled wisely and well over his people, who loved him very much. This king had four beautiful daughters who were all well respected by the people. One day he called them together and told them, "I am going to a far-off monastery to spend time in prayer with God. Therefore, I am leaving you in charge of the kingdom." While all the girls, one after the other, told their father not to leave, he insisted that it was necessary. Before he left on his journey, however, he gave each one a small gift, one single grain of rice. Then, after hugging and kissing his daughters, he set off on his journey.

Each of the daughters used the gift in different ways. The eldest thought the gift was special and wanted to display it. She went to her room, tied a long, golden thread around the grain of rice and placed it in a beautiful crystal box on her bureau. She could see it each day and it reminded her of her father, the king. The second daughter also believed the gift to be important. She placed her grain of rice in a wooden box and put it in a secure place under her bed. The third daughter, who was very pragmatic, looked at the grain of rice and thought, "What good is one grain of rice?" She simply discarded it. The youngest daughter took the grain of rice to her room and began to ponder what the significance of her father's gift was. She thought about it for weeks, then a month. After nearly a year had passed, she believed she understood the meaning of the gift.

Months turned into years and the four daughters ruled their father's kingdom. Then one day the king returned with a sparkle in his eye and a certain illumination in his face that he gained from years of prayer. After greeting each one of his daughters he asked to see the gifts that he had given to them. The eldest daughter retrieved the crystal box containing the grain of rice on the golden thread. The king accepted the crystal box and the grain of rice saying, "Thank you." Similarly, the king accepted the wooden box from the second daughter, saying to her, "Thank you." The third daughter rushed into the kitchen, found a grain of rice, and brought it back to her father who accepted it, again saying, "Thank you."

Then the youngest daughter came forward. She explained to her father that she had thought long and hard about the meaning of the gift and finally realized that it was a seed. So she planted it. Soon it grew and from it she harvested other seeds which she again planted. This continued over many seasons. She said to her father, "Father, look at the enormous crop of rice that we now have. It is enough to feed our entire nation."

Stepping before his daughter, the king took off his golden crown and placed it on her head. "You have learned the meaning of how to rule," he said softly. From that day on the youngest daughter ruled the kingdom wisely and well.

The story of the king and his four daughters demonstrates that privilege and responsibility come together; they cannot be separated. Each of the women received the same privilege, the honor of ruling their father's kingdom. The first three did not understand the responsibility that came with the privilege. The youngest, however, after contemplating the significance of her father's gift, realized the need to be responsible. Thus, she was the one chosen to succeed her father.

Today we close the Christmas season by celebrating the Baptism of our Lord. We are reminded not only of the Lord's baptism, as we hear described by all the synoptic evangelists, but possibly more importantly our own baptism. This sacrament brought us great privileges but significant responsibility is ours as well.

The Acts of the Apostles, from which our lesson is taken today, is really two books in one. Often referred to as the "fifth gospel," due to its probable authorship by Saint Luke, and its content, Acts presents two separate but important stories. In the early chapters we hear about the nascent Christian church, the formation of the community of faith, and some of the early struggles of these people, our ancestors in the faith. The latter portion of Acts chronicles the conversion of Saint Paul and then provides a detailed description of his three missionary journeys, for which he is often called the "apostle to the Gentiles."

The apostles and their close followers realized that they were privileged people. To walk in the footsteps of Jesus and to be his representatives on earth were indeed significant privileges. Persecution notwithstanding, these early Christians fearlessly and with great zeal and persistence carried on the work of their master amongst the people of their day and locale. Peter and John, two of the inner circle, realized that the privilege they had received in being apostles required that they take seriously their responsibilities.

Thus, as we hear in the reading, they brought the Holy Spirit, the same gift they had received at Pentecost to the people of Samaria. Recall that these people were the remnant of the so-called "ten lost tribes of Israel," overrun by the Assyrians and lost to history in 722 BCE. The apostles realized that Jesus' message of inclusivity went to all, even the long-despised Samaritans. Therefore, they unhesitatingly go to their natural enemy, realizing that they have a responsibility to carry forth the message of Christ to all people. Thus, they share the great gift that Jesus sent, the Holy Spirit, with others. Like the youngest daughter in the story, they understood that responsibility came with the privilege of carrying the message of Christ. Fortunately, through the efforts of people like the original apostles, Saint Paul, and many other brave men and women of that early Christian community, the message has been preached throughout the world. The Christian community has taken its responsibility seriously.

Baptism, the common denominator for all Christians, is a rare privilege. We have the privilege of being adopted children of God. Too often we brush over this significant prize of being children of God. However, only a few moments of reflection will show us how great a privilege God has bestowed upon all of us. We have the privilege of the church and all the many things it brings us — the sacraments, the word of God, the community of faith, fellowship, and assistance. We have each other as our friends, brothers, and sisters in the Lord, to celebrate our triumphs and to mourn our losses.

This great privilege of being a baptized Christian, however, has many responsibilities that come with it. Like Peter, John, and the other first-century Christians, we, the contemporary baptized, have the responsibility to carry forth the message of Christ to others. We are to preach the good news, both in formal and informal ways. We can teach an academic class, go door-to-door to evangelize, or even stand on a street corner and preach the message of Jesus. Clearly, these can be very effective methods, but they are by no means the only ones. In fact, meeting our baptismal commitment, fulfilling our responsibilities as Christians, happens each and every day of our lives in ways that are often routine, ordinary, and even seemingly mundane.

For example, simply walking along the street and sharing with a passerby a friendly smile and a cheery, "Good morning," is preaching the goodness of God to others. We can preach Christ's message of love, care, and peace through a gentle disposition, random acts of kindness, assisting those in need, or going out of our way to help someone, especially one whom we do not know. Parents and others in positions of authority carry out their baptismal commitment by being responsible for those whom God has given to them — children, grandchildren, fellow employees, and fellow travelers along the road of faith.

We have responsibilities to our places of work, the neighborhoods where we reside, and the community we call home, both on local and even national levels. Young people demonstrate their baptismal commitment by being responsible to their school work and classmates, their parents, and after school jobs. They show responsibility by avoiding the many pitfalls into which they are pressured: violence, drinking, sex, and drugs. In short, the privilege of being a baptized person necessitates we take seriously our Christian responsibilities.

Our fast-paced and highly technological world challenges us in many ways. Self-autonomy, desire for personal advancement, and the need to always shine above others often does not allow us to spend the time that is necessary to meet our responsibilities. Additionally, we fall victim to apathy, indifferentism, laziness, and even a sense of fatalism. We say, "Why should I get involved? Things will be the same with or without my effort." It is easy to take this road because it is well-traveled and quite popular, but for the Christian it is a dead-end street. We must accept the reality that responsibility is part and parcel of our lives as baptized Christians. All great privileges bring with them a sense of responsibility. We readily and with great joy accept the former, but only grudgingly, at times, fulfill the latter.

While the road will not be easy, nor the path straight, we must nevertheless push forward with vigor and persistence the Christian agenda that calls us to be responsible people, to be countercultural in a world that often does not understand or value the things we do or the beliefs we profess. Let us understand our responsibilities to family, neighbor, community of faith, and most especially to God. Let us as they say, "Take the ball and run with it," and sprint toward the goal, which is not a touchdown, but more importantly eternal life. Amen.

Epiphany 2
Ordinary Time 2
1 Corinthians 12:1-11

Strength Through Diversity

Recently on a British Airways flight from Johannesburg, South Africa, a middle-aged and apparently quite wealthy South African woman found herself sitting next to a black man. As the passengers were filing in and taking their seats she called a member of the cabin crew to ask about her seating. "What seems to be the matter, madam?" asked the attendant.

"Can't you see?" the woman responded. "You have assigned me a seat next to a *kaffir* (a pejorative word referring to a native black African). I cannot possibly sit next to this disgusting human being. Please find me another seat as soon as possible!"

The cabin attendant, hearing the words and observing the commotion that was clearly stirring among other passengers, commented, "Please calm down, madam. The flight is very full today but I will do what I can. I will go and check on availability of seats in business or first classes."

Meanwhile the woman, with a scowl on her face, looked at the black man beside her, who was outraged, not to mention many of the surrounding passengers. A few minutes later the attendant returned with good news that she delivered to the woman, who continued to look at her fellow passengers with a smug and self-satisfied grin. The flight attendant told the woman, "Madame, unfortunately, as I suspected economy is full. I have spoken to the cabin services director and business class is also full. However, we do have one seat in first class."

Before the woman had a chance to answer, the flight attendant continued, "It is most extraordinary to make this kind of upgrade;

I needed to receive special permission from the captain. But, given the circumstances, the captain felt that it was outrageous that someone be forced to sit next to such an obnoxious person." With that the flight attendant turned to the black man sitting next to the woman and said, "So if you would like to gather your things, sir, I have your seat ready for you." At that point, the surrounding passengers stood and gave a standing ovation as the black man walked triumphantly into first class.

This true event presents us with many lessons. Most obviously we learn of the reality of prejudice and intolerance in our world. The story also shows how one can learn a significant lesson from those with greater wisdom that such prejudicial attitudes do not gain us anything, but rather can shame us into realizing the callous nature of our attitudes. Somewhat hidden, but nonetheless present, the story also tells us of the great value diversity can bring, especially with the knowledge that all things have one source, namely God, and we are to work toward one common end, the building of God's kingdom. Although our methods will be different, we must use the gifts we possess and our varied cultures and racial ethnicities to assist others toward the common goal of life eternal. Openness to what is new and different is key to appreciating the power, goodness, and strength that can come from diversity.

Saint Paul addresses the issue of diversity in today's reading by describing the various gifts we have received, all of which have one common source, the Holy Spirit. First, Paul speaks of the necessity of the Spirit in our lives. He writes that we can only address Jesus as Lord by the inspiration of the Spirit. We are not autonomous operators; God is here to inspire and encourage us. God does not force us to do anything, but the inspiration is given to lead us in the proper direction — the one and only path that leads back to God. Thus, the Spirit is necessary to continue toward God. Paul also says that if we have the Spirit, we cannot speak ill of God. Living in the power and presence of God has its positive effects on us. We cannot go astray with God, but there are many lessons we need to learn in order to achieve this result.

The apostle then enumerates the many gifts of the Spirit. Each is unique and special; each is given, Paul says, as the Spirit chooses.

Each gift is different and must be used in a collective sense with others in building the kingdom of God. It is through this diversity of gifts that we find our source of sustenance. We need all the gifts, but none of us has them all. Thus, we need to appreciate the diversity, the differences, and the strength that we gain through sharing with one another. If all the world's people had the same gifts, human society would never achieve its potential. As Paul says, the manifestations of the Spirit's gifts are given for the common good.

We have all experienced the plethora of the Spirit's gifts, in our lives and the lives of those we know, love, and with whom we regularly associate. Some are given great wisdom; some are given significant knowledge. We know that these two gifts are very different, but both are necessary to build the kingdom. We need a certain amount of knowledge — that is people who are smart — but we definitely need people who know how to apply that knowledge, those with wisdom to apply facts and information.

Paul continues by describing many gifts, each given by the Spirit, each different and unique. Whether it is faith, healing, being a worker of miracles, prophecy, languages, or one who interprets languages, the gift is part of the breath of God's goodness. These gifts, together with knowledge and wisdom, show the diversity of our talents. All are important; all are necessary. While we might live without one of the gifts in our personal lives, our world would be somewhat less without any of them. We would all be deprived of something very special.

We have all heard the expression "Diversity is the spice of life." I think we can all verify the reality of this statement. Picture a world where all people looked, spoke, acted, and thought alike. It would be like entering a shoe store and finding only one style or going to a car dealership that offered only one make or model of automobile or finding only one brand of cereal or bread in the grocery store. Simply put, life would be boring and certainly less than satisfying. Yet, as is evidenced by the story of the passengers on the plane and, too often unfortunately in the world around us, indeed in our own lives at times, we reject diversity. We are selective.

Everyone makes choices; nobody likes everyone or everything. The rejection of diversity is not that we don't acknowledge differences in talents, ideas, ethnic or national backgrounds, or possess varied religious or political persuasions. Rather when we reject diversity we openly reject that which is different around us. Most of the time, our rejection of diversity is rather subtle. We choose not to associate with certain people, either individuals or collective groups. There are times we never consider another person's idea, way of doing things, or attitude if it differs from ones we hold. We isolate ourselves from what we do not like or simply do not wish to deal with. Most probably we don't even realize that we are rejecting diversity. Rather, we say to ourselves, "I simply have different ideas than others."

Too often, however, society and individuals openly reject diversity, even in a hostile way. That was certainly the case with the woman on the plane. We may not make a scene as did the woman, but in our minds and actions we are as closed as she was toward the black man. Such attitudes stunt our growth. Sometimes we are fortunate, like the woman, to be shocked or even embarrassed into understanding the problematic reality of our attitude. However, too often we do not learn and thus we continue down the path that leads nowhere. We miss out on many opportunities of life.

The destructive force of a world without diversity has, unfortunately, been repeated too often in history. The suppression of native people in the New World and the perceived need to have one and only one culture deprived the world of a few significant civilizations, such as the Aztec, Mayan, and Inca native people in Mexico and South America. Religious wars in Europe, the infamous crusades of medieval times, and many wars between rival Christian factions were fought basically because people were not open to varied understandings of God. Certainly such actions were an overt denial of Jesus' message of inclusivity. Intolerance in ways of thinking, politically and socially, generated the Soviet State's control of the "Iron Curtain" countries after World War II. Rejection of the Jews as a race, culture, and religion led directly to the Holocaust. These historical events stunted the world's ability to grow for a time. We were all the losers.

We need to root out the attitude of exclusivity, the idea that some people, ideas, opinions, and attitudes are acceptable while others are not. We may not agree with certain ways of doing things, but we cannot dismiss them out of hand. Such behavior not only contradicts the message of Paul and his diversity of spiritual gifts for the common good, but it betrays the whole life of Jesus, the head and guide of our faith. Therefore, let us learn a lesson today of the need to appreciate variations in our world. Let us truly believe that strength comes through diversity. As we continue to walk as one people, rejoicing in our different talents, gifts, ideas, let us do so in imitation of Jesus, our brother, friend, and Lord. Amen.

Epiphany 3
Ordinary Time 3
1 Corinthians 12:12-31a

Teammates In Building The Kingdom

"Outlined against a blue-gray October sky, the Four Horsemen rode again. In dramatic lore they are known as pestilence, famine, destruction, and death. These are only aliases. There real names are Studehler, Miller, Crowley, and Layden." Grantland Rice, a well-known sports columnist in the first half of the twentieth century, wrote those memorable words in October 1927 after attending a classic gridiron struggle between Army and Notre Dame, played at the Polo Grounds in New York. With these words a legend was started, for Notre Dame football, the team's immortal coach Knute Rockne and, that day especially, for the Four Horsemen of Notre Dame.

Who were the Four Horsemen? Elmer Layden, Harry Studehler, Jim Crowley, and Don Miller were the talented offensive backfield for the Notre Dame football team in the late 1920s. There is no doubt that they were great players. Football fans then and now remember their names and their exploits on the gridiron. All four have been enshrined in the College Football Hall of Fame.

Most people know, however, that there are eleven players on a football team. What about the other seven? Who were they; what did they do? History knows them as the "Seven Mules." Few if anyone remembers their names. Only one of them, a fellow named "Rip" Miller, is a member of the College Football Hall of Fame. Still, I am certain that the Four Horsemen knew them. In fact, the same Grantland Rice who immortalized the horsemen said that this talented backfield attributed all their success to the mules. They were the ones who stood in front, did the blocking, ran interference, and paved a way for the two halfbacks, the fullback, and quarterback to run the plays, score touchdowns, and bring victory to Notre Dame.

The Four Horsemen and the Seven Mules were a team. They knew that they needed each other. Without the mules the horsemen probably would have been an ordinary college football backfield. But the combination of the mules and the horsemen, working as a team, brought greatness, fame, and legend to Miller, Layden, Crowley, Studehler, and to Notre Dame football, as well.

The story of the fabled Four Horsemen of Notre Dame and the unheralded "seven mules," is a good illustration of how people need to work together to accomplish great goals. We are not solo operators in the world; we need each other. While we may be different and possess varied talents, in this case some to run with the ball and others to block and run interference, all are needed to achieve the desired common end. In a similar way, Saint Paul uses the famous image of the body to demonstrate that while we are different in many ways, possessive of various gifts and talents, we must be united as the body of Christ in our common effort to build the kingdom of God in our world.

Paul begins his famous analogy by describing the power of baptism in unifying the body of Christ. He says that our baptism in the Spirit unites us, whether Jews or Greek, slave or free. Thus, Paul touches on both of the critical bases: sacred and secular. Not only are the Jews, those who were the first converts to Christianity, part of the body, but also the Greeks, that is the Gentiles. Jesus' message of salvation goes out to all. He goes on to say slaves as well as free men and women are part of the body. Here Paul suggests that status in the world is of little or no consequence to Christ. Baptism is the great leveler, the right that is common to all. His message says that no one is more or less important in Jesus' eyes.

Paul's analogy of membership to the body continues by speaking of the contributions of hands and feet, eyes and ears. In both cases each part of the body is of significant value. One part cannot say of the other it is not part of the body or unimportant. All parts are members, all parts are important. He goes on to say that each part is essential. If the body were all an eye or an ear then other senses, such as smell and touch, would be lost. Indeed, Paul says that the parts that seem weaker are actually indispensable. Those with less honor are clothed with greater honor. God has arranged to give greater honor to those inferior members so that there will be no dissension.

God desires the body of Christ to work together. If it is truly united then when one part suffers the whole body suffers; when one member is honored the whole body rejoices. The body, therefore, must live, love, and cry together. The body is one; its strength comes through unity.

Paul concludes his analogy by providing examples of how the parts of the body are manifest. He mentions apostles, prophets, teachers as some of the many specific vocations of the body. Then he describes the many gifts, such as healing, assistance, forms of leadership, and tongues or languages. No one person possesses all of these gifts and, thus, there is a need to work together to maximize the potential of the body. Again, Paul stresses the need for unity.

Paul's analogy of the body working together clearly presents the message that we must be a team, working with Jesus, our leader and guide. Saint Augustine in his great work, *The City of God*, wrote that we are citizens of two worlds, human society and the church. In each of these domains it is necessary to be a team, to work on a united front. We must, however, realize that unity does not mean uniformity. We don't all march to the same drummer; we have various likes and dislikes, different ways of operation. Thus, our methods and ideas will vary, which is actually helpful to the progress of the body. We can and must approach situations and problems with various solutions. What is essential, however, is to remain on the same page with respect to the goal. There are many ways to skin a cat; achieving the desired end is essential. Thus, the body can use all its members to gain its goal, not only a few who are prominent, influential, or noteworthy.

But what is our goal? We are called to build the kingdom of God in our world. In essence we are to build a more compassionate, peaceful, and just world. We have been commissioned through baptism to do our share to complete the master's work. Jesus' work in our world is multidimensional but has been succinctly described by Father Basil Anthony Moreau, founder of the Congregation of Holy Cross, who wrote that our mission is, "to make God known, loved, and served."

We can carry out this mission in our world in many ways. We have varied locations, occupations, and gifts. We need doctors, attorneys, teachers, office workers, police and fire personnel, engineers, and a host of other peoples to make civil society one that functions properly. Each contributes in his or her individual and specific way. However, we must keep our eyes focused on the goal, to make God known, loved, and served.

Unfortunately, too many divisions exist in our world. We are not running the race together as a team, but rather, seem to be individual athletes in competition. This competition between groups and individuals is strong and even becomes counterproductive toward the achievement of the common goal. The body, therefore, is fighting against itself. Thus, society is not moving sufficiently toward its proper end. On the contrary, there is much evidence we are moving increasingly away from our common goal.

Such evidence is clear in the North-South economic division of our world that continues to grow, separating nations and people. Paul suggests that if the body of Christ must suffer, it must do so together. Unfortunately, this is not the reality. The vast majority of the world suffers and lives in darkness. The manifestations of this reality are many and widespread. Poverty, disease, ignorance, injustice, and violence are only some of the many significant ways the world suffers. We do not care sufficiently for our weaker members, as Paul suggests. Rather we place them on the margins of society, unseen and unheard. The majority feels better when such "problematic" individuals are kept out of mind and sight. Again, we contradict the body of Christ in our actions. On the other hand, a limited few exult. These possess not only what they need but in many cases have superabundance. While it is true that Jesus said, "The poor you will always have with you," we cannot use this as an excuse to ignore the inequalities in our world.

What is even sadder is that the majority of the world suffers and a few exult due in large measure to personal choice. Nations and individuals make decisions that create the world in which we live. It is not simply the progress of history that creates poverty and wealth. No, human society has chosen this route.

The lack of teamwork in human society is, unfortunately, replicated in our church. Rather than working together as a team, we are far too divided. Often, it seems, we are actually working against each other. Distinctions that divide communities of faith seem more important than ideas that unite us. Again, personal choice is, in large measure, the reason for this situation.

Solutions to this situation can and must be found. In society we can create a more compassionate and just world by focusing more on others and less on ourselves. While we cannot change a societal attitude on a systemic level overnight, we can and must change our own attitude. As the expression goes, "Think globally but act locally." If we can begin to move more toward an attitude of community and push away from individualism in our personal lives and that of society, we will have at least made a good start. In our churches we must move toward greater ecumenical and even interfaith dialogue. Again, we must begin with ourselves realizing that men and women of faith worldwide have good intentions. Thus, to concentrate on what is common and constructive rather than that which is divisive will get us started in the proper direction.

Saint Paul's image of the body of Christ, many members working together, sharing our joys and sorrows, is our goal. However, society and the church are far from this lofty summit. Let our goal be to work toward making the body one in our society. Let us work together as a team, like the Four Horsemen and the seven mules. Jesus' prayer to his Father can light our way: "That they may all be one. As you, Father, are in me and I am in you, may they also be in us, so that the world may believe that you have sent me" (John 17:21). Let us profess and believe the same. Amen.

**Epiphany 4
Ordinary Time 4
1 Corinthians 13:1-13**

Love — The Basic Christian Call

During the 56 years of his life, Adolf Hitler did incredible harm and was responsible for the death of millions of people. Yet in all of the horror that he unleashed, there were pinpoints of light and nobility. One German soldier, Private Joseph Schultz, was one of those pinpoints.

Schultz was sent to Yugoslavia shortly after the Germans invaded that country. He was a loyal, young, German soldier on patrol. One day the sergeant called out eight names, his among them. They thought they were going on a routine patrol. As they hitched up their rifles, they came over a hill, still not knowing what their mission was. There they encountered eight Yugoslavians, standing on the brow of a hill, five men and three women. It was only when they were about fifty feet away from them, when any marksman could shoot out the eye of a pheasant, that the soldiers realized what their mission was.

The soldiers were lined up. The sergeant barked out, "Ready!" and they lifted their rifles. "Aim," and the soldiers got their sights set. Then suddenly in the silence that prevailed there was the thud of a rifle butt against the ground. The sergeant, the seven other soldiers, and those eight Yugoslavians stopped and looked. Private Joseph Schultz walked toward the Yugoslavians. His sergeant called after him and ordered him to come back, but he pretended not to hear him. Instead, Schultz walked fifty feet to the mound of the hill and he joined hands with the eight Yugoslavians. There was a moment of silence, and then the sergeant yelled, "Fire!" Private Schultz died that day, his blood mingled with those of the innocent men and women. Found on his body was an excerpt from Saint Paul: "[Love] bears all things, believes all things, hopes all things, endures all things" (1 Corinthians 13:7).

This true story from World War II demonstrates the concept of love as articulated by Saint Paul in his famous passage from 1 Corinthians. The many manifestations of love are brought together by Paul who understood this powerful emotion through his imitation of Jesus and the latter's commandment of love. We are similarly called to love without reservation.

Saint Paul begins his teaching by describing the many ways love excels all other virtues. He says one may be able to speak with great force and angelic quality, but if there is no love behind the words, the person is a noisy gong or clanging symbol. Clearly, the intent, the reason one speaks is of great importance for Paul. One must speak with the proper intent — never to injure, but always to demonstrate love. This does not mean, at times, that hard words are not necessary. Tough love may demand words that others do not want to hear; to act in any other way would not be a demonstration of love.

The apostle then speaks of the power of love over prophecy. We may have been given the gift to understand great mysteries and the opportunity to proclaim them to others, but without love we are not utilizing the gift in an appropriate manner. Knowledge is given to aid others and to build the kingdom of God. If, however, we do not have love in our use of this knowledge it is easy to misuse it or to utilize it in inappropriate ways. It will not be used to build the kingdom.

Again, Paul says we may have faith so strong we can move mountains, yet without love we have nothing. Faith in God mandates that we have great love; faith without love cannot be faith in God, for God is love.

Lastly, Paul says if we give all we have away and give our bodies over for others to use in some way but do not possess love we gain nothing. There is no activity of charity or compassion that can be rightly done without love. We may give but if there is no love behind our gift, then most probably we are giving only to be noticed by others, not for the appropriate reasons.

Thus, Paul provides ample evidence to the reality that love is the basic Christian virtue. It is the foundation upon which all is built; it is the root from which all of Christianity blossoms. Love is absolutely essential if we are to live the Christian life as Jesus outlined it in his words and deeds. While Paul could not have read any of the gospels, he seemed to know a great deal about Jesus, including his new commandment of love. Jesus expresses it powerfully.

> *I give you a new commandment, that you love one another. Just as I have loved you, you also should love one another. By this everyone will know that you are my disciples, if you have love for one another.*
> — John 13:34-35

Paul's idea that love is the base of Christianity is clear, but how can we know we actually love as Jesus commanded? The apostle helps us answer this question by providing an important list of qualities present in one who loves. First, he says love is patient. We know patience is a virtue in short supply these days. The humorous little prayer demonstrates our difficulty with patience: "O, Lord, grant me patience and give it to me now!" We don't want to wait for anything these days, in our world and in our personal lives, both of which mandate instant answers and results. We are all impatient, especially when we have no control over responses or results. Paul suggests if we truly love we will demonstrate patience.

Next, he says love is kind. Often impatience leads to a very unkind attitude; we become angry quite readily. The way we approach people and situations is too often far less than kind. We are adversarial; we are right and others are wrong. We somehow believe if we are too kind we demonstrate weakness and others will take advantage of us. Yet, Paul suggests we are not people of love if we cannot demonstrate kindness to our brothers and sisters.

The apostle continues by saying love is never envious or boastful. There are certainly major problems in our society today. We are always trying to impress people with who we are or the things we do. We observe this in many professional athletes, television and movie stars, and politicians. But even more Paul is suggesting that a boastful or envious attitude will destroy relationships. True love for another cannot allow us to be envious of who others are or what they do. We are told by Paul that love is never resentful. If we are envious we are often resentful of what others have been given. We desire their power, wealth, prestige, or some combination of these three. We cannot "lord it over others" simply because circumstance or situation has placed us above others on the corporate or social ladders. True love is incompatible with attitudes that differentiate between peoples or place one person ahead or behind another.

Paul concludes his discussion of love's qualities by providing a list of attributes that demonstrate the positive nature and hopefulness of love. He says love bears through any hardship. We know love is greatly tested when problems and the vicissitudes of life come our way. The person of true love can look down the road and bear through to the end. This is possible because people who love can believe all things are possible. With love, meaning with God, all things truly are possible. We can hope in all things because with love hope is possible. As a popular expression goes, "Hope springs eternal." Love will endure to the end.

Yes, Paul believes love is eternal. While prophecies end through their fulfillment, tongues will fall into disuse, and even knowledge will be lost over time, love will endure. Prophecy, knowledge, and all other ideas are only found in part, but love is eternal. Love is the fulfillment of our life. Paul expresses this idea by seeing love as the adult response to life. In the end, he summarizes his teaching by saying, of all the great virtues of faith, hope, and love, the greatest and, therefore, the base of the Christian life is love.

How can we manifest this great love of God? Joan Baez, the famous folk singer of the 1960s, sang a song titled "Love Is Just A Four Letter Word." The lyrics of the song express the idea that because love is a short word of only four letters it might be thought to be a simple concept. We know, however, that this base virtue of the Christian life is anything but simple. Its manifestations are many. As Private Schultz understood by his heroic actions, love never delights in evil, but rather rejoices in the truth.

The Greeks, a wise and highly sophisticated ancient civilization, understood the complexity of love. Their language uses three words to express the one we have in English. The concept of *eros* speaks of specialized romantic love. Obviously this is an integral element of love where men and women demonstrate their total commitment to each other in marriage. All the qualities of which Paul speaks must clearly be put into a relationship of *eros*. Unfortunately, today we often see the consequences when one or both parties in such a relationship cannot fulfill the qualities and characteristics of which Paul writes.

The Greeks used the word *phileo* to describe brotherly and sisterly love. We have many relationships with members of our family, good friends, colleagues and associates at work, as well as neighbors in our city or town. We must show love for them as well. We cannot like all people; we will only choose to associate for social recreation with a limited group. Others, let us face reality, we might choose to avoid for a whole host of reasons, some of which might be appropriate, but others not very sound. Yet, we are called to demonstrate love to all. In essence we are called to respect people, to never seek our advantage over them, nor denigrate their person or the ideas they express simply because we do not agree. Love calls us to show this common respect.

Lastly, the Greeks use the word *agape* to express their highest form of love — service to one another. While Paul's exhortation on love, on initial examination, does not seem to speak of service, yet all of these qualities are endemic to it. Service requires us to go out of our way, beyond our immediate purview to meet the needs of some of our brothers and sisters. In such endeavors we must show patience and kindness. We must never be boastful or arrogant, placing ourselves above others. We have all heard the expression, "If not by the grace of God, there go I." Our Christian commitment to love calls us to serve others. We must never shirk this most important responsibility.

The manifestations of love are many. Few of us will ever be tested to love as was Private Schultz. His faith constitution was obviously strong, and he made his decision to stand with the Yugoslavians as an act of love. Still, we are challenged on a daily basis to show love, to manifest in our lives with spouses, friends, and associates, and God's people more generally the special qualities of love that Paul describes today. Let us take some time to look into our hearts and ask, "How have we loved today? What more do we need to do?" When we find the answers, let us have the courage as did Private Schultz, Saint Paul, and Jesus of Nazareth and manifest love to others in all that we say and do. If we can, our reward in heaven will be great. Amen.

Epiphany 5
Ordinary Time 5
1 Corinthians 15:1-11

The Great Sacrifice Of Love

In the fifteenth century, a rural village in Germany was home to a family with eighteen children. The family was poor, but despite the difficulty of making ends meet, two brothers in the family still held a dream, namely to pursue their talent as artists. With the financial situation bleak the two boys came up with their own solution to the problem. They agreed to toss a coin with the loser going to the local mines to work so he could support the other while he attended art school. When the first was finished with his training, he would support the education of the other, either by sale of his art works or by going to the mines himself. Thus, one brother went off to the dangerous mines while the other went to the art academy. After four years, the young artist returned triumphantly to a homecoming dinner. The artist rose from the table to drink a toast to his beloved brother for his years of sacrifice. He said, "Now Albert, it is your turn to go to the academy and pursue your dream; I will support you."

Albert sat at the table and tears began to flow down his cheeks. He began to repeat, "No, no, no." Finally Albert rose, wiped the tears from his face and holding his hands out in front of him said softly, "No, brother, it is too late for me to go. Look at what four years in the mines have done to my hands. The bones in every finger have been crushed at least once, and I suffer from arthritis so badly that I cannot even hold a wine glass properly to return your toast, much less make lines on a canvas with pen or brush. No, brother, for me it is too late."

Then, one day to pay homage to his brother who had sacrificed his life dream for him, the great artist, Albrecht Dürer, painstakingly drew his brother's hands with palms together and crooked fingers pointed skyward. He called his powerful painting simply *Hands*, but the entire world almost immediately opened its heart to the masterpiece and renamed his great work and tribute of love, *The Praying Hands*.

The story of the great sacrifice of Albert Dürer for his brother is truly inspiring. After hearing his story, whenever one sees Albrecht Dürer's masterpiece, *The Praying Hands*, it is impossible to not associate this work of art with the sacrifice of love it represents. In today's lesson from 1 Corinthians, Saint Paul describes the earliest account of the greatest act of sacrificial love the world has ever witnessed, the Paschal mystery — the passion, death, and resurrection of Jesus Christ. Jesus came to our world in obedience to his Father's will, becoming human in all ways, save sin, and willingly gave his life so we would have the possibility of life eternal. Not only does Paul describe the great sacrifice of Jesus' love for us, he also explains how he responded to this love through his energetic and unceasing missionary activity. Paul's words must challenge us to ask how we can respond in a similar way to the sacrificial love Jesus has shown us.

Saint Paul's encounter with Jesus on the road to Damascus and the long period of preparation (scholars dispute whether it was fourteen or seventeen years) after his conversion for his mission, filled him with the tradition of Jesus. Thus, he wants to educate the Corinthians, a people he knew very well as evidenced by his letters to the community and his residence in the city for a considerable amount of time. He explains to them the significance of the extraordinary sacrifice of love that Jesus performed for us. First Corinthians is the earliest source for these sacred Christian traditions. In 11:23-26, Paul gives the first account of the institution of the Eucharist, one of the basic and common rites in our Christian tradition.

In today's lesson Paul describes the Paschal mystery. He says the great traditions of Jesus were foretold in the scriptures. Jesus is the fulfillment of God's promise. It is through the promise and its fulfillment that the Corinthians and all others will be saved. Thus, it is essential that the community believe in Paul's message for it is the missive of life.

Paul then articulates specifically the great events of our salvation. First, he says that Jesus died. Jesus truly suffered and experienced death for the remission of our sins. But the tradition of Jesus' death and burial is followed by the elation that he was raised and appeared to the apostles and even later to Paul and many other disciples. This great sacrifice of God's love demonstrated the length and breadth of what God was willing to do for us. As Albert Dürer went to the mines so his brother could attend art school, and in the process sacrificed his own opportunity for greatness and personal fulfillment, so Jesus, the Son of God, fulfilled his Father's will and sacrificed his life for us.

Paul realized that such a great sacrifice requires a significant response from us. He understood how privileged he was to be chosen by God to be a missionary. He believed this was his mission as partial payment for the sacrifice Christ endured for him. He confesses that he was unfit to be chosen, let alone to be called an apostle, as his former life as a zealous persecutor of the "new way" was antithetical to the notion of Jesus and his message. Thus, he concludes, "But by the grace of God I am what I am" (v. 10). Paul's conversion and his commission came in response to God who first loved him. Realizing, as we have stated in earlier weeks, that responsibility and privilege go together in Christianity, Paul answered the challenge of Jesus by fulfilling his call as the first and greatest Christian missionary. Indeed, as he says, he worked harder than all others.

In the end, Paul attributes his ministry and his success to God, not to himself. All that Paul was given, especially his ability to respond to the Lord, has come from God. Clearly, Paul's message to the Corinthians is not only one of information, but equally, if not more importantly, one of challenge to respond to God who first loved us.

The scriptures consistently speak of our need, as Jesus' disciples, to sacrifice, to give our lives for others.

> *If any want to become my followers, let them deny themselves and take up their cross daily and follow me. For those who want to save their life will lose it, and those who lose their life for my sake will save it.*
> — Luke 9:23-24

Jesus is asking his followers to give their lives for the betterment of others. This is not a call to martyrdom, but rather a challenge to find ways we can use our lives, our talents, our opportunities, our time, and our resources to build the kingdom of God in our world.

The call to demonstrate sacrificial love is an everyday challenge to all, from youth in school, to men and women in the working world, and even those who are retired. Children have a special role to demonstrate love. Learning at an early age one's need to give up something desired so another good can be furthered is a fundamental lesson in life. Freely refusing to have some item, a new piece of clothing, the newest CD or DVD, some special food, and seeing in such action a solidarity with those who have little or none is certainly an act of sacrificial love. Children quite naturally form their own group of playmates, those with whom they desire "to hang," but sacrificial love means they need to be open to others. Many "outsiders" may wish to be part of the group, but because an invitation is never extended they can never break through and be recognized. Sacrificing for others means to reach out, as did Jesus, to those who are different, those we do not know, and those whom society has placed on the margins.

Working people and parents have different opportunities to demonstrate sacrificial love. While being a parent is certainly satisfying, this important task must be the most difficult work in the world, and one that becomes increasingly more complex as life becomes faster and more diverse, almost on a daily basis. Parents have been given children by God to raise in the faith and to educate in mind and heart. Such a responsibility requires sacrifice. Parents gladly give up their own agenda and often many of the things they would like so their children can have more. Seldom do you hear a parent not say that they want things better for the children than it was for them. Sacrificial love is more than giving up material things and time. It may actually cause us great pain, although we know it is necessary.

Tough love often needs to be applied when children or even spouses have gone astray. We do no one any favor by failing to address problems that arise. Surely it is much easier to ignore the problem, "sweep it under the rug" or do nothing. We might be able to keep peace by feeding one's addiction, but we are not demonstrating the power of sacrificial love that Jesus exemplified on the cross, the same love of which Paul writes in our lesson today.

Children and working adults are not the only ones who must demonstrate sacrificial love. It is a requirement of those who are retired as well. People who have spent the bulk of their life in education and work can now give back to society. Surely, the retired person has every right to rest and relaxation, but sacrificial love requires them to service of their brothers and sisters in public and private sectors. We can use the extra time we possess to help schools, both children in the classroom and other areas where our services can be utilized. We can assist in social service agencies for the poor and marginalized, such as a soup kitchen or a homeless shelter. We can assist our peers who might be less physically or psychologically capable and who reside in restrooms or frequent senior centers.

Sacrificial love, whether we are young, working adults, or retirees will require us to go out of ourselves. We will have to give up, as Jesus says, something we possess — valuable time, opportunity, or material possession — but the rewards will be great. Jesus says, "The measure you give will be the measure you get back" (Luke 6:38b). We recall Jesus' response to Peter when he asked what would be received for living a life of discipleship.

> *Truly I tell you, there is no one who has left house or brothers or sisters or mother or father or children or fields, for my sake and for the sake of the good news, who will not receive a hundredfold now in this age — houses, brothers and sisters, mothers and children, and fields with persecutions — and in the age to come eternal life.* — Mark 10:29-30

Albert Dürer did not know it at the time, but his agreement to go to the mines would not only produce a world-class artist, but at the same time ended any possibility he had to be an artist himself. His act of sacrificial love was an imitation of the heroic sacrifice of Jesus, which Paul describes in our lesson today. May we have the courage to do likewise as we continue to walk the journey of faith, one that leads to death, but eventually to resurrection and eternal life. Amen.

Epiphany 6
Ordinary Time 6
1 Corinthians 15:12-20

Raised To New Life Today

William Wilberforce was a privileged man. He was given a second chance; he was in many ways resurrected. Because of his efforts the world is a much more compassionate and just place. Wilberforce was born in 1759 in Hull, England, the son of a wealthy merchant. As a youth he led a rather dissolute life; his father's money allowed him access to people and things, yet he used his privilege to his advantage or abused it to the detriment of others. In 1780, he became a member of parliament representing Yorkshire. At this time he initiated what would become a lifelong friendship with William Pitt the Younger, who would later serve with distinction as Prime Minister. Still, he continued his self-indulgent ways; there seemed to be no stopping his actions that brought him further and further from God.

In 1784, however, Wilberforce received a great gift, although he may not have recognized it at the time. He met a group of evangelical Christians, a group called the Clapham Sect, who forced him to reevaluate his lifestyle. He was so transformed by his experience with this group that he completely changed his ways and became a leading proponent of social reform in Great Britain, especially the improvement of factory conditions.

Wilberforce's newfound Christian faith, his second chance on life, led him eventually to the door of Thomas Clarkson, a leading abolitionist in Britain. Clarkson and others were campaigning for an end to the horrific British slave trade that ferried Africans from their homeland to the New World. Through his position in parliament, Wilberforce had the power to do something about this intolerable institution. Despite strong opposition from many lobbies, he introduced legislation to abolish the slave trade and he reintroduced it for the next eighteen years in succession. Over time, more and more people began to join with the Clapham Sect and their allies, producing pamphlets and books and holding rallies and circulating petitions.

Finally, in 1807 the slave trade was abolished, but his work was not done. He became a leader in the Society for the Suppression of Vice, started in 1802. Wilberforce led campaigns for better education for children. He died in July 1833, literally a few days after slavery had been abolished in the British Empire. William Wilberforce was given a second chance; he was resurrected. Fortunately for the world he made the best of the opportunity God gave to him.

Wilberforce's ability to find a new direction, basically to rise to new life, stands as a good illustration of Saint Paul's message to the Corinthians in today's lesson. In chapter 15 Paul tells the Corinthians of the centrality of the tradition that he was given, namely the significance of the Paschal mystery, the passion, death, and resurrection of Christ. Now, he goes further, expanding on his earlier ideas of resurrection as a central focus of our Christian faith. This fundamental message of Christian faith is a source of consolation to us. Christ's resurrection will give us the second, the third, the hundredth chance. We need to respond to the opportunity of new life Christ has given to us.

Paul tells the Corinthians of his certainty that there is resurrection from the dead because Christ conquered death. This is the central article of faith for Christians. It is so central, in fact, that Paul tells his readers that if Christ has not been raised, his proclamation has been useless and so too the faith of those who believe. Moreover, he says that if Christ is not raised, then Paul is guilty of misrepresenting God, testifying to something that is not true.

The apostle also speaks of the essential need of Christ's resurrection for our future hope. Without Jesus' resurrection there is no reason to have hope in him for the resurrection was the event that secured our release from bondage. It was the action that released us from our sins. If Christ is not raised, one remains in sin; we have no hope to break the bond of sin that our first parents brought to the world through their disobedience of God. Christ's resurrection is our ticket to eternal life. Paul tells the Corinthians that if our hope in Christ is only for what the Lord can do today, if there is no possibility for future resurrection, then we are pitiable people. We have believed in a hoax. However, Paul reaffirms at the end of the passage that, in fact, Jesus was raised from the dead. He is the first fruit of those who have died. Jesus' action has brought release and new life to those who have died. The same can become reality in our lives today, as well.

Certainly there is no need to wait for life eternal to experience the possibility of new life today. As the life of William Wilberforce clearly shows, we can find and even should seek opportunities to be renewed, to be resurrected, and to find new life in our lives and that of the society and community in which we live. Yet, there is an important prerequisite; we must be open to transformation by God. Opportunities to find our proper road to God are given to us at certain special moments in life; they don't come every day! Thus, when the Lord provides the opportunity, we must be open and ready to respond. We must be attuned to the Lord's call since it is generally quite subtle. We must listen well. Remember the call of the great prophet Samuel. When he was just a boy, God called him twice, but he nor his mentor, Eli, recognized the Lord's call. Finally, when the Lord called a third time, Eli perceived it was God's call and told young Samuel, "Go, lie down; and if he calls you, you shall say, 'Speak, Lord, for your servant is listing' " (1 Samuel 3:9).

When God's call comes and we hear it, then we must be willing to respond. But this is often not an easy thing to do; it may require much of us. When the young man came to Jesus and asked what was necessary to find eternal life, in other words to be converted and resurrected, Jesus' answer was not received well. Much was required of the man who possessed many things. Mark reports, "He [the young man] was shocked and went away grieving, for he had many possessions" (Mark 10:22).

Yet, we have many positive examples of people, like William Wilberforce, who were given opportunities to change their lives and responded. The call of the apostles is certainly illustrative. When Jesus called, we are told they immediately left family, livelihood, home, and followed him (Matthew 4:18-22; 9:9; Mark 1:16-20; 2:13-14). Indeed, Peter was so taken with the miraculous catch of fish that he did not know how to respond. Thus, he told Jesus, "Go away from me, Lord, for I am a sinful man!" But Jesus told him that in the future he would be fishing for men (Luke 5:1-11). Saint Paul as well was given a second chance. Indeed, he claimed that he should never be called an apostle as he had been so fervent and zealous in his earlier persecution of Christians (1 Corinthians 15:9-10). Yet, God transformed him into the most famous evangelist and missionary of all time. Paul's efforts transformed Christianity from a sect of Judaism into the major world religion it is today. But this all happened because he was open to the call and accepted resurrection in his life.

Resurrection not only brings the possibility of a new direction in life, it also assists us to change our attitudes and perspectives. The general stance we take in life can be expressed by answering a basic question: Do we see life as a glass of water half empty or half full? The former attitude sees life in negative ways. We are never enough; we are always only half of what we need to be. The glass half full perspective, on the other hand, is very positive. This attitude places us on the proper road where we can make great progress. Rather than seeing things as lacking or inadequate, we can view life as fulfilling. True, we should never be totally content where we are and should push on to where we seek to be. But the glass half full tells us that resurrection to new life is possible for all.

Therefore, we need to approach life and the possibilities the Lord provides for us from a positive direction. Not only must we seek the positive perspective, we are challenged to help others to do likewise. Too often today people view the challenges and obstacles of life as a wall too high or difficult to negotiate. Thus, many choose not to engage the world. In these cases the individual has no opportunity to find God and thus the new life God brings. Surrender to the perceived inevitable problem will paralyze us; we will not be able to see our way out of the forest. Thus, we need to be persistent and engage the world. It will not be easy, but then the

Christian life well led should never be easy. We should recall how the famous British essayist, G. K. Chesterton, put it back in 1910: "Christianity has not been tried and found wanting; it is been found difficult and left untried."

The personal resurrection we seek gives promise to a collective resurrection for our world. If we start with ourselves we can initiate a tidal wave that can bring our world to new ways of acting and thinking. American society is dominated by the secular and a pervasive sense of apathy and indifferentism. Our nation trumpets its idea of the separation of church and state, but too often today this good idea, which was initiated to keep harm from occurring to either of these great institutions, now brings problems to both. The perception that the relationship between religion and politics is problematic has brought us to the re-exaltation of civil religion. Rather than honoring God, too often we honor the state, its precepts, and civic values.

The situation in our society, dark though it may be at times, can be transformed. William Wilberforce was only one man, but he led a campaign to transform the thinking of the most extensive and possibly most powerful empire in world history. But this only began when Wilberforce was resurrected to a new way of thinking. Similarly, we need to be open to God's message in our lives. The missive will be different for each person, but we all need to raise ourselves to a higher plane. Let us strive toward this lofty plateau. The goal that is our ultimate destination is worth every ounce of our effort. It is nothing less than life eternal with God. Amen.

**Epiphany 7
Ordinary Time 7
1 Corinthians 15:35-38, 42-50**

Formula For Eternal Life

George lives in Fort Portal, a town on the western front of Uganda, some fifty miles from the Congo. Like the Rwenzori Mountains (the Mountains of the Moon) that surround the town, George is a beautiful man in many ways. He works as a cook, among many other tasks, for a local school. There is actually little that George does not do. He is the one who washes, irons, and mends the students' clothes, cleans the dormitory, fixes what is broken, does the grocery shopping, and takes care of the outside yard. In short, George is a servant in the classic sense of that word. He serves the students and often the faculty and staff of that school from morning until after 8 p.m. each day.

He rides his bicycle to work over the dusty and narrow dirt road each day. He returns on the same road each evening after dark, a road with no lighting. One wonders how he can see in the pervasive darkness. But people in many similar regions of the world always say, "Oh people here know the area." One wonders how well he knows the ruts and chuck holes in the road that seek to swallow one who might walk the path, let alone dare to jog or ride a bike along the same road.

A visit to George's home would be a true experience for most Americans. In order to arrive one must first take that dirty and rut-filled road for more than one mile. Then you must veer off into a wooded and tropical land with no path at all. You simply have to know the way. When you arrive, you see an adobe shack of no more than 300 square feet. The walls on the inside are covered with newsprint; a cloth separates the two rooms of the home. The bathroom, if you could call it that, is outside, as is the kitchen, along with the chicken coop. There is no running water, no electricity, and no heat. However, George is lucky; his house has a tin roof.

In the main room there is a hanging string of Christmas lights. One might naturally ask how the lights are lit since there is no power. The answer is as simple as George's entire existence; he uses batteries. The home is filled with holy cards of saints and popes, rosaries, and other religious reminders. George lives in this house with his wife and five children, ages fourteen to one year. George has very little, or so it seems, but actually he considers himself rich. If you talk with George he will tell you how fortunate he feels to have a prayer life and family and friends with whom to share it. He is also grateful for the faith that was instilled in him by his parents. Believe it or not George is actually richer than most of us and he is grateful for it.

From a worldly perspective, especially here in the United States, George's résumé for life would not be considered very significant. In fact, most would rate his chances for advancement as rather poor. While I am sure that George would certainly appreciate having a few more things in this life, especially for his family, his concern is not on the here and the now, but rather the future eternal life which is God's promise to all who believe. Through faith George has the ability to look forward to his eternal life with God. In a similar way, Saint Paul writes to the Corinthians telling them that this life is transitory. Our lives truly are only a seed that will germinate and grow in the resurrection of the dead. He wishes to tell the Corinthians not to concentrate so much on our lives today, but rather to concentrate on a future eternal existence with God.

Paul starts his lesson by disavowing an idea the Corinthians apparently had concerning the resurrection. He tells them they should not be concerned with the kind of body they will have in the resurrection of the dead. Our earthly body must die in order to find eternal life with God. We do not sow our present body for the future; rather we sow a seed that matures later. God will give us a body as he chooses.

Then the apostle gives a series of contrasting ideas that show the difference between this life and the eternal life God has promised to those who believe and follow his pattern of life. First, he says what we have today is perishable, but in the next life all is imperishable. The finitude of this earthly life is transformed to the infinity of life eternal. All we know in this world is finite; all has beginnings and ends. But in the eternal life of God we will encounter only infinity. Similarly, Paul says in this life our body is sown in dishonor; we stand and make mistakes. In the life of resurrection, however, our body will live in glory. As finite human beings we are beset by weakness. Paul knew this very well. He wrote to the Corinthians: "I came to you in weakness and in fear and in much trembling" (1 Corinthians 2:3). Yet, in the resurrection of the just, we will gain great power.

In summary, Paul says we have a physical body now, but in the life to come we will have a spiritual body. We must experience the physical in order to find the spiritual. For Paul this transition is one of natural maturation. As neophytes of the "new way," the Corinthians are on the level of the physical. With time, knowledge, and the development of their faith they will find a spiritual sense of their existence. This will find its culmination in the eternal life of God. He illustrates his point by comparing the first man, Adam, who was physical and made from the dust of the earth, with Jesus, the man from heaven. As we start in a physical sense like Adam, we will one day come to a spiritual sense, as Jesus. He concludes by saying that flesh and all that is perishable is not found in the resurrection. Rather the imperishable, namely that of Christ, is found in the resurrection.

Our movement from the physical to the spiritual requires us to consider our preparation for this great event. Imagine picking up the Sunday paper, opening it and reading in giant, bold letters, **Jesus Christ Will Return In Two Weeks!** What would we do? How would we react to this astonishing information? I think there would be two basic reactions. Some of us, out of fear, would change our lives immediately. The Lord is coming and we are not ready. We might start going to church more often, probably every day. Prayer would become a much higher priority in life. We would pray not only in the morning and evening, but many times each day. We would seek reconciliation, with a member of our family, neighbor, coworker, and certainly with God.

Others might have a very different response. Some of us might do nothing differently. Some in a defeatist attitude might say, "There is nothing I can do at this late hour. God has already decided my fate. I might as well continue what I have been doing all along." There are still others who might not change a thing that they are doing, but not in a defeatist mode. Some could hopefully say, "Isn't this the event for which the world has been waiting? Isn't this the reason for which I came into the world?" Possession of such an attitude would allow us to continue doing what we have always been doing, confident that our preparations have been sound.

Most of us, I suspect, would be in the first category. As people of faith we have awaited the Lord's return, but we probably are not fully prepared. The revelation of the Lord's return would be greeted with much consternation as we would realize there is still much to do in our lives.

There is no doubt that we spend a lot of time preparing for the present life we live. This reality is part and parcel of our contemporary American world. We spend a lot of time in formal education, gaining knowledge in certain disciplines, and honing our skills in areas we have already developed. Generally the better our education, the more opportunities come our way. Professionally we attend seminars and various training sessions that will make us more confident and better able to do whatever our daily tasks ask of us. We spend a lot of time enhancing our physical appearance. Many people exercise regularly. This is obviously time well spent, and it helps us feel better and perform up to our capability. Others, however, simply spruce up our appearance so others will notice. We do this for gain today; we are generally not looking to our future life with God.

If we find ourselves in that category of people who are not ready for the coming of the Lord, then we need to start now to get our résumé in proper order, for as Jesus says very clearly in the gospel with respect to the day of the Lord's arrival, we know not the day or the hour (Matthew 24:36).

What needs our attention to prepare ourselves better? First, we need to review our relationship with ourselves. This might seem an odd way to begin, but if we do not have a good relationship with ourselves we can never progress in our relationships with God and our brothers and sisters. In this sense the parable of the prodigal son (Luke 15:11-32) is instructive. Before the young prodigal could begin his journey home he needed to realize his need for reconciliation. This process began with him. The résumé for eternal life requires us to love what God has created in us. Yes, the great commandment says we must love God and our neighbor, but we can only do this if we love ourselves first. Too often people show very little respect for themselves. This can be manifest in the way we treat our bodies through overindulgence of food, drink, or by driving ourselves so hard that we receive insufficient rest and relaxation. We need to take care of and respect our person.

Our résumé for eternal life must next address our relationship with others. As Paul says we are in the flesh, not in the spirit. This manifests itself in relationships that are fragile or broken. We find ourselves at odds with others and too often through pride we will not allow reconciliation to happen. Past hurts that we have inflicted or have been perpetrated against us weigh us down like a ball and chain. We are not able to move forward so as to further our relationships with others. The solution is simple, yet so very hard to affect: We must break the chain that holds us to the past. Jesus expressed this so powerfully when he raised his friend Lazarus from the dead: "Unbind him, and let him go" (John 11:44b). Once we are free from the past we can move forward and prepare our relationship with others and add to our résumé for eternal life.

The last and obviously most important element of our preparation of the résumé for eternal life is our relationship with God. We can build our relationship with the Lord in many ways. First, we must be in daily communication with God through prayer. The busy lives we lead can produce excuses for why we cannot find time to pray. But like the many things we "put off" in life, this is an excuse; priorities simply need to be set so that our daily conversation with God is never left out. Once we have established this ongoing conversation with God, when we speak with and listen to God, then we must have sufficient courage to act upon what God says. God generally does not hand us a blueprint for our life that precisely tells us what we must do. Rather, God speaks in subtle ways through the words and actions of others in the progress of our daily lives. But God does speak; he answers our prayers. We, therefore, must have the courage to respond so as to build our résumé for eternal life.

Our very comfortable first-world, twenty-first-century American existence presents a challenge to Christians. We live in the here and now; we seldom think about our future or eternal existence with God. Therefore, quite naturally we spend a lot of time, energy, and effort in building our résumé for life. Yet, when we observe the simplicity of one like George who lives not for today but for his future existence with God, we are reminded of what is truly important. Saint Paul in today's lesson forcefully contrasts our life today, one that is of the flesh, timely, and weak, with that of our ultimate life of God, which is spiritual, timeless, and powerful. We need to live in this world and do our best each and every day. God has given us talents and opportunities for this pursuit. Yet, we ultimately must find our life with God. Thus a résumé for eternal life is essential. Let us, therefore, consider our need to be more like George. Let us care less about today and build a résumé for tomorrow. The goal we seek, eternal life, is worth every ounce of our effort. Amen.

Epiphany 8
Ordinary Time 8
1 Corinthians 15:51-58

Christ: The Victor Over Death

In many ways, Nicholas Green was an ordinary seven-year-old boy, but he became a source of life for seven people and a beacon of inspiration for the world. Nicholas was born on New Year's Eve 1986, a new bundle of joy to greet the New Year. Along with his baby sister, Eleanor, and his parents, he enjoyed life and all the fun associated with being a child. With the help of his mother, Maggie, he read all seven books of C. S. Lewis' epic *The Chronicles of Narnia*. He loved to role play and considered himself a perfect Saint George, pointing out to his parents that he was half English. However, as his parents would often say, he fit the model of Saint George more because he always wanted to do what was right.

When Nicholas was seven years old his family took a vacation to Europe. Among many places they visited was the beautiful Swiss Alps where a family photograph captured Nicholas in front of the fabled Matterhorn. Four days later the family was in Italy sightseeing like so many other American tourists. The date was September 29, 1994. As Nicholas' father was driving a rental car, a band of robbers approached in a daring robbery attempt. In the process, Nicholas was shot in the head. He was rushed to the hospital and after a short amount of time the doctors told his parents that the boy could not survive. He remained in a coma for two days, but the doctors told his parents that Nicholas was brain-dead.

Although the shock and the trauma of the recent days' events could not be calculated, Nicholas' parents asked that their son's vital organs be transplanted into needy individuals. At the time, organ donation was a rare event in Italy. Thus, Nicholas' heart, liver, kidneys, pancreas, and corneas were used to bring new life to seven Italians, including several children who were near death. The resulting dramatic increase in organ donations in Italy has now been called "the Nicholas effect." In a very real way, Nicholas Green brought new life to several people, but the broader effect of his life and the decision of his parents to share that life with others might be incalculable.

The story of Nicholas and his ability to give new life in multiple ways to several people is truly inspiring. The selfless act of grieving parents who had lost their son was a true act of charity and love. More directly their decision to utilize Nicholas to assist others shows how new life can come in the midst of death and darkness. Thus, this heartwarming story serves as an excellent illustration of Saint Paul's message to the Corinthians in today's lesson — that Christ is the one who conquers death and brings new life. We can be confident that Jesus will bring new life to us. We, in turn, must do what we can, in our limited and finite ways, to bring new life to others.

In today's lesson, Paul continues his basic resurrection theme that he has expressed throughout the whole of 1 Corinthians, chapter 15. We first heard of the resurrection of Christ. We were taught that Jesus' death and resurrection was a supreme sacrifice of love for us. As Christ so sacrificed for us, so must we be willing to sacrifice ourselves, our material possessions, personal needs, and opportunities for the betterment of all. In this way we build the kingdom of God in our world. We were challenged to see the new life Jesus can give us and how we must adequately and properly prepare for this great event. The résumés for life today and for eternal life tomorrow are very difficult. We must spend as much time if not more on the latter if we are to find God at the end of our days. Today Paul concludes his message of new life by saying Jesus is the one who brings victory over death, transforming the perishable into the imperishable, mortal into immortal. As Paul says, God gives us victory through Jesus Christ.

Paul speaks of the new reality we will find at the resurrection of the dead. At the sound of God's command the dead will rise. As Nicholas gave new life to so many, so Christ will transform what is mortal and perishable about us into the immortality of God. Death will have no power; death will be vanquished. God's victory will prevail. The sting of death, namely sin, will be routed by God. Sin and death will no longer have power over us.

Paul concludes by saying that people must be steadfast in the Lord. If we remain faithful to God's command, our labor will not be in vain. Rather, to the contrary, we will move forward in our common efforts to build God's kingdom in our world.

Transforming hopeless situations into ones that find and generate life is not always easy, but there is ample evidence that such events have happened numerous times. Nicholas' story is rather dramatic in that through death he brought victory to so many. He made the impossible possible for others. History presents us with numerous examples of life and victory springing from the clutches of defeat and death. In the history of warfare this is certainly true. How was it in 480 BCE that a vastly inferior force of some 300 Spartans and about 1,000 other allies was able to hold off the entire Persian army at Thermopylae?

While the Persians eventually won the battle, the courage of the Greeks, the casualties they inflicted upon the Persians, and most importantly the time the battle consumed, afforded the Greeks time to consolidate their forces in order to win a decisive naval battle at Salamis. This brought Greece victory in the Greco-Persian War and halted the expansion of the Persian empire into Europe. How was it that the upstart American colonies with a ragtag group of soldiers and without sufficient supplies and divided loyalties among their people were able to defeat the finest military force in the world at the time? I'm sure that most common folks at the time felt the effort was futile. Yet, the colonists rallied behind their leaders and after eight long years of war managed to defeat the British.

There have been some famous political victories that also probably seemed impossible. In 1860, Abraham Lincoln was basically an unknown person on the national political scene. All of his rivals in the quest for the Republican presidential nomination were better known and generally speaking eminently more qualified than he: New York Senator William B. Seward, Ohio Governor Salmon P. Chase, and Edward Bates, a distinguished elder statesman from

Missouri. Yet through some excellent politicking and a sense of determination, not only did Lincoln win the nomination but the White House when the Democrats split their votes between two men (John C. Breckenridge and Stephen Douglas) and a third-party candidate, John Bell. In more recent memory the pollsters and the American populace in general gave Harry Truman no chance at all in 1948. Most were calling New York Governor Thomas Dewey the winner long before the voting even commenced. However, when people awoke to Truman's upset victory many thought the impossible had been made possible.

Sports also provides some important and improbable wins. In 1986, the New York Mets seemingly had no chance to win the World Series. Down three games to two and behind by five runs in the ninth inning, the end looked near. But an error by Boston Red Sox first baseman, Bill Buckner, gave New York new life. They won the game and the deciding seventh game; they snatched victory from the jaws of defeat. In a reverse role in 2004, the Red Sox were down three games to none to the New York Yankees in the American League championship series. Playing at home to close out the series, the Yankees looked like a shoe-in, but the Red Sox never gave up. Not only did they win four straight against the Yankees but continued their winning ways with a four-game sweep of the St. Louis Cardinals and their first World Series in 86 years. The infamous "Curse of the Bambino" had been broken.

We will face many difficult challenges in our lives, tasks that may seem to be impossible missions. In the journey of our working days we will face trying situations. We may face obstacles that will not allow us to work as we want. Coercion, threat, or the temptation of reward may "force" us to do things in a manner that we know might hurt or ill-effect another. We may be required to relocate in order to stay with the company or worse still our job might be lost. At such times we wonder what we will do and what the future will hold. Families experience many difficult challenges. Some people are asked to walk the road of ill-health with a spouse, child, sister, brother, or another relative. Tough love may be required in our relationship with one who suffers from addiction.

Many people must suffer the pain of observing a loved one reject God and the church and opt for the things of the world.

All of us will one day face the death of one close to us. The church will also bring us challenges. We pray fervently to God for our needs, yet our prayers are not answered in the way or time that we want; we might even feel God has abandoned us. Sometimes we lose sight of the road; we move off the track or even reverse course in our journey to God.

We will experience difficult times in our lives, with our jobs, our families, and the church, challenges that may seem to be impossible missions. But if we, like Abraham, Moses, the prophets, and Jesus, can persevere and continue on the road, then God will recognize and reward our efforts. The task will not be easy; the road to God has pitfalls and obstacles. Saint Paul advised his friend, Timothy, of this reality, "Do not be ashamed, then, of the testimony about our Lord or of me his prisoner, but join with me in suffering for the gospel" (2 Timothy 1:8). But he also assured him, "If we have died with him, we will also live with him; if we endure, we will also reign with him" (2 Timothy 2:11-12).

We must constantly reevaluate our lives and renew our determination to walk the journey of life, which one day will lead to union with God. It will not be an easy journey, if taken seriously, but it is the only path that will one day lead to eternal life. Let us, therefore, walk the road; let us take on what seems to be mission impossible. Certainly the parents of Nicholas Green had no desire to walk the road that came their way, but they realized their son could give new life to so many and thus, despite their grief, made a courageous decision. In a similar way, God will strengthen us, reward our efforts, and use us to complete his work on earth. Let us follow the lead of Jesus. If we can, our reward in heaven will be great. Amen.

Epiphany 9
Ordinary Time 9
Galatians 1:1-12

Don't Compromise Your Beliefs

William Jennings Bryan was truly a man who answered the call. Bryan, who was born in 1860 at the dawn of the Civil War, was an advocate for various causes throughout his life. As a young attorney he pleaded the cases of those who had little voice. Because he was so well appreciated, he was encouraged to run for Congress in the state of Nebraska and won a seat in House of Representatives in 1892. This was only the start of a long political career wherein he never compromised his beliefs.

The economic crisis of 1893, which generated the greatest depression to that date in the United States, created a backlash against government. Bryan was asked by his fellow Democrats to answer their call as a candidate in the 1896 presidential election. The Democratic platform advocated help for the common worker and the promotion of organized labor. Bryan lost that election to William McKinley, but he was not deterred, nor were his supporters. Bryan ran again in 1900, but again was unsuccessful. He was unwilling to change his message to suit others.

Despite his failure to win the presidency, the fame of William Jennings Bryan grew. His speeches and oratorical style became legendary. He traveled throughout the nation to promote the policies for which he stood. In 1904, Bryan established a newspaper that advocated many progressive causes in promotion of the social question, which was a front page issue at the time. Bryan edited the paper and again went on the road to promote its views.

Bryan continued to answer the call as the twentieth century began to unfold. In 1908, he again answered the summons of the

Democratic Party to run for president. Again he was defeated, this time by William Howard Taft. Later, in the administration of Woodrow Wilson, he served as Secretary of State. But when the United States entered World War I, Bryan, believing America's participation to be unjust, resigned his post rather than compromise his ideals. Bryan was the champion of many popular causes. He led the fight for the popular election of United States senators, where before it had been conducted by the various state legislatures, was at the forefront of the women's suffrage issue that culminated in the nineteenth amendment to the Constitution, and was active in the temperance movement and fought for prohibition.

The final episode of his life quite possibly will be the one most remembered. In the 1925 Scopes Monkey Trial in Dayton, Tennessee, Bryan was counsel for the prosecution, defending the fundamentalist Protestant cause against the teaching of evolution. Clarence Darrow, the famous lawyer, was John Scopes' defense counsel. The famous play and equally popular movie, *Inherit the Wind*, tells the story of this famous trial. Scopes was convicted; Bryan had won. It was his last opportunity to answer the call. He died from a heart attack one week after the trial ended.

William Jennings Bryan was a man who refused to compromise his beliefs; he was willing to pay the cost, no matter what it might be, to be a disciple of Jesus. This account of one of America's unsung political and religious heroes presents an excellent illustration of the message that Saint Paul delivers to the Galatians at the beginning of his letter. Paul wants the Christian community in that region to realize that there is one gospel and the people need to be committed to it. They are never to compromise what they believe; they must be willing, as was Jesus and Paul, to pay the full measure for their faith.

As with his entire corpus, Paul begins this letter with his usual salutation, but with an important addition. He states at the outset that his apostleship comes directly from Christ; he has received no human commission to preach the gospel message. This is vitally important, especially when we read today's passage where Paul's authority has been questioned by the Galatian community. It is important to Paul's argument that he possesses the true gospel message, which he proclaims comes directly from Christ. Since those who are proposing an alternative gospel message claim authority, Paul must stake his assertion to have the ultimate authority and, therefore, the true message.

Normally, following the salutation in Paul's corpus, the apostle gives thanks to the community to whom he writes. However, Paul is anything but pleased with the community at Galatia. Thus, instead of giving thanks, he immediately launches into a defense of his work and more importantly his message, namely to never compromise the faith in Christ that he instilled in the Galatians when he formed the community a few years earlier.

Paul chastises the Galatians for deserting the gospel he preached for one preached by false apostles. Paul presumably is speaking of the Judaizers, a sect of the "new way" that demanded full adherence to the Mosaic law. It seems the Judaizers had accused Paul of preaching a false message, one not from Christ, because he suggested circumcision was not essential. Paul's opponents believe he has "watered down" the message to make it more palatable to Gentile converts. But Paul defends his position, going so far as to call his enemies, those preaching another gospel, "accursed." He says he is not trying to please people; if he sought simply to make the message amenable to people, he would not be a servant of Christ. Thus, he reiterates his earlier claims that his message comes directly from Jesus. By implication he suggests it is the Judaizers who have misrepresented the message of Christ.

Paul's message to the Galatians, that there is only one gospel and the people must never compromise their faith, has inspired Christians for 2,000 years. William Jennings Bryan was a fervent Christian as well as a shrewd politician. While his fundamentalist belief may not be popular today, it was his total commitment to purpose and belief that was significant. He never compromised his person or his beliefs; lack of popularity, negative reactions, or political defeat were not important to him. He never counted the cost of his discipleship.

We live in a world today where Christians are constantly challenged by outside forces. These challenges come in two basic ways: apathy and indifference. How often have we heard a person say,

"It's not my responsibility, not my concern. I don't want to get involved; other people can worry about it"? The challenge that this comment, so often heard by us or even one we have used ourselves, can also be illustrated by a little story.

Fred Everybody, Thomas Somebody, Peter Anybody, and Joe Nobody were neighbors, but not the type that most would want to know. They were odd people and difficult to understand. The way they lived their lives was a shame. These men all went to the same church, but most people would not have wanted them as parishioners. Everybody went fishing on Sundays or stayed home and chatted with his friends. Anybody wanted to worship, but he was afraid that Somebody would speak with him. Thus, guess who went to church — that's right, Nobody. Actually, Nobody was the only decent one of the lot. Nobody did the parish census; Nobody joined the parish council. One day there was an announcement in the parish bulletin for a person to volunteer to teach in the Sunday school program. Everybody thought Anybody would volunteer; Anybody thought Somebody would take the job. So, guess who volunteered? You are right, Nobody! This is the apathetic attitude against which Christians must fight in our contemporary American society.

Apathy can be a significant concern for all of us. Many people feel they have no voice, no opportunity or position from which to present their views or ideas. If people have no voice, we might understand why their attitude would be rather apathetic or possibly indifferent. People often say, "You cannot fight city hall, so why try?" Oftentimes people surrender, not only because it is necessary in their minds, but also because they feel they have no option. These people are apathetic; they have given up.

We will encounter many people who for varied reasons have decided that they cannot use their gifts, talents, and time for a particular endeavor. Too often, however, we find apathetic people who, even with the necessary talent and time, choose not to get involved. Why? Because people believe, due to past personal experiences or by observations of others, that their efforts will make no difference in the outcome of events. We must guard against this apathetic attitude, because it is a trap into which one can easily fall. When society continually tells us not to get involved or that our efforts are of little value, we begin to believe that this is true. We become apathetic. However, we cannot allow society to drag us down to its lowest common denominator that refuses to get involved.

Christians today have an obligation to not allow apathy to reign. Some of us may be leaders in business, civic organizations, or even hold important positions within our church. Whatever path we choose, however, we cannot allow apathy to move us off the proper course of right action in seeking to continue Jesus' work of building the kingdom of God in our world. People look to us in varied ways; we cannot let others down. If we follow the road of apathy, it is almost guaranteed that those over whom we have influence will follow a similar path. We must always be conscious of our responsibility to others.

The struggle we have to remove apathy from our lives is also found in the contemporary tendency to be indifferent. How often have we heard people say, "If I live a good life, if I follow the teachings of Jesus, what does it matter what faith I practice; who cares if I go to church?" This tendency in today's society has been aptly described by the well-known sociologist of religion, Robert Wuthnow, at Princeton University. In his book, *After Heaven: Spirituality in America Since the 1950s*,[1] he describes the transition in spirituality as manifest in the United States, from the post World War II era to the present. He refers to this transition as a movement of spirituality from "indwelling" to "seeking."

He suggests that in the 1950s, American spirituality in general was centered in an institution, a physical place, such as a local parish. People found their spiritual sustenance by attendance at church. Not only did people frequent the church on Sunday morning, but it was the social center of their lives. Christians were physically present on the church grounds for numerous events each week. Wuthnow then contrasts this "indwelling" spiritual idea with the more common theme today of people seeking spirituality outside an institutional setting. People believe they can find God and their spiritual sustenance somewhere "out there"; there is no need to seek God in a physical place or within a particular faith community. Certainly the rejection of "traditional" religion is a complex question and there are many factors involved, but in general this new trend is an example of indifferentism.

If we can conquer the contemporary temptations toward apathy and indifference, we will be on the proper road to never compromise our faith. We will find ourselves in various challenging situations in the future, many of which may threaten our beliefs and faith. We may find ourselves, like the Galatians, under the influence of an individual or group who will seemingly "convince" us of the validity and merit of their ideology or ideas. Although we see the conflict with our faith, we can still be swayed. But we must remember Paul's message that there is no gospel other than that preached by Christ. Easy answers and solutions are often proffered for the challenges and problems of daily life, but the Christian life, while not always easy, has the answers we seek. G. K. Chesterton had it right in 1910 when he opined of society's "less than positive attitude": "The Christian faith has not been tried and found wanting; it has been found difficult and left untried."

Let us continue on the road we have chosen, the one that leads to Christ. May we never compromise who we are or what we believe. If we can stand strong, then when Christ calls us we will hear the words that, in the end, our whole lives have been lived to hear: "Come, you that are blessed by my Father, inherit the kingdom prepared for you from the foundation of the world" (Matthew 25:34b). Amen.

---

1. Robert Wuthnow, *After Heaven: Spirituality in America Since the 1950s* (Berkeley: University of California Press, 1998).

The Transfiguration Of Our Lord
(Last Sunday After Epiphany)
2 Corinthians 3:12—4:2

Transformed To Christ

One magnificent, moonlit night, a fisherman climbed the wall of a private estate to partake in the bounty of its fish-stocked pond. He moved with stealth and upon reaching the banks of the pond observed with keen awareness that there was no activity in the bungalow below. All the lights were out. With a sense of confidence, he envisioned his fishing needs taken care of for the full week. Thus, he cast his net into the pond making the light splash. The master of the house remarked to his wife from his deep stupor, "Did you hear a sound outside?"

His wife remarked, "My dear, it sounded like a net falling into the water."

In seconds, the owner sprang out of the stupor and visualizing his pond completely devoid of fish yelled, "Thief! Thief!" The servants of the house, hearing the master yell, scrambled outside toward the pond.

The fisherman gathered the net as swiftly as he tossed it and scrambled to find a safe hiding place. The workers' voices were near and the fisherman's desperation knew no bounds. His eyes caught a glimpse of a smoldering fire and he got an idea. He gathered some ash and rubbed it over his arms, body, and face. He quickly sat under the nearest tree in a posture of one in meditation. When the servants arrived at the scene and saw the man in meditation they asked for forgiveness and continued their search. Finally, they reported back to the owner telling him that there was only a *sanyasin*, a holy man, in the garden.

The owner's face lit up and asked to be taken to the site of the *sanyasin*. Upon seeing him, he was overjoyed and demanded that the holy man not be disturbed. The fisherman's fear turned to joy and then to pride thinking how smart he was to outwit the entire household. He sat under the tree until the shades of dawn began to sweep across the night sky. As he was preparing to leave he saw a small procession of people approaching; they had heard of the holy man. Now he could not leave under any circumstance. These people had come from a neighboring village and with total devotion had brought offerings of food, fruit, silver, and gold to invoke the blessings of the holy man!

At this very moment the fisherman realized that if by assuming the role of a holy man he had received so much respect and goodwill, how much more respect and goodwill would be received if he truly was a holy man. So the fisherman who was truly a thief turned in his net and became a true man of God.

It might have been quite by accident, but the fisherman experienced conversion in his life. He was transformed from a thief into a holy man through the action of others. The love, respect, and deference demonstrated toward him changed his heart. He realized he had been deluding himself to think others might respect him for his wealth, but he came to realize he could be held in high esteem by demonstrating kindness and those qualities that label people as "holy." In a similar way on this great feast of the Transfiguration, when we recall how Jesus was transformed in external appearance before Peter, James, and John, we must seek to be transformed ourselves. We must see our need to be converted into the person of Christ. We need to change our lives and conform them more to the one whom we follow and seek to serve by our service to one another.

Saint Paul continues his conversation with the Christian community at Corinth in today's lesson. Scripture scholars tell us that 2 Corinthians is actually a compilation of at least five and possibly six letters Paul wrote to that community. Over time, through the work of redactors, the partial fragments of these letters were put together in what we today call 2 Corinthians. Today's lesson comes from a letter where Paul seeks to defend himself against the theology of a band of "super apostles" who have infiltrated the

Corinthian Christian community preaching a theology different than that of Paul.

Paul tells the Corinthians that they should not become deluded with these false teachings but rather must stay on the true path. He uses the story of Moses in the desert and his conversations with God to illustrate his point. He says that Moses used a veil to cover himself after he spoke with God so the Israelites would not behold the radiance of God that was imprinted on his face. He suggests that the "super apostles" have veiled themselves like Moses. They do not see the truth; they hide behind a facade of their own ignorance and arrogance. Paul defends himself against such an attitude by saying if one truly turns to the Lord, the veil is removed.

Paul continues by saying that when the Corinthians see the Lord with unveiled faces, in other words, without the encumbrances of the "super apostles," they are being transformed into the same image one sees without the veil — the image of God. As he writes, "All of us ... are being transformed into the same image from one degree of glory to another; for this comes from the Lord, the Spirit" (v. 18).

Clearly Paul is telling this community of faith that they need to "see through" the false rhetoric of the "super apostles" who have placed a veil over their faces. They need to remove the veil and be transformed by the message of Christ. Paul says that his message is true; he is not to resort to cunning or false pretensions to communicate his message, but rather he produces the truth that he received from Jesus. His conscience is clear; he is to carry forth his mission to the Corinthians in a manner consistent with the commission Christ gave him, beginning from the day of his conversion on the road to Damascus.

The Transfiguration itself is a highly significant event in Jesus' life. All three synoptic writers, Matthew, Mark, and Luke, tell us the story. All three evangelists connect it in time to Peter's earlier profession of faith. When Jesus asked the apostles who he was, Peter responded, "You are the Messiah, the Son of the living God" (Matthew 16:16). Now six days later (Luke says eight days) Jesus is with the three special apostles on the mountain. Jesus wants to show that Peter's confession has merit. Some scholars suggest the

Transfiguration happened just as it is described. Others say the event was really a spiritual experience of the apostles. There are some, as well, who suggest that this is the narration of a post-resurrection appearance of Jesus that was intentionally inserted at this point in the gospel to make clear to the evangelists' readers the message that Jesus was Messiah and Lord. Jesus was physically transfigured for a brief amount of time. His clothes became dazzling white; his appearance was translucent. Moses and Elijah appeared in conversation with Jesus. Then God speaks from the heavens, "This is my Son, the Beloved; with him I am well pleased; listen to him!" (Matthew 17:5b).

Jesus' physical transformation was apparent, but it was momentary and not permanent. But what happened to Peter, James, and John? Most assuredly they were transformed. However, their conversion was not physical, but rather spiritual and permanent. From this time forth they could never look at Jesus and see only a man. Not only was their experience of Jesus and the two great Jewish figures of the past surreal, they heard a voice from heaven, God's voice, tell them who Jesus was and their need to listen to him. Peter, James, and John had the veil removed; they knew with total certainty who Jesus was and his mission and purpose in the world.

The transformation experienced by the fisherman thief, the same one described by Saint Paul and that experienced by Peter, James, and John, must be our goal as well. We might not want to admit it, but often we live our daily lives with a veil over our face that marks who we are and does not allow us to properly see the world around us. The fisherman thief thought crime would pay; it was his perceived ticket to greatness. But he learned through the goodness of others the fallacy of his idea. When he removed the veil he saw clearly the proper road to the goals he saw in life. Similarly, Paul tells the Corinthians to remove the veil the "super apostles" have placed over them. Then they will be able to "see" and hear the new message of Paul. Peter, James, and John were privileged to view the transfigured Christ. They were transformed in their understanding of Jesus.

What requires transformation in our lives? For some there is a need to transform attitudes — toward self and others. It is unfortunate but true that too many people have low self-esteem and do not respect nor love themselves sufficiently. These people need to be transformed to look into a mirror and believe fully that the person they see is a son or daughter of God. Some of us need transformation in our attitudes toward others. We think highly of ourselves; we place ourselves above others. Such an attitude needs to be transformed so that the attitude Jesus manifests and describes in the scriptures prevails. We need to be humble and sit at the low end of the table so, if we are fortunate, someone will call us up higher.

Many people need to be transformed in their habits. There are things we do that annoy others. There are habits we exhibit that are harmful to our health. We know what these problems are; now we need to have the courage to change.

All of us, to some extent, through prayer, need to be transformed in our relationship with God. Lent is the perfect time to root out sin and do our best to resist temptation — those near occasions of sin. We must do what needs to be done to improve our prayer life — our daily conversation with God — and stop making excuses for our failures.

All of us must seek transformation in our lives; we are also responsible to assist others in their transformation. The people who encountered the fisherman thief were instrumental in his transformation. Their respect, kindness, and goodness demonstrated to him that crime did not gain him the greatness he sought. The people removed the veil from his eyes; he was transformed in his vision. Our transformation can assist others to discover their own need to be transformed in Christ. May our words and actions be transformative for ourselves and others. May all that we do and say give greater glory and honor to God. Amen.

Sermons On The Second Readings

For Sundays In
Lent And Easter

But!

Steven L. Albertin

*To Reverend Jeff Iacobazzi
and his flock at
First Trinity Lutheran Church, Indianapolis, Indiana,
... whose faithful witness to the gospel
in a challenging urban context,
always insisting on God's "BUT"
in the face of contrary voices,
... has been an inspiration to me
and their partners in mission,
Christ Church, The Lutheran Church of Zionsville.*

Preface

"But" ... is one of the most important words in the New Testament. "But" ... is the foundation on which all the sermons in this section are based. "But" is the basis of Christ's resurrection from the dead, without which our faith would be in vain. The sermon titled "But!" preached for The Resurrection Of Our Lord, is the central sermon not only of these sermons but also the Christian church year and the Christian faith.

But

That is what God said when God raised Jesus from the dead. In the face of death, sin, the lies and power of the evil one ... and finally in the face of God's own righteous judgment, God says, "But!" They will not have the last word. God's grace and mercy will have the last word! And that last word is made manifest in the death and resurrection of Jesus Christ. Without Christ's life, death, and resurrection, life in this world would always and only be "the same old, same old." Sin would make us cynical. Death would make us fatalistic. The evil one would make us despicable. God's own law would leave devastated. *But* Christ changes all of that.

These sermons in this section from the season of Lent and Holy Week all look forward to God's big *but* on Easter. Lent and Holy Week would make no sense without God's contrary word, God's big *but* of Easter. Likewise the sermons from the season of Easter all begin with and are based on God's big *but* of Easter. This entire section of sermons is based on the fundamental conviction that the good news of the gospel is always a surprise, always unexpected, can never be deduced from the vagaries of human experience or the inevitabilities of nature. The gospel is always God's *but*, God's *au contraire*, *God's however*, *God's nevertheless*, *God's to the contrary notwithstanding*, God's protest against what the world would have us believe cannot be: That in Christ we are loved, forgiven, valued, and saved without qualifications, conditions, or strings attached. To those conditions, God says loudly and clearly in Christ: *But* ... I love you no matter what!

That glorious *but* creates a whole new kind of life the likes of which the world has never seen. Hopefully, these sermons will help their readers see how God's big *but* makes that possible.

Ash Wednesday
2 Corinthians 5:20b—6:10

Show Me Your Credentials

When you apply for a job, offer service to a customer, or try to get a license ... you will need to *show your credentials*. You will need to prove that you are who you say are and that you have the skills and abilities to deserve the job or get the license. The word "credential" is based on the Latin word *credo* that means "believe." Your credentials make you believable — credible.

My evangelism visits to prospective members are often very revealing. Lately, I have noticed that many of them are asking me a similar question. They want to know, "Is your church growing?" They want me to show them my credentials, the proof and the evidence that I have a growing congregation. Everyone wants to be a part of a successful organization. No one likes to be associated with a loser. Ten years ago the Indianapolis Colts could hardly give away tickets to their games because they were so bad. Today every game is a sell-out and you can hardly buy a ticket because they are so successful. People want to be a part of a winning organization.

People want religion to "work." If they are going to join your church, they want to see your credentials and the evidence that your religion "works." Visit many of our Christian bookstores today and you will see many books on their shelves selling "the prosperity gospel." One preacher after another claims that, *if* you are committed to their system or strategy, which is always God's system or strategy, *then* you will succeed; you will prosper. Then your life will be full and complete.

People flock to churches to be "saved." But I'm not so sure that it is their souls that they want to save. More often than not they expect the church to save their marriages, save their families, save their jobs, save their health, save their delinquent children, and so on. But before joining these churches, they want to know their credentials. Why should they believe that you can save them and their marriages, families, jobs, health, children, and more?

We want to appeal to a world like this. We want to be relevant. So we offer our credentials in the hope that they will make us believable. We present a positive image. We show that this is a happy place filled with nice people. Isn't that what we expect our nicely decorated and well-maintained church building to do ... to make us credible and appealing to our community?

Such sentiments are not new. Churches have always been concerned about their credibility. In today's second lesson from 2 Corinthians we see a snapshot of life in your typical messy church. As the congregation in Corinth began to be racked with conflict and disagreement, it turned on Paul and blamed him. They blamed him because his credentials were rather questionable. Paul was not very believable or credible. He was very ordinary looking. He lacked eloquence. He was not well-versed in the wisdom of the ancient world. He was not wealthy. He wasn't very popular and had this terrible habit of creating conflict and controversy wherever he went. In short, he just did not have the proper credentials to be a good leader and pastor.

Paul responded to these accusations in today's second lesson. At times he sounded a little defensive. Other times he seemed downright neurotic, even wacky.

Credentials? Paul, show me your credentials! Why should we take you seriously? Why should we listen to you at all? Why are you believable?

Paul strangely believes that all the suffering and hardship that he has undergone in his life lends credibility to his message and his authority.

> *But as servants of God we have commended ourselves*
> *in every way: through great endurance, in afflictions,*

> *hardships, calamities, beatings, imprisonments, riots, labors, sleepless nights, hunger....*
> — 2 Corinthians 6:4-5

How odd! Paul believes that those very things that would seem to undermine his credibility are his most compelling credentials. He is proud of things that would put us to shame and make us shrink with embarrassment. Nevertheless Paul insists that he is on top of the world. He knows that such experiences do not seem to be very compelling credentials, yet he is proud of them. In spite of appearances to the contrary, they are the very things that confirm his authority as an apostle.

> *We are treated as imposters, and yet are true; as unknown, and yet are well known; as dying, and see — we are alive; as punished, and yet not killed; as sorrowful, yet always rejoicing; as poor, yet making many rich; as having nothing, and yet possessing everything.*
> — 2 Corinthians 6:8b-10

Paul dares to make such outrageous claims about himself simply because of his relationship to Christ. God's love in Christ has transformed his troubled life and made it a success, even though in the eyes of others it seems like an utter failure. To many his credentials seem worthless, yet he believes that Christ has made his suffering and troubled life the most compelling proof of all that his message is true and his authority as an apostle is legitimate.

So, what are your credentials? You folks claim to be Christians. You claim to be the very sons and daughters of God. You claim to be members of the kingdom of heaven. You claim to be saints, holy ones, and the apples of God's eye. Now is the time to fess up. No more foolin' around. Show me your credentials.

Ironically, perhaps even surprisingly, you already have done that. In fact, you do that every time we gather for worship. But I must admit that they are rather strange and odd credentials. They are not the kind of credentials that members of a successful and prosperous organization would want to show others. When stockholders go to the annual shareholders meeting, when the board of directors holds its monthly session, when the Rotary gathers for its weekly luncheon at the local VFW hall, when the cub scouts have their monthly pack meeting in the church basement, what gets trotted out for all to see? Everyone wants to hear the success stories, that the bottom line is prosperous, that membership is growing, attendance is up, and everyone is happy. In fact, some companies spend a lot of money hiring a public relations staff just so that a positive and upbeat "spin" is a part of the company's public image.

What about the failures — the losses — the low morale — the shrinking profit margins — the political conflict between the company's executive staff? They are kept out of site. The chair of the meeting prays that no one will ask about them. Or if they do come to light, every effort is made to "explain them away." Everyone wants to look good. Nothing lends more to your credibility than a bright and shiny success story.

But ... that is not what we do here, is it? We started our public gathering by dragging out all of our dirty underwear for everyone to see. We confessed our sins, recognized our failures, and owned our despicable behavior and attitude. Even more, we visually and ritually demonstrated that by marking our bodies with ashes. We didn't use face paints or cosmetic makeup or something else that could cover our blemishes. We used ashes, something burnt and dead and utterly useless as if this best symbolized the state of our lives.

Could you ever think of anything more bleak? What a dark and dreary way to begin our worship. Shouldn't we be more positive and upbeat? This is no way to impress our friends and neighbors. "Pastor, why are you not more positive and upbeat? Why don't you tell us how good we are and point out all of our positive qualities? This is a downer! Who is ever going to join such a dark and dreary congregation?"

That is not the truth. And if there is anything the church is dedicated to doing, it is telling the truth. The ashes remind us of the embarrassing and uncomfortable truth that the rest of the world is dedicated to denying: We are sinners. All is not well. Life is irretrievably broken. We are at odds with God and doomed to the ash heap of history. "From dust you came and to dust you shall return."

Even this is not "the whole truth and nothing but the truth." There is an even bigger and better truth which ultimately is the church's only reason for being. This is truth on which we can base our credentials and our right to make such outrageous claims about ourselves: that we are righteous, upright, the beloved sons and daughters of God, prince and princess in his kingdom.

Look! These are ashes, but these ashes are in the shape of a cross. This is not just any cross. They are the cross of Jesus, the Christ. His cross makes all the difference in the world. Because of his cross, because of what he did for us, we are able to make the outrageous claims that we do about ourselves.

Oh, I know. When the world hears us talk like this, they think we are just a bunch of hypocrites. We are deluding ourselves if we think that trusting in Christ and his promises can make such a difference in our lives. These are not credentials that will make us more believable. They are liabilities that make us look like fools.

These are our credentials, and we are confident in them. Yes, we were made from dust and to dust we shall return. Our lives are fit for the ash heap. We know we are sinners and are willing to admit that ... and even joyfully confess that because our ashen lives have been marked in the sign of the cross of Christ. Because of him, we are not afraid to expose them. We are not so afraid that we must hide them. And the only thing that makes that possible ... and our confession credible ... is Christ and what he did for us on his cross. What we can sport as our credentials is not what we have done but what Christ has done for us!

We flock to this place to hear that good news, and we leave this place with our lives changed. Our lives changed? Our lives still remain a mess and the great unchanged mess they have always been. In fact, that is what the critics of our credentials are quick to point out. All this talk about forgiveness and mercy is just another lie to get us off the hook. We have heard this line before. It's just cheap grace, freedom to remain that same old sinners that we have always been. "God loves to forgive sins. We love to commit them. Isn't the world admirably arranged?"

That is not the case at all. Christ does change our lives. Our making the sign of the cross in ashes on our foreheads and our willingness to face up to our dirty underwear at the beginning of this service, the Rite of the Imposition of Ashes on this Ash Wednesday, is recognition that our lives have been changed. We now have entered a struggle, a struggle that will continue the rest of our lives, a struggle that will never leave us complacent, at ease, or unmoved. Yes, "God loves to forgive sins," but we don't *love* to commit them. We *hate* to commit them. Yes, "Isn't the world admirably arranged?" Because if it were not for Christ and his mercy, we would be stuck in our sins and the same old miserable world. Were it not for Christ and what God did for us in him, we would be most pathetic and all the charges of hypocrisy made toward us would be most certainly true.

Our lives are changed in another way. We no longer need only live for ourselves. We now can live for the world. We can care for and serve our neighbors with a genuine sense of love. Our good deeds of kindness and love are not about adding to our credibility or winning friends and influencing others. It's simply about giving ourselves away for others. Isn't that why Jesus says in tonight's gospel that when giving alms to the poor your right hand should not know what your left hand is doing? It's not about getting credit! It's simply about helping someone in need.

These are our credentials. This is all we need. This is what will finally make us believable. We live "cross-shaped lives." This is what reveals our identity. This is what makes us believable. We don't need to fake it. We don't need to pretend to be something we are not. We are nothing more than ashes and deserve nothing more. However, we are ashes marked in the sign of the cross, Jesus' cross ... and his cross makes all the difference in the world. Because this is his ashen cross, we can stand tall. We are righteous and holy, the beloved sons and daughters of God ... who can give our lives away in service to others, not needing credit or recognition. We already know who we are.

When our critics defiantly demand, "Show me your credentials!" We can point to the ashen cross on our foreheads. There is nothing that will ever make us more credible. Amen.

Lent 1
Romans 10:8b-13

Did God Really Say...?

Today is "Temptation Sunday." Every year on the first Sunday in Lent we focus our attention on the story of the temptation of Jesus. It is a story that has captured the imagination of Christians for centuries. They have sought to portray in art what it must have been like for Jesus to have been tempted by the devil. The picture on your sermon outline this morning portraying this ugly, grotesque, devilish creature is typical of the way the evil one has been portrayed. If the devil looked like this, you would never miss him. You would never be fooled. You would never fall into temptation.

We all know that is not the case. If the devil was so easily identified, then no one would ever succumb to his wiles and temptations. We look at people or pictures and we may choose to ask ourselves — Who are we looking at? One person may be looking straight ahead as the other whispers into the ear of the first person. Who is the face looking straight ahead? Is that Jesus? Or is that someone else? Is it one of us? Who is that other face standing off to the side? That must be the devil. That face looks so common and ordinary that it could be the face of just about anyone you might meet on the street.

That is exactly the point. When the devil shows up in the pages of scripture, his physical appearance is never described. It is unimportant. There is no mention of any ghoulish features, no horns, no pitchfork, no long tail, no monstrous fangs or claws that we would expect to see on the devil in a late night horror flick. Instead we can expect to meet the devil in the ordinary and every day. Sometimes the devil could even appear in the attractive and the beautiful. For example, in the Genesis 3 story of the temptation of Adam and Eve the serpent, whom we are so quick to identify as the devil, is actually described as "more crafty than any other wild animal that the Lord God had made." In the New Testament when Jesus angrily speaks, "Get behind me, Satan," it is spoken not to some threatening enemy but to one of the innermost circle of his disciples: Peter. Where is the monster with the horns and pitchfork?

What identifies the presence of the devil is exactly what we see portrayed in many pictures. He speaks. When he speaks he always begins by saying: *"Did God really say...?"* Whether it was in the Garden of Eden or to the Israelites wandering in the wilderness or to Jesus in today's gospel, it is always the same. To Adam and Eve in the garden he says, *"Did God really say ... you shall not eat from any tree in the garden?"* After Jesus had been in the desert for forty days he says, *"Did God really say ... you are the Son of God?"* After Jesus had predicted that he must go to Jerusalem and suffer and die, the devil again speaks but this time through the voice of Peter, one of Jesus' most trusted disciples. *"Did God really say ... you had to go to Jerusalem and suffer and die to be the messiah?"* When the devil speaks, he attacks his prey by sowing the seeds of doubt and trying to undermine the trustworthiness of God by implying that some how, some way God is pulling a fast one, that God is not completely on the up and up, that God is not keeping his promises.

"And because God is not trustworthy, you need to take things into your own hands. If God won't be God, then you need to be God and you do that by taking charge of your own life. You do that, Adam and Eve, by eating that forbidden fruit and deciding for yourselves what is good and evil instead of always having to trust God, who doesn't seem to be all that trustworthy in the first place.

"Because God is not trustworthy, Jesus, you need to take matters into your own hands and show the world that you are strong and powerful and in control of your own life. *Did God really say ...* back there in the waters of the Jordan that you were 'the Son of God, the Beloved, with whom I am well pleased?' If that is what he really said, then why did he send you out into the desert for forty days? After that kind of treatment, aren't you hungry? Why not turn these rocks into bread? Then I might believe that God really said that you were his beloved son. Then even you could believe that you were his son.

"*Did God really say* ... that you are his son? Prove it. Jump off the pinnacle of the temple and see if God's angels will catch you. After all, God himself says in his word, 'He will command his angels concerning you to protect you.' Do that and I will believe you. Even more importantly, Jesus, do that and you could believe God.

"*Did God really say* ... that this world is his? Jesus, you can't possibly believe that. God is not being straight with you. Just look at this world and what a mess it is. It obviously is in my hands. But being the generous fellow that I am (unlike your Father in heaven), I will give this world to you, if you will just worship me."

In each case there is the lie, the insidious lie, that God can't be trusted, that you are on your own, that you have got to take matters into your hands and look out for yourself. You can't count on God anymore.

"*Did God really say*...? No, of course he didn't. Now, what are you going to do about it, Jesus, Steve, (*call out names of people in the congregation*)?"

In today's reading, Paul addresses the same issue with the Romans. They, too, are grappling with the trustworthiness of God. The problem was that God's chosen people, the people to whom he had made such an incredible promise, the Jews, had rejected Jesus as the Messiah. They had turned their backs on the very God who had chosen them. As a result many Christians had come to the conclusion that the Jews were no longer God's chosen people. They had rejected their election and were lost.

That posed a very troubling problem. Did that mean that God had reneged on his promise to the Jews? Had God now turned his back on his own people? If God had rejected the people who had formerly been his people, what assurance is there that the same thing wouldn't happen to them? God had made a promise to Abraham and his descendants that would never be revoked. Now, if God has chosen to reject the Jews for their failure to accept Jesus as the Messiah, how can they be sure that God someday might not do the same thing to them? How can anyone be sure of God's promises, if those promises can be revoked?

You can just hear between the lines of Paul's letter the voice of the tempter, sowing the seeds of doubt and peddling his lies to the Romans. *"Did God really say ...* that he would keep his promises? If he did, he lied, because he hasn't kept them. Look what has happened to the Jews. The same thing could happen to you. Can you afford to trust a God like that? Isn't it time to take matters into your own hands?"

Is our situation any different? The devil is going to peddle his lies. You can count on it. And you can be sure that he isn't going to show up in any talking snake in the garden or in some horned beast wielding a pitchfork. Instead he shows up in the familiar voice of an old friend, our beloved spouse, our own children, the leader that we trusted, the company that had promised so much. *"Did God really say ...* did you really think that you were someone special? Well, what about that pain in your chest, that lump that wasn't supposed to be in that part of your body, that pink slip you thought you would never get, that coworker who got the promotion that was supposed to be yours, that raise you deserved but didn't get, a society in which the rich get richer and the poor get poorer, where children die too young, where terrorist bombs rip apart the lives of the innocent?"

Maybe we aren't so special after all. How can we trust God in a world like this? So we take matters into our own hands and make choices shaped not by what is right but by what we can get away with. Who cares what it does to others? We are now in charge. We have the knowledge of good and evil, that is, our version of good and evil and in our version we are always good. We are always God.

It gets worse. The devil uses God's own words to poison our faith. Imagine that! The devil quotes scriptures! In today's gospel the devil used God's word against Jesus to undermine his trust in God. When he took Jesus to the pinnacle of the temple and dared him to jump and then to a high place to show him the kingdoms of the world and promised to give them to Jesus, he quotes scripture,

God's own word, two times, to undermine Jesus' trust in God. He quotes God against God.

Doesn't the devil do the same thing to us? He uses God's own words to lead us into temptation and undermine our trust in God. God's word says, "It is easier for a camel to go through the eye of a needle than for a rich man to enter the kingdom of God" (Mark 10:25 RSV). We are all in trouble when we realize that a rich man is anyone who has enough money to be afraid to lose it. And who of us doesn't do that?

God's word says, "You have heard that it was said to the men of old, 'You shall not kill.' But I say to you that everyone who is angry with his brother or sister (is a murderer) shall be liable to judgment" (Matthew 5:21-22 RSV). We are all murderers. We all have hands covered with blood. We are all liable to God's judgment.

God's word says, "Not everyone who says to me 'Lord, Lord' shall enter the kingdom of heaven" (Matthew 7:21). We thought our confession of faith and our flawless recitation of the Creed for memory mattered, but now we can't even be sure of that.

The voice continues to speak softly, gently, persuasively, *"Did God really say* all that? But you know the truth. You know that you *can't* count on God. You are on your own. It is time to do what is best for you." And so we reach out and eat of the forbidden fruit. Before we have a chance to cover our shame and nakedness, God comes walking in the Garden in the cool of the evening and he is no longer our friend. He has become our enemy. We have to run and hide or we will surely die.

When the Romans felt vulnerable, unsure, uncertain, and afraid, when we feel vulnerable, unsure, uncertain, and afraid ... because the devil has had his way with us, like he has had his way with every human being before us, Paul is determined that we not be left standing there, hiding in the bushes, embarrassed and ashamed. He responds with the bold words of today's reading. Like an attorney rushing to our defense in a court of law, Paul quotes God's word against the devil and his ilk who use God's word to threaten and terrify us.

But the evil one won't give up easily. *"Did God really say ...* that you were special, that you could trust him, that you are his chosen people, his beloved sons and daughters? That can't possibly be true. Just look at your life. You ought to be ashamed of yourself. Look at the skeletons in your closet. Look at the wounds you have inflicted on your family. Look at the failures that litter your past. Look at your pride, your arrogance, the way you gossip and destroy the good name of others. Look at your love of money."

Paul will not let the devil have the last word. *"Yes, God really did say that!* God really did say that we are special. The promise of your baptism remains. The forgiveness of sins you receive at his table will never be revoked. His desire to forgive is eternal." Paul, too, can quote God's word: "No one who believes in him will be put to shame" (Isaiah 28:16) and "Everyone who calls on the name of the Lord will be saved" (Joel 2:32). Clinging to these promises, Paul is certain that we can count on God no matter what.

However, the devil persists. He will not give up easily. *"Did God really say* that? How do you know that for sure? How can you trust one word of God and disregard the other?" Paul boldly responds by pointing to Jesus, the one who went before us. He is the word of God, the last word of God, to which we cling. He resisted the wiles and temptations of the devil and we don't. We fall for them, hook, line, and sinker. Even on the cross the voice continued to whisper into Jesus' ear, *"Did God really say ...* that you are the Son of God?" Three times on the cross Jesus again is tempted. This time it is not about turning rocks into bread or jumping off the temple or worshiping the devil, but it is about daring to believe that God is his Father even though he is suffering this brutal fate. Three times the "father of lies" speaks: "If you are the Son of God, come down from the cross." Again Jesus resists. He had already refused to turn rocks into bread, jump off the temple, and worship the devil. He continues to do what he has always done. He believes. He refuses to come down from the cross. He would rather die. Even in death he still believes. His God has not lied to him. "Father, into your hands I commit my spirit."

When he died, he looked like a fool, just another misguided martyr. But "on the third day" he was raised from the dead. His faith was vindicated. God said, "That's my boy!" Jesus had staked his life on that promise. He was not mistaken. He was no fool.

So also for us. *"Did God really say ...* that you, the people of this church, are the beloved sons and daughters of God, that you are the apple of his eye, that your sins are forgiven?" We hesitate. We wonder. Is it true?

Listen to Paul: "The word is near you, on your lips and in your heart." Go ahead. Say it. Confess it. Confess this faith and you will never be put to shame. God did not let Jesus down. God will not let you down. You will never be embarrassed for the faith that is "on your lips and in your heart."

The old Reformation hymn puts it well.

> *A mighty fortress is our God,*
> *A sword and shield victorious ...*
> *Though hordes of devils fill the land*
> *All threatening to devour us ...*
> *Let this world's tyrant rage ...*
> *His might is doomed to fail ...*
> *God's Word forever shall abide,*
> *No thanks to foes who fear it;*
> *For God himself fights by our side*
> *With weapons of the Spirit.*
> *Were they to take our house,*
> *Goods, honor, child, or spouse,*
> *Though life be wrenched away,*
> *They cannot win the day,*
> *The Kingdom's ours forever!*[1]

The evil one whispers, *"Did God really say...?"* And before he can finish his sentence, we shout, *"Yes, he did!"* Amen.

---

1. "A Mighty Fortress Is Our God," words by Martin Luther, ca 1529. In the public domain.

Lent 2
Philippians 3:17—4:1

Enemies Of The Cross

Whenever I lead an inquiry class for those who want to learn more about my congregation and the faith we confess, I try to keep things very simple and boiled down to the basics. I call it an inquiry class because by exploring their questions I hope to help them to see what is at the heart and core of the Christian faith.

What is that heart and core? It is revealed by a shocking answer to a simple question. It is a question that every human being asks: What do I have to do to be saved? It is a question that gets asked in a variety of ways in a multitude of circumstances: What must I do to have a worthwhile and meaningful life? What do I have to do to have a life that matters? Can I do anything of eternal significance? What must I do to be happy? These questions all seem to be different but, in fact, they are all asking the same fundamental question: What do I have to do? The shocking answer that the Christian faith offers to that question is ... *nothing*! I don't *have to* do anything to be saved or to have a meaningful and purposeful life or be happy or be somebody. Why? Because God has already given me that in Jesus Christ! It is a pure gift. What I can never achieve on my own, God freely gives me with no strings attached, no conditions to be filled, or obligations to be met.

Immediately there are always those in the class who raise their eyebrows. If they are especially bold, they might even protest. Even lifelong Christians in the class might be uncomfortable with this answer. "But, pastor, I *have to* do something, don't I? At least I *have to* believe, don't I?" But I stick to my guns and keep on insisting on the *nothing*.

The problem is with the question. It assumes that we *have to* do something. Yes, faith is important. Yes, it is only by faith in Christ that we are saved. But faith is something that we *get to* do, willingly, freely, joyfully in response to what God has first offered us in Jesus Christ.

There is an underlying fear shared by all of us that such a message goes just too far. If I don't *have to* do something to be saved, then I can do anything. What is to prevent me from just going out and doing anything I please, having a grand old time sinning and carousing knowing that it really doesn't make any difference because God is going to save me anyway? It's like that streetwise corner newsboy who upon hearing the gospel shouts, "God loves to forgive sins. I love to commit them. Isn't the world admirably arranged?"

In the face of such an "anything goes" kind of attitude, there are those who go running to "law and order," to the rules and regulations, convinced that people will always abuse such freedom for their own selfish gain. You have to crack down on them. You have to keep them in line. You just have to lay down certain duties and obligations, otherwise they will turn the Christian faith into one big joke. But as we all know, sometimes the best of intentions ends up creating results we never expected. A noble attempt to prevent chaos turns the Christian faith in to a "bunch of do's and don'ts." We thought we had good news to offer but all the rules create only a bunch of guilt ridden do-gooders who never can escape their sense of failure. Or we create a bunch of hypocrites who are very good at lying to themselves and to anyone else who is foolish enough to believe that they don't have any skeletons in their closets.

It seems that we are trapped between a rock and a hard place, between "letting it all hang out" and "nailing it all down."

It is just this sort of problem that Saint Paul addresses in today's second reading. The congregation at Philippi was one that he dearly loved and it gave him great joy. But it seems that the congregation is threatened by those in their midst whom Paul calls "enemies of the cross of Christ." In very harsh language he describes them as those whose "end is destruction, their god is the belly, and they glory in their shame, with minds set on earthly things." Who are these terrible "enemies of the cross" of Christ?

Scholars have debated this question *ad infinitum*. On the one hand, there are those who see them as libertines, the "let it all hang out" crowd. For them "anything goes" in the name of Christian freedom. They indulge in every sort of excess and immorality, all in the pursuit of their own self-gratification. In pursuit of their own pleasure they have little concern for the welfare of others.

On the other hand, there are those scholars who see the "enemies of the cross" as Jewish Christians who insist that followers of Jesus must still adhere to the law of Moses. In other words, one must become a Jew before he could become a Christian. "Their god is their belly" when they insist on enforcing all the Jewish food laws. And "their glory is in their shame" when they demand circumcision for every male. They believe that the performance of such "earthly things" guarantees them their salvation.

The debate between the scholars is interesting but ultimately it doesn't matter. In fact, both groups are "enemies of the cross." In fact, there may have been members of both groups in the congregation in Philippi that Paul had in mind when he wrote this. Like two dogs fighting each other, biting at each other's throat, they are mortal enemies with nothing in common ... other than their desire to destroy the other. That is exactly the point! They are fighting each other, but they have their tails tied together. They both share the same assumption: they *have to* win; they *have to* be right; they *have to* succeed ... and it is up to them to do something about it.

They are just like us living their lives under the tyranny of the *have to*. Isn't that the way we all live our lives? In fact, we have no choice. There is no escape. We *have to* justify our lives, carve out our own niche, be somebody, *win*! We cannot but live our lives any other way than by serving our own self-interest. On the one hand the libertine tries to "save" himself through all sorts of self-indulgence. On the other hand, the moralist tries to "save" himself through all sorts of discipline. They do it with a passion that betrays its ultimate source: the empty and searching heart that feels compelled to have a life that counts. There is no escaping the sense that they *must*, that they *have to* do something or else they will disappear into oblivion.

Paul would say in terms of today's reading that we cannot escape serving our "belly." We *have to* always eat. Some people in this world eat to live. We live to eat, to feed our "belly." We live in a society that glamorizes conspicuous consumption. For as much as we love the delights of a flashy lifestyle or the thrills of our latest gadget, we still crave being right. Our "belly" demands that we feed its cravings and desires. We cannot escape its gnawing hunger, its demand for always more and more. We cannot live otherwise.

And what is the result? Paul says "their end is destruction." What is the result of a "belly" that can never be satisfied? We end up destroying ourselves.

The biggest epidemic in our society today, a society where we can never get enough, is obesity. We eat too much of the wrong foods, always hoping to satisfy our hunger, and it kills us. We get hypertension, heart disease, and diabetes, the diseases, ironically, of affluence! The affluence that billions of the world's hungry crave, ironically, is killing us.

Our economy may already be in a recession partially aggravated by the burst of the housing bubble. Too many people in pursuit of satisfying their "belly," never convinced that they have "enough," always feeling that they *have to* have more and more, lied about their incomes, took on mortgages they couldn't handle, and were all too willing to receive loans they never should have received. Lenders, also, were unable to resist the cravings of their "belly." In pursuit of a more robust bottom line they made loans that never should have been made. Foolishly believing that the "bubble" could expand forever, they were unprepared for the burst that was inevitable.

We live in a society that glamorizes immediate gratification. Commitments are ridiculed. Loyalty is scorned. Pleasure is a right. We *have to* satisfy our "belly." But what are the results? Paul's words sound prophetic. "Their end is destruction." Over half of all births in our society are to single mothers. Over one in two marriages crumbles. Children come into this world unwanted. People flee to the suburbs to escape social problems but only end up creating clogged freeways and more pollution. What kind of society are we creating? What kind of future will we have with such massive social dysfunction? "Their end is destruction."

We would like to think that Paul is pointing his finger at all the people out there. In this season of Lent we are reminded that the finger is also pointed at us. There is no escape. So we mark ourselves with ashes. We drape our sanctuary in the mournful shades of purple. We refuse to sing "Alleluia" for six weeks. We confess that we are simply getting what we deserve.

We realize that when Paul speaks of "enemies of the cross," he is talking about us. Clinging to our pious deeds, obsessed with having to prove ourselves and be right, unable and unwilling to leave behind the cravings of our "belly," we are finally thumbing our noses at the cross. We don't really need Christ and his cross. We like the challenge of the *have to* and the *ought to* because we think we can do it. We are proud of our accomplishments: our incomes, our beautiful homes, our children who are always on the honor roll, our latest promotion, our four-star schools, our beautiful church (or at least the new one that is rising out in the parking lot). Who needs Jesus ... except to maybe fill in the blanks, cover the mistakes, and pick us up when we slip? After all, who is perfect? We *have to* be appropriately modest because we all know how everyone is turned off by arrogance. God forbid that we should not be liked!

The problem gets worse. When we insist that there are parts of our lives that are pretty darn good after all and can stand on their own, we are living dangerously. We are thumbing our nose at God. We are telling God, "Thanks but no thanks for Christ and his cross. We don't need them." Are we serious? Do we know with whom we are messing? We are inviting God to give us what we deserve. We should not be surprised that our end is our destruction.

That is not a particularly appealing fate. We were sure that when Paul referred to the "enemies of the cross of Christ" he was talking about all those other folks. When we realize that Paul is talking about us, we want to run and hide. Instead Paul invites us to "join in imitating me." On the one hand this sounds incredibly arrogant on the part of Paul. Just last week we heard how this guy's life was such a mess, pockmarked with failures, rejections, shipwrecks, beatings, and loss. Do we really want to imitate this? On the other hand this sounds like just another *have to*, like just another appeal to our "belly" that is eternally craving to be somebody.

But this is something entirely different. When Paul asks us to "imitate" him, this is not a *have to*. It is a *get to*! Paul is not asking us to imitate his virtuous life. He is keenly aware of his shortcomings and failures. "For I do not do the good I want, but the evil I do not want is what I do" (Romans 7:19). "Yet whatever gains I had, these I have come to regard as loss because of Christ" (Philippians 3:7). Instead Paul is inviting us to imitate his trust of "the cross of Christ."

That cross is everything. God could have simply given us what we deserve. We continue to bring upon ourselves daily destruction. Just look at the newspaper, watch cable news, see a good film, read a good book, or listen to what those closest to us are really telling us about ourselves, and we will see the deadly fate to which God is handing us over. The cemeteries are filled with evidence. But that is not the fate God desires to give us. God is determined to love us. God's love will not be thwarted, even by our "bellies" and our stubborn desire to always go our own way. God sends Christ to bear the wreckage of our sin and suffer the judgment we deserve. He carries them to the cross where he bears the fate we deserve.

It is no accident that the cross is the focal point of this worship space. It is at the cross where God does the unthinkable. There God chooses not to give his enemies (enemies of the cross like us) what we deserve. No, instead God chooses to bear what we deserve, paying the price, biting the bullet, for us ... and our salvation.

When we gather here to eat and drink, to be washed and "born again," to receive the words of peace and consolation, it is under the cross. For it is here at the foot of the cross that we are given the status we crave. The hunger in our "bellies" is satisfied. Here God welcomes us home with the hug we thought we could find elsewhere. Here God dresses us in the finest clothes, kills for us the fatted calf for the feast in our honor, puts a ring on our finger, and declares to the whole company of heaven that the lost have come home. Those who once had been his enemies are now not just his friends but his beloved sons and daughters.

When Paul invites us to imitate him, it is an invitation in the best sense of the word. It is an invitation to a party where we will receive a gift and enjoy a blessing. This is no burden. This is no demand we *have to* meet or else. On the contrary, this is a *get to*, a privilege, an honor, a blessing that we will surely *want to* make our own.

When we do, we discover that we *get to* live our lives differently. Paul uses an interesting image to portray that here. He reminds us that even though we live in this world, "our citizenship is in heaven." When our life has been changed by the cross, we no longer belong to this world. Because we are citizens of heaven, we *get to* live in this world as foreigners, immigrants, strangers, never again to feel at home, no longer able to truly fit in. We will never be able to totally assimilate, but we will always be like the immigrant who is never able to shake his foreign accent. We gather on Sundays here in our ethnic neighborhood, to eat our ethnic foods, to practice our ethnic customs, to sing our ethnic songs, and to speak the foreign language of grace, mercy, and forgiveness.

We live "in" the world but are never "of" the world. When we leave this place, we will always be out of step. We will never quite shed our strange customs and practices. We can live with less. We can say "No" to conspicuous consumption. We don't need to hoard but can give ourselves away in lives of service to those with less. We welcome the stranger. We do what is right and not just what is expedient. We turn the other cheek. We go the extra mile. Why? Because our "bellies" are full. At the cross it has been satisfied. We are no longer hungry. We know who we are. We who once were enemies of the cross now embrace it.

This ... is now the shape of our lives! *(make the sign of the cross)* In the name of the Father, the Son, and the Holy Spirit. Amen.

Lent 3
1 Corinthians 10:1-13

Passing The Test

"Students, it is time to get out your pencils, close your books and remove any notes from your desks. The test is about to begin."

Those are words that make us shudder, our hearts start to pound and the palms of our hands begin to sweat. From our earliest days in school, we all have had to learn to deal with tests. It may begin with a simple first grade spelling test. But it doesn't take too long before it morphs into ISTEP, the SAT, the Bar, the Boards, or a doctoral qualifying exam. Or it might be as ordinary as a driver's test or as basic as remembering the correct password on your email account. No wonder the Boy Scouts insist that their young men must "Be Prepared!" (If I remember correctly from my scouting days, that is the motto of the Boy Scouts.)

The worst situation you can be in when taking a test is not being prepared. Maybe you forgot to study or maybe you never understood the subject matter or worst of all you were so sure of yourself that you never bothered to study. But then after taking the test you knew you were in over your head. You knew that your grade would be a disaster. You were embarrassed to admit that your complacency got the best of you. You knew you could have done better, if you just hadn't taken things for granted.

Every year in Faith Inkubators we struggle with giving tests. We don't want the students to be obsessed with grades or scores. We tell them that this is all about the gospel, which has nothing to do with grades or scores. So we call the tests "X-rays" because we are trying to send them the message that this is less about us "testing" them for a score or giving them a grade than it is about us trying to find out how much they have learned and how well we have taught them. The gospel is not about how well you can memorize the Creed. It is not about reciting the catechism. Rather, the gospel offers good news in the form of a radical answer to a simple question: "What do you *have to* do to be saved?" Answer: *"Nothing!* because God did it all for you in Christ and you *get to* believe that." The students, after they get over the initial shock of that answer, often get the impression that, since they don't *have to* do anything to be saved, they can literally *do nothing* for Faith Inkubators. Do they need to learn their memory work, read the assigned materials, participate in discussion, or even remember to bring their Bibles? No, they don't need to do any of that because ... the pastor told them they don't *have to* do anything! They feel justified in their complacency.

You can see the pickle we have gotten ourselves in. We want the students to study and learn. But what we are ultimately trying to teach them, faith in God, is something that has little to do with academic prowess or the ability to pass a test. As Jesus once reminded his disciples when they protested his spending time with little children who were too young to pass a test or memorize the catechism, "Let the little children come to me; do not stop them; for it is to such as these that the kingdom of God belongs" (Mark 10:14). It is the simple trusting faith of a child that God wants and not the sophisticated, measured, calculated, and qualified faith of a reasoned commitment. God wants our heart and not a flawless recitation of the Ten Commandments or the 66 books of the Bible. So how do we motivate youth or even adults for that matter to learn and study without the "carrot and stick" of a test or the threat of a grade?

Paul faced a similar problem in today's second reading. There were those in the Corinthian congregation who had become complacent. They were treating the sacraments, baptism, and communion as if they were some sort of magical and mystical guarantee of their eternal salvation. They could tell you all about God's grace and forgiveness. They could extol the benefits of baptism. They loved to celebrate communion, so much so that sometimes their celebrations got a little out of hand. They had no problem with participating in the immoralities and excesses of one of the most notorious cities in the entire Roman empire. No matter! They were baptized! They received holy communion! They could do anything they pleased because these sacraments guaranteed their privileged status. You can just imagine them standing around the narthex on Sunday morning sipping on their cups of coffee and telling one another what a "good deal" this being a Christian was. "God loves to forgive sins. We love to commit them. Isn't the world admirably arranged?"

But Paul could smell a rat. The Corinthians had lulled themselves into a dangerous situation. Today's reading is Paul's word of warning to them. "So if you think you are standing, watch out that you do not fall!" (v. 12). They had become so complacent that they had lulled themselves into thinking that nothing bad could ever happen to them. They were automatically in. Nothing could ever touch them, not even the displeasure of God. They could pass any and every test. No big deal! But they were kidding themselves. God will not be mocked. Or as that great modern "prophet" and humorist, Erma Bombeck, once said, "Life is *not* a bowl of cherries."

Sooner or later the roof falls in on all of us. No one goes through this life unscathed. Despite the incessant sales pitches of our consumer driven, immediate gratification culture, every one must eventually suffer. Everyone must deal with those stretches of life where we are in the wilderness, utterly alone, where no one seems to care. In those dark and dreary expanses of the desert it seems that even God has forsaken us. The sad story of human history is that more often than not in such times of darkness we will turn to anything but God. Instead of trusting God, we will make just about anything else we can get our hands on our god. Such idolatry has deadly consequences and does not go unnoticed by God.

To make his point, Paul calls the Corinthians' attention to the history of their brothers and sisters in the faith, ancient Israel. Through some rather deft biblical interpretation he points out several parallels between the Corinthians and the Israelites. Just as the Corinthians were rescued through the waters of baptism so also the Israelites were rescued by passing through the waters of the

Red Sea. In a sense the Israelites were "baptized" into Moses, just as the Corinthians were baptized into Christ. Just as the Corinthians were spiritually fed and nourished by the bread and wine of holy communion, so also were the Israelites fed with manna in the wilderness. Just as the Corinthians "drink living water" from Christ, so also the Israelites drank water from the rock that Moses struck in the wilderness (Exodus 17:1-17). Paul then cites an ancient rabbinic tradition that said that this rock followed Israel during their forty-year sojourn in the wilderness providing them water on a daily basis. It was the first "rolling stone." Paul then compares this "rolling stone" to Christ who continues to nourish the Corinthians and satisfy their thirsty hearts.

The problem is that Israel became unfaithful. She became complacent taking her privileged status as God's chosen people for granted. She turned to other gods and practiced idolatry. Remember the "golden calf" that the Israelites made to represent their god when they became impatient with Moses and his long stay on Mount Sinai? God didn't overlook that sin and destroyed many of the Israelites by swallowing them up into the earth. When the Israelites practiced sexual immorality with some Moabite women, 23,000 of them were struck down. When the Israelites complained in the wilderness and became impatient with God, God destroyed many of them by sending an invasion of poisonous snakes.

Throughout her forty years in the wilderness, God repeatedly tested Israel with all kinds of hardships to see if she would remain faithful. All too many times Israel flunked the tests and suffered the consequences. Not all that unlike the Corinthians, she thought that her privileged status permitted her to do anything she pleased without suffering the consequences. She was wrong. She paid dearly for her presumption and her complacency.

Paul cites these examples from the history of Israel in order to warn the Corinthians of the fate that awaited them, if they continued in their complacency and indifference, doing as they pleased. They would be tested. If they flunked, dire consequences awaited them.

Paul directs this same warning to us. We had better not take our faith for granted. We had better not be too complacent. We had better stay alert and on our toes, because God is going to test us. God is going to send trials, temptations, and tribulations our way to see how we handle them. If we pass the tests, if we remain faithful, we are okay. If we don't, look out!

But what about all this talk about grace and the gospel? We thought we didn't have to do anything to be saved. Is grace conditional after all? It appears that what Paul gives us with one hand, he takes away with the other. "So, if you are standing, watch out that you do not fall!" In other words, we still have to do something. We still *have to* stay on our toes, pass those tests when they come and, as the Boy Scouts say, "Be Prepared" ... or else!

We need to clamp down on those Faith Inkubator students who don't do their homework. We may say that they don't *have to* do anything to be saved, but we really don't mean it. The bottom line is that they still *have to* do something: They still *have to* believe, they still *have to* show up in church, they still *have to* pray, they still *have to* try to be good, they still *have to* pass confirmation ... or they won't be good Christians and respected members of this congregation. Why? Because God won't tolerate complacency! You *have to* be committed and prepared because you never know when God is going to tell you, "Students, it is time to get out your pencils, close your books, and remove any notes from your desks. The test is about to begin."

The tests come in a multitude of ways. You are not welcome at anyone's table in the school lunchroom. You tried too hard to make the team and you got cut. There is that sudden pain in your chest. You become a casualty of corporate downsizing. You receive that unexpected phone call at 3 a.m. and it is the police with a message you never wanted to hear. The promotion that you know you deserved goes to someone else. The friend you thought you could count on betrays you. The depression everyone tells you to do something about only gets worse, slowly strangling what little hope you had left in your life. Your children, you had such high hopes for them, only continue to disappoint you. You wake up in the middle of the night crying because you never thought that your life would turn out like this. You are in the wilderness ... thirsty, hungry, alone ... even God seems to have forsaken you. This wasn't supposed to happen to Christians. This wasn't supposed to happen to those who believe in God. Wasn't going to church and saying your prayers supposed to fix all this stuff? This is not what you signed up for.

Then to add insult to injury, someone quotes verse 13, "He will not let you be tempted beyond your strength." Really? You have to be kidding! What kind of a God would do this to you? Does God really think you are strong enough to handle this? You know your strength and it sure feels like God is now crushing you. It must be your fault. You must be letting God down because God surely wouldn't be laying these burdens on you if he didn't think you were strong enough. This is a test and you are flunking it. There is no way you are ever going to pass it.

It is then that God has us just where he wants us. Jolted out of our complacency, pushed to the edge, about ready to collapse, having had everything we thought was so important stripped out of our hands, all we can do is cry for help. All we can do is open our hands to receive ... for we have nothing. It is then that Paul's words begin to make sense.

Paul boldly declares, "God is faithful. He will not let you be tempted beyond your strength." He is not just telling us to "grin and bear it." No, these are words to comfort. God is coming to the rescue. "With the testing he will also provide you with the way out, so that you may be able to endure it." What is the "way out"? How can we possibly hope to "endure it"?

Christ is the "way out." Christ is the one who enables us to "endure it."

It must be because Paul was under the influence of the Holy Spirit that he is able to see in these ancient stories of Israel's wandering in the wilderness something Israel never saw. Paul sees Christ. At two places in today's reading Paul makes this explicit connection.

First, Paul knew of that ancient rabbinical tradition that spoke of the rock Moses struck, which brought forth water to quench the thirst of the Israelites (v. 4). According to the rabbinical tradition the rock followed the Israelites throughout their forty years in the wilderness giving them fresh water every day. Paul says the rock was a symbol of Christ, the same Christ who now satisfies the spiritual thirst of the Corinthians.

Second, Paul recalls another story from Israel's wilderness wandering (v. 9). In that story the Israelites so complained and murmured against God that God sent poisonous snakes among them. Stripped of their pride and complacency, realizing their desperate plight, the Israelites cry for help. God in his mercy relents and tells Moses to mount a bronzed serpent on a pole. Whenever someone who was dying from the snakebites would look at the serpent, they would be healed. Just when they were about to completely bomb the test, God rescues them.

In this season of Lent we recall that Christ and his cross are the signs that God is present with us in the wilderness of our lives. When we suffer, when we are alone, when our soul is parched and we long for someone to tell us that all is okay, when we are convinced that God has handed us over to the poisonous snakes because we have once again failed our test, Christ, like that bronzed serpent, is lifted up on the cross to assure us that God is faithful. Christ is our rock, our "rolling stone," following us wherever we go in the wilderness of this world giving us a drink, soothing our snakebites, helping us to pass the test, giving us an A when we deserve an F.

In the midst of our trials and temptations, even as we are tested, God is there coaxing out of us the right answers so that we can pass the test with flying colors.

Doc Christman underwent a test. He was a pillar of the community. The old, retired teacher had been awarded Teacher of the Year by the State Teachers Association in 1982. Everyone admired and respected him, but now he was a shadow of himself. He had shrunk to less than 100 pounds. His life was slowly consumed by cancer.

Doc had to leave the hospital. He had to decide where he wanted to die: at home or in a nursing home. His pastor, Reverend Braun, came to help him decide. His pastor wouldn't tell him what to do but helped him to decide.

Reverend Braun leaned over the hospital bed and whispered into Doc's ear, "Doc, where is your home?"

Doc mumbled, "321 North Maple Street." That was the house he had lived in for fifty years.

Reverend Braun once again leaned over the bed and asked, "Doc, where is your home?"

Again, Doc mumbled, "Oh you must mean 200 Eastgate Drive." That was the address of the nursing home.

Again Reverend Braun spoke into Doc's ear but this time with a firm prosecutorial tone, "Doc, *where ... is ... your ... home?*"

This time Doc perked up. His eyes glowed as if a light had just gone on in that tired mind of his. This time he didn't mumble but spoke with conviction, "*... with ... the ... Lord!*"

That is just what Paul is talking about in today's reading. God keeps on testing us, pushing us, questioning us, so that we can discover the faith that is already within us, so that, when the time of testing comes, we can pass the test. We can confess the faith that he has already given to us. God doesn't need us to prove our faithfulness ... or else. God is testing us for our benefit and gain, so that we can better understand, appreciate, and confess the hope that is by God's grace in our hearts. God wants us to pass the test ... and does everything to make that possible, even to the point of sending his only Son to the cross, so that all our F's might be forgiven. God even gives us his very own Spirit who, when the time of testing comes, will help us to speak all the right answers.

So what about the Faith Inkubators? We will continue to give them "X-rays" and not tests. We won't give them grades. We are not interested in shaming them into working harder. No, we will continue to teach them, to prod them, to question them, to coax out of them the childlike faith we believe is already within them. We will whisper into their ears, "Where is your home?" Why? So that when they find themselves in their wilderness, when they must face their trials and tribulations, which they surely will as they become adults and continue to live their lives, they will *get to* confess their faith and say with old Doc Christman, "with the Lord." And then they will have discovered that they have passed the test. And God will smile and all the company of heaven will sing with joy. Amen.

Lent 4
2 Corinthians 5:16-21

A New Point Of View

In 2000, Mel Gibson appeared in the comedy, *What Women Want*. The film was fairly successful at the box office because it built on a fantasy that I think all of us have indulged in at one time or another. He plays an executive who works at an advertising agency in Chicago. His life dramatically changes when he is jolted by electricity and develops the ability to read women's minds. It leads to some absolutely hilarious and humorous situations. Sure enough, it transforms him into a great lover who knows exactly what to do and when to do it to please a woman. Likewise his ability to read women's minds enables him to advance his career by developing ads for products that women want. But his ability to read the minds of women also has a down side. He is horrified to find out that many of the women in his office pretend to like him but really don't.

The whole premise of the film is based on the assumption that what others think of us is important. Despite the playground mantra ("Sticks and stones may break my bones but words will never hurt me."), words do have great power. It indeed does matter what the other kids on the playground think of us. We like to think that growing up and becoming mature means that we have become self-confident, that we know who we are, that we have become a "self-differentiated adult" immune to criticism of others. But that is simply not true. Unless we move to a deserted island or to the middle of the desert and live life in utter solitude, we can never escape the opinions and evaluations of others.

If you have ever held a job (and it is hard for me to imagine any of us making it through life without having some kind of job), your performance is always graded, evaluated, praised, criticized, rewarded, and penalized. Who of us has never been told by our spouse or our children, "That looks ugly!" and we run to put on a different shirt? We cannot escape the human point of view.

Likewise, we can never escape forming opinions and making evaluations of others. We are constantly judging others on the basis of gender, race, economic status, age, appearance ... and whether they are a Colts' fan or not. The political frenzy, as we get ready to elect a new president each four years, reminds us that at the heart of our democratic process is the assumption that what the electorate thinks of you matters.

At the heart of the way we humans evaluate one another is "keeping score." And at the heart of such scorekeeping is our need to score points for ourselves. We want to score points on the job because that is the way to a pay raise or a promotion or the growing success of our business. We decide to change our shirt because we not only want the approval of our spouse and children but also the neighbors and coworkers who will see us in that shirt. Their opinion matters. We choose to associate with people who are like us because they are safe. Safety counts. We hang around with people who are rich and famous because they make us look good. The Indiana Pacers lose fan support not just because they are losing ball games, but because their players are hanging out with the wrong kinds of people, in some cases, criminals. It doesn't look good and looking good matters to management and the fans.

According to the human point of view such score keeping inevitably makes winners and losers. That is the down side of it all. Some are more beautiful and popular than others. Some are smarter, faster, taller, and stronger than others. Some come in first and others go home. None of us wants to lose or come in second or be left behind because someone else was better. We all want to know that we matter, that we count, that we are loved, that we are right. There is no escaping that need. It is what makes us human.

So we build our empires. We plan our careers. We plot against the competition. We make our case for being right. We draw our lines in the sand. We divide the world into those who are for us and those who are against us. That brings to mind the old office joke: "What's the difference between God and Mr. Z? God never acts like he thinks he is Z."[1]

That raises the most important question of all: the God question. What does God think of us? Some of us just avoid the question all together. We just "brush God off." Even though we might show up in church every once in a while, even though we say we believe in God (as most Americans do), we live most of our lives as functional atheists, as if God doesn't exist or as if God's opinion of us doesn't matter. We live with this huge disconnect between Sunday morning and the rest of the week.

However, if your life is anything like mine, you know that we are kidding ourselves. If that is the case, then why do we work such long hours? Why do we complain that we are always under pressure? Why do we say there are not enough hours in the day? Why are we always worried about tomorrow? Why does our lifestyle always have to keep up with the Joneses in Zionsville or Carmel? Because the truth of the matter is that the "human point of view" has become the most important thing in our lives. "The human point of view," what others think of us, has become our god. The problem is that those humans can never give us what only God can give us. The pressure never relents. The hunger is never satisfied. There are never enough pats on the back or smiles of approval to silence the fear that that we will never be good enough.

Do we honestly think that God is going to let us "brush him off" and let us leave him behind in the walls of this sanctuary while we go off living our lives as if he didn't exist? Of course not! The truth of the matter is that God is there with us seven days a week. There is no place in this universe where we can hide from God's scrutiny. Talk about pressure! Talk about measuring up! Talk about scoring points! It's tough enough to measure up to the "human point of view." Measuring up to God's "point of view" is impossible.

This dilemma lies behind Paul's words to the Corinthians in today's lesson. The people in the Corinthian congregation were splintered and divided because all they seemed to care about was living according to the "human point of view." All they wanted to do was score points. All they could do is pass judgment on one another. All they could do is divide their congregation into those who were on their side or not on their side, into those who were winners and losers. Some spiritual gifts were better than others. Some were fans of one preacher instead of another. Some had more money than others. Some were smarter than others. Some were more eloquent than others. The scorekeeping went on and on hopelessly dividing the congregation into a bunch of warring factions. It had made their lives miserable. But their plight was not just self-inflicted. They were also suffering God's own judgment for being so faithless. They were not only failing according to a "human point of view," they were failing according to "God's point of view." They were in big trouble.

But all is not lost because at the heart of today's lesson is Paul's appeal to regard one another according to **a new point of view**. He reminds them that it is possible to live their lives differently because of what God has already done for them and to them in Christ. They don't have to be always keeping score, counting up trespasses, measuring accomplishments, both theirs and others, as they shamelessly pursue their own success. They no longer need to tear up their congregation with one backroom deal, one secret meeting, one slanderous conversation after another. All of that is no longer necessary. They no longer have to build themselves up at the expense of others because they are a new creation!

They are part of a new world, a new way life, marked not by the scorekeeping of the "human point of view" or even the scorekeeping of God's own judgment. God in his grace and mercy has decided to end it all and make a new world, a new creation.

At the heart of that new creation is Christ and what God has done in Christ. Paul describes that marvelous action of God as "reconciliation." Where there previously had been division and conflict, there now is unity and peace. Where previously there had been competitors and enemies, there now are companions and friends. And, the amazing thing about this new creation is that God so loved the world, even those who were his enemies, that God decided to take it all upon himself to end the conflict. God paid the price. God reconciled himself to us.

How did that happen? Paul puts it so clearly at the end of today's lesson: "For our sake he made him to be sin who knew no sin, so that in him we might become the righteousness of God." Luther calls it the "froehlicher wechsel," "the happy exchange" or what a dear teacher of mine once called, "the sweet swap." This is the strange, utterly odd and amazingly gracious thing that God did at the cross for those conflicted and faithless Corinthians ... and for us who are hopelessly unable to escape from our obsession with keeping score.

In this season of Lent as we make our trek to Holy Week, Good Friday, and Easter, we are reminded of Christ's sole mission and purpose. At the heart of Christ's mission was the bold declaration, "The kingdom of God is at hand, repent and believe this good news!" What was it about the kingdom that would cause us to repent, to so change our lives that we would be an utterly new creation, no longer regarding the world from a "human point of view"? Watch Jesus. See how he treats others. Listen to what he says. And soon it becomes very clear that he is not viewing this world according to a "human point of view." He is not even viewing it according to God's point of view as reflected in Moses and the prophets. Instead of judging sinners, he is the friend of sinners. He eats and drinks with outcasts. He embraces those who seem to be utter failures and losers. He takes upon himself everything that is wrong and sick with this world. He bears it all. He "who knew no sin" ... was "made to be sin." By whom? By God, himself! Why? "For our sake" (v. 21), because God loves us that much.

On the cross Christ suffers for us the fate we deserve. And in exchange for that fate, God gives us his righteousness, "so that in him we might become the righteousness of God" (v. 21). We who were last are now first. We who were poor now are rich. We who were dirty now are clean. We who were dead are now alive. We who were lost now are found. We who were sinners now are forgiven. We who once were enemies of God now are friends. And God who was once our enemy because of our sin is now our "Father," our daddy, our papa. What a "happy exchange!" What a "sweet swap!"

It is the beginning of a whole new world, of what can only be called a "new creation." "So if anyone is in Christ, there is a new creation; everything old has passed away; see everything has become new" (v. 17). That means that we no longer look at the world from a "human point of view" but from the way God looks at it ... in Christ! The pages of the New Testament are filled with examples of what that new creation looks like. A man born blind, who was thought of as nothing more than a beggar, an outcast, a sinner condemned to live his life off the generosity of others, Jesus sees in a totally different way. He sees him the way God sees him. Jesus loves him. Jesus gives him his sight. And as that blind man opens his eyes and looks at Jesus, for the first time he can "see" God for who God really is (John 9).

A son demands his inheritance, leaves his father, and wastes it all in a life of decadence. From a "human point of view" he deserved to be on the street begging for crumbs. He deserves to eat pig food. In desperation he decides to return home hoping that his father might be willing to accept him as a slave. From a "human point of view" that is all he could hope for. But his father does not look at him from a "human point of view." No, he looks at him from God's point of view ... in Christ ... and welcomes him home with a new robe on his back, a ring on his finger, sandals on his feet, and a fatted calf for dinner (Luke 15).

From the cross Jesus looks down at his enemies who had brutally abused him and ridiculed him. A crown of sharp thorns had cut into his brow. His back had been filleted by a vicious beating. His hands had been pierced by nails. According to a "human point of view" those who had inflicted this suffering and pain on him were deserving only of his disdain. But Jesus did not look at them like that. Instead he looked at them through the eyes of the kingdom of God. He could only see people crushed by the weight of their own hatred. This was no time for revenge. This was time for reconciliation. "Father, forgive them, for they know not what they do" (Luke 23:34).

An auctioneer holds up an old violin, battered and scarred. He looks at it wondering why anyone would ever think that it was worth his while. But he holds it up anyway and cries, "Who will start the bidding? How about a dollar? Anyone a dollar? How about two dollars? Only two dollars? Two dollars? Will anyone make it three? Three dollars anyone? ... Three dollars once, three dollars twice. Going for three...."

Suddenly he is interrupted by a voice from the back of the room. A gray-haired man comes forward and picks up the bow of the old violin and wipes off the dust. He tightens the strings and then plays a melody so pure and so sweet on that old violin that it sounds as sweet as a song the angels of heaven might sing.

When the gray-haired man finishes playing, the auctioneer continues with a voice that is quiet and low. He says again, "Who will start the bidding for the old violin?" He holds it up high with the bow and cries, "A thousand dollars? Do I hear a thousand dollars? Who will make it two? I hear two thousand dollars. Who will make it three? Do I hear three thousand dollars? Three thousand once. Three thousand twice. Going and going and ... gone!"

The people cheer! The crowd is exuberant! But some of them ask, "We do not quite understand — what changed its worth?"

> *Swift came the reply,*
> **"The touch of the master's hand."**
> *And many a man with a life out of tune,*
> *And battered and torn with sin*
> *Is auctioned cheap to a thoughtless crowd,*
> *Much like the old violin.*
> *A mess of pottage, a life of shame,*
> *A game and he travels on.*
> *He's going once, and going twice,*
> *He's going and almost gone.*
> *But the Master comes and the foolish crowd*
> *Never can quite understand*
> *The worth of a soul and the change that's wrought*
> ***By the touch of the Master's hand.***[2]

With this new point of view, we live our lives no longer keeping score, no longer counting their trespasses against them, no longer dividing the world into losers and winners. We like Christ on the cross, welcome the world, forgive our enemies, turn the other cheek, and welcome home the prodigals.

And when the folks gather around the water cooler in the office and ask, "What's the difference between God and Mr. Z?" some will say "It's hard to tell the difference." Amen.

---

1. Frederick Niedner, *New Proclamation, Year C, 2003-2004* (Minneapolis: Fortress Press, 2003), p. 173.

2. Myra B. Welch, "The Touch of The Master's Hand," *For All The Saints* (Delhi, New York: American Lutheran Publicity Bureau, 1995), pp. 893-894.

Lent 5
Philippians 3:4b-14

Running The Race

Every week in our country millions of people go to stadiums and arenas to participate in the thrills and chills of athletic competition. Athletic competition attracts people as participants and spectators for a variety of reasons. Perhaps the most universal reason for the appeal of sports is the similarity between what goes on in the arena of athletic competition and the arena of life. Athletic competition is a microcosm of life, because we all love to compete and win.

In our second lesson for today, Saint Paul uses an image from the arena of athletic competition to describe the nature of the Christian life. Paul compares the Christian life to running a race. In a series of very carefully chosen verbs Paul dramatically describes the Christian life like a race as he "presses on" toward victory. He "strains forward" to the finish line. He "presses on" to reach "the goal" to capture "the prize."

However, if we take a close look at what Paul is saying here, it becomes less and less clear as to why Paul would ever want to choose this kind of an image to describe his life. He hardly looks like an Olympic track star about to capture the gold medal. He hardly looks like a champion about to seize another victory. He is writing this letter from prison. He is accused of being a criminal. He is in grave danger of losing his life. He looks more like a loser than a winner, more like a weakling than a champion. Nevertheless, he is confident and certain of victory. He is not the least bit worried or fearful of defeat.

Athletic competition appeals to so many because after the final gun has sounded and some have enjoyed "the thrill of victory" and others have suffered "the agony of defeat," we can always walk away from it. Unlike the rest of life, it is "only a game." It was only "just for the fun of it." It was not a matter of life and death.

Once the contest moves out of the contrived "make believe" world of the gymnasium or the gridiron, the stakes increase dramatically. It is no longer "just a game." Instead of taking our positions on the court or on the field, we take our positions in the office, the factory, the classroom, the lab, the family. Suddenly we are "playing for keeps." Suddenly whether we win or lose does matter. It matters to our family, our friends, our coworkers, our colleagues, our customers, and all those who depend on us and our success. It even matters to God. As we contend with the pressures and demands of living, we are not only contending with the marketplace, quotas, profit margins, peer reviews, and crabby children, but with the demands of God.

Vince Lombardi supposedly said it: "Winning isn't every thing. It's the only thing!" It could just as easily have been said by God who insists that unless our "righteousness exceeds that of the scribes and Pharisees, you shall not enter the kingdom of heaven."

Whew! That ups the stakes significantly. Life is tough enough without having God breathing down our necks.

We all seek to cope with these demands in different ways. Sometimes we make excuses and "pass the buck." Sometimes it is easier to blame our poor finish on someone else than to accept responsibility for ourselves. Sometimes it's easier to blame our poor grade on a poor night's sleep or the distraction of a television show than to admit that we just didn't study. Sometimes it is easier to blame our failure to get promoted on work place politics rather than to admit that we just didn't do a good job. We think we have run the race well but the reality is that we are not track stars. We are more like molasses in January than a jack rabbit in June.

Some of us wouldn't think of making excuses. We are competitors. We like winning. We are willing to make sacrifices. But while running down the backstretch, we feel our legs getting heavy.

Our lungs are short of breath. We start falling behind. We start to panic. The thought of not winning terrifies us. So, we bend the rules a little. We cut off an opponent. We "accidentally" trip the runner beside us. We reason that we had no choice because, when winning isn't just everything but the only thing, all is legal. "All is fair in love and war" — a little lie, a slight overstatement, a wee bit of exaggeration, the carefully placed rumor, an unfortunate slip of the tongue, a timely deletion on the computer — all become a way of life. Suddenly the race that we loved to run has become the burden we cannot bear. The innocent bending of the rules has become a cancer destroying not only the joy of competition but our relationships with our friends, our neighbors, and our fellow competitors. Infected with distrust, suspicion, jealousy, and even hatred, friendly competition has become a war.

Some of us like to compete because we like to win. We are proud of the fact that we do it fair and square. We can point to our great successes and manifold victories. We have a fine collection of trophies and medals to show for it: a big house in the right neighborhood, the perfect family with children all above average, a successful career and lifestyle that suits our lofty status. But all good things must come to an end. The glory of victory is always passing. The recent teary-eyed retirement announcement of Brett Favre, one of the greatest quarterbacks in the history of the NFL, reminds us that "all things must pass." There is no mistaking the fact that "from dust we came and to dust we shall return." Brett Favre even acknowledged that his retirement was like dying. We spend more and more energy holding on to our fragile victories. But sooner or later they all fade into oblivion.

Years ago, when I used to jog in the cemetery, to pass the time as I ran I would carefully look at the names, dates, and sculptures that adorned graves there. Some of them were magnificent, large, ornate, and probably very expensive for their day. I used to think that the people buried here must have been big shots who wanted to be remembered. Now, most of them are forgotten, their names no longer remembered by anyone, their lives swept away by the seas of time. They must have worked so hard to be able to afford these magnificent monuments, but ultimately it all counted for nothing.

The thought of this can make us angry and bitter. It is enough to make us scream, "Foul!" This is no way for a winner to be treated! But such bitterness only further reveals the fact that we have trusted more in our blue ribbons and shiny medals than the promises of God. Such a trust will always be in vain and will always be disappointed.

If any one should have had a reason to cry, "Foul!" it was Paul. He had certainly been a success, a winner, a righteous man. Paul says that if anyone had a reason to be confident and proud of himself, it was he. He was the consummate Jew, "circumcised on the eighth day, a member of the people of Israel, of the tribe of Benjamin, a Hebrew born of Hebrews; as to the law a Pharisee; as to zeal, a persecutor of the church; as to righteousness under the law, blameless." In other words, he had a closet full of trophies and gold medals. He was admired by his peers. And he was sure that God was proud of him, too.

But he found himself in prison, in danger of losing his life. What kind of justice was this? Bitterness and anger could have poured from his lips. Yet, with an amazing sense of grace and peace, Paul felt no need to lament his fate. He felt no need to parade his trophies and ribbons for all to see and demand better treatment. What many of us would cling to at any cost, Paul simply dismissed as worthless, only so much garbage. In fact, the Greek word he used is quite a bit more graphic than that. *Skibulla* is the Greek word for "excrement." You can substitute in your own mind our popular four-letter equivalents that all too frequently pollute speech today. In other words, Paul minces no words when it comes to jettisoning the things that many of us would see as the things that really matter in life.

It might seem that Paul felt this way because he had lost everything. Of course, he regarded all of his accomplishments as so much *skibulla*. We would, too, if we had lost everything. I imagine that is exactly the way many felt along the gulf coast after experiencing the devastation of hurricane Katrina several years ago. All those possessions, those gorgeous homes, automobiles, hotels, resorts, and beautiful cities with their manicured neighborhoods were turned into rubble and ruin, so much *skibulla*. If you had lived there, you would have counted it garbage, too, just like Paul did who found himself in prison.

That is not the reason why Paul felt this way about his accomplishments. In fact, what many of us would see as the mark of defeat (being in prison), Paul regarded as a badge of honor. In spite of being behind bars, in spite of having lost everything, he thought of himself as a star athlete, running his race on his way to victory.

Paul certainly seemed to have some rather strange ideas about winning and losing. He talked like a winner when he looked like a loser. Paul wasn't just rationalizing away his defeat. He believed that he actually was a winner, even though he appeared to be running dead last. Why? Because he believed that he had already won the race!

Listen carefully, people. Now is when you get to see what a strange and wonderful race it is that we Christians get to run. In every other kind of race we couldn't dare to claim victory for ourselves *because someone else won*! Former Indiana coach, Bob Knight, already has his critics and those who think he is a little crazy. But can you imagine what everyone would have thought of him last year while he was still at Texas Tech if he had claimed to be the champion of the NCAA Tournament even before it started because Florida had won the year before? That sounds ludicrous! Even loyal Bob Knight fans might have wondered if he hadn't gone a little off the deep end. Yet, that is precisely the kind of claim Paul, and we, can make for ourselves while we are running the race of life.

In any other kind of race, it is *our performance* that really matters and counts for everything. How fast we run, how much money we put in the bank, how much power we command, how many gold medals we have in the closet are what really matter. We can't claim victory on the basis of some one else's performance. Even God won't let us get away with that one. As we are often reminded, it is the Ten Commandments not the ten suggestions. God is holding us accountable for our performance. We are judged on the basis of our performance. Every day we see people suffer because they think they can thumb their nose at God's commandments and get away with it. God will not be mocked. We might think we have accumulated a lot of trophies. We might be frantically trying to think of ways that we can explain away our lack of trophies. But the bottom line is that no one gets out alive. No one is able to finally win the big race of life and go on forever. I have yet to see a person who has escaped the cemetery.

Except for one! Someone has already crossed the finish line and won the race. And he did it *for us*! Of course, that winner is Jesus of Nazareth, Jesus, the Christ. God in Christ defeated the powers of sin and death. Christ carried the sins of the world to his grave and suffered their consequences, even God's own judgment, *for us* so that we might be free. Ever since that day he rose from the dead, he stands at the finish line, at the end of history, promising to share with us the consequences of his victory. When water was poured on us at the font in his name, we not only died and rose with Christ, we crossed the finish line as victors even before we got there. When we eat and drink at the table, we eat and drink the body and blood of the one who has already crossed the finish line ahead of us. We receive a foretaste of the victory to come. When we hear those glorious words, as we did today at the start of this service, announcing that all of our sins have been forgiven, we have been declared winners before we ever cross the finish line.

Trusting this promise makes all the difference in the world as we run the race. All the victories and accomplishments along the way are nice, but finally they are so much garbage, so much *skibulla*. They simply don't matter because of the surpassing value of knowing that Jesus Christ is our Lord. He has already won the race for us. Our eyes are focused on the prize that Jesus holds for us standing there at the finish line. We press on toward the goal looking forward to that day when we finally can claim what has already been promised to us.

I can assure you that when we start to live our lives like this, eyes will roll. Our neighbors will snicker. The critics will shake their heads. Many will wonder if we haven't gone off the deep end. But as they watch us run our race and the way we are free from all the stuff that weighs everyone else down, they might also begin to wonder why we don't care about the gold medals and blue ribbons. Under their breath we can hear them mutter, "They must think that they have already won the race." The truth of the matter is that we have!

We may not find ourselves behind bars and in prison like Paul. But when we do find ourselves losing ground and falling behind, when it seems that we not only will lose but come in last, we don't need to break the rules. We don't need to resort to making excuses. Why? Because coming in second or third or fourth or even dead last doesn't matter. We have already won. We have nothing to lose, everything to gain, and nothing to hide.

The fourth-century desert monk, Agathon, tells a story about what it is like to live your life and run your race when you have nothing to lose.

> *Some thieves came one day to the dwelling of an old man and said to him, "We have come to take everything that is in your house."*
>
> *He said to them, "My children, take what seems good to you."*
>
> *So they took what they found in the house and went away. Now they forgot a purse which happened to be hanging there. The old man picked it up and ran out after them, calling out, "Take this which you have forgotten from my house."*
>
> *Filled with wonder at the old man's long suffering, they put back everything in its place in the house and begged for forgiveness from the old man, saying to one another, "Truly this is a man of God."*[1]

Let us run the race. Let us press on to the prize that awaits us. We have nothing to lose. We have the world to gain, because in Christ we have already won. Amen.

---

1. *The Sayings of the Desert Fathers*, translated by Benedicta Ward, SLG (Cistercian, copyright 1975 by Benedicta Ward), p. 55.

Passion/Palm Sunday
Philippians 2:5-11

A Bloody Cheer!

Today is a strange and peculiar day. It reminds me of a film clip that I am sure many of you have seen. It was November 22, 1963, in Deele Plaza, Dallas, Texas, just outside the Texas Book Depository. There was a parade. In that parade was the limousine with Jackie wearing her famous pink dress and pink pillbox hat. And there was her husband, JFK, waving to the cheering crowds. As we watch them go down the street we shudder, because we know that a disaster is about to happen.

Today we remember another parade, very much like that one with which we began today's service. Jesus had deliberately staged this parade. Accompanied by his entourage, he deliberately stirs up messianic expectation and the crowd responds with shouting "Hosanna to the Son of David! Blessed is he who comes in the name of the Lord!" These were the words from Psalm 118, which the crowds had always greeted the arrival of a triumphant king to the holy city of Jerusalem. They waved palm branches as an expression of nationalistic fervor, just like you see people today waving flags and shouting, "God Bless America!" But like the parade in Dallas, we know that disaster is about to happen. We want to yell to Jackie and JFK, "Stop!" We want to yell to Jesus, "Stop!" Danger lies ahead.

But Jesus' parade is different! Jesus knew what was coming. There was a hint of that already in the parade. Unlike other kings who have made entries like this into Jerusalem, Jesus entered not on a war horse, not wielding a sword, not with a clenched fist raised in defiance, but riding on a *donkey*! Matthew sees this as an intentional allusion to Zechariah 9 and the prophet's portrayal of a king of peace who enters the holy city in utter humility riding on a donkey. Yes, Jesus was a king, but he was a different kind of king. Jesus knew that, but the crowd didn't! Instead it had visions of grandeur and a return to the glory days of King David.

Throughout this week in Jerusalem, Jesus will make it clear that he is a different kind of a king. He commands no army, brandishes no weapons, and exerts no brute force. Yet, in the temple he is confrontational. He harasses the religious leadership. He stirs up controversy. He is deliberately provocative. Therefore, we should not be surprised that by Thursday he is betrayed and arrested. It is no wonder the crowds that cheered him on Sunday were crying for his blood on Friday. They did not get the king they wanted!

On this Passion Sunday we read the entire passion story. You, the congregation, speak the parts of the crowd. Why? Because if there is anyone in this story that most reflects our situation, it is the crowd. Just like them, our lives often turn out to be not what we wanted. So much is simply not fair. This is not what we thought God was going to give to us in our lives. This is not the God, the church, and the religion we wanted.

I remember Ed. He was a middle-aged member of my congregation who one day was stunned to find out that he had ALS, Lou Gehrig's Disease. For years he was tenderly cared for by his wife. I used to visit them almost weekly and watch how he was gradually wasting away. I was there on his last day in his last hour as he gasped for breath and finally choked. He was dead, far short of the three score and ten we all expect to get.

They were a jovial, senior citizen couple, German immigrants, both of them. On slow summer afternoons, I used to stop by their house and drink German beer with Henry. One day I got the panicked phone call from Elizabeth, his wife. Henry had been ravaged by a stroke and was now hardly more than a vegetable. For months, Elizabeth visited Henry every afternoon in a nursing home to tenderly clean him, soothe him, and minister to him. One afternoon when I came, she was sobbing. She looked up at me with rage and grief in her face. "Pastor, they stole everything! What few earthly possessions Henry had in his drawer and closet are gone." She continued to sob and then spoke to me with utter disappointment, "Pastor, they never told me that the golden years were going to be like this."

How many of you have had days like this? You come expecting just another day at work, when you are called to a surprise meeting with your manager. When you take your seat in his office, he asks you for your keys, gives you your pink slip, and then escorts you back to your desk. Everyone now is watching as you empty out your drawers and are led to the door. It is humiliating. You are embarrassed and ashamed. It is all so unfair. This is not at all what you expected or wanted.

How many of you young students have studied hard for a test, even studied together with your friends late into the night? It was a hard test. You were glad when it was over. You felt lucky to get a B. Then you hear others brag how they had cheated, outwitted the teacher, and got an A! That's just not fair!

That was the reaction of the crowd, a reaction not all unlike ours when things go bad. This is not what we wanted! This is not what we expected! So, we get angry. We want revenge. This is not fair. We want pay back. We want our "pound of flesh." The same crowd that had cheered on Sunday praising Jesus was cheering again on Friday. But this time they were cheering for blood! They wanted Jesus' blood. So they shouted these memorable words: "May his blood be on us and our children!" They felt so angry, so betrayed, and so disappointed with Jesus that they were willing to take full responsibility for his death.

But, be careful what you ask for! Be careful what you cheer for! You wanted it to rain. But when it starts, it never ends and you have a flood. You wanted sunny skies. But when the sun shines, it never seems to stop and you have a drought. You love snow. You pray for a white Christmas. But when it starts, it never stops and you have a blizzard. You are preparing for the grand opening of your business. You worry that not enough people will show up. But when you open the doors on that first day, a few hours later you have to shut them because they bought you out of everything. You get a flat tire on the freeway. You pull over to the side, get out, and wonder how you are ever going to get help. Finally someone does stop. When he gets out of his truck, you see one of the dirtiest, greasiest thugs you have ever seen. You want to take back your prayers and run.

When we yell our bloody cheer, we think that we know better. We know what is right and wrong and no one else does. We know what is best not only for ourselves but for everyone else. By golly, we ought to be God! The biblical tradition is very clear about the consequences for such arrogance. We saw what happened to the former governor of New York. He paid dearly for his arrogance. We all do. Not one of us escapes the cemetery. God will not be mocked!

But things are even worse! When we join the crowds cheering for his blood, this is not just Jesus of Nazareth, the carpenter's son. This is the Son of God! This is the second person of the Trinity! This is the Son of the creator of the cosmos! We are playing with fire here. We are courting disaster. God will not be mocked!

This is a strange, odd, and peculiar day. How ironic! What a surprise! When that crowd cheered, "His blood be on us and our children!" it was actually a declaration of good news ... not only for them but for the world. There is no more wonderful and life-giving thing than to be splattered by the blood of Jesus!

In today's lesson, Paul quotes a wonderful hymn that surely was sung by first-century Christians in gatherings like this one. That hymn proclaims that this splattering of Jesus' blood was not the dark tragedy it appeared to be. On the contrary it was God's marvelous way of saving the world. In a world where everyone is grabbing, grasping, pushing, shoving, arguing, where only the bottom line matters, where only winning counts, where everything is measured by monetary success, where everyone shouts, "What's in it for me?" Jesus comes riding on a donkey! Jesus enters the holy city humbly, not counting equality with God as a thing to be grasped, not grabbing, grasping, pushing, shoving, or insisting "What's in it for me?" but humbling himself, taking the form of a servant, obedient to death, even death on a cross. If there was ever love, it was this!

We call today "Passion Sunday." In the context of this Sunday, we think that "passion" means "suffering," in particular the suffering of Jesus during this most holy of weeks. But "passion" also means "a deep feeling and commitment." We speak of people being passionately committed to something. During the last month, as we have had interviews with a variety of musicians to fill our organist position, it has been amazing to see how so many of them are passionately committed to music. Their lives are all about music, even at the expense of other things. For the sake of their music, they forget themselves and lose themselves in their craft. That is passion. Throughout this Holy Week as we once again hear those ancient stories of our Lord's suffering, we will see the passion of love, a love that forgets itself, that leaves behind its own needs for the sake of someone else.

This love is so passionate that the New Testament virtually invents a new word for it: *agape*. The Greeks had several words for "love." There was *eros*, erotic and romantic love. There was *philos*, love between friends and companions. There was *storge*, the love you might have for your favorite food. In each one of these loves, something is loved because it is worth loving. "I love you because you are attractive, because you are beautiful, because you make me feel good about myself." But God's *agape* is different. Something is loved not because it is worth loving or because it is beautiful or attractive. In fact, it might be ugly and unlovable. Rather, it is loved simply because the lover chooses to love it. The beloved becomes lovable because of the love of the lover.

That is exactly what God is up to in Christ. God in Christ empties himself, takes the form of a servant, and immerses himself totally and deeply in this broken world. Christ carries all that is wrong and ugly with this world. He bears ALS, strokes, thefts, the most distasteful of sins, jealousy, hatred, and even those impersonal economic forces that crush so many, that bites them off, grinds them up, spits them out, and then calls them "a tax write-off." Even Jesus dies on a cross. He goes all the way to the cemetery and joins us in that ultimate state of oblivion, all because he loves us.

That will be remembered this coming Friday. It will be a dark day. This sanctuary will be draped in black because that was a tragic day. We will remember that Jesus did not come down from the cross. There were those angry voices that taunted, "You can't even save yourself and come down from the cross!"

But that's precisely the point! Jesus was not in the business of saving himself. He was all about saving us! For that reason it is a good thing that he didn't come down from the cross. That is *agape* love!

Therefore, God raised Jesus from the dead! Therefore, we can look back at Friday and the cross and not see tragedy or only black or just another bad day, but *Good* Friday!

Now his name is exalted above every other name! At his name every knee shall bow! Every tongue will confess that Jesus is Lord! And every voice will join us in that bloody cheer: "May his blood be upon us and our children." Yes, that is exactly what happens when we come here. We are gloriously splattered with Jesus blood at his table, at the font, when we hear that wondrous promise: "Your sins are forgiven!" That is good news for a world afflicted with sin, disease, and death and longing for new life.

Paul has one more gift to offer to the Philippians and to us: a new way of living. The special grammar of the gospel makes it clear: "Because ... therefore...." *Because* we have been splattered with the blood of the crucified and risen Christ, *therefore* we *get to* pour ourselves out in service to the world.

When we leave this place, we are reminded that we are "now entering the mission field." The most important ministry of this congregation does not take place within these walls but out there, Monday to Saturday, wherever you are called to make a difference in the lives of other people. You get to do amazing things out there because the bloody cheer of the crowd on that Good Friday was true in ways they never anticipated. Because you have been splattered with the blood of Christ, you can pour yourselves out in love for others, splattering the world with the blood of Christ. And then maybe even our neighbors might join us in that gloriously bloody cheer "May his blood be on us and our children!" Amen.

Maundy Thursday
1 Corinthians 11:23-26

Meal Of Death

There it is. No one can enter this sanctuary without noticing it. Because of the events we remember tonight, the night that our Lord was betrayed, this object is so central to our worship.

What is it? Is it an altar? Or is it a table? I am not just nitpicking. What we call it probably reflects our understanding of what goes on there when Christians gather around it. There are dramatically different understandings of it within the Christian church. The gigantic high altar of St. Peter's Basilica in Rome is a far cry from the simple, plain table that you will find in the sanctuary of many American Protestant churches.

I suspect that most American Christians today are more comfortable with a table than with an altar. An altar brings to mind grotesque images of some wild, dark-skinned natives isolated in the darkness of a remote jungle offering a bloody sacrifice of an animal to placate an angry god. We are much more comfortable with the image of a dining room table. At the dining room table we are the friendly family of this congregation gathered around the cozy table, just like our families at home, to share some good fellowship and a little bit of food.

When the people of this congregation built this church, they were too Christian to have just a small table in their sanctuary. They had a strong suspicion that there was something more going on here than simply table fellowship. It looks like a table, but its sheer size and dominating presence indicates that there is something big and powerful associated with that table. There is something about this table that reminds us of an *altar*. In fact, even though it looks like a table, we still call it an altar. Perhaps if we knew why it is an altar rather than a table, we would better understand what we are participating in when we gather around it. If we knew its origin, then we would know why it is an *altar*.

As an experiment sometime, when you are at home sitting at the kitchen table with one of your children, ask this question: "Where does that slice of bread in your stomach come from?" You will probably get a variety of answers, none of which really tell the origin of that slice of bread. Your child might say, "From this plastic package." "From the supermarket." "Oh, I know ... the bakery!"

Like that slice of bread, there are so many things in life that are just "given." We accept them without really thinking about their origin. In a recent magazine article I read one man's account of just how difficult it is to get back to the origin of things. He described how once he was walking through the streets of a Mexican village at dusk, when he heard the calm of the fading day shattered by the sound of an unearthly scream. Was it a child in pain? A dog in heat? No! On the back stoop of a simple stucco house, an old woman was calmly wringing a chicken's neck. It was suppertime and she was preparing the family's evening meal. In a short time it would be ready to be eaten on her family's table. Now, compare her children who were standing in the doorway watching this bloody slaughter ... with our children who think that their fried chicken comes from a kindly old Kentucky colonel with a white goatee. There is something to be said for the mother who let her children see the real origin of their evening meal. When they ate their chicken, it meant something much more to them than just a means to satisfy their appetite.

Our technological society insulates us from the truth of so much of life. Why? Perhaps because our world with all of its conveniences and pleasures is really the end product of a long line of suffering, toil, and pain. It is not easy to live with the constant awareness of such misery staring us in the face. It is carefully concealed in plastic and cellophane, brightly colored wrappers, and cardboard packaging. If we can't see it, we don't think about it.

Perhaps that is why so many modern Christians, when they decide to build a church, shy away from building something like this large altar. A table is so much more "user-friendly." At a dinner table there is harmony, unity, and pleasant conversation. The only sounds are the sounds of polite talk and the clink of sterling china. But at an altar the sounds are so much more disturbing. One does not hear the polite table conversation of friends but the braying and screaming of beasts being slaughtered. At the table there is the coziness of family relationships. At the altar there is cry of anguish as the beast sighs its last before the blade of death finally pierces its breast. At the table there is bread, wine, and the conviviality of good friendship. At the altar there is blood, carnage, and death. When we see ourselves gathered only around a table instead of an altar, we forget the true origin of this meal. I fear that it is more than a matter of mere forgetfulness. Perhaps it is the deliberate intention of those who do not want to face the horror, the blood, the carnage, and the blasphemy ... that is the origin of this sacred meal.

The real reason for our gathering in this place around this object this evening is not just that we like each other's company (although I hope that we do!). It is not just that we like to party together (although that also may be true!). No. We gather because we cannot forget the blood, the carnage, and the death of which this important object reminds us. It was the death, not just of another beast, not just of another man ... but of the Son of God!

What a strange lot we Christians are. We gather to worship our God gathered *not* around a garden of flowers, not under the sunny blue sky, not in view of a towering majestic mountain. No, we gather around the place of death, a place that calls our attention to a life that was slaughtered. We must wonder what kind of God this is who invites us to meet him at such a place.

In tonight's lesson we see how God has always had a habit of doing things this way. There we read of the instructions God had given to his people to celebrate the Passover. That annual eating, drinking, remembering, and praying was intended to remind the Israelites that it was by means of the bloody slaughter of that unblemished lamb whose blood was splattered on the door posts and lintels of their homes that they were spared death and delivered from bondage in Egypt. The Passover meal was a meal of death, the death of the unblemished lamb, the death of the Egyptian first born, the death of Pharaoh's soldiers in the waters of the sea, deaths that ironically brought life and freedom to Israel.

The shadow of death also hangs heavy over Jesus and his disciples as they gathered for the Last Supper. It was the Passover Seder for which Jesus had gathered his disciples to eat on this dark and ominous night. Because we have the advantage of hindsight, we know that this was a meal of death in more than one way. A great horror and carnage was about to break out again. Jesus was going to be betrayed by one right there in their midst. Jesus was going to be slaughtered like a sacrificial beast upon the altar, the altar of the cross.

Why? Why was such a bloody fate necessary for the Son of God? Why would there have to be the sacrifice of that unblemished lamb of the Passover?

The answer we often utter much too blithely, too conveniently, and much too matter-of-factly. The answer reveals a truth we so often want to avoid and ignore. He died because he came to bear the sin of the world. There, I said it so easily, didn't I? But like the chicken we conveniently pop into our mouths at the colonel's, we don't realize all the brutal bloodletting it took to get it there. Jesus died because that is the bloody fate we all must suffer for being such sinners and scoundrels. Jesus died because he became entangled in the maze of lies, fears, worries, hatreds, and sins that make up the fabric of human life. Jesus died because we all must die. No one likes to admit that our world is so flawed, so fallen, and so doomed. If the Son of God was to become like us in every way, then he had to suffer such a fate.

For all of its horror and carnage, this altar and the death it symbolizes is also a place of refuge. Because of the death of the one whose life was sacrificed on the altar of the cross, God himself promised to one day deliver us from the horrible fate every sinner must endure.

In Kurt Vonnegut's novel, *Slaughterhouse Five*, during World War II a group of allied soldiers is captured and herded into a defunct meatpacking plant near Dresden, Germany. They are incarcerated in "Slaughterhouse Five." Vonnegut vividly describes how the prisoners dread going into the dark basements of a place they could only associate with death. But the slaughterhouse no longer seems so cold and inhospitable. Sheltered deep in the basements of this house of death, Slaughterhouse Five ironically becomes a place of refuge and shelter when the fire bombing of Dresden began. The city above them was incinerated. But sheltered deep beneath the firestorm above, this place of death became a place of life.

Can we not say the same about this altar? Our church is built around the altar of death, a place that reminds us of the carnage and slaughter of Golgotha. We are repelled by such a bloody place not only because of the blood that was shed there by Jesus of Nazareth, but also because we are reminded that it was because of us and our sin that such a bloodletting was ever necessary. But at the same time we are attracted to this place, because this altar of death is also for us the altar of life. It is a place of refuge and shelter for us in the midst of a world that is doomed to burn in the fires of judgment.

The sacrifice has been accomplished. The judgment of God has been silenced. The blood has been let. So, let us come to eat of the meal of death. Let us come to the altar and die. Let us join the sacrifice. Let us offer up ourselves and die with Christ ... the Christ who not only died a bloody death but who also was raised in a glorious resurrection. Let us eat and drink and be joined to the same fate suffered and enjoyed by our Lord.

Yes, this is the meal of death, our death, and the death of our Lord Jesus Christ. But because of him, the crucified and risen Christ, the meal of death is also the meal of life. It is our taste of eternity, a foretaste of the feast to come! Amen.

Good Friday
Hebrews 10:16-25

A Bloody Sacrifice

It is a sad commentary on the state of our world that we are far too familiar with those who have shed their blood ... for noble and ignoble causes. The media has been reminding us of the bloody sacrifice that thousands of our soldiers have made in the war in Iraq. Our country is still bitterly divided over whether that sacrifice has been worth it or not.

The last two summers I have had the privilege of visiting two of our national cemeteries: Jefferson Barracks on the shore of the Mississippi south of St. Louis and Arlington Cemetery on the shore of the Potomac across from Washington DC. Visiting those cemeteries was a moving and sacred experience. The beautiful hills in both those magnificent places are covered with thousands of white crosses marking the lives of those who shed their blood to save our country. It seems inevitable in the course of human events that blood must always be shed if lives, if countries, if the world is to be saved.

We remember another bloody sacrifice: Jesus of Nazareth, the king of the Jews, carpenter from Nazareth in Galilee, one who was acclaimed by his followers as Yeshua ... the Messiah, the Son of God. The lesson for today from the letter to the Hebrews is filled with such sacrificial imagery. Because we are not first-century Jews, the imagery seems utterly odd and strange to us. On the one hand we do not live in a society and world where all of life is ordered around visits to a temple and making bloody sacrifices to our God. On the other hand, as the bloody soils of Gettysburg, Normandy, and Baghdad testify, we live in a world in which the bloody sacrifices are still very much required, if not to appease the gods then at least to appease the forces of evil and wickedness, which always seem to be terrorizing our world.

The letter to the Hebrews centers on the bloody sacrifice that Jesus made not in the temple of Jerusalem but on the Place of the Skull outside of Jerusalem. His sacrifice, unlike the sacrifices made by the priests in the temple, did not need to be repeated day after day, year after year. It was once and for all, for all time and every place. What is so surprising about this bloody sacrifice is that it was not a holy sacrifice offered in a sacred temple or a noble sacrifice offered on the fields of battle, but it was a bloody sacrifice offered in an utterly unholy and ignoble place — the first-century equivalent of the gas chamber, the gallows, the guillotine.

It was the execution of a criminal, at least in the eyes of the first-century religious and political establishment. There was nothing noble or sacred about this bloody sacrifice. This was a sacrifice that was intended to rid the world of a cancer. It saved no one. That is what a crucifixion was supposed to accomplish. There was nothing glorious or redeeming about it.

Yet, with the author of the letter to the Hebrews, with all the sacred writers of the New Testament, with all the Christian believers of every time and place, we believe that this crucifixion of this common criminal was more than what it appeared to be. This crucifixion, this execution, saved the world.

A missionary in Kenya wrote of an experience he had thirty years ago, the closest thing he ever saw to a crucifixion. It happened one day at a government outpost in an isolated rural region of that wild and untamed country.

> *I happened to be leaving the small frame office building which also served as the police station, when I saw a lot of people running toward the office. Leading them was a man running from a woman holding a knife in her right hand as she chased him. A crowd was running alongside them.*
>
> *She chased the man around the building before the police came out and caught hold of her. They took her*

knife away and pushed her to the ground, where they started kicking her with their boots. She didn't try to defend herself. She just lay there and took it.

I was at the road then, getting into my Suzuki jeep. When I saw the policemen start to kick her, I got out of the jeep. I flinched each time they landed a kick on her defenseless body. But I didn't do anything more. I was afraid. They were armed. I was an outsider. Whatever, I drove home feeling sick.

Years later, as I reflect on that moment, I imagine the concentric circles of guilt for the evil I witnessed, with pain at the center.

At the center, the woman and her husband. I have no idea what the man had done to his wife to make her so angry with him. I don't know who started it all, or when. I'm sure there was enough blame for everyone.

The first circle, the police who broke their rules to kick her, and seemed to enjoy it. And the police who stood by. The next circle, the neighbors-become-spectators, some of them snickering.

The expanding circles of sin and guilt included me, too, for not helping. And then the tribe and its culture, for allowing this type of thing. And other nations, for the tragic byproducts of colonial rule. The dark circles of guilt get thinner as they get farther out, maybe ... but in a way they come all the way to include you. Where were you? What were you doing to help her?

Of course, the woman being brutalized by the police in Kenya was not the only thing in the world that went wrong that day, thirty years ago. Or since. The world is awash in sin and guilt. If you don't see it, it's because you are not looking. You cannot opt out.

When I read that, I felt very uncomfortable. You see, the repercussions of each episode of sin are more episodes, whole chronicles, whole cultures, whole civilizations, a whole humanity afflicted with inhumanity, infected with sin. It is like a stone hitting the surface of a pond and then concentric circles of waves inexorably rippling across the surface. There is no place in that pond that escapes its impact.

God sees it all!

And God says (and this is where Good Friday comes in), "Let me be the one who takes the kicking, so we can stop this. And instead of guilt and blame, let forgiveness radiate from my crucifixion, to heal the past of the nations, the past of cultures, the past of families, the past of individuals. Let righteousness ring! Let peace swell around the globe, to stop the kicking and the knifing."

They say, if you want something done right, do it yourself. So God sent himself to the government outpost in Jerusalem, hounded by his enemies, cut by whips, and hung finally on a cross. And because God says, "The buck stops with me," it does! We do not carry the burden for Jesus' dying. No, his dying carries the burden of our sin, so we can stand up and be at peace with each other.

Then husbands and wives can love each other. Parents and children can hear each other. Communities can pull together. Nations can work together.

They snickered, while Jesus hung on the cross. He heard it. They said, "You can't even save yourself!" They were right. He was too busy saving you and me with his bloody sacrifice, the most holy and noble sacrifice ever!

Thanks be to God! Amen.

**Easter Day
1 Corinthians 15:19-26**

But...!

I think anyone who has tried to teach a class or make a presentation to a group has experienced something like this. You have a perfectly planned lesson. You have your presentation all worked out. Then as you begin, there is always this one student, this one participant, this one character in the audience who interrupts you and begs to differ with what you have to say.

"*But* pastor, what about this? What about that? I see things differently."

At first you may be pleased that there is actually someone who is paying attention and is giving what you have to say some thought, even if they beg to differ with you. But the interruptions persist. Their questions become an irritation. Suddenly what you thought you had under control is rapidly becoming chaos.

Likewise, many of us think we have Easter all figured out and everything is under our control. Then we miss the fact that this day is essentially a celebration of the unexpected, unnatural, and uncontrollable. Today is God's big *but*, God's great "nevertheless," "however," "on the other hand," "to the contrary notwithstanding" ... to a life we thought was well planned and under our control.

Isn't it interesting how most in this world prefer to call this day "Easter" and not "The Resurrection Of Our Lord"? You are not going to be able to go into the CVS/pharmacy and buy "Resurrection Of Our Lord Chocolate Rabbits." There are no "Resurrection Of Our Lord Sales" at JC Penney this week. The name "Easter" comes from a name used by the ancient nature religions to refer to the season of Spring. As a result, our society finds it easy to celebrate this day with eggs and bunnies and flowers, all those symbols of new life that everyone can understand. It doesn't matter if you are an orthodox Christian or a tree-hugging Wiccan, you get the picture. I heard a commercial in which a child asks his mother if the Easter Bunny comes down the chimney just like Santa Claus bringing gifts. And he wanted to know why a rabbit brings eggs. Wouldn't a chicken do that? He was all confused. Whatever the confusion that might be in the symbols and rituals of Easter, it is our rite of spring that celebrates the return of life and warmth after the death and cold of a long winter.

The fact that the Resurrection Of Our Lord is the only festival of the church year that is set by the cycle of nature (Easter always falls on the first Sunday after the first full moon on or after the vernal equinox) reinforces this tendency to understand this day as merely a commemoration of the larger cycle of nature and the change of seasons.

As complicated as that sounds, it makes good sense, since it means that Easter coincides with the greening of the earth. Christ is risen and the whole, natural world around us seems to come to life. Sap will be rising in the dormant trees and bushes. The crocus and daffodils will be peeping out of the soil and bringing the first colors to the brown, dead landscape. The lilies that adorn our sanctuaries with their fragrant smell remind us of the flowers and fragrances that soon will be filling the spring air. It seems like a natural connection between faith and the creative power of God.

It is also a misleading connection. Spring is a natural event. Its return every year is inexorable and irreversible. Buy a tulip bulb in fall and it looks dead. Well maybe it looks a little like an onion with its thin skin and scraggly roots. That's the way bulbs are. You know that all you need to do is plant them and wait for spring. When spring comes, sure enough, they will shove through the soil alive and burst with color. It seems like a miracle, however we know that it is a completely natural and inevitable process.

Resurrection is another matter! It is utterly unnatural. When someone dies and is put in the ground, that's it. We do not wait for the person to reappear next spring along with the daffodils and crocus. When someone dies, we say, "Good-bye" and go on with our lives trying to adjust to a life without someone you know will never return. As far as we know the only place spring happens in a cemetery is *on* the graves and not *in* them.

For much of the church's history there have been those who have tried to make the Christian faith less offensive by reinterpreting the resurrection of Christ to make it easier to swallow. Some ask, "Is it really necessary to believe that Easter took place to be a Christian?" After all, most Americans believe they will live on automatically after death. Out-of-body and near-death experiences certainly prove that. Why add the unnecessary baggage of belief that Christ was raised from the dead?

And that story of the empty tomb? Was that not just a symbol that the writers of the gospels made up to affirm the fact that love is stronger than hate and life stronger than death? Is it really necessary to believe in the bodily resurrection of our Lord? Is not resurrection impossible from the point of view of modern science? So is not the New Testament story of the empty tomb simply a symbol of the continuing spiritual presence of Jesus whom the disciples felt to be with them after he died? Surely that is just a pre-scientific belief that we can now discard as primitive and superstitious!

If it happened, fine. So this wonderful event happened in the distant past but it does not have anything to do with how we live our lives now. Maybe it assures us that when we die, we will go to heaven. But in as far as this world goes and how to survive in this dog-eat-dog world now, it is a nice thought but ultimately irrelevant.

Saint Paul in today's lesson has a different point of view. If Christ has not been raised from the dead, if we have only hoped in Christ and his body is still dead in the grave somewhere, then we ought to be pitied for being such naive fools. Then we are still stuck with our sin. Then we are doomed to the cemetery with no hope of life ever being anything else than dog-eat-dog, grab all you can, eat, drink, and be merry for tomorrow we die ... and that's it.

But ... and what a big *but* it is. It is God's big *but*, God's protest against this world as it is. It is God's way of reversing the inevitable: irreversible and inexorable. "*But*," says Paul, "in fact Christ has been raised from the dead!" The ironclad law of cause and effect, the ironclad law created by God himself, "that the wages of sin is death," has been broken and shattered by the resurrection of Christ. And as a result, the world is different. Now we can be the ones who raise our hands and ask those embarrassing questions of those who thought they ran the world. Now when the rest of the world assumes that you only go around once in the life so grab all you can, that you get what you pay for and there is mercy for no one, we can beg to differ. We can join Paul in declaring, "*But* ... Christ has been raised from the dead." A new kind of world has now begun!

I have had this article in my files for years. It comes from some *USA Today* article in the mid 1990s. It exemplifies so well the foolishness and absurdity of our resurrection faith to the modern world. The article was about the family of the Reverend Scott Willis, a Baptist minister in Chicago. In a freak accident with a truck on I-94, the Scott car exploded killing their six youngest children. The headline was "Still Thankful in a Sea of Sorrow: Family's Faith Unshaken By The Loss of Six Children." In the account, Willis and his wife testify to their abiding faith in Christ and the eternal hope that tempers their grief. Apparently this was confusing to the *USA Today* reporter, so she consulted a psychiatrist.

"Different people have different ways of dealing with grief," says Dorothy Starr, a psychiatrist who had not met with the Willises. But she expected they would have an angrier reaction at some point. "They may well be numbed, and it may take some time for it to sink in," Starr said. "I would still expect these people to have trouble, even with their incredible faith."

I found this whole article terribly condescending toward Christianity. On the other hand, maybe the reporter and her editors were genuinely puzzled by the phenomenon of vibrant Christian faith in the face of tragedy. It is after all, a form of deviant behavior. Perhaps it is admirable in some ways, but nonetheless deviant. It required explanation by an expert, and the relevant expert in a therapeutic/feel-good society is the psychiatrist. Enter Dr. Starr, who sympathetically explained that the Willises had not yet had time to understand what really happened. The inference was that their affirmations of Christian faith were a form of denial. Such denial disguised as faith is a common stage in the grieving process, and so forth.

However, the Willises spoke forthrightly about their grief and their loss. There was no evidence of denial. The sticking point with the *USA Today* people was that the Willises confidently confessed the great "*but*," the great "nonetheless," "however," "to the contrary notwithstanding." They had suffered a great tragedy, *but* they were confident of God's continuing love that triumphs over tragedy. It was that apparent confidence, combined with a readiness to forgive the truck driver who caused the accident, that *USA Today* thought needed to be explained by a psychiatrist. The "healthy" and "normal" reaction to what happened to them was anger and rage against the meaninglessness of the universe.

It is the Christian thing that poses the problem. I can just imagine the exchange in the newsroom.

"Yes, maybe it's true that the great majority of Americans go to church and sing songs like 'Jesus Christ Is Risen Today,' but these Willis people actually seem to believe that stuff. It isn't real. Anyway, we can't go with a story that looks like it is pushing religion. We need to get a more impartial take on this. Better call Dr. Starr to give you something to put this in perspective. We frequently run across this kind of thing in the grieving process. They may well be numbed and it may take some time for that to sink in."

But ... and what a big *but* it is ... *but* not for the Willises, *but* not for you and me! We know precisely what Reverend Willis is talking about. Jesus lives! He is not to be found among the dead artifacts and dusty memories of history. He is alive! He is here now ready to greet you in the waters of the font and the bread and wine of the table in people like Reverend Willis and his wife ... and in the people gathered with you this morning.

You may have difficulty believing ... not just the resurrection of our Lord but how God can continue to love you in the midst of the mess that is your life. *But* you came here this morning because you knew that here you would once again hear that unnatural, unexpected *but*. You came longing to hear that this world and your life are not inexorably, irreversibly, and inevitably bound for death.

And you were not disappointed. "*But* ... in fact Christ has been raised from the dead!"

There is only one way to respond to that good news. For the last six weeks we haven't been able to shout it, let alone say it. *But* ... because of God's big *but*, we can. Let us say it. Let us shout it: Hallelujah! Hallelujah! Hallelujah! Amen.

Easter 2
Revelation 1:4-8

Cracking The Code

Have you ever seen one of those prison break movies? They all seem to follow a formula. You are introduced to the hero. You learn his name. He has been unfairly incarcerated. He is depressed and dejected. He believes that there is no way out from his life behind bars. Until one day a secret is revealed to him. It changes his life.

There is a secret, hidden group of prisoners that is planning an escape. A tunnel is being dug under the walls. It soon will be completed. Those strange clanking sounds on the water pipes in the middle of the night, which he thought meant nothing, now mean something. Those spoons tapping on the plates in the dining room, which he thought were just expressions of boredom, random rhythms to accompany the Muzak on the PA system, now are the Morse Code of a developing conspiracy. That door left ajar. The stones arranged in odd shapes in the recreation yard. They are no longer the haphazard of someone in a hurry and someone trying to break his boredom. They are part of a secret code! They are bursting with meaning!

This all had been a hidden mystery until someone befriended our hero and revealed to him the secret code. Once able to crack the code, our hero realizes that the inmates are constantly communicating with each other in a strange and hidden language undetected by their captors. They are planning an escape. They have created a secret society with a secret language, secret plans, secret rules, secret customs, secret rituals, and secret hope. He willingly joins the conspiracy and joyfully anticipates the coming day of freedom. Hidden beneath his sullen face is newfound hope, a child with a secret he can't wait to tell friends.

The prison guards gloat and take every opportunity to humiliate the inmates. But those who have cracked the code and are in on the conspiracy are buoyed by a quiet strength. Outwardly they may be bruised and beaten but inwardly they are strong. They may appear to be imprisoned but in fact they are already free. The freedom that is now theirs in hope will soon become theirs in fact. With every late-night clank on the water pipes, with every tap on the dinner plates, with every door left ajar, with every odd pattern of stones on the ground, they are comforted. Their faith in the future is renewed. Every brutal blow from their captors is easier to bear because it is a reminder that they are getting closer to the new birth of freedom.

This well-known cinematic formula is a picture of the book of Revelation, its context and its purpose. For the remaining Sundays of this Easter season the second reading will be taken from the book of Revelation, one of the most controversial, enigmatic, and disputed books of the New Testament. Throughout its tortured history the book of Revelation has been a bane and a blessing. There have been those who have made it the centerpiece of their faith. There have also been those who would just as well have it burned. For centuries there were many who strongly questioned whether the book even belonged in the New Testament. For example, Martin Luther didn't have much use for it largely because of the way it was abused by such crazed prophets and social revolutionaries as Thomas Muntzer. However, there have also been those who have seen it as a blueprint for history and have constantly turned to it for guidance and consolation.

The book has a legitimate place in the New Testament. It offers a voice that the church needs to hear. But it is neither the most important book of the New Testament nor does it need be tossed on a pile of condemned books about to be burned. The book of Revelation is intended to speak a word of comfort and consolation to God's people in times of suffering and persecution. That word of comfort is nothing more or less than the gospel of Jesus Christ. For that reason alone (regardless of the way it has often been abused over the centuries in the hands the misguided), it belongs in the Bible.

Most agree that the book of Revelation was written by one of Jesus' disciples, John (the one whom Jesus loved). During the last years of his life John was exiled to the island of Patmos in the Mediterranean Sea where he died as an old man. John was exiled because his enemies wanted to silence him. The Roman government was increasingly suspicious of Christians like John and did not want their strange religion spread throughout the empire. So he was condemned to spend the rest of his life in exile on the island of Patmos. However, John was not about to be silenced. He wrote this book as a word of comfort to suffering and persecuted Christians throughout the empire (specifically to seven congregations in Asia Minor).

In order to not make the situation for them worse and aggravate the ire of their enemies, John wrote his book disguised in the secret code language of *apocalyptic*. In that respect it resembles the secret code of inmates planning to break out of prison. It is filled with secret code language, bizarre images, and far-out symbols, the exact meaning of which remains hidden to us today. The images and symbols are the equivalent of the late-night clanking on water pipes, the tapping on the dining room plates, the door left ajar, and the stones left in odd patterns that made up the secret code of the inmates in prison. To the outsiders it is a hidden code. It is only so much random noise and routine activity without any meaning or significance. But to the privileged insiders, to those who have been able to crack the code, it is the secret language of the gospel. It is the good news. It is hope for those who were without hope.

But we don't live at the end of the first century. To a large extent we remain outsiders. We don't have the "dictionary" or ability to crack the code and its rich and complex system of meaning. That is why much of Revelation remains an unsolved mystery. Some if the images are so bizarre that it almost seems as if John was in some kind of trance or high on drugs.

This was typical of the *apocalyptic* literature of the day. This kind of literature was widespread in the ancient world. People back then, just as many of us today, wanted to know what the future held. They felt helpless in a world they did not understand and were powerless to do anything about. They may have looked to *apocalyptic* literature just as we look to the zodiac or palm readers, desperate for a word that will prepare us for the future and help us to unlock the mysteries of life.

In that first-century world many looked at the universe as a two-story building. What happens down here on the ground, on the first floor, in the tangible world that we can see, feel and touch, is a reflection of what has already happened in the world above, on the second floor, in the invisible and intangible world of eternity. Of course, what has gone on in the world above is hidden and invisible to us stuck on the first floor. *Apocalyptic* literature pulls back the veil, opens the curtain, lifts up the window, so that we can see what has happened on the second floor, in the realm of eternity. Such literature "revealed" the truth of what lies behind events of this world. Hence the title of the book of *Revelation*.

The world of eternity was often filled with all sorts of bizarre creatures and odd places that seemed to be utterly unrelated to what was going on in this world. A prophet might offer a revelation filled with such images. But someone was needed to crack the code and interpret the vision. Without being able to crack the code, the revelation would remain an impenetrable mystery. Unfortunately for many today the book of Revelation remains just that, an impenetrable, if not frightening, mystery.

All is not lost. Though much of it remains a mystery, though its frequent frightening imagery makes it a disturbing and even scary book, we do have the key that can crack the code. We do have the key that can unlock the door and take us inside the world of those persecuted first-century Christians and see that this book is not simply a warning for a frightening future but a word of comfort for a glorious future.

The key to cracking the code is right there in today's reading at the very beginning of this marvelous and mysterious book:

> ... *Jesus Christ, the faithful witness, the firstborn of the dead, and the ruler of the kings of the earth. To him*

> *who loves us and freed us from our sins by his blood, and made us to be a kingdom, priests serving his God and Father, to him be glory and dominion forever and ever. Amen.*   — Revelation 1:5-6

Even though John, as a visionary and prophet, is pulling back the veil and giving us a glimpse into the realm of the eternal, he actually is redirecting our attention to a different place. He directs our attention to Jesus, to his life, death, and resurrection that took place here, in this world, in this time and space, down-on-the-ground. John claims that the worldly suffering, death, and resurrection of Jesus was more than what it appeared to be. It was more than just another execution of another criminal by the brutally efficient Roman empire. It was a first-floor event with second-floor consequences. It pulled back the veil and opened the window so that we could see the real meaning not only of Jesus' life but of our lives.

Even though those first-century Christians were suffering much at the hands of their enemies and the empire, the conflict was already over. God had already defeated all the forces of this world: sin, death, and the power of the devil. The mighty and brutal Roman empire had already been put down. All those things that would destroy God's people and tear them away from his care had been overcome. The death and resurrection of Jesus defeated all those enemies. John's revelation tears back the veil. The window is opened. Eternity is revealed. What did John's revelation show them? The lamb who shed his blood for the world now sits triumphantly on his thrown in heaven.

> *"I am the Alpha and Omega," says the Lord God, who is and who was and who is to come, the Almighty.*
>   — Revelation 1:8

Christ is the key to cracking the code. Christ enables us to not only unlock the mystery of the book of Revelation, but he enables us to unlock the code of our life in all of its mystery, confusion, and pain.

Our life on the first floor, in this world, often seems like a mess. It is filled with confusion, suffering, and death. An unexpected disease shatters our plans. A pink slip slams the door on a career that we thought was so promising. A collapsing stock market abruptly thwarts our plans for retirement. Our best friend is killed in auto accident because he just had to have one more beer. We are continually reminded, if not ridiculed, that we do not have what it takes to succeed. Shrill voices, angry faces, biting criticisms, all shred our self-esteem. We can identify with John on Patmos and all those first-century Christians who were persecuted for simply trusting in Jesus. We long for a word of comfort and consolation. Is there any sense in this madness? Or is it all random, aimless, without rhyme or reason?

It is then that today's reading cracks the code. It pulls back the veil. The window is opened. The truth of what was really going on "upstairs," on the second floor in eternity, is "revealed."

> *Look! He is coming with the clouds; every eye will see him, even those who pierced him; and on his account all the tribes of the earth will wail. So it is to be. Amen.*
> — Revelation 1:7

In a world where suffering and "persecution" are too much a part of our lives, where fear and uncertainty make living with hope so difficult, where so much seems random and senseless, at last the mystery is solved. At last the code is cracked. Christ has triumphed. On Good Friday and Easter, God defeated all that would separate us from his love. All this suffering, hurt, pain, confusion, and persecution are just the "mopping up" actions of a war that has already been won.

The code is cracked. So now we can see things that remain invisible to the world. It is only so much random noise or meaningless chatter to our captors who don't have a clue. Water is poured at the font "in the name of the Father, and of the Son, and of the Holy Spirit." Bread is broken. Wine is poured. "This is my body given for you. This is my blood shed for you." A hand is offered. A smile is shared. "The peace of the Lord be with you ... And also with you." Sins are forgiven. Prayers are spoken. Time and talent and treasure are freely offered. Casseroles are baked and delivered. Tears are wiped away. The heartbroken are hugged.

To our beleaguered and embittered world and our captors who think we are just a bunch of fools, it only seems like clanking water pipes in the night. It is only so much tapping on our dinner plates. That door left ajar? Someone must have forgotten to close it. Those stones oddly arranged in the recreation yard ... someone was just bored. But for us, those for whom the code has been cracked, those who know the truth of eternity, those who know what has really happened upstairs on the second floor, this is a "revelation"! This is good news! This is what happens when you have cracked the code! Amen.

Easter 3
Revelation 5:11-14

The iPod Vs. The Larynx

The book of Revelation is a vision that occurs on the Lord's day. When you read the book, it feels like a worship service. In fact, in the historic liturgies and worship services of the church (regardless of one's denomination or tradition), more passages from the book of Revelation are used than from any other book in the Bible. The book is filled with hymns, sections of hymns, colorful and vivid images, and metaphors that simply beg to be used in a service of Christian worship.

Today's reading is one such passage. When reading it, one image just jumps out and slaps you in the face. **Worship is ultimately not intended to be a solitary activity.** It is foremost an activity in which *the people of God gather together and as a corporate group* (not just as the sum total of solitary individuals) to offer their praise to God. John in his visionary book repeatedly pictures the people of God, the saints, the angels, the elders, and all the company of heaven and earth, literally the whole creation gathered together to thank God for what God has done in Jesus Christ.

> *Worthy is the Lamb that was slaughtered to receive power and wealth and wisdom and might and honor and glory and blessing!* — Revelation 5:12b

I suspect that this was an important point for John to make as he penned his message to the embattled and persecuted Christians of the late first century. One of the most cynical and vicious strategies that persecutors like to inflict on their victims is "divide and conquer." Isolate your victims from their community, from the support of their friends and fellow believers, and the more likely you are to get them to capitulate. Many of those first-century Christians refused to capitulate and joyfully went to their martyrdom. There were even more who did cave in. Many of them probably did it because they were afraid to be alone. They were cut off from their fellow believers. Their enemies even convinced them that they were cut off from their God who could no longer help them in their hour of need. So, they gave in. They caved in. They burned their incense to Caesar rather than burn at the stake or be lunch for the lions. They fell for the lie that God had abandoned them. There is nothing worse than being alone.

That is why corporate worship is such an essential part of being the church. The community nourished and fed by "the blood of the Lamb" (a favorite image of Revelation) together gathers to pray, to read and hear scripture, to eat and drink around the table, to bathe its initiates in the font, and ... as Revelation portrays so vividly ... to *sing together*.

Recently a pastor friend of mine and I visited another congregation. The experience got me thinking about this passage from Revelation and the importance of corporate worship and a congregation singing together.

We visited the congregation with my friend's musician to check out their digital organ for possible purchase for their new sanctuary. While there I discovered that the congregation has had the organ mothballed and unused for about five years.

Why would they have done that to such a fine musical instrument? Because, as their pastor told us, they had made the commitment to "contemporary praise music" in all their worship services. While we were there, the pastor was proud to show us their "new" worship space, which was their "old" gymnasium.

When we walked into the space, something struck me as being very odd. As we talked to one another, it sounded as if we were talking in a clothing closet. We could hear each other, but we sounded very muffled. I noticed that there were panels of baffling hung all over the ceiling and the walls were covered with fabric.

As a result, there was no echo in our voices whatsoever. Acoustically it was one of the most "dead" rooms I had ever been in.

When the pastor left us to answer a phone call, I turned to friends and asked, "How in the world can a congregation sing in a room like this?" My friend's musician smiled and said to me, "They don't. This entire space is designed for the electronically amplified praise band and the song leaders standing in the front of the congregation on the stage."

The musician's observation reminded me of a conversation I had with my friend about the interview process he and several members of the building committee held during their search for the sound engineers and consultants who would help them craft the acoustics of their new sanctuary. During the course of those interviews it became very obvious that some of those engineers did not understand what they were trying to do in their new worship space. Some were trying to sell them all kinds of electronic equipment with a huge mixing board because they assumed they were trying to support a praise band and song leaders. But that was not their goal. They wanted a sanctuary to support the natural acoustic sound of the human voice and unamplified musical instruments. They wanted a space that would not just electronically amplify the voices of a few song leaders but magnify the unamplified natural acoustics of the voices of an entire congregation.

My friend and I have a similar understanding of worship and church music. Therefore, it was not surprising that all three of us commented that for us church music and congregational song is not just a matter of personal taste. It is not just that we prefer the natural sound of unamplified voices over the sound of the electronically amplified voices. On the contrary, we want a worship space that reflects our understanding of the nature of the church. Congregational singing can greatly affect one's understanding of the church. In other words, there is a lot more at stake here than meets the eye. Or should I say the ear?

The world has changed dramatically during my lifetime. It always seems that when it comes to technology, I am the last one to figure out the changes. I still buy CDs for my music. But my children tell me that mode of sound reproduction is slowly dying. Now it is time to welcome the age of the iPod and the digital download. I am sure you have seen many people, not just necessarily teenagers, walking around with plugs in their ears attached with skinny long wires to a little box in their hands or in their pockets. Welcome to the iPod where anyone can digitally download their favorite music into their own personally customized musical "library." Now everyone can customize their own personal entertainment. Now you don't have to put up with someone else's bad taste in a noisy room. Now you can escape and hide in your own personal musical world.

As a result we are creating a world of musical consumers. Vocal music teachers have been complaining to me for years that people just don't seem to be able to sing or are interested in singing like they used to. *In the age of the iPod, the larynx is losing out to electronics.*

Years ago when I lived in Fort Wayne, Indiana, I made a discovery that dramatically portrayed to me this major change that has slowly taken place in our society over the last century. Some of the members of my congregation lived down the street from a quaint little city park called "Packard Park." One day I asked them if that park was named after the old Packard automobile. They said, "Oh, no! That was the location of the old Packard Piano Company." I had never heard of the Packard Piano Company before. So, I did a little research.

At the turn of the twentieth century, about 1900, America was filled with hundreds of piano manufacturers. Many, many homes had their own pianos. And the biggest, most widely produced printed matter in the country was not books or magazines but sheet music! Why? Because in the age before radio, television, computers, and iPods, families would actually get together in the evenings around the piano and sing. If you didn't have someone who could play the piano, you would buy a "player piano." It was then that I realized that as wonderful as our modern musical technology is, we have lost something in the process. Those must have been great days to experience family and community as everyone gathered around the piano to actually sing. That sense of "togetherness" and community is so difficult to create today as we race through our frantic weekly schedules. We are lucky if the whole family gets to sit around the table to eat together. Sitting together to sing ... that is unheard of! We might join in humming the melody of a popular song that we hear on the radio. We might be able to mouth a few words. Have you ever tried to get several people to join in "singing" the latest rap or hip-hop song? It is virtually impossible.

We live in a world dominated by "individualism." The days of the "Top 40" hits are long gone. The music market has been splintered into dozens of different styles and demographics. There are only a few piano manufacturers. Who buys sheet music besides choral directors? What do we sing together anymore? "Take Me Out To The Ball Game" or "The Star Spangled Banner"? It seems that there are fewer and fewer who can even sing those anymore. But everyone loves music and has their own, private and personal favorites downloaded onto their individual iPod so that they can go off in their corner and listen alone.

I am concerned that in this rush to speak to the world of the iPod, its language of electronically amplified and personalized music and its core entertainment values, we will abandon being the church. The church is a kind of community that ought to never totally "fit in" to the world because to do so would abandon who we are as the people of God.

The church in the New Testament is called the *ekklesia*, that is the "called-out ones." The church is not just a collection of individuals. We are called as individuals into a community by the voice of the gospel. The gospel holds us together into a community and collection of people that is greater than the sum of its individual parts. John's picture in the second reading of the whole creation worshiping God and the lamb reflects just this kind of community.

We come together not just as people of northern European ethnic extraction, not just as upper-middle-class suburbanites, or as people who prefer a given style of music or church architecture. We are called together because we have heard the good news of Jesus and Christ and have staked our lives on it. For as much as we might share common tastes and preferences or as much as we might like each other as friends, what ultimately holds together this diverse congregation is Christ and the message of his gospel.

That sense of being a community called together by a message is reflected in the most important thing we do as community every week: worship. We are gathered as a community to be a community. We come together not just as individuals, living in our own private space to have our own private needs met. We are a community that has been called together and remains glued together by the grace of God. Therefore, our worship ought to reflect that reality.

That means worship is not merely "entertainment." We come not to just sit in seats to watch and listen to a "show" that is taking place before us on a stage. Worship is not like going to a concert where we are entertained by performers on a stage. If it were, then we would want our churches to be modeled after a good concert venue, such as good sight lines, visually stimulating, good sound amplification that enables us to clearly hear the music of the performers and eliminates any distracting noise from the audience. The audience is welcome to sing along but clearly amplification of the sound of the performers is most important.

The church that I visited with my friends was modeled exactly on that kind of experience. They no longer needed an instrument like this large organ that was designed for congregational singing. They needed a space that inhibited and even silenced congregational singing since everything is about the performance of the worship leaders who were positioned in front of the congregation on a stage. It is no accident that many such churches will call their worship not a "service" but an "experience." Personal, subjective, individual involvement is of paramount importance. Unless "I can feel it," the worship experience is of little value.

Worship portrayed by John in this passage from Revelation is very different. Yes, we want worship to be lively and not boring. We want music to be performed well, regardless of its style. (The so-called distinction between "contemporary" and "traditional" music is not very helpful. All music is "contemporary," performed and heard in the here and now. The question concerning music ought to be quality. Is it done well? Does it fit the occasion? Can the corporate group sing it?) Yes, we want it to be relevant to our daily lives and not simply an exercise in some unintelligible, mysterious cult. But the focus of worship first and foremost is not on us but on God and the good gifts God so graciously showers on us, beginning with God's love for the world in Jesus Christ. Therefore, our songs, prayers, words, drama, dance, and music are "served" (in a worship "service") to God. Our worship is to honor, praise, and glorify God. It is not about us and our "experience." It is not a "performance" that we put on for one another's benefit or entertainment. Our musicians and vocalists do not stand in front of us so that we can "watch" them.

Our attention is directed to God. If we applaud, it is not for a good performance done well but because we are thanking God for making possible such marvelous music. But I suspect that, when worship is done "well" and honors God, we will also find it pleasing to our sensibilities. It will have been something that was a pleasure to "experience."

Most of all weekly, corporate worship is something the "community" does. It is something that we do together as a group. That is certainly reflected in John's glorious picture of this massive community of all the creatures in heaven and on earth gathered in a community worshiping God as a community. Congregational song, singing where all join together raising their voices in a common melody, making a sound that is simply impossible to create as individuals, is essential and fundamental not only to Christian worship, but also it is a reflection of how we understand ourselves as the church of Jesus Christ.

Every congregation is an amazing collection of people. If you closely look at any Christian congregation regardless of its size, this particular group of people would probably never choose to associate with each other were it not for the voice of the gospel that has called them together. But since they have been "called out," since they are an *ekklesia*, expressing themselves as a community is important to them. When they raise up their voices in common song, when they actually can hear each other sing and reinforce and encourage one another in their singing, they give powerful testimony to the power of Christ and his Spirit that has created this amazing and marvelous community.

Perhaps some of you have walked into a worship space that is very conducive to making this happen. It is usually a space that has good height and has a lot of hard surfaces. Such a space is anything but "dead." It does not "muffle" sound. Instead, it makes sound come "alive."

A few years ago I had the privilege of worshiping in the chapel at Valparaiso University, which is just this sort of acoustically friendly space with a high ceiling and lots of hard surfaces. The service began outside the chapel in the open air. We processed into the chapel singing a hymn. I distinctly remember what happened to our singing as we entered the new sanctuary. Outside our singing got "lost" in the open space. But when we entered that space, everything changed. Without the aid of any electronic amplification, the sound literally "exploded." It was as if someone had turned up the volume tenfold. The congregation's song literally took on a new form. It sounded much different as the sound reverberated around that glorious space. We were able to vividly hear each other sing in a way that did not happen when we were outside. Because we could hear each other, we encouraged one another to sing even louder and clearer. We created a unique sound that was more than just adding individual voices together. That day I literally experienced "auditory evidence" for this new reality called "the church."

Just think of it. There are very few places in our society where people gather together to sing as a group. The days of families gathering together to sing around the piano are long past. Our individualistic world has made us pay a great price and lose something that was truly precious. *But* not the church! Here we still gather together around the piano, the organ, the table, the font, and the sacred text to hear the good news and experience a sense of togetherness, family, and community that can be found no other place in this world.

In the church as we gather for worship we can literally leave behind our iPods, flex our larynx, and join the angels, archangels, seraphim, cherubim, all the company of heaven, and the myriads of creatures (as John reminds us).

> *Then I heard every creature in heaven and on earth and under the earth and in the sea, and all that is in*

them, singing, "To the one seated on the throne and to he Lamb be blessing and honor and glory and might forever and ever!"   — Revelation 5:13

Amen.

**Easter 4
Revelation 7:9-17**

The Blood Of The Lamb
And The Voice Of The Shepherd

Who is Jesus? How are we to understand him? In the novel, *The Brothers K*, David James Duncan tells the story of the Chance family, a family of four boys, two girls, an agnostic father, and a mother of passionate fundamentalist faith. They all have very different ideas about who Jesus is. One of the boys, Kincaid, describes how each family member tries to make sense of Jesus and religion:

> *It's strange the way everybody has their own pet notion about Jesus, and nobody's pet notion seems to agree with anybody else's. Grandma, for instance says He's "just a defunct social reformer." Then there's Papa, who once said He's God's Son all right, and that He survived the crucifixion just fine, but after the two-thousand-year-old funeral service his cockeyed followers called Christianity probably made Him sorry he did. Meanwhile, there's Freddie, who's six now, and who told me she saw Christ hiding under her bed one night ... And Bet, who spent a whole day making a Christmas card for Uncle Marv and Aunt Mary Jane last year, then got so proud of the card that she refused to mail it to anybody but herself ... Then we looked to see what she was so proud of, and it turned out to be this whole army of crayon angels, in this gold sort of football helmet, charging into Bethlehem while in the sky above them huge red and green letters copied from a Christmas carol book Bet couldn't yet read proclaimed: "JOY TO THE WORLD! THE SAVIOR RESIGNS!"*[1]

And elsewhere in the novel one of the children says:

> *Personally I'm not sure just who or what Christ is. I still pray to Him in a pinch, but I talk to myself in a pinch too — and I'm getting less and less sure there's a difference ... Mamma tried to clear up all the confusion by saying that Christ is exactly what the Bible says He is. But what does the Bible say He is? On one page He's a Word, on the next a bridegroom, then he's a boy, then a scapegoat, then a thief in the night; read on and He's the messiah, then oops, He's a rabbi, and then a fraction — a third of the Trinity — then a fisherman, then a broken loaf of bread. I guess even God when He's human, has trouble deciding just what he is.*[2]

In the midst of all this confusion, today's scripture lessons make it very clear who Jesus is. When you see Jesus, you see God. In the gospel, Jesus says, "The Father and I are one." When you have seen and heard Jesus, you have seen and heard as much of God as you ever hope to see and hear. Then Jesus uses what has become among Christians one of the most important of all these biblical images to describe our relationship to God: the shepherd and his sheep. We call John 10 "The Good Shepherd Chapter." Today's gospel brings to a conclusion Jesus' extended use of what for Christians over the centuries has been one of the most important images to describe Jesus and his relationship to us: the good shepherd. Jesus is the good shepherd, and we are his sheep.

That same image is used in today's reading from Revelation. Jesus, on the one hand, is a lamb. Recalling images of the sacrifice of the Passover Lamb of the Hebrew scriptures, Jesus is the lamb whose blood was shed on the cross to set free all of God's people who have ever suffered. Then John takes the image one step further. Jesus is not just the lamb but also the shepherd who "will guide them to springs of the water of life, and God [the shepherd] will wipe away every tear from their eyes."

This must have been an amazing word of comfort to those suffering and persecuted Christians at the end of the first century to whom John addressed these words. In the midst of a world that was falling apart, John reveals to them the truth: Jesus is the good shepherd reigning victoriously from his throne in heaven. That victory will soon be theirs.

With the way today's lessons are filled with images of sheep and shepherds, we should not be surprised that this fourth Sunday of Easter has historically been designated by the church as "Good Shepherd Sunday."

I once knew someone who actually grew up on a sheep farm. He said that, contrary to popular opinion, sheep are not that dumb. He said that cattle ranchers are the ones responsible for spreading that ugly misunderstanding because sheep do not behave like cows. He said that cows are herded from the rear by hooting cowboys with cracking whips, but that won't work with sheep. Stand behind sheep and make loud noises and all they will do is walk around behind you, because they want to be led. You push cows but you lead sheep and they will not go anywhere that someone else does not go first — namely their shepherd — who goes ahead of them to show them that everything is all right.

The implication of this relationship for understanding our relationship to Jesus is obvious. When John calls Jesus our shepherd reigning over the universe from his throne in heaven, he is reminding us that there is no place in this universe that he has not gone before us, including death itself. And look what happened to him. Like the Passover Lamb, his blood was shed, but that was not the end of him. He was raised from the dead. He reigns as king on a throne in heaven. All the enemies of him and his people have been destroyed. Therefore, we can follow him, we can trust him, and we can walk in his steps with complete confidence. We have nothing to fear, not even death itself. For as Jesus lives, so also will we.

There is even more to the relationship between the sheep and their shepherd. Sheep tend to grow fond of their shepherd. Any shepherd who has grown up among sheep will tell you that he can walk right through a sleeping flock of sheep without disturbing a single one of them, while a stranger could not put one foot in the fold without causing total confusion and chaos. Sheep seem to consider shepherds part of the family and the relationship that exists between the shepherd and his sheep is quite exclusive. They develop a language of their own to which outsiders are not privy. A good shepherd learns to distinguish a bleat of pain from one of pleasure, while the sheep learn that a cluck of the tongue means food or a two-note song means that it is time to go home.

In Palestine today, it is still possible to witness a scene that Jesus almost certainly witnessed 2,000 years ago — that of Bedouin shepherds bringing their flocks home from the various pastures they have grazed during the day. Often those flocks will end up at the same watering hole around dusk, so that they get all mixed up together — eight or nine small flocks turning into a convention of thirsty sheep. But the shepherds do not worry about the mix-up. When it is time to go home, each one uses his or her own distinctive call — a special trill or whistle or a particular tune on reed pipe, and that shepherd's sheep withdraw from the crowd to follow their shepherd home. They know whom they belong to. They know their shepherd's voice, and it is the only one that they will follow.

It reminds me of some of the research done by Harvard's Dr. Barry Brazelton I once saw demonstrated on television. He showed how even very young infants quickly become aware of the identity of their parents and can recognize their parents just by the sound of their voices.

He took an infant in his arms and asked the audience to watch the infant's eyes. He spoke to the baby. Then he asked other people to speak to the infant. There was little reaction or recognition from the baby in both cases.

When the mother of the baby spoke, the baby's eyes visibly brightened, and the infant turned toward the sound of the mother's voice. It was obvious that the child knew her mother's voice in distinction from other voices.

We are the sheep of God's flock. God is our loving parent. We are God's beloved children. We know the voice of our shepherd when we hear it just like we know the voice of our mother when we hear it. We have been listening to the voice ever since we heard about Jesus. For some of us that may be have been ever since we were baptized as an infant when all we were able to distinguish was the voice of our mother or father from the sound of others voices we did not know and often may have frightened us. But not this voice! It has been assuring us and comforting us as long as we could ever remember.

This voice, unlike any other voice, has been saying, "You are the apple of my eye. You are the crown of creation. You are my beloved son and daughter. I love you always and forever. Nothing in the whole universe can separate you from my love. Have you had to earn it? Have you had to prove yourself? No, I love you simply because I want to. And just in case you don't believe me, look at Jesus, the good shepherd, the lamb who shed his blood and what he did for you. You belong, no matter what!"

That doesn't mean that believing this voice has been easy. Our own self-doubt and insecurity are constantly gnawing on that belief. A world that only seems to honor those who can climb to the top of the mountain ridicules such belief. Even the evil one, who is alive and well in this world, chips away at such belief. As a result, we know that our trust in the good shepherd often wavers and at times even seems to disappear.

But your belief or unbelief is not the point. The point is that you are here this morning. You may think that there were many reasons for your coming: your parents made you, this is your Sunday routine and you wouldn't feel right without it, you would feel guilty if you didn't. The real reason you are here is that once upon a time you heard the voice of Jesus, the good shepherd, the lamb who reigns over the universe from the throne of heaven. You came because you wanted to hear that voice again. You have heard about God's love for you before. You know that you need to hear it again.

You have had a tough week and you needed to hear a word of comfort. You needed to hear someone assure you that everything is all right in this messed up world, that all is right, not because you have been so right but because Jesus is right. Because you know that because Jesus suffered, died, arose, and reigns from his throne, all is right for you. You know that you aren't going to hear that kind of good news any other place, but you know that are going to hear it here.

I remember back in my first call when I complained to the senior pastor about the poor church attendance. What was wrong with those lazy, irresponsible, indifferent church members who couldn't get their bottoms out of bed on a Sunday morning to come to church? He then gently put me in my place. He reminded me that we have no right to expect a single person to walk through the doors on a Sunday morning. That they come at all is a miracle of the Holy Spirit. It's not about us and our attractiveness or about their commitment to support this organization or their lack of it. It is about the voice of the shepherd. It is about the lamb who reigns from his throne. They have heard his voice and have come.

Therefore, people, let me assure you of this. You are here. You are here because you have heard the voice of the good shepherd and have come to hear it again. Jesus has called you because you are one of his sheep.

The lamb who reigns from his throne in heaven is *your* shepherd. He "will guide [you] to springs of the water of life, and [He] will wipe away every tear from [your] eyes." Amen.

---

1. David James Duncan, *The Brothers K* (New York: Bantam Books, 1993), p. 61.

2. *Ibid*, pp. 58, 61.

**Easter 5
Revelation 21:1-6**

Heaven On Earth

Many years ago when I was going to prep school in Milwaukee, the students loved to walk past a nearby factory from which often emanated some simply wonderful smells. The factory made a product whose name seemed to perfectly fit the heavenly aromas that would occasionally fill the atmosphere of the neighborhood. The factory made *Ambrosia Chocolate*! For a chocolate lover like myself, there could be no better name for such a delectable food. You see, in ancient Greek mythology *ambrosia* was the name of the food of the gods!

But how does one know that something is "heavenly"? I don't know of anyone who has been to heaven and come back to tell about it. Yet when we find a food that tantalizes our taste buds, we are not afraid to pretend that we know all about heaven. An exquisite piece of chocolate, a luscious slice of our favorite fruit pie, or a bite of tender steak ... what else could we possible call them? They must be *ambrosia*, food fit for the gods!

As a pastor you often have the privilege of answering the most curious questions. There always seems to be a child who asks "Pastor, what is heaven like?" Even though I haven't been there yet (and I don't intend on going there any time soon!), they must figure that one such as myself, one who dares to speak for God, must somehow know more about heaven than anyone else. The stock answer will refer to angels sitting around in the clouds playing their harps and singing songs. There must be streets paved with gold and lined with precious stones. It always seems, just when I start to have fun with my imagination going wild with heaven speculations, the child wants to know if his pet cat that was run over by a truck last week will be in heaven. Or if that isn't enough, what about Grandma or Grandpa? And what about Uncle George who was cremated and whose ashes were scattered on his favorite golf course? How is God going to find all those ashes that have long since been washed into the creek and put George back together again in heaven? In heaven will Aunt Polly still have a limp and walk with a cane?

What can I do? I always try to comfort them with answers that assure them that all will be well, even though I have never been to heaven.

Today's reading continues our journey through the book of Revelation in these Sundays after Easter. Like all the others, today we have another picture of heaven. The book of Revelation is filled with wild, fantastic, and bizarre images of heaven and what it will be like when God finally brings the world to an end. The images are not meant to be literal pictures but imaginative poetry and metaphor that make it almost seem as if the author, Saint John, the evangelist, was on some kind of psychedelic drug when he wrote it. In today's reading John gives us another picture of what it will be like when that last day arrives. There will be an end to the suffering and pain that has afflicted life in this world. Instead, there will be a new heaven and a new earth. Even the seas, which in the minds of people of the ancient world were places that harbored horrible and dangerous monsters, would be no more. And most of all, there would be no more tears, mourning, suffering, or pain.

What makes the imagery of Revelation even more challenging to decipher is that it is written to persecuted Christians at the end of the first century in a kind of secret code. At that time many Christians in the Roman empire were suffering under the brutal persecution of Roman Emperor Diocletian, who hated the Christians and wanted to blame them for many of the problems that were afflicting the empire. The secret code was used in order to protect the Christians from further persecution by their enemies. The code disguised a marvelous message of hope intended to comfort these Christians in the midst of their terrible ordeal.

In a world that literally seemed to be under the control of beasts and demons, John comforts his readers with this wonderfully subversive message: Contrary to appearances, the hated Roman empire and its supporters were not in control of the world and would not be able to crush the Christians. These beasts and enemies have already been destroyed. Christ in his death and resurrection has already disarmed all the powers of this world. The day is coming when Christ will make visible to all the victory he achieved on the cross and at the empty tomb. Now that victory remains hidden, but the day is coming when it will be visible to all. In the meantime the Christians addressed by this book can live with hope. Even though they must endure great suffering, they can look forward to the day when God will finally deliver them to a new heaven and a new earth. In spite of appearances to the contrary, a blessed future awaits the people of God!

Over the centuries, Christians have been criticized for propagating an "other worldly" hope at the expense of the suffering and pain of this world. Do you remember that old hymn, "I am but a stranger here, heaven is my home"? Karl Marx in his infamous *Communist Manifesto* attacked a society in which religion had become "the opiate of the people." Religion anesthetized people, making them numb to the suffering and injustice of this world. Christianity promised heaven in the next life at the expense of justice in this life.

Today's psychedelic reading seems to justify just this kind of criticism. It seems focused only on life in heaven. The other-worldly images of a new heavenly Jerusalem can easily numb people to the suffering of this world. However, the focus of this reading is not this at all! In fact, it speaks a meaningful and comforting word to *this* world, to people suffering *here* and *now*.

In verse 3, John hears a voice from heaven announcing to the suffering Christians of the first century that God is coming to "dwell" on this earth among his people. The word "dwell" actually means "to pitch a tent." To Christians familiar with the stories of the Hebrew scriptures, this word would immediately remind them of God literally "dwelling" among his people in the tabernacle.

The tabernacle actually was a tent pitched in the midst of the people of Israel as they wandered for forty years in the wilderness.

This is also the same word that John uses in the opening chapter of his gospel. Speaking of the birth of Christ, John writes "The word became flesh and *dwelled* [pitched a tent] among us" (emphasis mine). John is not talking about the end of the world but the Jesus whose coming brings about something wonderfully new. With his coming there is a new Jerusalem, a new universe, a new heaven, and a new earth.

In these words John is assuring suffering and persecuted Christians at the end of the first century that their hope is not just up in the clouds or when they die and go to heaven ... but already now, here, in this world, in this time and place as Jesus Christ "pitches his tent" among them.

In today's gospel, Jesus is with his disciples in the upper room, the night of his betrayal and arrest. The disciples are anxious about their future. Jesus has openly spoken of his departure. But Jesus assures them that they will not be left behind. He will give them the gift of his Spirit who will continue his work among them. In addition he gives them "a new commandment." This commandment is not like the old commandments, filled with threats and demands. This commandment is new. It is something they *get to* do. They will *get to* love as Jesus loved them. In so doing, the world will see in them not only Jesus but also (and this is the shocker!) ... heaven on earth! In their love for one another, they will reflect the new kind of world that Jesus has made possible.

That same gift is ours. In the midst of lives that are often confusing and painful, in a world that is often dangerous and deadly, Jesus is among us making a new world, a new heaven, and a new earth.

A few weeks ago I took some unwanted household items to a place where they will be distributed to needy people. When I was at the rear door dropping off my stuff, up pulled a beat-up jalopy. Inside were two Hispanic mothers and their children. They were patiently awaiting some bags of groceries from the food bank. I tried to make some small talk with them but I knew no Spanish. The rear door suddenly opened. A grouchy-looking, gray-haired lady came out with two bags of food and handed them to the mothers. She was obviously ill at ease and seemed to want to run right back into the building.

You should have seen the faces of those two mothers! They were so excited, so grateful, so filled with joy that they ran up and gave that grouchy-looking, gray-haired lady a big hug. In their broken English they joyfully cried over and over, "Thank you! Thank you!" I had never ever seen anything like this. When you go to a food bank, the "clients" or "needy folk" or whatever you call them always keep their distance. They are suspicious of the donors and the donors are suspicious of them. You sense their shame. You sense the mistrust of those handing out the food, but that day something amazing happened. The wall of suspicion crumbled. That bag of food touched them with what John in Revelation would call the love of the lamb. For a short time, this ministry of Christian compassion and charity was able to bring a little heaven to earth.

I recently heard a story about an urban congregation in a changing neighborhood of one of our eastern cities. The congregation had decided not to flee to the suburbs but to stay in the city and serve the needs of its crumbling neighborhood. The congregation had decided that in order to save souls, it had to start by saving its neighborhood. As a result, the church council decided that instead of repairing aging stained-glass windows, it would simply replace them with a more functional clear glass. Repair would not only have been costly but also would have meant repairing the glass of an image of the heavenly Jerusalem. The council felt that such an image was too otherworldly for a congregation committed to justice in the city.

Then someone pointed out that when you stood in the sanctuary and looked out through that old stained-glass image of the heavenly Jerusalem and saw the neighborhood surrounding the church, suddenly that decaying neighborhood appeared in a whole new light. That window literally reflected the mission of that congregation. Through their ministry of compassion and to the needs of their neighborhood, they would be a bit of heaven on earth. Through them the people in their neighborhood, struggling to eke out a meager living in a hostile world, could catch a glimpse of the victory already won through the blood of the lamb.

Is that not what all of you will *get to* do through your daily work in the week ahead? As you leave this place, renewed at the Lord's table, refreshed by his promises, strengthened by his Spirit, through your deeds of love and kindness you will give this world all too often suffering in its own kind of hell ... a glimpse of heaven on earth. Because Christ has triumphed, already now a new world is beginning to take shape, a world in which every tear will be wiped away, where death will be no more, where mourning, crying, and pain will be a distant memory, where there will be heaven on earth. Amen.

Easter 6
Revelation 21:10, 22—22:5

A Glimpse Of Glory

(Sing the first verse and chorus of "The Battle Hymn Of The Republic.")

> *Mine eyes have seen the glory of the coming of the Lord;*
> *He is trampling out the vintage where the grapes of wrath are stored;*
> *He has loosed the fateful lightning of his terrible swift sword;*
> *His truth is marching on.*
>
> *Glory, glory! Hallelujah!*
> *Glory, glory! Hallelujah!*
> *Glory, glory! Hallelujah!*
> *His truth is marching on.*[1]

Every time I hear these words from the "Battle Hymn Of The Republic," I have visions of some old Civil War movie with soldiers marching off to meet their fate in the glory of the battlefield. Such a hymn would truly soothe any of the doubts or fears a soldier might have as he enters the bloody conflict. As the battle was about to commence, he could be sure that he was on the right side, the side of truth, of God's truth. Whether he would die or survive, simply being involved in such a holy war would assure him that he would catch a glimpse of the glory of God. That glory would come either in the victory of the battlefield or in the giving of his life for a holy cause, which, of course, would assure him of his place in heaven. And there in heaven he could at last see God in all of his glory.

Perhaps one of your children has perplexed you with this question. Perhaps you have asked yourself the same question, unable to find a satisfactory answer. "Is there really a heaven? And if so, where is it?" Your grade schooler is having her first science class on outer space. She comes home one day, obviously troubled. After some gentle probing by you, she shares with you her problem. "Dad, if astronauts travel to outer space, if we have sent people all the way to the moon, if telescopes can see billions of miles into outer space ... then where is heaven?"

In Sunday school she had heard the story of Jesus' ascension, his rising up into the skies, disappearing into the clouds, and going to heaven. She had seen artists' imaginative paintings of heaven with angels, relaxing on the clouds, fluttering their wings, adjusting their halos, and playing their harps. If that heaven is "up" there, why hasn't it been discovered?

I still remember it well, when I was in grade school in the late 1950s at the height of the Cold War between the US and Russia. Russian cosmonaut, Yuri Gagarin, the first man in space, had triumphantly announced to the world that he had been "up there" and he had seen neither God nor heaven. Where is heaven? Is it "up," "down," or "beyond"? Of course, his comments pleased the leaders of the communist government and supported their official atheism.

The church has always referred to heaven as the abode of God. Heaven is where God is. But where is God? Isn't God supposed to be everywhere in creation? Yet God is transcendent and far beyond the most distant galaxy. Then where is heaven? Everywhere? Nowhere? Somewhere? It is so difficult to speak of a dimension of existence that is very different from life as we know it. Yet, to deny the existence of heaven would make our Christian faith and hope for the future empty and meaningless.

Such questions about the nature of heaven are more than just expressions of our curiosity. They are reflections of a much deeper anxiety, something that touches each of us in a very personal way. Such questions take on a special sense of urgency not only because we are concerned abut the destiny of our departed loved ones (Has God abandoned them? Are they in misery or ecstasy or somewhere in between? Do they have a future?), but also because we are anxious about our own destiny. What does the future hold? What about us? What lies beyond death for you and me? Is this life all there is? Or is there more? And if there is, is it heaven or hell or somewhere in between?

Maybe what we need to do is stop thinking of heaven as a place somewhere "up there," above, in the sky. When we confess in the Apostles' Creed that Jesus "ascended into heaven and is seated at the right hand of the Father," we don't literally mean that there is a specific place in heaven where Jesus is sitting. We don't literally mean that God actually has a right hand, a left hand, a right foot, a left foot, and so on. What we are really saying is that Jesus has been honored by his Father for the job he performed faithfully on earth. "At the right hand" means a place of privilege and honor. With apologies to any left-handed people here, as a right-handed person uses his right hand to do what he does best, so also for God. When God is doing that for which he wants to be best known, he does it through the risen and ascended Jesus "at his right hand." Jesus is God's "right-hand man," so to speak.

So, where is heaven? It is wherever Jesus is present acting as God's right hand man. And where is that? Jesus is present doing his heavenly thing wherever the forgiveness of sins is being offered. Martin Luther once said, "Where there is forgiveness of sins, there is also life and salvation." In other words, heaven is where Jesus is present doing God's right-handed thing, such as forgiving sinners.

Where is heaven? Heaven is where the waters of baptism are poured and the name of God is spoken. Heaven is where the body and blood of Jesus are offered in bread and wine. Heaven is where the guilty are released from their deadly past through the granting of forgiveness. Heaven is where the stranglehold of death and hopelessness is broken. When enemies embrace, when spouses reconcile, when neighbors are neighborly, when victims refuse to get even, when the powerful offer to serve instead of demanding that they be served, there is heaven.

When we sing "Mine eyes have seen the glory of the coming of the Lord," we are not just singing of some glory we have yet to see, some glory that lies somewhere in the distant future. No, we are making the outrageous claim that we have *already* seen the glory of the Lord! We have already caught a glimpse of heaven! We have already seen that place where death has been defeated, where there are no more tears, where there is only joy and celebration.

We have seen Jesus seated at the right hand of the Father. We have seen that Jesus already, here in the ministry of this congregation and not just in the clouds or galaxies above. When the word of the gospel is proclaimed in our midst, when bread is broken and wine is poured at the table, when bodies are bathed at the font, when sins are forgiven, when the sick are visited, when prayers are spoken, and when deeds of love are freely offered, there is Jesus. There is heaven. There our "eyes have seen the glory of the coming of the Lord."

Today's reading from the book of Revelation, the last book of the Bible, reports a grand and glorious vision of heaven. It is written in the code language that fills the book of Revelation. Contrary to those who try to turn the book of Revelation into some secret prediction of the future, it quite simply is a word of comfort to persecuted Christians in the first century. It was written in the code language of apocalyptic because Christians at the end of the first century were being put to death for their faith. They used the code language of apocalyptic to communicate the faith to one another.

The bizarre and fantastic images of Revelation are not just a promise of "pie in the sky in the sweet by and by." If the faith of those first Christians was just a hope that when they died, they would go to heaven; if their faith was just in the life hereafter, then their enemies would have considered them harmless. Everyone in the ancient world believed in some sort of afterlife. The Roman government didn't care what you believed about the hereafter. What they did care about was now and whether you would submit to Roman power now in this world. What made those early Christians so dangerous and even subversive in the eyes of the Roman establishment was their belief that Jesus was Lord and not Caesar.

They dared to believe that Jesus had already defeated Caesar in his death and resurrection. They believed that they were free from Caesar and refused to give him their ultimate loyalty. That was radical. That was dangerous. That was subversive. That made them enemies of the state. That made them candidates for execution.

Revelation through its bizarre and fantastic images of heaven described so vividly in today's reading, through its secret code language understandable only to Christians, assured them that they had nothing to fear. Jesus had already defeated Rome and the other empires and evil powers of this world. That victory was hidden to the rest of the world. But to Christians, to those with they eyes of faith, it was clear. Jesus reigned. Regardless of what the future held, they could wait patiently and with faith to that last day when Jesus would make is his victory visible to all. At that last day their eyes would finally get to "see the glory of the coming of the Lord."

The book of Revelation also offers us a glimpse of glory. Jesus, who died, rose again, and is seated at the right hand of the Father, is already now exercising his reign over the world through the ministry of the church. Here, in this place, the vision of Revelation is coming true. Here, in this place, we get to see a glimpse of the glory of heaven. Here "mine eyes have seen the glory of the coming of the Lord."

But wait a minute! This sounds great, too great, too great to be true. As my daddy used to say, "If something sounds too good to be true, it probably is." How in the world can we make these great and wonderful claims about the ministry of the church? The church? The church? You've got to be kidding! As our critics continually remind us, the church all too often looks like anything but heaven. Our lives are often as flawed and imperfect as the atheist down the street. We have more skeletons in the closet than we would ever like to admit. And despite our efforts the church isn't anymore effective than any other organization in changing this world. There is as much suffering, injustice, and death as ever. Where is heaven? Where is the "glory of the coming of the Lord"? How can Revelation possibly be true? And the saints? Where are the saints? Where are these special people who according to the second reading see the face of God and have their name on his foreheads?

Every year, when I meet with the confirmation students, I try to help them come to grips with this problem. When they complete their confirmation instruction and come forward to confess their faith before the congregation, they will be doing a pretty outrageous thing. In a sense they will be claiming that their "eyes have seen the glory of the coming of the Lord...."

One year this exercise was especially effective. In that class were twins, brother and sister, Simon and Sarah. Contrary to what you would expect, Sarah was the more precocious of two. She was the better athlete, better student, more outgoing, more popular, and she let you know it. Even though he was the twin brother, Simon always seemed to live in her shadow.

As I do every confirmation class at the beginning of the year, I asked the class if anyone knew what a saint was. There was silence, so I gave them a definition. A saint is someone special. A saint is someone chosen by God. A saint is someone perfect, sinless. A saint is not just someone dead in the ground. A saint is someone bound for heaven.

Then I asked them the big question: "Does anyone here think he or she is a saint?"

The class was silent for a few moments when to no one's surprise Sarah raised her hand.

"Pastor, I think I might qualify. I mean I try to do my best. I say my prayers every day. I do my homework. I made the basketball team. I come to church almost every Sunday. I think I keep the commandments most of the time."

"Well, Sarah, that is pretty impressive," I responded. "I'm sure that the rest of the class is pretty impressed, too."

That was all Simon needed. This was his chance to puncture the balloon of his precocious sister and have his day in the sun.

"But, pastor," blurted out Simon, "don't let Sarah fool you. She is not all she thinks she is." Then began a long litany of Sarah's transgressions from a brother who was obviously harboring a lot of hurt and hostility. He put the topping on the cake with, "And if you don't believe me, just ask my mom and dad. They will tell you the truth about Sarah."

Turning to Sarah, I spoke. "Sarah, are you still so sure that you are a saint? After listening to your brother, you seem a lot more like hell on earth than heaven on earth. Sounds like you have a lot to work on. Sounds like you are not always what you appear to be. Sarah, do you still think you are a saint?"

Mumbling and letting her gaze drop to the floor, "Well, pastor, maybe not a saint. I guess I am not a saint. But if I'm not, then I don't know who is."

"Well, Sarah, lets see what the rest of the class thinks. Class, let's ask the question again. Who here thinks they might be a saint?"

Silence. No hands are raised. This time they know the answer. This time they know what the pastor wants. They have learned their lesson. No one is a saint.

But I ask them again, "Does anyone here think he or she is a saint?"

Certain of the right answer and that they have learned their lesson well, no one raises a hand. Okay, now it is time for the punch line.

"Class, I want you to listen carefully. I want all of you to raise your hands."

And they all stare at one another ... in disbelief. What is the pastor doing? Has he gone off the deep end? This doesn't make any sense. Did I not just show them and Sarah that no one is a saint. No one is perfect. This doesn't make any sense at all. What is wrong with the pastor?

"Yes, I want all of you to raise your hands. C'mon, class. Let's see everyone's hands." Slowly they raise their hands with a look of total confusion and bewilderment on their faces.

I explain the shocking implications of what I have just done. "Yes, you are all saints. Even Sarah is a saint. Why? Because I said so! Why? Because Jesus says so! Why? Because God says so! You are all saints. You are perfect, sinless, the apples of God's eye. You are already bound for heaven to be with all the saints and angels ... not because you are better than anyone else, not because you have kept the commandments, not because of your good works. You are saints *because God says so!* God first said that to you the day you were baptized and were marked with his name on your forehead. He has been telling you that every day ever since. You are saints because what of Jesus did ... for you! Because of Jesus' suffering, death, resurrection, and ascension to right hand of the father in heaven, you are saints."

That surprising announcement is the good news of the gospel. I continually remind the kids during their confirmation instruction that this is the most important thing about the Christian faith. This is the good news they are invited to believe. And when they believe it, they receive God's greatest gift: a place next to Jesus in heaven ... already now! When they believe this startling announcement, they are seated at the right hand of the Father in heaven. They already now have a glimpse of glory.

(Show a large book that lists the congregation's "official acts.") This is the "book of life." Its name comes from the book of Revelation. In this book are recorded all the "official acts" of this congregation: baptisms, confirmations, weddings, funerals.

The hardened skeptic will look at this and wonder "What is the big deal? Let's face it. These are only the congregation's 'records.' Why make such a big deal and call it the 'book of life'? Isn't this a bit of exaggeration?"

No! This is no exaggeration because through the simple acts of the ministry of this congregation, people literally do have their names put in the "book of life." God reserves a place in heaven for them. Through these simple acts done on behalf of God, the church makes and sustains the saints. These actions give us a glimpse of heaven.

(Organist begins playing quietly "The Battle Hymn Of The Republic.") That day when water was poured over you and a few words were uttered, "In the name of the Father, and of the Son, and of the Holy Spirit," a saint was made. Your name was written in the "book of life" forever. You were given a glimpse of glory.

In a few moments you will come forward to eat and drink at the Lord's table. You will eat bread and drink wine. But even more you will meet Jesus, God's right-hand man, sitting at the right hand of the Father in heaven.

The words of that famous hymn will have literally come true. Then you will be able to sing with all confidence and certainty, "Mine eyes have seen the glory of the coming of the Lord...." Amen.

(All rise and sing "The Battle Hymn Of The Republic.")

---

1. "The Battle Hymn Of The Republic, words by Julia Ward Howe, 1861. In the public domain.

**The Ascension Of Our Lord
Ephesians 1:15-23**

It's A Good Thing He's Gone!

Today I want you to participate in the proclamation of today's message. Perhaps it will help you to remember the spectacular event and its significance that we are commemorating today.

Today is perhaps the most misunderstood and forgotten holiday of the entire Christian church year. Today, forty days after the resurrection of Jesus, the church for millennia has commemorated the ascension of Jesus. The first reading reports that memorable day when Jesus took his disciples to a hill outside of Jerusalem where he ascended into the clouds and disappeared from their sight. It used to be one of the biggest holidays of the church. Churches were packed for worship. In Germany, it is still a national holiday, *Himmlefahrts Tag*. Today only a few churches bother to have worship services. Nevertheless, it commemorates an important event in the life of Christ. In order to impress upon you the importance of this day, this sermon is going to employ some audience participation.

Every time I raise my hand like this *(demonstrate)*, I want you to say this: **It's a good thing he's gone!** You may wonder as to the significance of these words. You may question whether the pastor has gone off the deep end. But by the end of this message you will appreciate the wonderful significance and glorious good news proclaimed by these words.

No doubt that when Jesus ascended into the heavens and disappeared into the cloud, there were plenty of people around to say, **"It's a good thing he's gone!"** They were glad to get rid of him, to no longer have this Jesus of Nazareth walking around and disturbing their orderly little world.

There were people like Pontius Pilate who may have said, "It was bad enough that this Jesus got everyone worked up by claiming to be some sort of a king. And then there was that messy trial and death sentence. I got manipulated into releasing that troublesome Barabbas. I know I'm going to regret that some day. I didn't want to put the man on trial, but I really had no choice. If I hadn't, there certainly would have been a riot and it was my job to keep law and order. Most of all, there was this strange talk of the empty tomb. Now I hear that he has disappeared into the clouds! What a relief! I'm finally rid of him. Yes, **it's a good thing he's gone!**"

Then there were people like the religious leaders who may have said, "It was bad enough to see all the common people flock after him. For someone who claimed to be a man of God, he certainly could have chosen to associate with more respectable people than tax collectors, thieves, harlots, lepers, the blind, and all other such notorious sinners. Then to do it all in the name of God! And to claim to be able to forgive their sins! And to show such disrespect for the religious traditions of our fathers and the customs of our people! Why, the man was sacrilegious! Dangerous! A heretic! Yes, it was too bad that we had to railroad him to a death sentence, but there was just too much at stake. He gave us no other choice. It was the right thing to do. And then all this foolish talk about an empty tomb? His crazy disciples just wouldn't admit that they had lost, that their dreams were in vain. Well, **it's a good thing he's gone!**"

There are people like the sophisticated cynics of our day who say, "Who needs Jesus and his religion? It's just for women and children, for the weak and puny, this talk of God and mercy and forgiveness. We can make it on our own. We can do it ourselves. We know how to succeed. We can achieve and make money and be good people and be happy without this Jesus. Yes, **it's a good thing he's gone!**"

Then there are the intellectually elite, the highly educated, and worldly wise of our day who say, "I never believed in God anyway. Where is God? What proof is there that God even exists? If

God does exist, why does God permit so much suffering and sorrow? Why is there so much injustice and oppression in this world? Jesus? ... ascended into heaven? Up there somewhere in the clouds? Well, if you're foolish enough to believe in some heaven 'up there,' good riddance! **It's a good thing he's gone!**"

There are also those who live and die by the bottom line, those me-first, looking-out-for-number-one kinds of folk who say, "We don't want somebody always bugging us to give our money away to the poor. Let the poor take care of themselves! We don't want someone telling us to love our enemies. Let us give them what they deserve! We don't want someone reminding us to take up our crosses and follow him, about working for peace and justice, even if we don't get anything in return! Yes, **it's a good thing he's gone!**"

As a matter of fact, **it *is* a good thing that he's gone!** All of these people are right about that, *but*, of course, for all the *wrong reasons*! Yes, we Christians can join in with all these people and say, **"It's a good thing he's gone!"** Yes, he has ascended into heaven. Jesus of Nazareth, the Son of God, with flesh and blood just like you and me, who lived in a particular place in a particular time, who spoke with an audible voice with a certain tone and timbre, who weighed so many pounds, who had such and such color of hair, this *one* is no longer here! He has ascended into heaven!

Because Jesus is gone does not mean that he is absent or has abandoned us to struggle in this life on our own. It means that he is in heaven "sitting at the right hand of the Father," as the creed reminds us. Today's reading affirms that he is at the "right hand in the heavenly places." That means that Jesus is now in charge of this whole broken world. His victory of the cross and resurrection is now complete. Being in heaven doesn't mean he is absent and gone, but rather that he can be everywhere and anywhere and any time in the universe to share with us his victory. It means that he can be with us in our sufferings and temptations. It means that he can be with us in our joys and successes. Being at the right hand of the Father in heaven means that time and space no longer confine him. Sitting at the right hand of the Father means that he can even be with us now as ascended Lord to share with us his victory over death.

I cannot be standing here in the sanctuary and be out there in the parking lot at the same time. I cannot be in Indiana in the year 2010 and be in medieval Europe at the same time. That is impossible because I am confined to this body at this time and place. That is the nature of living in time and space. But not for Jesus! Because Jesus is now ascended in heaven and sits at the right hand of the Father, he is no longer confined to space and time. Because Jesus is ascended, because he is not "here" in time and space but in heaven, Jesus is everywhere in the universe. There is no place and no time where Jesus is not present to share his love. "He has put all things under his feet!" From the most distant black hole light years removed from this place and time to the personal privacy of your bathroom, Jesus is there.

Oh, oh! Is that really good news? Do I really want Jesus with me all the time? Do I really want him there when I am doing shameful and embarrassing things? Do I really want Jesus there when my sins are getting the best of me? Do I really want Jesus there when doubt and despair are haunting my soul?

Yes, **it's a good thing he's gone**, because as the ascended Jesus, he is with us in a new way, not as a judge or prosecutor out to find all the dirt on us. No, on the contrary, he is present through the power and presence of his Holy Spirit. Just before Jesus ascended into heaven, he told his disciples to wait in Jerusalem until they would be "clothed with power from on high." Jesus was speaking of the coming gift of the Holy Spirit that he would shortly give to his disciples. That giving of the Holy Spirit to his disciples we will celebrate next Sunday, the Day of Pentecost. Through the power and presence of the Holy Spirit, Jesus was going to be able to be present with his disciples in a more personal and intimate way than he was when he walked around with them on the hills and dirt roads of Palestine. He would be present as risen Christ who had defeated the powers of sin and death. He would be present as the friend of sinners, as the one who suffered and died and rose again so that their sins, shames, and embarrassments might be forgiven.

Yes, **it's a good thing he's gone!** It is good news that he is gone because that means whenever we are ashamed and embarrassed and want to run and hide, he is there to forgive us, to clothe us in his righteousness, to make us clean and whole again.

Yes, **it's a good thing he's gone!** It is good news that he is gone because that means whenever we feel alone and forgotten, whenever we feel that God is distant or absent, Jesus can be with us to comfort us in our loneliness.

Yes, **it's a good thing he's gone.** It is good news because that means that he can be present with us in the ministry of this congregation today even though he ascended into heaven 2,000 years ago, 10,000 miles from this place.

Yes, **it's a good thing he's gone.** This is a good thing because that means whenever the gospel is preached or the sacraments are administered, whenever bread is broken and wine is poured at this table, whenever water is poured at this font, the risen ascended Jesus is present here ... for us ... now! What had been hidden is now made visible for us through the eyes of faith!

Yes, **it's a good thing he's gone.** Why? Because wherever and whenever the gospel is preached, the hidden presence of the risen and ascended Jesus who fills the universe is revealed.

It's like this. I carry around my wallet in my pocket wherever I go. But you don't see it, even now, because it is hidden in my back pocket under my robe. When I pull that wallet out of my pocket and show it and its contents to you, I have revealed what was hidden. I have revealed the presence of a wallet that was with me everywhere I went. Even though it was hidden, it gave me confidence. I had money to help out, even when I was in a fix. So also does the risen and ascended Jesus comfort and assure us. There is no place in the universe where he is not with us. But we may not know that or believe that. We might doubt that. The evidence is not clear, like that wallet hidden in my back pocket. When Jesus is proclaimed and shared, when the wallet is pulled out of my back pocket and its contents revealed, we are blessed and comforted ... wherever we go. Because Jesus is in heaven, there is no place in the universe where he can't be to reveal his love for us.

Yes, **it's a good thing he's gone** because then this congregation can be the body of Christ. Because Jesus now is no longer confined to space and time, he can be here in this place, in the life of this congregation, whenever we go about doing God's "right handed thing," such as bringing this world the life and love of the risen Jesus. It is literally through the actions of this congregation, of any congregation, that the body of risen and ascended Jesus appears in this world.

Even though you must live in a world that often mutters to itself, "it's a good thing he's gone" for all the wrong reasons, you know because of what we celebrate today, **it's a good thing he's gone!** It's a good thing he has ascended to the right hand of the Father, because then he can be with you always, everywhere, forever, as you struggle with the never ending tasks of being his body in the world.

Let's say it one more time? It is good news to our ears: **It's a good thing he's gone!** Amen.

Easter 7
Revelation 22:12-14, 16-17, 20-21

All In God's Time

"Why do bad things happen to good people?" is the way we say it today.

That surely must have been a question on the hearts and minds of those first-century Christians as they suffered under the brutal persecution of the Roman empire. It is a question that surely was on the hearts and minds to whom John had written this extraordinary piece of literature we call the book of Revelation. Many of them were convinced that they were innocent and righteous sufferers sent to their deaths in the coliseum because they had refused to "burn incense to Caesar" and acknowledge that any one else was Lord of their life than Jesus, the Christ.

But there is even a more troubling question than "Why do bad things happen to good people?" that must have bothered them. "Why does a holy, righteous, and loving God permit the unrighteous to swallow the righteous, the wicked to devour the innocent? Why does God permit such suffering and seemingly do nothing about it?"

It is bad enough if some outsider is the villain. It is intolerable when the villain is homegrown. It's like having the fireman start the fire, the policeman rob the bank and murder the citizens, the government extort money from its subjects, and the armed forces ravage their own country. Outsiders we could excuse by saying that they are outsiders. But how does one excuse the insiders? This is the most haunting question of all raised by those to whom John wrote his book.

"God, how could you do this to your own people?"

How could God be a god of love and still permit this kind of suffering? Either he is not an all-powerful God ... or worse yet, not loving.

These first-century Christian martyrs were not the first nor would they be the last to raise this poignant question. When our Lord Jesus Christ cried in anguish from the cross, "My God, my God, why have your forsaken me?" it was the same question. Why should God turn on the one who without question has been faithful? The fact that he does makes this question very important. Easy explanations are out. We should not be surprised or ashamed to find ourselves crying out with the same question.

How do God's people excuse God, the righteous God, for letting the righteous, good people be victimized at will by those who scorn him and them?

That same cry was raised by many in our land after the attack of September 11, 2001. Over 7,000 people, just going about their daily business, were suddenly destroyed by these four flying bombs. They were innocent victims who bore no malice toward those terrorists. It is easy to understand our anger and our desire to get back and get even. In the same way many Christians in the Roman empire were angered and infuriated. Many were outraged by what had happened to their brothers and sisters in the faith at the hands of the brutal and ruthless Romans, and God seemed to be doing nothing about it!

This problem also vexes us. We just don't understand the ways of God. We especially *do not understand God's timing*! We want quick, immediate action when someone has been wronged or injustice has been inflicted. Especially when we have been wronged, we want immediate retaliation. We grow impatient with God's inaction, with God's seeming reluctance to balance the scales of justice. We want God to follow our timetable. Instant justice! Immediate eye for an eye, tooth for a tooth!

But ... would we ask for the same, immediate solution when we are the ones who have done the wrong, when we have been unjust, when we have used power to serve only ourselves? Then, it is a different matter, isn't it? Then we are quick to plead "extenuating circumstances," give explanations and beg forgiveness. Then we are not unlike the criminal who refuses to extend mercy to his victim but who pleads weeping for mercy when he has been caught. Perhaps God might be rejecting the instantaneous response because that would mean wiping out just about everyone with his judgment, including those who were pleading for swift retaliation as long as it was not directed at them.

God understands time much differently than we do. Since we measure time in milliseconds, a little time seems like a lot of time. In our demand for justice *now*, we forget that God is the inventor, the creator of time. His relationship to time differs from that of ours. "A thousand years as one day, and one day as 1,000 years," says scripture. His timing is not like our timing.

For example, the people of Israel were in bondage in Egypt for an inordinate number of years. They cry out to God to free them. Then God remembers his promises to Abraham, Isaac, and Jacob. When did that promising take place? Only 400 years before! His delivery of the people of Israel is regarded as fulfilling that 400-year-old promise! That is certainly a different way of keeping a promise and that certainly is a different sense of timing than ours.

A guide at the Wailing Wall in Jerusalem once explained it this way, this divine sense of timing that is so different from ours. A devout Jew who lives far from Jerusalem has his heart set on getting to the Wailing Wall during his lifetime. He dies without having made the journey. His children then take up the wish and the dream. They do not make it. Then the grandchildren. They are not successful. Then the great-grandchildren, the great-great grandchildren and the great-great-great grandchildren. At last one of the great-great-great-great grandchildren makes it to the Wailing Wall. In the person and presence of this child, the hopes and dreams of all that went before him are fulfilled. The devout father who died hundreds of years before is at the Wailing Wall, as this child now prays there.

That is why God said he had fulfilled his promise to Abraham, to Isaac, and to Jacob, when we would say that he only fulfilled it for those Hebrews he brought out of Egypt some 400 years later.

We are impatient with God's timing. Individualism has become such a strong religion in our world that we cannot work very well with the idea that promises made to us are fulfilled when they come true in the life of our offspring generations later. Because we were never able to taste them personally, they were promises broken and not promises kept.

Our sense of time has a much shorter fuse. We like it when God's timing agrees with ours. When it does, we gloat over the misfortunes of the unjust, the wicked, of those whom we are convinced deserved it. And so we rejoice at the downfall of a religious leader, at the resignation of a politician, the suicide of Adolf Hitler, the stroke-induced death of a Joseph Stalin, the execution of Sadaam Hussein ... or even on a much lesser scale, the crushing of a sports hero by one still younger, or by the aging of the beautiful, or the bankruptcy of a tycoon. We delight when the great are brought down. We are sure they had it coming.

More often than not God's sense of timing does not agree with ours. God's timing seems so slow and it is so painful to wait for it. Just ask those first-century Christians, the audience of John's book, who had lost brothers, sisters, parents, and friends in the bloody persecutions of Nero and Domitian. Just ask the parents of missing children, the families keeping vigil at the deathbed of their loved ones, the poor who are longing to flee from their ghetto of deprivation, the widows and widowers and divorced who are still trying to fill the emptiness in their lives ... all who find it so difficult to wait.

We want God to act *now*! And when he doesn't, we often find it necessary to take matters into our own hands. We get angry. We abuse our children, our spouse, our neighbor. We lose our tempers. We become violent. Or worse yet, we give up ... as all too many Christians did at the end of the first century when they decided to burn incense to Caesar and deny that Jesus was Lord when faced with their own martyrdom.

Most often our impatience results in our reluctance to forgive. Forgiveness requires a willingness to be patient, the willingness to wait, to wait out our own anger and the anger of those with whom we are in conflict. Forgiveness requires the willingness to withhold judgment, getting even, and extracting our "pound of flesh." Forgiveness means that we must be willing to forgo the impatient race of our time for the gentle flow of God's time. It means to be patient enough to forgive one another, to never stop forgiving, to withhold cutting off the brother, to resist lashing out in righteous wrath, because you never know according to God's timetable when your forgiveness may finally be able to reclaim your enemy.

There were also many of those about-to-be-martyred Christians who cried out in desperation for God to increase their faith. Without an increase in faith, they would never be able forgive their enemies or their friends who had betrayed them. They sensed that it was going to be very difficult to live according to God's time, not just because they were used to their own time, but ultimately because they did not trust God and his time schedule.

If the first-century Christians to whom John addressed his book cried out to God to increase their faith, so also do we. When bad things happen to good people, when the world is riddled with violence that so often strikes the innocent, when we find ourselves the victims of injustice and oppression, it takes a lot of faith to still trust God. It takes a lot of faith to trust his time schedule, to curb our own impatience, and lust for revenge. It takes a lot of faith not to be anxious and worried when you lose your job or the company is losing money. It takes a lot faith to trust the promises of God when so much in life seems to contradict them. To risk ostracism, ridicule, humiliation, and even our jobs because we won't "burn incense to Caesar" takes a whole lot of faith, more faith than you or I could ever hope to muster on our own. So, we get tired of waiting. We get tired of God's timing. We join those first-century Christians in Asia Minor crying out for more faith. We are about to give up on God.

But God's time is not our time. In his time, he truly does keep his promises. In his time, he rights the wrongs and saves his people. In today's reading, the dramatic conclusion to the entire book of Revelation, God speaks to John and shows a vision of the future when in God's time, in the fullness of time ... all things shall be accomplished. All shall be set right.

Yes, the delay between the sin of Adam and Eve and the coming of Christ was a long time. Yes, three hours on the cross was a long time, especially after you have first been beaten until the white of your backbone and white of your ribs shows through the mangled flesh that once covered them.

Yes, God's time is difficult to understand. And, as if to heighten the confusion even more, what Jesus seemed to call an injustice ("My God, my God, why have you forsaken me?") was the ultimate working out of justice. This was God finally keeping his promise. And he did it in a way that was utterly different from the way we usually understand justice. We expect God to just sock it to the evil ones of this earth. But that would be nothing more than the same old routine. That would be God caving into the demands of our time and our cries for revenge. *But* what if God finally vented his justice not on all the sin and evil of this world but on himself, on his only begotten Son? What if the cries of all the innocent victims of history for justice and righteous destruction of all the bad guys of this world were finally answered not by blasting them to smithereens but in the cross, in the dumping of all that righteous anger on his Son?

What would that mean? That would mean the end of anger. That would mean forgiveness, mercy, new life! That would mean salvation ... for you, for me, for our enemies, for the world.

That is exactly what happened on Good Friday and Easter, on the cross and at the empty tomb. All in God's time God kept his promise. God finally made good on what he had promised to Abraham, Isaac, Jacob, Moses, David ... and those first-century victims of persecution. God acted decisively, once and for all, for you and for me. For all the lives lost in the rubble of the World Trade Center, for the broken bodies and lives of the Pentagon, for those trapped under the debris of all the unjust suffering and hurt of this world, for the victims of Katrina, of cancer, for the starving in Darfur, for those crushed by the screeching tires, shattered glass, and smashing metal on a slippery, midnight road, God acts once and for all. God offers not with an explanation as to why these things happen, but with a solution, with a way through them, with a deliverance from their ability to crush the faith of their victims and with a promise of rescue from their eternal consequences.

Do you now begin to see the wonder of God's timing, that his timing is not our timing? Isn't it good that God chooses to be so merciful and patient ... not only with those scoundrels who deserve hell, fire, and brimstone, but with you and me?

Just think of it. Do we really want God's timing to be so quick and swift when we too are standing among the wicked? Thank God that his timing is different, that the fullness of time arrived at the cross and empty tomb, instead of the last time we wanted to pop our enemy in the nose. Thank God that his timing is so different that he is so patient with us, that he does not take pleasure in the death of the wicked, that he permitted his only Son to die, raised him again and promised that he would come again, so that we might live!

We complain, "Why do bad things happen to such good people?" when we ought to be praising God with "Why has such a *good thing* happened to such *bad people*?"

God's timing is not our timing. That is difficult to accept. Some times it seems to defy all common sense. Sometimes it seems down right cruel. We can't wait. We can't help but get angry. We can't help but shed tears over the immense suffering that afflicts so much of human life. We can't help but doubt and wonder if there is a God at all. But God is patient. God is patient with us. The faith that seems so weak now will grow strong, strong enough to not only refuse to bow down and worship the powers of this world, but to save our souls. God has promised to make it that strong ... all in *his* time!

John, in today's second reading, declares that this time has arrived ... *now*! As he pens these words, as he declares the victory of God that has already been accomplished at Good Friday and Easter and these words are trusted by his readers, God's time is fulfilled!

That time has also arrived *now* as you come to this table. Here you receive a foretaste of the feast to come ... now. Now God makes you his beloved sons and daughters. *Now* he says,

> *The Spirit and the bride say, "Come." And let everyone who hears say, "Come." And let everyone who is*

thirsty come. Let anyone who wishes take the water of life as a gift.... The one who testifies to these things says, "Surely I am coming soon." Amen. Come, Lord Jesus! — Revelation 22:17, 20-21

Trusting that promise, you can move mountains, thumb your nose at the empty promises of this world, defy the threats of "Caesar," love your enemies, turn the other cheek, go the extra mile, feed the hungry, clothe the naked, change the world, all in God's time! Amen.

Sermons On The Second Readings

For Sundays
After Pentecost
(First Third)

Led By The Spirit

April Yamasaki

To Gary,
with all my thanks
for all your support and encouragement

Preface

"Sermons don't sell!" said one publisher.

"Is the sermon dead?" asked one denominational magazine.

In our multi-media world with the internet, TV, DVDs, video games, MP3 players, and other high-tech gadgets, is there still a place for the human voice?

I preach shorter sermons now than I did when I first began preaching years ago. I've learned to use PowerPoint to outline a sermon as it unfolds or to project a passage of scripture so people can see it without having to flip from place to place in their own Bibles. I've come to realize that adding a map or photograph, a movie clip or other visual can help a sermon communicate in a new way and often more clearly.

Yet there is just no substitute for the human voice, for the personal stories and the personal relationship that are so much a part of the preaching moment. My narrow miss of a car accident on my way to church might find its way into a sermon on God's grace. A letter from a friend might work its way into a sermon on Paul's letter to the Galatians. Or the time our annual youth retreat was rained out and they spent the night in the church gym might serve as an illustration of prayer.

But my car accident wouldn't make sense in your voice. You didn't receive my friend's letter. Your church may not have an annual youth retreat or it may never have gotten rained out. So I haven't included these more personal elements in this small collection of sermons. Instead, I offer these sermons more as a biblical framework, as an aid to your own reflection on the text.

In that way, they're really not quite finished. Without the human voice, a sermon is not really a sermon. Without a more personal interaction with the text and with the congregation, what appears on the printed page can only be a place to start.

So as God continues to lead you in prayer and preparation, may you also add your own voice to this modest beginning. "Let the word of Christ dwell in you richly; teach and admonish one another in all wisdom; and with gratitude in your hearts sing psalms, hymns, and spiritual songs to God. And whatever you do, in word or deed, do everything in the name of the Lord Jesus, giving thanks to God the Father through him" (Colossians 3:16-17).

— April Yamasaki

The Day Of Pentecost
Romans 8:14-17

Getting The Big Picture

A "global positioning system" can tell you the fastest way to drive from Point A to Point B — which streets are one-way only, which streets to avoid due to construction or too much traffic, where to park once you get where you're going. Like a street map, it can show how the roads run north, south, east, and west; which roads are dead ends, or go over a bridge; how they curve and then straighten out again. Like the yellow pages of a telephone book, it can tell you where to find the nearest coffee shop, Chinese restaurant, or grocery store. Like a radio, it can give the latest traffic update. It even provides a bit of company in the form of an audible voice telling you where to turn right or left.

For this Day Of Pentecost, our scripture text describes the Holy Spirit, who guides us as children of God. Only the Spirit's leading is not about getting from Point A to Point B in the fastest way possible. It doesn't necessarily mean hearing an audible voice, and it's not mainly about finding the right restaurant or grocery store, although it might make a difference in the way we make some of those choices, too. Instead, our scripture gives the big picture of what it means to be led by the Spirit of God. Instead of focusing more narrowly on the thousands of individual decisions we make each day, it describes more broadly a way of life.

When We Are Led By The Spirit Of God,
We Are No Longer Afraid
Wherever we may go in life, we need never be afraid. The Spirit of God goes with us, is behind, and before us. As Paul

preached to the Athenians at the Areopagus, "In him we live and move and have our being" (Acts 17:28). As he wrote to Christians in Rome,

> *For I am convinced that neither death, nor life, nor angels, nor rulers, nor things present, nor things to come, nor powers, nor height, nor depth, nor anything else in all creation, will be able to separate us from the love of God in Christ Jesus our Lord.*
> — Romans 8:38-39

In our scripture text for today, it is "a spirit of adoption" that banishes fear from our lives.

On a practical level, when it comes to the thousands of decisions we make each day, we can relax in the knowledge that God will lead us and never leave us. We don't need to be overly anxious about life, about what we will eat or drink or wear, or even how long we will live. As Jesus himself points out in the Sermon on the Mount, God cares for the birds of the air and the lilies of the field. "Are you not of more value than they?" he asks (Matthew 6:26). As adopted children of God, we have a special place in God's care, so we need not worry or fear.

Yes, we are called to make good choices. In Romans 7, Paul shares his own struggle to do good. In Romans 8, he gives his readers a long list of instructions to give to the needy, practice hospitality, live at peace with others, and other good works. But as we make these and many other choices in our lives, we make them not out of fear, but out of God's love for us and confident of God's leading.

When We Are Led By The Spirit Of God, We Have A New Relationship With God

There are many different names for God in the Bible. In the book of Psalms alone, God is addressed in many different ways as "God of my right" (Psalm 4:1), "O Most High" (Psalm 9:2), "my light and my salvation ... the stronghold of my life" (Psalm 27:1), "my rock and my fortress, my stronghold and my deliverer, my shield, in whom I take refuge" (Psalm 144:2). In all of scripture, the most personal address for God is used by Jesus as he prays in the Garden of Gethsemane shortly before his arrest: "Abba, Father, for you all things are possible; remove this cup from me; yet, not what I want, but what you want" (Mark 14:36).

In this most intimate moment before his arrest and crucifixion, Jesus prays to God as "Abba, Father." It's like saying "Father" twice — first in Aramaic with the word *Abba* that means father and is left untranslated, and then again with the word "Father" that Jesus also uses at the start of the Lord's Prayer (Matthew 6:9; Luke 11:2). In Aramaic, *Abba* was a form of address that a child might use with his own father or a student might use to address his rabbi teacher. It was a title that expressed both respect and close relationship, and it appears only three times in the entire New Testament — in Jesus' prayer before his arrest, in our scripture text for today, and in Galatians 4:6.

In our text for today and in Galatians, "Abba, Father" is the heart's cry of God's children. No longer slaves to sin or the law, no longer strangers, we have been adopted into God's family by the Holy Spirit. We are now joint heirs with Christ, and we echo Jesus' own personal prayer to God as "Abba, Father." We have a new relationship with God — a relationship of respect and love, as close as any parent and child or rabbi and student.

This new relationship with God can also make a difference to the way we make decisions in daily life. Do you face a challenging situation at home or work or school? Is there some concern that keeps you up at night? Instead of struggling with these things on our own, we can bring them to God in prayer, just as Jesus himself prayed in the Garden of Gethsemane, asking for God's will to be done. We may not hear an audible voice in reply, but we can have confidence in our "Abba, Father" who hears us and leads us in every situation.

When We Are Led By The Spirit Of God, We Know That This Life Is Not All There Is

As adopted children, we enjoy a close relationship with our Abba, Father. By the Holy Spirit, God is always with us, hears us when we call, and provides us with every good gift. These are very present mercies. But as adopted children, we also have an inheritance that is yet to come. This life is not all there is!

Our inheritance is described immediately after our text as "the glory about to be revealed to us" (Romans 8:18) and "the redemption of our bodies" (Romans 8:23). Ephesians speaks of "our inheritance toward redemption" (Ephesians 1:14) and our "inheritance among the saints" (Ephesians 1:18). Other portions of scripture refer to inheriting "the kingdom" (1 Corinthians 6:9, 10; 15:50).

It's not entirely clear what this inheritance is exactly, but it is clearly some time in the future, and this life is but a foretaste. Ephesians 1:7 says that redemption and forgiveness are already ours, yet a few verses later, Ephesians 1:14 says redemption is still to come as part of our inheritance. Colossians 1:13 says we have already entered God's kingdom; yet in the letter of 1 Corinthians, God's kingdom is part of our inheritance (1 Corinthians 6:9, 10; 15:50). This life is not all there is! There is yet more to come.

On a practical level, this eternal perspective can make a difference in the real decisions we make each day. We don't need to be focused on getting ahead in this life and keeping up with the Joneses, for this life is not all there is! We don't need to be consumed by our consumer culture, for this life is not all there is! So maybe we can choose to pay a little extra for a cup of free-trade coffee instead of our regular. We can choose to support the mom-and-pop restaurant that cooks real food instead of the fast-food chain. We can choose to get out of the fast-lane of life in favor of spending more time with family and getting to know our neighbors. In these and many other ways, having an eternal perspective can help shape the life we lead every day.

When We Are Led By The Spirit Of God,
We Share A Family Resemblance With Christ Himself

Throughout his earthly life, Jesus experienced suffering at the hands of others. Religious leaders criticized him for healing on the sabbath. The crowds and even his closest friends and disciples misunderstood his teaching and mission. Although the people initially welcomed him to Jerusalem, he was arrested, tortured, and executed by crucifixion. Philippians 2:8 describes Jesus' suffering this way:

"He humbled himself and became obedient to the point of death — even death on a cross."

Philippians 2:9 completes the story.

> *Therefore God also highly exalted him and gave him the name that is above every name, so that at the name of Jesus every knee should bend, in heaven and on earth and under the earth, and every tongue should confess that Jesus Christ is Lord, to the glory of God the Father."*
> — Philippians 2:9-10

The suffering of Jesus gave way to glory! As "heirs of God and joint heirs with Christ," we share this family resemblance with Jesus. Like him, we may have some suffering in this world. We, too, may be misunderstood for doing what we think is the right thing. We, too, may face criticism or ridicule for reaching out to those on the margins of society. All this may be very mild in comparison to our Lord, but we know that around the world even today some Christians still suffer persecution and martyrdom. Suffering is part of our family resemblance as God's adopted children.

The other characteristic that we share is future glory. Just as the suffering of Jesus is mirrored in our own lives, so too, the glory — not in the very same way as the exalted Lord we worship, but the glory of our final redemption and eternal life that is still to come. When Christian conviction leads us to take an unpopular stand, when we speak with Christian compassion against exploitation or other injustice, if we should suffer criticism or even worse at the hands of others, we can take heart that one day we will also share in Christ's glory.

As God's adopted children then, we receive the strength and courage to face the tough questions in life, to make the difficult decisions, to do the right thing. Whatever we might suffer as a result, it is only for this life. Our scripture text for today stops just short of Romans 8:18, but that verse provides a fitting commentary here. Immediately after our text, Paul writes, "I consider that the sufferings of this present time are not worth comparing with the glory about to be revealed to us." Both are part of our family resemblance.

So what does it mean then to be "led by the Spirit of God"? Can we think of God's Spirit as a kind of global positioning system for our spiritual lives? This is the big picture: When we are led by the Spirit of God, we are no longer afraid; we have a new relationship with God; we know that this life is not all there is; we share a family resemblance of suffering and glory. "For you did not receive a spirit of slavery to fall back into fear, but you have received a spirit of adoption" (Romans 8:15).

Let us pray: Abba, Father, we come to you as your children, trusting that you hear us and will lead us by your Spirit. In this world of great confusion and uncertainty, lead us forward with the confidence and courage that comes from being your adopted children and joint heirs with Christ. Amen.

The Holy Trinity
Romans 5:1-5

God's Chain Reaction

In 1980, NBC introduced a new television game show called *Chain Reaction*. Since then, the show has appeared in different forms, but the main idea has always been for different teams to fill in a chain of words. For example, the first word in a four-word chain might be "light," the last word "spring," with the team needing to guess the two words in-between. In this case, "light" comes from a light "bulb," and out of the bulb grows a "daffodil," which comes up in the "spring." It's a chain reaction of words, where one word leads to another, and "light" turns into "spring."

In Romans 5, there is also a chain reaction of words that begins in verse 3 with "suffering" and ends in verse 4 with "hope." How might suffering turn into hope? Is that kind of divine chain reaction really possible? Or is this just another word game?

For Christians living in Rome, there seemed to be some evidence of their suffering. Romans 8:35 mentions "hardship, or distress, or persecution, or famine, or nakedness, or peril, or sword." Romans 12:12 directs its readers to "be patient in suffering," and Romans 12:14 adds the encouragement "bless those who persecute you." In the midst of hardship, distress, persecution, and peril — in the midst of that kind of suffering — how could they possibly have hope?

Today, we might well ask the same kind of question — perhaps not from the same kind of persecution for our faith, but from whatever troubles and afflictions that we might face in the world and in our own lives. When violence erupts again in any part of the world with all of the suffering it causes, how can we have hope?

With the ongoing suffering of poverty, disease, and war in so many places around the world, how can we have hope? As we face our own personal challenges — raising our children in an increasingly complicated world, facing our own aging and health issues, and confronting our own mortality, how can we have hope? With the Romans long ago, we might also ask: Can suffering really lead to hope?

It does in God's chain reaction — for the first Christians who received this letter and for us today, suffering is the first element of a chain that leads to the second element of endurance. Other English translations use the word "perseverance" — like the persistent widow that kept going back to the judge for justice again and again and again. Or the Energizer Bunny that goes on and on and on. Endurance means we keep putting one foot in front of the other, we keep taking it one day at a time, we keep holding on even if it means we're holding on only by our fingernails.

When there is suffering and perseverance, the third element in the chain is character. The Greek word for "character" here is *dokimas* that literally means someone or something that has been put to the test and been approved. If you take driver training and pass your road test to receive your license, you are *dokimas* — you have been put to the test and been approved. Or if your toothpaste has received the stamp of approval from the American Dental Association, it is *dokimas*. It's been tested and approved. So, too, character is tested and proved by suffering and perseverance.

In turn, character leads to the fourth element of the chain: hope. Hope is forward looking. It takes us beyond suffering, beyond perseverance, beyond character, into the future. Hope takes us beyond ourselves and whatever concerns we might have to place our trust and confidence in God.

This is God's divine chain reaction — suffering, perseverance, character, hope. It appears in other parts of the Bible as well.

> *My brothers and sisters, whenever you face trials of any kind, consider it nothing but joy, because you know that the testing of your faith produces endurance; and let endurance have its full effect, so that you may be mature and complete, lacking in nothing.*
> — James 1:2-4

In God's chain reaction, the testing of your faith develops endurance, which makes you mature and complete — in other words, that gives you character.

In a similar way, 1 Peter 1:6-7 says:

> *In this you rejoice, even if now for a little while you have had to suffer various trials, so that the genuineness of your faith — being more precious than gold that, though perishable, is tested by fire — may be found to result in praise and glory and honor when Jesus Christ is revealed.*   — 1 Peter 1:6-7

Suffering is faith tested by fire, which results in praise, glory, and honor.

It's not that we rejoice *for* suffering in the letters of James or 1 Peter or here in our text from Romans 5. We don't rejoice *for* suffering in any kind of sadistic or masochistic way. But we can rejoice *in the midst of* suffering because there is a divine chain reaction — suffering that leads to perseverance and character and hope. We can rejoice because suffering is not the end, but it can lead us to something much better.

There is a second chain reaction in our text for today, beginning in verse 1 with "justified by faith" and ending in verse 2 with "our hope of sharing the glory of God." Again, we might ask — is this chain reaction merely a matter of words, or is it really possible in our own lives today? How do we get from being justified by faith to boasting in the hope of the glory of God?

The first step in this divine chain reaction is that being justified by faith leads to peace with God (v. 2). This is a simple statement of fact: When we are justified through faith, we have peace with God. At times we may not feel very peaceful. On the global scene, we may feel helpless and overwhelmed by world events that are so much larger than ourselves and beyond our control. Closer to home in our own community and personal lives, we may also face situations of conflict or distress. There may be so much happening in our lives we may feel anything but peaceful. But our feelings don't change the reality. Because of Jesus' death on the cross, our sins have been paid for and forgiven. If we have faith in Jesus, we have peace with God whether or not we feel that way.

Peace with God means we stand and live in God's grace (v. 2). This is a third element in the chain. It's not a one-time thing that lasts for a moment or a day or a year or two. Peace with God is ongoing, so we can stand in God's grace our whole lifelong, and even beyond this life, we can have hope of sharing the glory of God. Again, God's chain reaction is made complete by hope.

For both of these chain reactions, the end result is hope. In verses 1 and 2, it's justification by faith that leads to peace with God and standing in grace and results in hope. In verses 3 and 4, it's suffering that produces endurance that produces character that leads to hope.

Today we use the word "hope" very loosely in a number of different ways. I hope it's sunny this afternoon. I hope my mother will be well enough to go home from the hospital this week. Some of you may be hoping to pass math this year or hoping to get your driver's license; hoping for a new job or hoping to retire. Some of these hopes may come true. Others may lead to disappointment. As we well know, not all of our hopes in this life are satisfied. But the hope described in our text today always comes true!

It is the hope of eternal life. Romans 5:2 describes it as the "hope of sharing the glory of God." That's another way of saying the hope of eternal life. As Titus 3:7 puts it, "so that, having been justified by his grace, we might become heirs according to the hope of eternal life." This life with its suffering is not the end. When we place our faith in Jesus, we have peace with God in this life and in the next, where there will be no more pain and suffering, no more sorrow, no more grief, but endless joy and praise in the presence of God. That's part of our hope of sharing the glory of God in eternal life.

It is the hope of God's love. Romans 5:5: "God's love has been poured into our hearts." God is not a stingy God using an eyedropper to measure out love drop by drop. Instead, God's love has been so generously poured out that it reaches into our very being.

> *For I am convinced that neither death, nor life, nor angels, nor rulers, nor things present, nor things to come, nor powers, nor height, nor depth, nor anything else in all creation, will be able to separate us from the love of God in Christ Jesus our Lord.*
> — Romans 8:38-39

It is the hope of God's presence. Verse 5 of our text continues, "God's love has been poured into our hearts through the Holy Spirit that has been given to us." This is another statement of fact. When we place our faith in Jesus, the Holy Spirit is given to us. We may not always feel that God is with us, especially during times of suffering and trial. We may feel alone and abandoned. But at those times we can hope in the Holy Spirit who is always with us, no matter how we may feel. As Jesus himself says in Matthew 28:28, "And remember, I am with you always, to the end of the age." Since Jesus' death, resurrection, and ascension, he is no longer physically present on earth, he is no longer physically with us. But he sent the Holy Spirit to be with us to the very end of the age, no matter what sufferings and trials we may go through.

This kind of hope will never disappoint us! The hope of eternal life, the hope in God's love, the hope in the Holy Spirit's presence — through faith in Jesus, this hope is ours today. When we place our faith in Jesus, there is a divine chain reaction that leads to peace and grace and hope. Even when we suffer there can be a divine chain reaction that leads to endurance, character, and hope, a hope that will never disappoint us.

Let us pray: Our gracious and loving God, we pray for your divine chain reaction in our lives. Pour your love into our hearts. Give us a hope that will never be disappointed because we hope in you — in your promise of eternal life, in your love that never fails, in your presence that is always with us. Amen.

**Proper 4
Pentecost 2
Ordinary Time 9
Galatians 1:1-12**

An Uncomplicated Gospel

*Dear John,
I have decided that I can no longer see you. Our relationship has ended, and I wish you well in your future.*

*Good-bye,
Jane*

Whether you've ever written or received a "Dear John" or "Dear Jane" letter, the basic outline and intent is clear. It begins with a basic greeting — not "Dear Johnny" or "Sweetheart" or some other form of endearment, but simply "Dear John." There is a very brief and to-the-point body of the letter that makes it clear the relationship is over. Then the letter writer signs off with his or her own name. The "Dear John" or "Dear Jane" letter is a variation on the standard letter format used in other personal letters and even business correspondence today. Each letter has a clear beginning, a middle, and an end.

In the ancient world, letters also tended to have a standard form. Instead of opening with a greeting to the recipient of the letter, ancient letters would normally begin with the name and brief description of the letter writer, then a greeting to the recipient, followed by a prayer for their well-being, and sometimes a few words of thanks. After the main body of the letter, there would be a few words of farewell, which often included additional greetings to other people.

The apostle Paul used this ancient form for his letters that would later become part of our New Testament. So for example, his letter to the Romans begins with his own name, "Paul, a servant of Jesus Christ"; followed by the recipients of the letter, "To all God's beloved in Rome, who are called to be saints"; a wish for their well-being "Grace to you and peace from God our Father and the Lord Jesus Christ"; followed by words of thanks, "I thank my God through Jesus Christ for all of you" (Romans 1:1-8). This basic letter form appears again and again in most of the letters of the New Testament.

It's not surprising then that our scripture text from Galatians 1 would follow the same form. The letter begins with "Paul an apostle"; is addressed "To the churches of Galatia"; and includes Paul's traditional prayer for their well-being used also in his letter to the Romans and elsewhere, "Grace to you and peace from God our Father and the Lord Jesus Christ" (Galatians 1:1-3). But instead of the expected words of thanks, Paul goes directly to the purpose of his letter: "I am astonished that you are so quickly deserting the one who called you in the grace of Christ and are turning to a different gospel" (Galatians 1:6).

Unlike most of his other letters, there is no expression of thanks in the opening to Galatians. There are no words of thanks at all in the entire letter! What made Paul depart from his usual practice? Was there a problem in his relationship with this young church?

It seems as if Paul had a chip on his shoulder from the outset. In his opening words identifying himself, he immediately asserts that his authority is not from any human origin but comes directly from God. He is anxious to remind his readers that he does not rely on them or on anyone else, and this assertion is again repeated at the end of our text for today — Paul received the gospel directly "through a revelation of Jesus Christ" (Galatians 1:12).

What's more, Paul addresses himself simply "To the churches of Galatia" without additional comment. They are not "beloved" or "saints" as he describes the church in Rome (Romans 1:7). He does not refer to them as "faithful brothers and sisters in Christ" as he describes the Christians of Colossae (Colossians 1:1). Paul's greeting is as bald and bare as any "Dear John" or "Dear Jane" letter — only Paul does not wish to end his relationship with these churches, however strained their relationship might be. Instead, Paul writes them a stern rebuke that even includes a curse against anyone who would lead them astray.

Paul's great concern can be summed up in just one word: gospel. In the English translation of our text for today, the word "gospel" appears six times: in verse 6, it is "a different gospel"; in verse 7 "another gospel" in contrast to "the gospel of Christ"; in verse 8 "a gospel contrary to what we proclaimed to you"; in verse 9 "a gospel contrary to what you received"; and finally in verse 11 "the gospel that was proclaimed by me." Paul is so disturbed that his different expressions pile up one on top of the other, and the net effect is enough to make your head spin! Is the gospel really that complicated?

The word "gospel" is literally good news, and it's summarized in our text.

> *Grace to you and peace from God our Father and the Lord Jesus Christ, who gave himself for our sins to set us free from the present evil age, according to the will of our God and Father, to whom be the glory forever and ever. Amen.* — Galatians 1:3-5

This is good news — that God offers us grace and peace, that Jesus has set us free! That's the heart of the gospel that lies at the heart of Paul's concern and at the heart of all his many words. That's what he means by "the gospel of Christ" and "the gospel that was proclaimed by me."

For Paul, the gospel was God's grace in action. He often wrote the word "grace" in his letters, but it was much more than part of a standard opening or closing line. Grace was God's undeserved favor that transformed his own life and was freely available to all.

The movie *Seabiscuit* gives a picture of grace in action. On one level, the movie is about Seabiscuit's rise as one of the greatest race horses in American history. It's a story about the Great Depression, about the possibilities and the triumph of the little guy in America. But on another level, it is very much a story about grace

— the trainer who rescued a horse that was going to be destroyed and somehow found himself as well; the horse Seabiscuit who was too small and thought to be too wild to ride but when treated well became a record breaker, a jockey who was too big and blind in one eye but was allowed to continue riding, an owner broken by the death of his son and the failure of his marriage but who found new purpose. A common thread runs through all these different parts of the story, illustrated by one line that is repeated in the movie: "You don't throw something away just because it's a little beaten up." That's grace. God didn't throw Paul away or throw the Galatians away, and God doesn't throw us away. Instead, God offers us grace and peace and sets us free in Jesus Christ. That's good news!

In the case of the Galatians, the people were in danger of deserting this gospel of Christ for something else — for "a different gospel," "another gospel," a "contrary" gospel. They had received the good news of God's grace and freedom in Christ, but instead of continuing to rely on God's grace, they were in danger of distorting it and turning it into something else. It was becoming God's grace-and-circumcision, God's grace-and-the-law, God's grace-and-their-own-works.

Paul was so disturbed by this distortion of the gospel that he could hardly contain himself. He could not offer his usual words of thanks at the beginning of the letter or even later. Instead, he jumped directly to what he saw as a most grave and dangerous situation.

Now fast forward to our own day and age. Today, the heart of the gospel is still God's grace in Jesus Christ and the new freedom we have through faith in him. And today, we still have the same tendency as the Galatians to make God's good news into something else. Circumcision is no longer the flash point in our culture as it was for the Galatian church. The distortions of the gospel that we face are very different, but they are distortions just the same.

For some of us, it may be God's grace-and-going-to-church, God's grace-and-making-a-living, God's grace-and-family. In some parts of the Christian church, it may be God's grace-and-the-government and in other parts God's grace-and-protesting-the-government. It might be God's grace-and-good-works, God's grace-and-the-environment, God's grace-and-whatever our own pet project or concern might be. But is the gospel really that complicated even today?

Paul wrote to the Galatian church to recall them to the gospel of Jesus Christ — not the gospel-and-anything-else. They were not to be confused by any other teaching. They were not to seek the approval of others by adding anything else. He used all the apostolic authority he could muster to convince them in his letter. In the same way, this text of scripture challenges us and recalls us also back to the heart of the gospel. We are saved by God's grace. We are set free by the work of Jesus Christ.

There are many good works to be done in this world, many urgent needs and situations that need to be addressed. But these are not the center of our faith. They cannot save us. They are not the heart of the gospel. Instead, all of the good works and urgent concerns that we might be tempted to add to the gospel are actually the outworkings of the gospel. They are an essential part of our response to God's grace and freedom, but they are not the same thing.

Paul's own life was a vivid example of this. Once he had persecuted the church, but soon after his dramatic conversion on the road to Damascus, he became a tireless evangelist and church planter. During his ministry he experienced imprisonment, beatings, stonings, shipwrecks, and many other trials. Yet he knew that it was not his own efforts that absolved him of his past life. It was not God's grace-and-evangelism, God's grace-and-church-planting. It was God's grace that saved him and gave him this new ministry.

The words of the well-known hymn, "Amazing Grace," were penned by John Newton, a former slave trader who later became an ordained minister and wrote over 200 hymns. Leaving the slave trade did not save him, but it was an outworking of God's grace in his life. Becoming an ordained minister and writing hymns did not save him, but they were an outworking of God's grace in his life. For John Newton, it was not God's grace-and-anything-else, but "Amazing grace, how sweet the sound that saved a wretch like me!"

We may not all experience a dramatic conversion like Paul or like John Newton. But God's grace and the uncomplicated gospel of Christ Jesus are still at the heart of our faith. At times we may be tempted to add to it, as if God's grace is not enough. At times we may be tempted to take it for granted, too pre-occupied with ourselves and other things to notice. Our text for today challenges us to recognize these things as distortions of the gospel and take hold again of God's grace in Jesus Christ.

Paul was so disturbed that he was not able to include a word of thanks in his letter to the Galatians. It was a marked departure from his usual practice that signaled the seriousness of the situation in the Galatian church. Today, let's take the opportunity to write a word of thanks into our own lives. That's really all that is left for us to do. God has already done it all!

Let us pray: Gracious God, we give you thanks for your will and work in our lives. When we act as if your grace is not enough, recall us to the heart of your gospel. When we are distracted and busy with many things, remind us of your amazing grace. Thank you ... thank you ... thank you.... Amen.

**Proper 5
Pentecost 3
Ordinary Time 10
Galatians 1:11-24**

But When God ...

In the early Christian church, there were no pulpits. It wasn't until the Middle Ages that pulpits were first introduced in churches and not until the Protestant Reformation of the 1500s and 1600s that the pulpit became a central symbol for the authority of scripture and the preaching of the word. But it hasn't always been that way. Instead, the very first Christian churches were house churches, where there were no pulpits, and everything was done face-to-face without a piece of furniture in between.

The apostle Paul was very used to that. In his missionary travels, he generally started with preaching in the synagogues. But he was also very used to telling the story of Jesus out in the streets, in the marketplaces, and even down by the riverside wherever people would gather. When Paul could not speak in person, he would often write a letter as the next best thing. Without webcams, telephones, or texting, in the ancient world, letter writing was the next best thing to being there.

In the first chapter of Galatians, Paul writes out his personal testimony as part of a letter to the Galatian Christians. Many scholars read these verses as Paul's defense of his authority as an apostle. There were some in Galatia who questioned Paul's authority, who opposed his teaching, who were very critical. In these verses, Paul takes great pains to show that his authority and teaching come from God. But in defending his apostolic authority, Paul also provides a thumbnail sketch of his own personal testimony.

Galatians 1:11-24 takes just over a minute to read out loud. So we might think of it as Paul's one-minute testimony. It wasn't delivered from what we know today as a traditional pulpit. It wasn't given face-to-face. Instead, it was a very brief written testimony as part of a letter to the church. It was really just a refresher for the Galatian Christians, because as Paul points out in verse 13, they had already heard of his previous way of life. They already knew him. But just as a reminder, and for anyone who might not know, Paul describes his former life.

In his former life, he used to persecute the church of God and tried to destroy it. But God gave him a new way of seeing, and now he is preaching the faith and planting churches. In his former life, Paul had been advancing in Judaism beyond many Jews of his own age. But now he is being thrown out of synagogues for preaching Christ. In his former life, he had been extremely zealous for all the religious traditions that had been handed down generation after generation. But now he is telling everyone that faith in Christ means they do not need to keep the religious law. This was a dramatic change — from trying to destroy the church to planting new churches, from advancing in Judaism to advancing the cause of Christ, from living by the law to living by the Spirit.

What made the difference? How did Paul's life change so dramatically? And what might we learn about how God can change our lives?

The key is verse 15 of our text: "But when God" — it was God who dramatically changed Paul's life. Paul was advancing in Judaism, Paul was keeping the law, Paul was dismantling the church, Paul was going full speed ahead — but when God — when God stepped in, everything changed! Paul did not change because of something someone made up. He did not change because of what other people said. He did not change because the other apostles told him to change his way of life. Some scholars speculate that Paul's three years in Arabia were part of the reason for his dramatic change — that he spent those three years on an extended retreat, out in the desert, spending time with God in prayer. Others argue that Paul had already radically changed by that time, that he was already involved in mission, preaching, and making converts in Arabia. But all of that is speculation, because Paul doesn't say what he did in Arabia. He gives very little detail in this personal testimony. Instead he paints everything in broad strokes to make his point about the power of the gospel: "but when God" — when God stepped in, Paul received a new way of seeing, a new way of living that changed everything.

In a similar fashion, today we may be just as busy in our own way as Paul was in his. Just as Paul had been concerned to advance in Judaism, maybe we are also focused on advancing in some way — getting ahead at school or in business, excelling in our work or playing a sport. Just as Paul was very zealous, maybe we are very zealous about a certain project in the community or in the church or about our family life. Just as Paul had been concerned about the religious traditions that had been passed down generation after generation, maybe we are focused on certain family traditions or church traditions that we think are important. We might be going full speed ahead on the things that we care deeply about, just as Paul had been in his life.

We may not receive a vision of the risen Christ out on the street the way Paul received a vision of the risen Christ on the road to Damascus. We may not have such a dramatic change in our lives. We may not go off to Arabia and refuse to talk to anyone else in the church. In fact, in contrast to Paul's experience, we'd all be better off if we would be able to share our experiences of faith together and learn from one another. But what we do have in common with the apostle is that God is also at work in our lives, to give us a new way of seeing and a new way of living. Paul came to understand Jesus in a new way, he understood the church in a new way, he was able to redefine success in a new way, he saw people in a new way — not divided between Jew and Gentile, slave and free, men and women, but as one new humanity in Jesus Christ. He came to a new understanding of the law, a new understanding of the Old Testament and how it points to Jesus.

In a similar way, when God breaks into our lives, we too can receive a new way of seeing, a new way of living that changes everything. A new way where real success is not measured in dollars and cents, but in the character qualities of love, patience, kindness, and goodness. A new way where getting ahead is not as important as being faithful. A new way where the kind of clothing we wear doesn't count as much as the kind of people we are. A new way where we see people in a different light — not divided between different races or different denominations, between old and young, men and women, but as one new humanity in Jesus Christ. Just as God gave Paul a new way of seeing and a new way of living, so too, God can change us.

Paul describes God's work in his life this way: "But when God, who set me apart from birth ..." (v. 15). In other words, God was at work throughout Paul's life — not only on the Damascus Road when the risen Christ appeared to Paul in a vision, not only when Paul was in Arabia on retreat or preaching, or whatever it was that he was doing there. God had been at work from Paul's birth and throughout his entire life. In the same way, God is at work in our lives all along, too. You and I are a long-term project. God doesn't just fly in at moments of crisis or during times of intense need or intense prayer. God is at work in our lives from birth to death, even when we're sometimes unaware of it, even when we're sometimes at odds with the church and at odds with God's purposes as Paul once was. God is at work throughout our lives.

> *But when God, who set me apart from birth and called me through his grace, was pleased to reveal his Son in me, so that I might proclaim him among the Gentiles, I did not confer with any human being....*
> — Galatians 1:15-16

For all the drama of Paul's conversion, for all of the dramatic changes in his life, it is also very clear that for Paul some things actually remained the same as before. He was just as stubborn and independently minded as he was before. He was just as energetic and just as zealous and still going full speed ahead. Only now it was in a different direction. He was still a very passionate and headstrong person — but what was new was Paul's direction and Paul's purpose.

Some of us are also very passionate and very active just like Paul. When we decide to do something, we don't consult anyone else, we just go ahead. Some of us are a little too full of ourselves just the way Paul was. As he says in verse 24, "and they glorified God because of me" — that may very well have been true, but it was also a rather self-centered way of putting it.

For all the changes in his life, for all the great work that he was doing, Paul was still a work in progress. There were still plenty of rough edges left in his life. God wasn't finished with him yet. For us, too, each of us is unique, each of us has our own rough edges, and God isn't finished with any of us. Whether we've lived for nine years or ninety, whether we're very passionate and very active like Paul or maybe not so much, God's work in our lives continues, and God isn't finished with us just as God wasn't finished with the apostle Paul.

His one-minute written testimony was actually much more than that. It was a lifelong testimony that he was living out — in his preaching, his letter writing, in his daily work as a tent-maker, as a friend, as a traveler from city to city. Each of us is also living out a lifelong testimony in whatever daily work we do, in whatever service we're involved in, as a friend and family member, wherever we might live or work or go to school or travel.

As you reflect on your own life today, what changes has God already made in you? Where is God's work in you still unfinished?

These are very open-ended questions — where the answers for each person are very different. For each of us has our own unique, ongoing, lifelong testimony. As we live that out in the coming week, may we reflect on what that means for each of us: What changes has God already made in your life? Where is God's work in you still unfinished?

Let us pray: May the Spirit of the living God who set you apart from birth and called you by his grace continue that good work in you. May God's transforming power bring renewal to your life and glory to God. Amen.

**Proper 6
Pentecost 4
Ordinary Time 11
Galatians 2:15-21**

Living With Integrity

"Justification by faith" — to a theologian these words express one of the most basic principles of the Christian faith. But to many people today, they're simply one more example of Christian jargon that seems to brand the church as too complicated and out of touch for our time. Is it real? Is it relevant? Does it matter? To the apostle Paul in our scripture reading for today, "justification by faith" was so important that he repeats it over and over again like a football coach going over and over the same drill again and again. To him and to his first readers, "justification by faith" was not primarily a theological concept. It was not meant as a technical term to be understood only by a select few. In fact, it was a response to a very real situation in the life of the church.

It all began with Peter, who had been one of Jesus' closest disciples. At one time, Peter had been a fisherman, but when Jesus called him, Peter immediately followed. He saw Jesus perform many miracles, including the raising of a little girl from the dead (Mark 5:37-43). He witnessed Jesus' transfiguration on the mountain top (Matthew 17:1-8). He was with Jesus in the Garden of Gethsemane (Matthew 26:37), followed Jesus after his arrest as far as the courtyard of the high priest (Luke 22:55), and ran to the empty tomb after Jesus' resurrection (Luke 24:12).

Just as Peter had been a leader among Jesus' first disciples, he also became a leader in the early church. It was Peter who preached the sermon on the day of Pentecost when the Holy Spirit came with power on the gathered believers (Acts 2:14ff.). Peter healed a crippled beggar at the temple gate in Jerusalem (Acts 3:1-10). He was arrested and testified to Jesus' resurrection before the religious authorities (Acts 4:1-22). When one of Jesus' followers in Joppa fell ill and died, Peter even raised her from the dead (Acts 9:36-43).

One day, Peter received a strange vision of something like a huge sheet filled with all kinds of animals. A voice said to him, "Get up, Peter; kill and eat" (Acts 10:13). As a proper Jew, Peter was horrified. He was well-schooled and practiced in the strict dietary code of Judaism. Certain animals were "clean" and could be eaten as long as they were slaughtered in accordance with Jewish law. Other animals were "unclean" and were forbidden to eat. He could barely look at the strange mix of animals in his vision, and he refused to eat any of them once, twice, three times, before the vision finally ended.

As Peter soon learned, this vision was not only about food, about what to eat and what not to eat. By the leading of the Holy Spirit, he came to understand that his vision was also about the people who had been declared "clean" and "unclean" according to the food laws. As the voice had said to him in his vision, "What God has made clean, you must not call profane" (Acts 10:15).

For Peter in his time and for his people, that meant accepting both Jews and Gentiles into the fellowship of the church. By faith in Jesus Christ, both had been made clean! They were no longer separated by the laws concerning food and other religious rituals. They could now eat together at the same table. They could now worship and fellowship together under the same roof. They could now celebrate the Lord's supper together for they were part of the same body. Peter himself demonstrated this by eating with Gentile believers, hosting them in his home, and granting them baptism on confession of their faith.

Yet at some point between Acts 10 and Galatians 2, Peter reversed himself and began to hold back from eating with Gentiles. Just before our scripture reading for today, in Galatians 2:11-14, the apostle Paul criticizes Peter for this reversal. We don't have Peter's side of the story here, but Paul clearly interprets this as fear on the part of Peter. He was afraid of what others might think! So Peter acted against the vision that he had received, against what had been revealed to him by the Holy Spirit, against what he knew to be true. What's more, since Peter was a leader in the church, his actions influenced other Jewish Christians to separate themselves from the Gentiles. Paul was so incensed over this that he accused Peter of hypocrisy in front of everyone.

This is the backdrop for our scripture reading for today. Peter and others had begun to separate themselves again from the Gentiles as if the old dietary laws were still in effect. They were acting contrary to the gospel that had set them free and had made them one with all who believe. They were acting as if Jesus' life, death, and resurrection had not happened!

No wonder Paul was so incensed. No wonder he used such strong language over and over again in our text for today. He wanted to be very clear — it was not keeping the law that made a person right with God, but justification came by faith in Jesus Christ. The crucifixion of Christ had changed everything! His resurrection had changed everything! So now all who have faith in him are dead to the law and dead to sin and live in newness of life before God. As Paul writes later in Galatians 3:28, "There is no longer Jew or Greek, there is no longer slave or free, there is no longer male and female; for all of you are one in Christ Jesus." In Christ, there is no reason for Jews and Gentiles to eat separately, no reason for Paul or Peter or any of the others to break fellowship with the rest.

Although it might sound like complicated Christian jargon to our ears today, "justification by faith" was actually a response to this very live and very practical issue in the life of the early church. "Justification" was another way of saying "being made right" with God, being declared righteous and acceptable to God. Like the margins of a book might be "justified" — they line up together and form a straight line up and down the page — being justified in God's sight means lining up with God.

The word "justified" appears three times in verse 16 alone: "a person is justified not by the works of the law but through faith in Jesus Christ"; "we have come to believe in Christ Jesus, so that we might be justified by faith in Christ"; "no one will be justified by the works of the law." Then in the strongest words possible, our text ends in verse 21: "for if justification comes through the law, then Christ died for nothing."

Justification does not come by what we do. It is not a product of our own work. Instead, it is a result of the work of Christ. It is "the grace of God" as Paul says at the end of our text. In other words, it is a gift, undeserved and freely given. It is not something that we have to earn but something to accept by faith. God is the one who lines us up, who makes us justified.

Our part is to live that way — to live in a way consistent with God's grace, to live in a way that expresses the truth of the gospel, to live as people who have been justified by faith. That's where Peter had fallen short. That's where the Galatians were also in danger of falling into the same error.

Today, hypocrisy and personal integrity continue to be challenges for the church and for all of us. Peter has lots of company! In our own day, some church leaders have also been taken to task in very public ways for their failure to live according to the very truths that they have preached. The issues today are not so much about food and eating together, but revolve around the big three of money, sex, and power. Church leaders have preached about giving, but have sometimes spent too much on themselves and in some cases have even embezzled funds. Some have preached about faithfulness in marriage and then later been caught in adultery or prostitution. Some have preached on the lordship of Christ, while at the same time misusing their own authority in a church or parachurch organization.

It's true that these are isolated instances — in fact, they are newsworthy in part because they are isolated instances. But they are also cautionary tales for all of us, since the challenges of faithful living and hypocrisy are not limited to those in church leadership. There are times when each one of us has acted against our better judgment, against what we know to be true, against God's grace and gospel in our lives. We may not make any headlines, but we also sometimes fall short of faithful living in our use of time and money, in our marriage and family life, in our work life, in the way we treat other people, in the choices we make for leisure and recreation, and in many other ways both large and small.

Some might say, "The church is full of hypocrites!" — and in a way they're right. From the pulpit to the very last pew, all of us stumble and fall and must plead guilty. Like Peter, there are times when we also need to be confronted, when we need someone else to point out our own blind spots. We need to be reminded that if we are justified by faith — *since* we have been justified by faith — we need to live that way with integrity.

At the same time, we might also say, "The church is full of forgiven hypocrites!" From the pulpit to the very last pew, there is hope for all of us. By God's grace, we can repent and change our ways; we can receive God's forgiveness and be made right with God again; we can live a new life! Not because we are justified by the law and our own ability to live with integrity but because we have been justified by faith in Christ Jesus.

We don't know how Peter responded to Paul's rebuke. Did he continue to avoid eating together with Gentiles? Did he get defensive and try to explain away his bad behavior? Did he immediately recognize his fault and mend his ways? Did he talk with Barnabas and the others who had followed his lead and redirect their misguided actions as well? We don't know the answers to these questions in Peter's life, but what of our own response? Do we get defensive and try to find excuses for our own bad behavior? Do we recognize our own failings and seek to turn ourselves around? Do we make amends with anyone that we have misled?

These are very real and relevant questions for our own time. "Justification by faith" is not just a bit of dusty theology or Christian jargon. It makes a real difference in the way we live — with faith in Jesus who has set us free from sin, with trust in God who justifies us by the free gift of grace, with integrity in all we say and do.

Let us pray: Lord, we confess that we often fall short in living out the truth of your good news. In this moment, we receive again your forgiveness and grace. We remember again that we have been justified by faith in Christ Jesus, and now we live in him. Amen.

**Proper 7
Pentecost 5
Ordinary Time 12
Galatians 3:23-29**

Thicker Than Blood

In the classic movie, *Mary Poppins*, Julie Andrews plays a no-nonsense, yet delightful, nanny to two young children. As a nanny to a wealthy family, she is part teacher, part parent, and part disciplinarian. She gets the children up in the morning, puts them to bed at night, supervises their many adventures, and guides them in many ways. While they are in her care, she is responsible for their overall safety and well-being.

In the ancient world, wealthy Greek and Roman families would assign this kind of responsibility to a slave called a *paidagogos*. He was usually an older male slave, charged with the responsibility of caring for a young boy through childhood into adulthood. At times, he might need to be a disciplinarian; at other times more of a teacher; at other times more of a supervisor. It was an important role, but also a temporary one that ended once his young charge reached adulthood.

In Galatians 3:24, the apostle Paul calls the law a *paidagogos*. In some English translations, this word appears as "disciplinarian"; in others, it's translated more broadly as "schoolmaster" or "guardian." But like the *paidagogos* of a wealthy family, the law was really more than any of those things. It provided discipline, teaching, supervision, and overall caretaking — but only for a time.

With the revelation of Jesus Christ, the people were no longer subject to the law. Like a child who had outgrown his *paidagogos*, the people had been set free from the law through faith in Christ. It was not a license to do whatever they pleased whenever they pleased — it was not lawlessness. After all, the grown-up child minus his *paidagogos* was still meant to live as a responsible adult. So, too, those who had been set free from the law through faith in Christ would now live according to their new identity in Christ. Once they had been under the law, but now they were baptized into Christ, clothed with Christ, belonged to Christ, and they were meant to live that way. From now on, the law would no longer separate Jew and Gentile, slave and free, male and female. From now on, they were all joined together in Christ.

Whatever physical, social, ethnic, cultural, historical, and other differences there might be, these were no longer the defining and dividing qualities they once were. Instead, all those who were baptized into Christ and clothed with Christ had received a new identity and a new way of life that brought them together in Christ Jesus. That ringing affirmation remains true for us also today: "There is no longer Jew or Greek, there is no longer slave or free, there is no longer male and female; for all of you are one in Christ Jesus" (Galatians 3:28).

In our contemporary experience, we might well add: There is no longer first world or third world, urbanite or country dweller, black or white, young or old, rich or poor, healthy or unwell, able-bodied or disabled, immigrant or citizen — not that all of these very real differences would disappear, but that they would make no difference to our identity and unity in Christ Jesus.

Cast in those terms, this affirmation is also clearly a challenge. Can we really bridge these divisions in the church today? Can we live out such a transcendent vision of unity in Christ Jesus?

If we think of this as a new "law," it becomes clear how much we have failed! Our world is full of examples of racial hatred, ethnic cleansing, the wealthy oppression of the poor, and other situations of hostility and conflict. Even in the church, there is division, quarreling, one-upmanship, and other behaviors contrary to our unity.

If being one in Christ Jesus were a new law, clearly we have failed — and the law is unable to save us. Instead, if we are to live out this vision of unity, we need to turn to Jesus himself.

In Romans 7, the apostle Paul describes his personal struggle to do what is right — the good that he wanted to do, he could not do; and the wrong he wanted to avoid, he ended up doing in spite of himself. "Wretched man that I am! Who will rescue me from this body of death?" he asks in Romans 7:24. Instead of answering this directly, in the very next verse Romans 7:25, he immediately turns to God with a word of praise: "Thanks be to God through Jesus Christ our Lord!"

In the same way, as we struggle and fail to live out the unity in Christ that we know to be good and true, we might also ask, "Broken church that we are! Who will rescue us from our all-too-human failings?" And our answer is the same: "Thanks be to God through Jesus Christ our Lord!"

If we are to become more unified, to live as a more unified people, we need to look beyond ourselves and beyond our differences to focus on our common Savior and Lord. We have been baptized into the same Christ Jesus. We belong to him, and so we belong to one another.

An old proverb says, "blood is thicker than water" — meaning that the ties between family members are stronger than the ties between people who are not related to one another. But here in Galatians, the apostle Paul argues just the opposite — that through faith in Jesus Christ, the water of baptism forms a closer bond than anything else. By God's grace, the water of baptism *is* thicker than blood — for we are joined to one another with a spiritual bond that is stronger even than the ties of family and biology.

In Ephesians 5:32, the oneness of Christ and the church is described as "a great mystery." It's beyond all human understanding. It cannot be fully explained in any book let alone a single sermon. There is no scientific formula or set of how-to instructions to manufacture unity in Christ Jesus. Yet within that mystery, there are also some practical things that we can do to acknowledge and live out a greater unity with one another.

Look To Jesus

On Sunday mornings, people see me dressed for worship. During the week, when I clean the house, work in the garden, or wash the car, I might wear jeans and a T-shirt. If you play any kind of organized sport, you might wear a team uniform. Or if you work in a hospital or fast-food restaurant, you might wear a different kind of uniform when you're on the job.

What we wear can change our behavior and also change the way that other people respond to us. I don't wear my Sunday best to wash my car. The fast-food cashier out of uniform on her day off doesn't step behind the counter to open the cash drawer. If you're wearing the uniform of my favorite sports team, I'll cheer you on. If you're wearing the uniform of our arch rivals, I'll groan when your side scores.

As Christians baptized into Christ, we have clothed ourselves with Christ. We have a new uniform! We have a whole new wardrobe! If we have put on Christ, then we need to act as he did — with love for God, with love for neighbors and even enemies, in humility, with respect for the needs and interests of others. If we have put on Christ, then we need to see Christ in one another and treat each other as we would treat Christ himself.

Our unity with one another is reinforced and demonstrated as we put on Christ and have the same mind as he did, when we can look beyond our differences to see Christ in others.

Live As If

A child playing make-believe might act as if he were a dinosaur or as if she were an airplane. At other times, their make-believe might be more realistic as they pretend to be shopkeepers or doctors or teachers or take care of their own baby doll children. Some of this make-believe is pure fantasy — the child will never really be a dinosaur or an airplane. But some of this pretend play is actually rehearsal for their future lives as adults. It's a kind of practice for when they really will have children of their own or become a teacher one day.

In a similar way, we can also "live as if" we are one in Christ Jesus even if we sometimes don't feel that way or it may seem awkward at times. It's not pure make-believe, and it's not a false hypocrisy, either. Instead, we can think of it as a kind of practice as we continue to grow into the kind of people that God has called us to be. It's our dress rehearsal for the future. It's not pure fantasy, and it's not fake — it's faith!

By faith, we can choose to think well of one another. By faith, we can cooperate and work together. By faith, we can offer one another mutual respect. By faith, we can live as if we are one in Christ Jesus — because we are!

Pray

In John chapter 17, Jesus prays to God that his followers might be "completely one, so that the world may know that you have sent me and have loved them even as you have loved me" (John 17:23). When he taught his disciples to pray, he said, "*Our* Father ... Give *us* this day *our* daily bread. And forgive *us* our debts, as *we* also have forgiven *our* debtors. And do not bring *us* to the time of trial, but rescue *us* from the evil one" (Matthew 6:9-13, emphasis mine). There is a sense of unity in this prayer, that we are all in this together as we pray for ourselves and for one another to *our* Father.

In keeping with Jesus' example, we also may demonstrate our unity in prayer. We also may pray for unity — in our own congregation, in our denomination, and beyond to the wider Christian community around the world.

The vision in our text — "for all of you are one in Christ Jesus" — was not only for the churches in Galatia. It's not only for our own local congregation in our own community or even for our own denomination. It's not only for those Christians who believe and worship and live in the world in exactly the same way as we do. There is a larger unity in Christ that is greater than the old law, greater than any of our differences.

So as we look to Jesus who has set us free from the law, as we live out our unity in Christ, let us also join together in prayer.

Let us pray: Thanks be to God through Jesus Christ our Lord! Through faith we have a new identity and a new unity, so we pray for our own congregation and for the church around the world; beyond our own denomination to churches of other denominations or no denomination; for the large megachurch and the two or three believers that meet together at home or in a coffee shop. We acknowledge this great mystery of oneness with Christ and with one another, and we ask that we might grow into this mystery and live it out in a new and deeper way. Amen.

Proper 8
Pentecost 6
Ordinary Time 13
Galatians 5:1, 13-25

Freedom Calling

Free! No obligation, no sales person will call! Free! Don't miss this opportunity! Free! Two sets for the price of one! In the world of advertising, something is free if you don't have to pay for it; if there's no money down, no payments to make; if you get something for nothing — or at least two for the price of one!

Galatians 5:1, 13-25 describes a different kind of freedom. It isn't free in the sense of no cost — in fact, this freedom was purchased at the great cost of Jesus' own life. It isn't something for nothing — in fact, it means becoming like slaves ourselves by giving our lives in love and service, just as Jesus did. Yet the apostle Paul dares to call this freedom and challenges his readers — and us — to live that way.

In the English language, an oxymoron is a phrase that puts together two words that would normally contradict each other. As Shakespeare's Juliet says, "Parting is such sweet sorrow." Or in more everyday language, we might give a child some milk in a "plastic glass," or order "jumbo shrimp" at a seafood restaurant. In Galatians, freedom is also presented as a contradiction in terms — it is "costly freedom," a "voluntary slavery."

To understand this oxymoron of Christian freedom, it might be most helpful to think first of freedom as the free gift of God. In this letter to the Galatians, Paul is very clear that this freedom comes from Christ himself. In his opening greeting, he describes Jesus as the one "who gave himself for our sins to set us free" (Galatians 1:4). Chapters 3 and 4 of the letter contain extended arguments on how the coming of Christ has made believers free from the law. So we are no longer slaves to sin, or slaves to the law, but we are children and heirs of God (3:29; 4:7). All this is the free gift of God — we have done nothing to deserve it, we can't buy it at any price, it is ours to receive with faith and gladness.

Yet the other side of the oxymoron reminds us that this free gift for us came only at a very high price. In this letter to the Galatians, Paul is quite clear that Jesus' suffering and death on the cross were critical in securing our freedom. Galatians 3:1 reminds his readers: "It was before your eyes that Jesus Christ was publicly exhibited as crucified!" Galatians 3:13 adds, "Christ redeemed us from the curse of the law by becoming a curse for us."

As a result, Paul's readers and all who believe have been set free — free from slavery to sin, free from the law. Yet for all their very real freedom, they are not free to do whatever they please. Instead, they have entered a kind of "voluntary slavery" where they are to use their new freedom to love and care for one another, to follow God's way instead of their own way.

This was important for the Galatians to hear, because they were in trouble as a community. They were a community in conflict — some argued that the cross of Christ wasn't enough and that you still had to keep all of the Jewish religious laws. Some disagreed over Paul's leadership and some refused to eat with others in the church. The conflict was so severe that Galatians 5:15 describes it as "you bite and devour one another." Verses 19-21 list some of their destructive behaviors: "fornication, impurity, licentiousness, idolatry, sorcery, enmities, strife, jealousy, anger, quarrels, dissensions, factions, envy, drunkenness, carousing, and things like these." They thought they were exercising their freedom by engaging in such behaviors, but they were actually destroying themselves as a community. They were actually destroying one another.

Instead, the biblical view of freedom is not freedom to sin in these ways but freedom from sin. By his life, death, and resurrection, Jesus had set them free. Instead of indulging themselves and behaving in ways that destroyed their relationships with one another, they were to practice the fruit of the Spirit that would strengthen their community: "love, joy, peace, patience, kindness, generosity, faithfulness, gentleness, and self-control" (vv. 22-23).

To a community in conflict that was being destroyed by jealousy, ambition, and spiritual pride, this was good news!

Today, our community is also in trouble — whether we define community as the church or the neighborhood in which we live, our own families and households, or the world community. On so many levels, we also have the tendency to act as if freedom means doing whatever we please, instead of loving and serving one another. As a result, we also "bite and devour" and destroy one another.

In the world community, we destroy one another when the desire for cheap products ignores the exploitation of those forced to provide cheap labor, often child labor. We destroy one another when the desire for more and more leads to deforestation and other forms of environmental damage, when the desire for more and more leads to the expropriation of land to the detriment of local people. We destroy one another when we use far more than our fair share of energy and other resources at the expense of others. Whenever those with power use it for their own benefit without regard for other people, that kind of "freedom" is not really free. Instead, the abuse of power exacts a very high price in the destruction of peace and well-being for communities around the world and for the world community as a whole.

Closer to home, the community of our own neighborhoods and households is also in trouble. Spousal abuse, child abuse, drug addiction, homelessness, and other social ills are still very much with us, and whether or not they touch our lives personally, they affect us directly as part of the communities in which we live. If freedom is defined only as the freedom to do whatever we please, to "live and let live," there will be little improvement on any of these fronts. To address them will require social and structural changes to be sure, but the kind of Christian freedom described in our text for today can also play an important role.

One example from history is the life of William Wilberforce, who at the age of 21 was elected as a British Member of Parliament. The year was 1780. Great Britain was in the middle of the American Revolutionary War. The slave trade was still very much a part of its commercial activities, but that was about to change.

During his second term of office, Wilberforce experienced a Christian conversion, and he became convicted to apply his Christian principles to his political life as well. Within the next several years, he joined the movement to abolish the British slave trade, and soon became a leading spokesman in Parliament. As a result of his advocacy along with the efforts of other social reformers, in 1807, Parliament finally passed legislation to end the slave trade. Wilberforce continued to work against slavery for the rest of his life, and in 1833, a few days before his death, legislation was passed to abolish slavery entirely. The freedom of slaves in Britain was thus accomplished in part by Wilberforce and others exercising their freedom in Christ — not using their freedom for self-indulgence but for the good of others.

You and I may not be another William Wilberforce. We may not have the same gift for speaking, or the same energy, or the same kinds of political connections and opportunities. But you and I can also make a difference in building up good community wherever we are, instead of destroying it. We, too, can use our freedom to love our neighbor as ourselves — within our own households and church, and in the world around us.

Our scripture text challenges us to turn away from "what the flesh desires" to "the fruit of the Spirit." That means replacing hatred with love, replacing strife and quarrels with peace. On a very practical level, it means refusing to engage in adultery or domestic violence, out of respect and faithfulness to our marriage partner. It means saying no to excessive drinking, to recreational drugs, and related excesses in favor of self-control.

It can mean diffusing road rage by exercising patience and allowing another car to go first. It can mean saying a kind word instead of complaining or passing on gossip. It can mean giving generously to relief and development efforts to bring about social and structural changes. It can mean demonstrating self-control in our consumer culture instead of insisting on more and more things at better and better prices. It can mean finding peaceful solutions to bullying instead of automatically striking back in anger.

In the face of serious social ills in our own communities and around the world, these small things may hardly seem like enough.

"What can one person do?" we might well ask. What can one church do? Can we really make a difference to world peace and to the environment or eradicate homelessness in our community and keep everyone safe? Put that way, the needs of the world are clearly beyond any of our small efforts, either as individuals or as a church. Yet you and I have been given the wonderful gift of freedom in Christ, and we are called to use that freedom not to indulge ourselves, but to love and care for our neighbors. In response to that call, we need to at least start somewhere!

One time, Jesus was having supper when a woman came to him with an alabaster jar of expensive perfume. She poured the whole jar of perfume on Jesus' head and anointed him with it. When some of the disciples and others saw what had happened, they became very critical. How could Jesus accept such an expensive anointing? Why wasn't this expensive perfume sold and the money given to the poor instead?

In response to these criticisms, Jesus defended the woman and her actions. He replied, "Let her alone; why do you trouble her? She has performed a good service for me.... She has done what she could" (Mark 14:6-8).

In the same way, as we exercise our freedom in Christ to love and serve others, we may not be able to do much, and what we do may even seem foolish or wasteful to others, but we can do what we can as a service to God. We are free to serve, free to love our neighbor as ourselves, free to express all the fruit of the Spirit.

Free! No self-indulgence, God calls us to use our freedom to love others! Free! Don't miss this opportunity! Free! Now live in the freedom of God's Spirit.

Let us pray: O Spirit of God, by your mercy, may we set aside all jealousy, anger, envy, and other destructive thoughts and behaviors. Fill us instead with love, joy, peace, patience, kindness, generosity, faithfulness, gentleness, and self-control. So may we live in your freedom, for Christ has set us free. Amen.

**Proper 9
Pentecost 7
Ordinary Time 14
Galatians 6:(1-6) 7-16**

On Not Giving Up

A word of encouragement came from an unlikely source the other day in a television interview with Dwayne "The Rock" Johnson. The former football player, wrestler, and now actor was asked about a low time in his life when he was very discouraged about his career and future.

"How did you make your way back from that?" he was asked.

The Rock replied, "You have to put yourself out there. You have to get out there and fail, and learn from your failures."

What advice would you give to someone who is discouraged by life? How do you deal with discouragement yourself? Whether it's a low point in your work life, a serious health issue, a difficult family situation, something you've been working hard at and yet you're not seeing results, doing the right thing in the face of criticism, being disappointed in a friend, struggling in your personal spiritual life, frustrated with the state of the world at large — whatever the source of your discouragement, how do you cope?

Is it enough to tell yourself to get out there and try? Or do we sometimes need a break to get away from it all? Take a hot bath, get a good night's sleep, pray, keep a journal, go for a walk, eat healthy foods, develop a hobby, work out, learn deep breathing — all these things can all help us deal with the discouragement and stress of life. But is there something more for the challenges we face?

Toward the end of his letter to the Galatians, the apostle Paul addresses this very issue. At the beginning of chapter 6, he instructs his readers to work for the good of their community — restoring anyone who has fallen into sin, guarding themselves against temptation, acting responsibly, taking care of one another including those with the responsibility of teaching. It might seem like a lot of obligation — especially in light of Paul's insistence on their freedom in Christ! To counter any sense of discouragement they might have, Paul goes on to offer them encouragement to persevere in this good work.

Beginning in Galatians 6:7 and following, Paul cheers them on. In effect, he says, if you're tempted to give up — don't! Don't be deceived by your feelings of discouragement. Don't be deceived by the difficulties in your life. Don't be deceived by the hardships in this world. Instead, take God seriously and keep on doing good, because one day there will be a great harvest — a harvest of compassion and good works in this hurting world, a harvest in a growing family of believers, a harvest of eternal life. If we do not give up.

Instead of focusing in on ourselves, on our own discouragements and failures, on whatever challenging situation we might face, we need to take the long view. Our immediate concerns are just that — immediate concerns. But they are also part of a much larger context, a bigger picture that can give us hope beyond ourselves.

The rhythm of sowing and reaping was a familiar one in the ancient world. To gain a harvest required the hard work of sowing, the careful work of weeding, the patient work of waiting, and finally the joyfully tiring work of the harvest. Here, Paul applies this familiar process to the spiritual realm: if you sow bad deeds, you will eventually reap corruption, if not in this life then in the next; if you sow to the Spirit — though you may have suffering for a little while and though you may grow weary — you will reap eternal life.

So don't give up — in fact, "whenever we have an opportunity, let us work for the good of all, and especially for those of the family of faith" (v. 10). The churches of Galatia had been disrupted by conflict between those who insisted the Jewish religious law must still be followed and those who did not; between those who recognized Paul's role as an apostle and those who criticized his leadership. Perhaps that's why Paul adds the special note about "the family of faith" — to heal their divisions, they especially needed to work for the good of their own community.

Paul interrupts himself at this point with verse 11: "See what large letters I make when I am writing in my own hand!" There is a break in his train of thought here, but it's a wonderful human detail, a reminder that the book of Galatians is not primarily a theological textbook, even though it reads that way in part. This is a personal and pastoral letter addressed to a church in need of admonishment and encouragement.

In the ancient world, people would sometimes have a scribe write a letter for them, and then at some point they would switch to their own handwriting as a way of making it more personal, and as a guarantee that the letter was genuine. For example, 2 Thessalonians 3:17 says: "I, Paul, write this greeting in my own hand. This is the mark in every letter of mine; it is the way I write." Here in Galatians, it seems that Paul does the same thing — he takes over from his scribe and writes the end of the letter himself.

There's some speculation that Paul wrote in large letters because he needed glasses! But it may have been more deliberate than that. He might have written in large letters to emphasize this next part, the way we might write something all in capitals or bold print. He didn't want anyone to miss this last part of his letter.

In these final verses, the apostle summarizes everything else he's said in Galatians so far: about circumcision and the law, about persecution and the cross of Christ, about crucifixion and new creation. He draws together the different strands of his letter here, but the heart of our passage is verse 15: "For neither circumcision nor uncircumcision is anything; but a new creation is everything!"

For the Galatians, one of the key issues in this letter was that some people were pushing them to follow the Jewish law, specifically circumcision. Established long ago in the time of Abraham and Sarah (Genesis 17:9-14), circumcision was the sign of God's covenant with them and with all the generations that would follow. It was the essential mark of following the law. It was the mark of being a real Jew. And these Galatian Christians were being pushed to practice circumcision as if the cross of Christ was not enough.

Paul writes in large letters to be very clear: To be a Christian you don't have to become a circumcised male baby first. In Christ, there is a new creation, a new order of things. There is a new freedom from the old religious law. Even those who were pushing for circumcision didn't keep the whole law, Paul argued. As he writes earlier in Galatians 3:28: "There is no longer Jew or Greek, there is no longer slave or free, there is no longer male and female; for all of you are one in Christ Jesus." All those distinctions no longer make sense because there is a new creation. Second Corinthians 5:17 says, "If anyone is in Christ, there is a new creation: everything old has passed away; see, everything has become new." Ephesians 2:15 describes it as a "new humanity." Ephesians 4:24 and Colossians 3:10 talk about it as putting on a "new self."

Illustrations of this new creation are often drawn from the natural world. Like the caterpillar that spins a cocoon is hidden away for weeks or months and suddenly emerges as a butterfly. Or the bulb that is planted before the snow of winter that grows into a bright red tulip in the spring. These are variations on Paul's earlier image of sowing and reaping. If you plant a bulb, you get a flower. If you patiently wait, the caterpillar will turn into a butterfly.

But God's new creation in Christ is radically different. It's more like planting a bulb and getting a mountain or the caterpillar turning into a star. It was so radically new that even circumcision with its long history and all its religious significance no longer applied. For Paul and for the Galatians, what counted was being this radically new creation! For us today, what counts is being a new creation!

In my own strength, I can never do enough. In your own strength, you can never do enough. In this world, there is always another failure. Even when we learn from our failures, there is another one just around the corner! There is always more good work to be done. When we face difficulties of various kinds, when the world seems spinning out of control, when our prayer list keeps getting longer and heavier, discouragement can set in.

There is a word of encouragement from our scripture this morning. Don't be deceived by your discouraging feelings! Don't be deceived by your apparently overwhelming situation! Do not grow weary in doing good — you are a new creation! Do not grow weary in dealing with whatever challenge you are facing — you are a new creation!

It's not about trying to make a good impression, which Paul mentions as one motive in our text. That's what he means by making "a good showing" (v. 12) or boasting about the flesh (v. 13) — those are only attempts to look good on the outside. Nor is it about avoiding persecution, which is another motive he mentions (v. 12). Instead of worrying about what looks good, instead of trying to avoid persecution or criticism from others, we need to do the right thing and keep on doing it. For the things of this world — keeping up appearances, being anxious about what others might think — these things are part of the world that has been crucified to me, and I to the world as Paul says here (v. 14). Instead, we live to Christ. We live according to a new creation!

So when discouragement descends and weighs us down, when we weary of doing what is right — yes, let's get a good night's sleep, go for a walk, or try one of the many other healthy options. Over and above those things, let's also remember that our efforts are not in vain — we have a share in the coming harvest of eternal life. Let's remember who we are and whose we are — we belong to Christ, and in him, we are a new creation. In him we receive new strength and life and find God's blessing of peace and mercy if we do not give up.

Let us pray: O God of new creation, re-create your faith and hope in us. Where there is failure, let us sow forgiveness and the restoration of community. Where there is temptation, let us sow perseverance in doing what is right. Where there is pain, comfort. Where there is discouragement, hope. We rest in your peace and mercy. Amen.

Proper 10
Pentecost 8
Ordinary Time 15
Colossians 1:1-14

For All The Saints

What picture comes into your mind when you think of a saint? Is it a portrait of a medieval saint with a golden halo? Or a cartoon character wearing a white robe and carrying a harp standing on a cloud? Is it a solemn picture of someone dressed all in black with a pinched look of long-suffering on his or her face? Do you automatically think to yourself, "It's hard to be a saint — but it's even harder to live with one"?

In the New Testament, the word "saint" is used to describe the early Christians. It actually doesn't have anything to do with white robes or shiny halos or acting holier than thou. In fact, when we read the stories of the early church, we discover that these "saints" had all the same stresses, all the same warts that we do — and maybe even more! They also struggled with questions about how to relate to the world around them; they experienced their own fair share of doubts on matters of faith; they had to work through their own personal disagreements, family problems, and church issues. These saints were real Christians with all of the struggles of real life.

The word "saints" appears three times in Colossians 1:1-14: as part of the opening address (v. 2); with reference to love for all the saints (v. 4); and with thanks to God for the inheritance of the saints (v. 12). The same word appears also in the book of Acts, in Romans, in 1 and 2 Corinthians, and in Hebrews. Throughout the New Testament, the believers are referred to as "saints," which means "holy ones." Just as God is called the "holy one" in the scriptures, those who live as God's people through faith in Jesus are called the "holy ones." It's very similar to the way the early believers acquired the name Christian — not because they were perfectly Christlike, but because they followed Christ. In the same way, the believers were called the saints, the "holy ones" — not because they were perfectly holy, but because they were the people of God, set apart to worship and serve the "holy one" revealed in Jesus Christ.

In the language of the Bible, if we have faith and follow Jesus, we might also think of ourselves as saints today — not as still-life portraits or cartoon characters, but as people set apart for God. If it were up to our own individual effort, none of us would qualify for sainthood. Not you, not me, not Mother Teresa, not Billy Graham. But through faith in Jesus, by the power of his life, death, and resurrection, we can qualify together with the saints past and present and around the world. All those who have faith and follow Jesus are saints in the New Testament understanding of the word.

Now you may or may not know all of the saints in this congregation, let alone all of the saints in a neighboring church, and certainly it's not possible for us to know all of the saints around the world. In the same way, it's quite likely that the writer of Colossians did not know all of the saints he wrote to in the city of Colossae. The first line of the letter identifies the primary letter writer as the apostle Paul. He was well travelled for his day and age and knew many people in many churches. Yet he writes to the Colossians in verse 4: "we have heard of your faith." Theirs was a long-distance relationship. He hadn't seen or experienced their faith because he wasn't there — but he had heard about it. Then later in Colossians 2:1, Paul addresses "all who have not seen me face-to-face" — in other words, those who had not met him personally. He and many of his first readers had never met face-to-face. They knew one another only by word of mouth, only on paper.

Yet in spite of this, Paul writes this letter and offers a prayer for the saints at Colossae. His example is an encouragement to us today — we may not know all of the saints in our own congregation, or in the next church, and we do not know all of the saints around the world, yet we also may be encouraged to pray on their behalf. This is Paul's example in our text from Colossians. It is echoed also in Ephesians 6:18, which instructs us to "persevere in supplication for all the saints."

How can we pray meaningfully for people that we do not know and may have never even met? What can we pray on their behalf? Can we read our text from Colossians as a model for our prayers today? There is much more in this portion of scripture, of course. It has much to say about the grace of God and our hope in Christ. But it also has much to teach us about praying for others — in fact, in these verses prayer is really the main point. Before Paul, the theologian, turns to the big theological ideas in this letter, he is first off Paul, the apostle, praying for the saints, and we would do well first off to be grounded in the kind of prayer that Paul demonstrates.

The apostle focuses on four specific items of prayer: giving thanks for the Colossians' faith and love (vv. 3-4); asking that they might be filled with the knowledge of God's will (v. 9); that they might lead lives worthy of the Lord (v. 10); and that they might be strong and endure and also give thanks (vv. 11-12).

It's interesting to note what Paul does not pray for. He does not give thanks for food or shelter, for families or jobs, or for anything that we might think of as more material or more physical. He doesn't pray for numerical growth in the church or for the success of a particular ministry. Instead, he gives thanks for the evidence of faith and love that he has heard. He prays for growth in knowledge and good works, for perseverance.

It's not wrong to pray more specifically about material and physical needs. Jesus himself taught his disciples to pray, "Give us this day our daily bread" (Matthew 6:11). Jesus himself gave thanks for bread and fish before he fed the crowds (John 6:11). He prayed over those who were crippled and blind so they would be healed. But Jesus' concern was also for those who were spiritually blind and spiritually hungry. When the Samaritan woman came to the well for a bucket of water, he offered her living water for her spiritual thirst (John 4). When he opened the eyes of a man born blind, the man received both physical and spiritual sight (John 9).

So, too, we are challenged in our prayers for the saints to enlarge our prayers even beyond the more physical concerns to pray also for spiritual matters. Yes, we pray for the brother in the church who has just been diagnosed with cancer. Yes, we pray for the sister in the church who is struggling with chronic pain. Yes, we pray for those who are dealing with disaster around the world. Yes, we pray for those who suffer under grinding poverty, oppression, and war. We pray that those who are hungry would receive food. We pray that those who need clean water would gain access to clean water. We pray for relief efforts that provide shelter and clothing and medical care and other forms of practical assistance. These are urgent prayers for urgent physical needs.

Yet, as human beings, we are more than our physical bodies, and Paul's prayer here in Colossians challenges us to pray even beyond the physical. Even as we pray for the physical needs of our world, let us also pray for spiritual concerns. Just as Paul gave thanks for the saints in Colossae, we also may give thanks for the saints in our own church and around the world. We also may pray that they might know God better, that their lives would be pleasing to God, and that they would endure whatever challenges they face.

At the time Colossians was written, the saints did not face the kind of physical suffering that Christians would face some years later under Nero. At this point, their need for endurance was related more to overcoming false teaching. In Colossians 2:4-19, the apostle instructs his readers not to be deceived but to remain firm in their faith. That's the kind of endurance and patience he prayed for them. Yet in the book of Revelation, endurance and patience are applied also to situations of intense persecution (1:9; 3:10; 13:10).

Today, saints around the world and here at home also face the challenges of false teaching, of violence and persecution, and other forms of suffering. So like the apostle Paul, we also may pray for the perseverance of the saints, that they might continue to be faithful. We also may pray for their encouragement and spiritual growth and strength to carry them through the challenges they face. These are urgent prayers for urgent spiritual needs.

For the apostle Paul, praying for the saints in this way was not a one-time exercise. In verse 3, his prayers are plural. In verse 9, they are unceasing. In the same way, we also may continue to pray for those saints we may not know personally — not just one prayer on one Sunday morning, but over and over again, and during the week. Our prayers may also be plural and unceasing.

As we pray beyond ourselves, we are also challenged and changed. We look beyond our own narrow world and our own personal concerns to the concerns of others. We pray for physical needs and also more broadly for spiritual needs. As we pray for others to grow in the knowledge of God, to live in ways that please God, to persevere, we are challenged also to live and grow in the same way. Like the apostle Paul and the Colossian church, may we also demonstrate our love for all the saints and share in our mutual inheritance, by giving thanks and offering our prayers to the one who has redeemed us and brought us into the kingdom of his beloved Son.

Let us pray: O God, we give you thanks for your people, for saints sitting next to us and saints around the world. May they be encouraged in leading lives that please you — in doing good works, in growing in your knowledge, in being strengthened by your power, and giving thanks. For those living in dire physical circumstances, we ask for your special care. By your mercy, grant food to those who are hungry, clean water to those who are thirsty, relief to those who are oppressed or suffering in any way. Even as we pray for others this morning, we know that our prayers also challenge us. So we ask that you would also lead us in good works, in a deeper knowledge of you, in drawing on your strength to endure the challenges that face us, and in giving thanks for all the saints. Amen.

**Proper 11
Pentecost 9
Ordinary Time 16
Colossians 1:15-28**

Sing Praise

Theologian Karl Barth was once asked to sum up his life's work. Instead of quoting from one of his many books, sermons, or university lectures, he responded with the words of a children's song: "Jesus loves me, this I know, for the Bible tells me so." Whether we sing a children's song like "Jesus Loves Me," or a great hymn of the church like "How Firm A Foundation," the songs we sing can express what we believe. In turn, they also shape our understanding of God, of who we are as human beings, and of the world around us.

One of the ancient hymns that expressed the theology of the early church and shaped its understanding is found in the first part of our scripture reading for today. Colossians 1:15-23 is written in regular paragraph form in some English versions of the Bible, but many scholars believe that it was actually an ancient song of praise. Like the well-known hymn, "Fairest Lord Jesus," or a praise song like "Here I Am To Worship," this ancient hymn was meant as praise to the Lord Jesus Christ.

We no longer have the original title or melody of this song. The rhythm of the words doesn't translate well from the original Greek to English, and the words don't rhyme as they do in many of our songs today. But one mark of this ancient hymn that we can still identify is its use of repetition.

The most obvious example of this is the repetition of the word "first" to describe Jesus as "the firstborn of all creation" (v. 15), "the firstborn from the dead" (v. 18), "first place in everything" (v. 18). In the Bible, the word "firstborn" most often refers to the oldest son in the family, quite literally to the one who was born first. So Esau was the firstborn in his family, born just before his twin brother, Jacob. But there is another sense of the word "firstborn" in the Bible, to describe someone who is in first place, who is the greatest. So in Psalm 89:27, God speaks in a vision about David, "I will make him the firstborn, the highest of the kings of the earth." In his own family, David was actually the youngest of eight sons, but as a king he would be "firstborn" in the sense of reigning supreme over all.

In our text for today, Jesus is not "firstborn" in the sense of being created first, before light and darkness and everything else that God created. As the gospel of John points out, Jesus "was in the beginning with God. All things came into being through him, and without him not one thing came into being" (John 1:2-3). This ancient hymn in Colossians makes the same point that all things were created in Christ Jesus, through him, and for him. Jesus was not created first, but he is "firstborn" in the sense of being in first place and reigning supreme over all of creation, over all those who have died, over everything.

A second example of repetition in this hymn is the word "created," which appears once at the beginning of verse 16 and once at the end: "for in him all things in heaven and on earth were created" and "all things have been created through him and for him."

As the eternal Christ, Jesus existed before creation, and he was part of creating all things. He did not begin as the baby born in a manger — he was already present at the creation of heaven and earth. As part of another ancient hymn of praise, Philippians 2:7 says that Jesus "emptied himself, taking the form of a slave, being born in human likeness." The great mystery and wonder of the incarnation is that the Lord of heaven and earth through whom all things were created, humbled himself to become a human being!

A third repetition: in verse 15, Jesus is "the image of the invisible God," and in verse 19 "in him all the fullness of God was pleased to dwell." Today we use the word "image" in a more superficial way — like a politician might get new glasses or a new haircut to change his or her image, or a businessperson might drive a luxury sedan to project a certain image. But the biblical word "image" goes much deeper — it means an "exact replication" — not only on the surface and what we can see, but outwardly, inwardly, and in every way. So Jesus as the image of God, was an exact replication of all God's love, all God's compassion, all God's holiness and righteousness. That's why verse 19 says "in him all the fullness of God was pleased to dwell." The exact words are not repeated, but the idea is the same: having the image of God means having all the fullness of God. In Jesus, the invisible God became visible!

The climax of this ancient hymn comes in verse 20: "And through him" — the one who has first place in everything, who created all things, who is God — through him "God was pleased to reconcile to himself all things, whether on earth or in heaven, by making peace through the blood of his cross." The hymn ends on this high note with Jesus' death bringing peace and reconciling "all things" to God. This peace means forgiveness from sin and being made right with God (Ephesians 1:7; Colossians 1:14), but it also means much more than that. It's a peace that embraces all the war-torn and hurting world around us, peace on earth and peace in heaven, peace for all creation.

For the apostle Paul, these were not just the words of a song once heard and easily forgotten. They were so profound and so full of meaning that he wove them into his letter as he tried to express the mystery and glory of Christ Jesus. The eternal Christ — the firstborn of creation, the head of the church, the one who holds all things visible and invisible together — this is the one who brings about reconciliation for us and for the world.

For the Colossians, that reconciliation meant they were no longer "estranged and hostile" — now they were "holy and blameless." They were no longer engaged in "doing evil deeds" — now they were "irreproachable" and beyond criticism. For Paul's own life, it meant that he was no longer an enemy out to destroy the gospel — now he had become its servant. He even understood his own sufferings in the light of Jesus — not that Jesus' suffering and death on the cross were somehow insufficient, but since Jesus was no longer physically present on earth, Paul saw himself joyfully continuing to suffer for the sake of the church as the body of Christ.

For us too, reconciliation with God is not only something to sing about, not only something to move us to praise, but something for us to live out.

We Live Out God's Reconciliation When We Extend Forgiveness To Others

In 2006, there was a tragic shooting in Nickel Mines, Pennsylvania. A 32-year-old truck driver, who had never gotten over the death of his own daughter a number of years earlier, entered a one-room Amish school and shot ten schoolgirls. Several were killed, others seriously injured, before he himself committed suicide.

The story made headlines in the United States and around the world — both for the tragic shooting and for the way the Amish community responded with forgiveness. In the midst of their own great pain and loss, the Amish people offered words of forgiveness to the family members of the man who shot and killed their children, they attended his funeral, and even contributed to a fund set up for his family.

They did not condone what had happened, but at the same time they refused to compound the tragedy by seeking revenge or becoming bitter. Instead, they lived out the reconciliation they had already received from God and had prayed so often in the Lord's Prayer: "And forgive us our debts, as we also have forgiven our debtors" (Matthew 6:12).

We Live Out God's Reconciliation As We Care For God's Creation

Climate change, world energy prices, and other concerns have highlighted the need to take better care of our environment. "Reduce, re-use, recycle" have become common practices for many, and they make good sense practically, economically, and also spiritually. Economics and politics aside, caring for God's creation is another way of living out God's reconciliation of all things to himself.

This might take the form of growing your own vegetables; composting fruit and vegetable scraps; taking your own re-useable bags to the grocery store; walking, biking, or taking public transit instead of driving everywhere; carpooling; driving a smaller vehicle; recycling newspapers; taking shorter showers; installing more energy efficient lighting. I don't mean this to sound like an environmental awareness campaign, but caring for the environment in these and other very practical ways are reminders of God's reconciliation even with creation.

These might seem like small things — and they are — but they are related to the much bigger idea of God's peace for all creation. Just as we long for and await our final redemption, so the whole of creation is longing to be set free (Romans 8:19-25). Our care for creation is a sign of God's peace to come.

**We Live Out God's Reconciliation When
We Work For Peace In The World**

Violence and warfare are so much a part of our world that we even have special terms for certain kinds of violence: bullying, genocide, ethnic cleansing, terrorism. These and other forms of violence tell us that God's peace has yet to be fully realized in this world. We are still watching and waiting — and we can also work for peace.

That means saying no to bullying, finding nonviolent answers to disagreements, working at solutions to homelessness, building community, feeding the hungry, supporting victim-offender reconciliation efforts, and finding alternatives to warfare. Idealistic? Yes! Overwhelming? Definitely! Impossible? Well, just as impossible as turning Paul from an enemy of the gospel into its servant, as impossible as transforming the Colossians from estranged and hostile to holy and blameless, as impossible as Amish forgiveness, as impossible as caring for all God's creation. We may not be able to do all of these things, or to do them completely, yet once we receive God's grace and peace, we are called to live them out in our real lives in the real world. That's God's reconciliation!

For this ministry of reconciliation that we have been given (2 Corinthians 5:18), we can find hope in the vision of Christ Jesus presented in our scripture text for today. The one who is before all things, the head of the church, who holds all things together, is the one who holds us. In the face of the overwhelming challenges in our world and in our own lives, as we live out God's reconciliation in the world, we can still have hope — not in our own small efforts, but hope for God in Christ Jesus.

Let us pray: Reconciling God, the One who has brought us together in this place and who holds us close, grant us a larger vision of your fullness in Christ Jesus, a larger vision of your work of reconciling all things to yourself. As we seek to live out the reconciliation that we have received, grant us wisdom, courage, and hope. So may our lives be a song of praise to you and reconciliation for the world. Amen.

Sermons On The Second Readings

For Sundays After Pentecost (Middle Third)

Faith, Hope, And Love: From Paul And After Paul

Charles L. Aaron Jr.

Proper 12
Pentecost 10
Ordinary Time 17
Colossians 2:6-15

When God Adds Insult To Injury

So many things separate Christians into groups: denominations, different ways of practicing the sacraments, different understandings of how to organize the church, different attitudes toward social issues like sexuality and money, even different perceptions of who Christ was. With all of that disagreement and separation, what unites us? Is there any common ground among us, other than simply calling ourselves Christians? Are we hopelessly divided, or can we push aside some of these barriers and embrace as brothers and sisters under one Lord?

A little quirk in this passage from Colossians may hold some answers for us. The quirk is highlighted by the way the passage appears in the NRSV translation of the New Testament. In the printing of this passage in the NRSV, there is a small gap between verse 7 and verse 8. It is not a chapter break, of course, but just a small bit of white space. This gap indicates that the NRSV editors thought that a transition occurred between verse 7 and verse 8, so they put a gap. Even though the gap on the page is only a quarter of an inch or so, the gap in subject matter is huge. The gap between what verses 6-7 talk about and what verses 8-15 talk about is significant. This gap has been around from the earliest days of the church. We still live with it. Among denominations, among congregations within denominations, among groups within any congregation, this gap exists, causes friction, and leads to much pain in Christ's body.

What is this gap represented on the page by a tiny bit of white between the blobs of ink that go before and after it? Verses 6-7 encourage us to live our lives in Christ. The NRSV translates it as, "live your lives in him." The image behind the phrase is a common saying among Christians. In any Christian bookstore you can find posters that teach the essence of this phrase from Colossians. Often the saying on the poster goes like this, "If you talk the talk, you have to walk the walk." Colossians exhorts us to walk in Christ. The image of walking makes us think of exercise. We have to keep our relationship with Christ in shape. Walking implies movement. We cannot stay in the same place. Our relationship with Christ takes effort; it is not static. This is sound teaching for all Christians.

The next image in verse 7 comes from the construction industry. Colossians encourages us to be rooted, built up, and established in Christ. To be rooted in Christ is to have a firm foundation. This phrase makes us think of the two builders in Matthew 7:24-27. One built his house on the sand, the other on rock. One house had a firm foundation, the other did not. The basics of prayer, reading scripture, receiving the sacraments, all contribute to a firm foundation. Sometimes we need to clear out space for a foundation by letting go of the past, or coming to terms with the past, so that it does not wreck our foundation. Once we have the foundation, Colossians teaches us to be "built up in him." We are always a work under construction. We may look at our Christian "house" and decide we need to redo the patience room, or remodel the forgiveness wing. We are always under construction.

The final little bit of teaching in this section is the call to abound in thanksgiving. Thanksgiving does not always come easily for us. We have to learn to be thankful. We have to pull thankfulness from within us. We would never say to someone who is in the immediate crisis of grief or tragedy to be thankful, but even in the wake of the disruptions of life, we can choose to be thankful. Being thankful cleanses our souls, lifts our spirits, and eases our hurt. Thankfulness reconnects us to God, even in the valleys of life. Studies have shown that terminally ill people, who know they will not become better physically, can find solace in making note of the things they have to be thankful for.

This part of the passage above the white space is about matters of the heart. These two verses are about our relationship to the risen Christ. They are about building our faith, a sense of trust that comes from within us. A recovering drug addict, writing to her pastor about the faith she and her husband — also an addict — had found, described faith in terms as eloquent as we can find anywhere.

> *For us, faith is not a warm, comforting, fuzzy, feel good. Faith was gritting our teeth, walking through the agony and helplessness of addiction recovery, and continuing to put one foot in front of the other, doing what we were told was the right thing to do, and trusting, praying, and hoping that God was in control, that our tortuous journey would end, and that on the other side was a life worth living. Faith happens when we are at our most desperate moments, and we hold our heads up, doing what we hear God tell us in our hearts, and trusting that he will take care of us. Faith is not smarmy and glowing with happiness. It is an action, not words. It is a very small space we go to within ourselves, among all the bad emotions and feelings and self-loathing — a place that we cling to, while listening to that small voice, the voice of a loving, forgiving power greater than ourselves, outside of ourselves, that will, eventually heal the bad, walk us through the emotions, help us feel better about who we are and what we stand for.*[1]

We do not have to be drug addicts to resonate with that description of faith. Even those who have never taken a drink in their lives can find inspiration in those words. Verses 6-7 of this passage are about that kind of faith. Do we draw upon Christ for the resources we need? Are we building our trust and our thankfulness? Do we let Christ cultivate joy in us? We share these things with all Christians, no matter what denomination, or theological position. We seek to grow this kind of faith whether we are liberal, conservative, or something in between. We can set the foundation of our faith, be rooted and built up in Christ, and abound in Thanksgiving whether we would rather read Billy Graham or Bishop Spong!

Haven't we all known Christians with whom we disagreed, but whose trust, thankfulness and joy we admired? Haven't we known people who faced grief, or disability, or some setback in life with courage and serenity? Didn't they inspire us, even if we didn't see eye to eye with them on every point of biblical interpretation or theology? A pastor friend once told me of a woman named Betty who came to every Bible study the church offered. She and the pastor frequently disagreed on interpretation, but my friend said that her faith was moving. She had arthritis, causing pain with every step she took. Nevertheless, her face glowed with a deep joy that came from within. She taught her pastor that verses 6-7 unite all Christians.

Now, if we leap across the chasm between verse 7 and verse 8, we are in different territory. We are not so much in the realm of our hearts as in the realm of our heads, our intellect. We are not talking so much about the sense of trust, joy, and faith that we feel deep in our souls as we are about what we think in our heads. What we think in our heads is not totally unrelated to what we believe in our hearts. If we believe in an implacably angry God with our heads, we may feel the wrong kind of fear of God in our hearts. We will not have the fear of God that is healthy respect, but the fear that sees God as unapproachable. Nevertheless, two Christians can have different belief systems and still have deep faith in their hearts. Here, Colossians urges us to be careful about what we think.

In the situation behind the letter to the Colossians a heresy has popped up. Behind the heresy is a problem the church confronted early on. Shortly after the beginning of the church, Gentiles began responding to the message about Christ. We should be glad of that, since most of us are Gentiles. The problem we Gentiles brought in was our old belief systems. Gentiles were used to thinking of life in terms of Greek philosophy. Greek philosophers belonged to a number of schools. You may recognize the names of the schools from the ways we used these terms in everyday speech. Among these schools were the Cynic School, the Stoic School, and the Epicurean School. When Gentiles came into the church, they brought these belief systems with them. That was both a good thing and a bad thing. Some of the New Testament writers used Greek philosophy to make a point. If we read the gospel of John we see in the first line, "In the beginning was the word" (John 1:1). There is much Old Testament thought in that sentence, but also some Greek philosophy. The bad thing that Greek philosophy did was to confuse early Christians about how to think like Christians. They had trouble unlearning the Greek philosophy systems.

If you know anything about philosophy, you know that philosophers do their work by asking questions. That is what Socrates did. He would ask a question like, "What is justice?" His students would try to answer. Socrates would point out the weakness of their answers by asking another question. The students would refine their answers. Socrates and his students would keep this up until they came to a better understanding of justice. The question behind the heresy in Colossians is the question, "What holds the universe together?" That is not a question we ask very often, but it was a hot topic to Greek philosophers. One answer to the question is that elemental spirits held the universe together. The Gentile Christians came into the church with the belief that elemental spirits held the universe together. These elemental spirits could keep you from getting to heaven. You had to deal with these spirits now in order to get to heaven later.[2]

This passage in Colossians was written to squelch the worry about elemental spirits. That's why verse 9 says that the whole fullness of deity dwells bodily in Christ. The elemental spirits are nothing. Christ is all you need. Then the passage reminds the first readers that they have been baptized and raised with Christ. They are Christians now. They don't need to worry about elemental spirits. Christ opens the door to heaven for us.

Even though we don't spend too much time worrying in the same way about elemental spirits of the universe, we do recognize that the evil of the world has a spiritual dimension. We know the natural explanations of the suffering of the world, of disease, of drug addiction, of child abuse, of cruelty, of war. Christians should not argue with these natural explanations of the causes of suffering. We go to the physician for treatment for our illnesses. We also recognize a spiritual dimension to the suffering of the world. That is why we pray for people who are sick. In trying to debunk the belief in the scariness of the elemental spirits, Colossians uses a strange image. In verse 15, the passage affirms that God has disarmed the rulers and authorities and made a public spectacle of them. The image behind this phrase is the practice of conquering kings to parade the defeated king and his army through the streets, while those loyal to the victorious king made fun of the defeated army. The passage puts the elemental spirits in a ridiculous light.

How well do we connect to the image of God as one who taunts, gloats, mocks, and even humiliates? Usually, we think of such behavior as kind of immature, sort of like the athletes who do a little dance after a score. Yet that is how Colossians sees God treating the spiritual causes of the world's suffering. We should take hope in that image, because it is an unmistakable image of God's triumph over the suffering we endure now. For all of the things that hurt us now, God will gloat over their defeat, adding insult to injury. We will be the ones standing on the street laughing at the things that used to make us suffer.

This second part of the passage teaches us to be diligent in deciding what we believe. If the first two verses call us to feed our faith as trust of the heart, this half calls us to think through what we believe, not necessarily accepting what we have always heard and thought. We can never agree on everything, but we can agree together to seek the truth, respecting each other's opinions.

What do we do with all of the divisions within the body of Christ? Is there any hope for unity? Can we call other Christians our brothers and sisters, even if we think differently? This passage shows us two things to cling to in that hope. First, we are one in our call to trust Christ in our hearts. We can live and walk in Christ together. We can be rooted and grounded in faith, abounding in thanksgiving together. We can support one another in that effort. I do not have to agree with you to encourage you to feed your faith and trust in Christ. Secondly, we can build on the idea in this passage that one area of thinking that is common to us all is that God is stronger than the evil of the world. God will triumph over evil and suffering. God has ultimately defeated the spiritual dimension to evil and will cause its humiliation. That's a reason to rejoice. That brings us together. That is a message that will feed our hearts and satisfy our heads. Amen.

1. This quote comes from Mrs. Cheryl Anderson, a member of First United Methodist Church of Farmersville, Texas. It was contained in an email sent to the author and used with permission.

2. For a discussion of the elemental spirits, see Lewis R. Donelson, *Colossians, Ephesians, 1 and 2 Timothy, and Titus* (Louisville: Westminster John Knox Press, 1996), p. 38.

Proper 13
Pentecost 11
Ordinary Time 18
Colossians 3:1-11

Killing What Is Already Dead

Every pastor has had this experience. It doesn't have to be the husband in a marriage, but let's just say that it's the husband. The man comes to the pastor's study clutching the report from the physician's office: high blood pressure, overweight, danger of heart disease. The physician has ordered the man to lose weight and to stop smoking. Sitting in the pastor's office, the man swears he is going to take better care of himself. He's said it before, but this time he really means it. He wants to be around for his wife and to watch his kids grow up. The pastor prays with him and wishes him luck. A few days, weeks, or months later, the wife comes in. She is beside herself, angry and hurt. Despite her best efforts, she can't get her husband to stop smoking, to exercise, or to cut back on the calories. "What else can I do?" she pleads.

Is the husband just a hypocrite? Was he full of hot air when he sat in the pastor's office promising he would take better care of himself? Perhaps that is too harsh a judgment. We often feel pulled in two directions. We can't always live up to our own expectations. We are weaker than we want to be. The husband in the pastor's office wants to live, but old habits die hard. It's hard to change. Even with the best of motivation and the best of intentions, our worst selves clutch onto us, refusing to let go.

We can get our heads around the notion of one person trying to quit a bad habit, trying to become a stronger, healthier person. The book of Colossians won't let us stop with just that, however. For the author of Colossians, our attempts to become better people have to fit into the big picture. Colossians is a big picture kind of book.

College students sometimes joke about having been assigned a research topic on "You, the Universe, and Other Related Subjects." That's what Colossians tries to do. Our passage this day begins with the word, "so." In order to understand what comes after the "so," we have to look at what comes before the "so."

Before the "so," Colossians writes of the creation of the universe. We have read the creation stories in Genesis, of course. In the first story, God creates with just a word (Genesis 1:1-5). In the second, God brings water to thirsty ground (Genesis 2:5-6). The book of Proverbs adds the idea of God using Wisdom as an instrument to create the world. With Wisdom itself speaking in first person, Proverbs teaches, "The Lord created me at the beginning of his work, the first of his acts of long ago. Ages ago I was set up, at the first, before the beginning of the earth" (Proverbs 8:22-23). Colossians picks up on the idea and interprets Christ as the instrument of creation, "He is the image of the invisible God, the firstborn of all creation; for in him all things in heaven and on earth were created..." (1:15-16).

Having established that Christ was the instrument of creation, Colossians goes on to say that Christ is also the means of reconciliation, "and through him God was pleased to reconcile to himself all things, whether on earth or in heaven, by making peace through the blood of his cross" (1:20). We are reconciled to God; we are reconciled to each other. That is profound enough. The way Colossians sees it, everything in creation is reconciled to what it should be.

These are both profound ideas. If Christ is the instrument of creation, then the universe has meaning and purpose. It is inherently good, even if it seems that nothing makes sense. If God has reconciled everything in Christ, then all of the conflict we see around us and even within us will eventually pass away. God's good creation will live in harmony. Neither of these ideas is self-evident. Only the eyes of faith can see the inherent goodness of creation. Only Christian hope can affirm that all of the conflict of the world will be healed in God's time, in God's way.

God will achieve this reconciliation through the cross and resurrection. The cross and resurrection change the whole universe.

All of the parts that were in conflict now come together. That's the universe part of what Colossians teaches. After that part, we come in. We participate in Jesus' death and resurrection through our baptism (2:12, 20). In baptism we die to the old self, and we are raised to a new self. I know all of this has sounded complicated, but it really is a nutshell version of what comes before the "so" that begins chapter 3. Christ is the instrument of creation; Christ's death and resurrection reconcile all things; we participate in Christ's reconciling work through our baptism, by which we die to the old self.

Before we go on to talk about what comes after the "so," we have to stop to say something that will sound funny. Some things are true, even though we have to make them true. Does that sound like I don't know what I'm talking about? When we talk about God's ways, when we talk about Christ, we have to admit that some things are true even though we have to make them true. Here's an example. We often affirm in the Christian faith that Christ's church is one. In God's eyes we are one. Nevertheless, we have to make it true that we are one with each other. We have to work together and worship together to make ourselves one, even though we affirm in the faith that we are one.

Here's how this idea of something being true even though we have to make it true works out in this passage. The passage says that we are dead to our old selves. Verse 3 of our passage says, "For you have died, and your life is hidden with Christ in God." That's the part that's true. The part we have to make true is in verse 5, where it says, "Put to death, therefore, whatever in you is earthly." We have died to the old self, but we have to put it to death. Baptism enacts what is true in God's eyes: We have died to the old self. We have to make true what is true in God's eyes. We have to put to death whatever in us is earthly.

The passage has two lists of what to put to death. The first list, in verse 5, concerns our sexual urges. Sex is one of God's most precious gifts. Sex between a husband and wife should be tender and loving. Sex creates a bond, even down to the chemical level of our bodies. Sex sustains love. Throughout much of American society we have taken God's good gift of sex and distorted it, corrupted it.

We have divorced sex from love, we have cheapened it. We have turned sex into recreation, simply another way to relieve boredom. In our distortion of sex, we have robbed even very young girls of their innocence. Our sexual drives are inherently good, part of God's good creation, but they must be treated with discipline. Sex without love leads to hurt and anger, not to the joy and fulfillment that sex is intended to provide. We in the church model for the world the joy of sex inside a relationship of true love. We model the building of a relationship with all of its complications. We model self-discipline and restraint. Self-discipline and restraint are not prudish or self-righteous, but the means by which we enable sex to become the blessing that it was intended to be.

The second list of things to put to death concerns our moods: anger, wrath, bad attitudes (v. 8). Anger can be a necessary part of life. We are angry at injustice, at exploitation, at mistreatment of others. Anger can also be a destructive force. Our anger often comes from the bad things that have happened to us. Anger can be hard to control. Bad tempers often defy our best attempts to tame them. Our anger breaks through the cages we try to put it in and takes over. We say or do things before we realize what has happened. Nevertheless, we must learn to control our tempers. Anger can ruin marriages and friendships. A parent's anger can leave a child with emotional scars for life. Our bad tempers often go back many years to some damage done to us a long time ago. Sometimes we need help understanding our tempers. Scheduling time with a counselor can be the greatest gift some people can give to their families.

Many of the things that can hurt us — our lust, anger, self-destructive ways — can be hard to overcome. That is why this passage talks the way it does. It tells us to put the old self to death. Using the language of murder gets our attention. Our old habits can be like the creature in a science fiction movie that refuses to die. That is why we should use every weapon in our arsenal to kill the parts of us that hold back our spiritual growth. Prayer, Bible study, counseling, willpower are all part of becoming the self God calls us to be.

When Colossians tells us to put to death the old self, it is not telling us we are worthless. It is telling us that we can become new selves, new people, better, happier, stronger, healthier people. We have to put away the old self so that the new self can grow. This passage tells us in verse 1 to seek the things that are above, but it doesn't tell us what those are until verse 12. Verse 12 draws on the other image that the passage uses. One part of the passage tells us to kill the old self. The other part of the passage tells us to strip off the old self, like taking off old, worn out clothes (v. 9). We put on the new clothes of compassion, kindness, humility, meekness, and patience. Colossians goes on to tell us to show love and to let peace reign in our hearts (vv. 14-15). The reason to strip off the old clothes of lust and anger is to make room for things like compassion. That is the new self God can create us to be. We should not despair if we have been unable to build this kind of self, full of kindness and compassion. We may have to make small steps to become more loving and more peaceful, but God can get us there. God can work in us, making us into a self we never imagined.

    God is reconciling all things in Christ. We are invited to come along. With good aim, we can kill the parts of ourselves that hurt us and others. We can grow a self full of compassion, love, and peace. Verse 4 of this passage has a curious comment. It says that in the resurrection when Christ is fully revealed we, too, will be revealed. Which self will it be? When Christ is revealed will our old self, angry and self-indulgent be revealed, or will it be the peaceful, loving self? Let us begin now to build the self we want to be revealed in the resurrection. Amen.

Proper 14
Pentecost 12
Ordinary Time 19
Hebrews 11:1-3, 8-16

The Assurance Of Things Hoped For

In the movie, *Cast Away*, Tom Hanks' character, Chuck, is stranded on a desert island in the Pacific Ocean. To keep himself company, he finds a volleyball that has washed up from the wreckage of the plane he had been flying in before becoming stranded. Chuck paints a face on the volleyball with his own blood and names him "Wilson." Wilson becomes Chuck's only companion while he remains on the island. He talks to and sometimes even *for* Wilson to keep himself company during the lonely months. After four years on the island Chuck builds a raft that he hopes will take him out to sea, where maybe someone will find him. He puts Wilson on a wooden post on the raft, because he can't leave without his friend. At one point, as they are floating on the sea, far from the island, Wilson falls off his post while Chuck is sleeping. When Chuck awakens, he notices that Wilson is missing. He looks out at Wilson on the horizon. We see the depth of his attachment to Wilson by the anguish he feels trying to recover the wayward volleyball. Despite his efforts, he cannot reach Wilson. Chuck cannot let go of his raft, because he might not be able to return to it. He watches helplessly as Wilson bobs off into the distance, gone forever.

The author of Hebrews is afraid that the same thing that happened to Wilson is happening to Christians. He fears that the Christians, perhaps in Rome, who are reading the letter, might drift away from the faith (2:1). The whole purpose of the book of Hebrews is to swim out to rescue church members who are bobbing off into the distant horizon away from the faith they have professed. Perhaps they are weary of persecution. Perhaps they were tired of waiting for God to establish the full dominion, the time when God will bring peace and justice to all creation. Early Christians had been promised such a time, but the wait was beginning to weigh on them. At least some of them wanted to go back to their old faith. Maybe they just weren't as diligent as they once had been. In any case, they are in danger of drifting away.

The author of Hebrews remains a mystery to us, but he was passionate about bringing the church back to a strong, vibrant faith. The author of Hebrews was a brilliant person who had studied deeply. He draws on the Greek translation of the Old Testament, philosophy, and Jewish traditions to convince his readers to maintain their faith.

Before we zoom in on chapter 11, our text for today, it might be helpful to look just briefly at what the rest of the book of Hebrews accomplishes. We can't really understand any one part of Hebrews until we get some understanding of what the whole book is trying to accomplish. We often call this book the letter to the Hebrews, even though it doesn't start off like a letter. It may well have been a sermon. Whatever it was, the author dives right in from the very first verse. Without any pleasantries, the letter launches into a deep reflection on who Jesus Christ was. Within the first three verses, the author associates Jesus with prophets (God speaks through the son, v. 1), priests (purification for sins, v. 3), and kings (seated in majesty on God's right hand, v. 3). In the first chapter, the author uses some of the most creative ideas in the New Testament to describe Christ's divinity. Christ is the reflection of God's glory, the exact imprint of God's very being. Christ is the instrument of creation. With this cascade of ideas, the author firmly establishes Christ's place in the Godhead. Then, in the second chapter, the author works just as hard to communicate the humanity of Jesus. Jesus became lower than angels, tasted death, endured testing and suffering. Throughout the book, these two aspects of Christ's identity — exaltation and humanity — affect every argument the author makes for maintaining faith, for not drifting away. The very reflection of God's glory knows what it is like to live in our skin.

When we come to chapter 11, the author recounts the history of some of the heroes of the faith from the Old Testament. Chapter

11 condenses these stories into a highlight reel. He writes out of a conviction that these stories feed our faith. The church is coming to the point where not many of us know these stories by heart anymore. Hebrews encourages us to reread them.

He introduces these stories with a remarkable sentence. "Now faith is the assurance of things hoped for, the conviction of things not seen" (11:1). In a sense, each part of the sentence reinforces the other parts. Let us start with "things hoped for." We hope that God forgives our sins through Christ. We hope that God will heal creation of its sin and pain. We hope that God will redeem our present suffering. We hope for these things because of who Christ is, as Hebrews has worked so hard to explain to us. These things are still not seen, because they remain to be fulfilled. Faith is the persistent trust that these things will come to be in God's time, even though we do not see them. Faith keeps us going when the hope is not yet realized. Our faith can be strong because the hope is so well grounded in Christ. Faith feeds our hope and hope feeds our faith.

In looking back to the Old Testament, Hebrews begins with creation, "By faith we understand that the worlds were prepared by the word of God, so that what is seen was made from things that are not visible" (11:3). Sometimes the creation can inspire us. That anything exists at all is a miracle. Looking at God's creation can give us new insight into God's power and sense of beauty. A mountain, the ocean, the stars at night, the tender fragility of a newborn bird can touch something deep inside of us, and our faith perks up.

After talking briefly about Abel and Noah, he lifts up the example of Abraham. Abraham was the great patriarch who left what was familiar and comfortable to set out for the place God instructed him to go. His story begins in Genesis 12:1, where the Lord tells him, "Go from your country and your kindred and your father's house to the land that I will show you." Abraham set out into an uncertain future. He went in obedience, in trust, in a sense of adventure. The Abraham story raises an important question for us. Can our faith grow if we are too comfortable? Do we not have to take some risks in order to find our faith? Don't we have to venture out into the unknown if our faith is to stretch? Does faith grow in the soil of comfort? We do not have to move physically to grow our faith, but if we find ourselves too comfortable — in our thoughts, in our attitudes, in our ministries, in our relationship with God — will our faith grow into what it could become?

Hebrews wants us to understand something about these heroes of the faith. Despite their obedience and their courage, their trust and devotion, they did not experience fulfillment of their hopes and expectations. They only saw them and greeted them from a distance (v. 13). Abraham went through trouble after trouble, threat after threat, test after test. As just one example, when Abraham arrived at exactly the place God told him to go, he encountered a famine (12:10). Striking out with God on a great adventure wasn't always easy. Hebrews wants to make that point, because when his community has experienced persecution and trouble, they have been tempted to drift away.

We may feel a similar temptation. Church members rarely decide that they no longer believe the elements of the faith. They don't sit down one day and decide that they don't believe in God anymore. They don't consciously decide that the church has no mission. They don't decide that Jesus was just a man after all. That kind of thing is rare. Christians move away from the church in a different process. They tend to drift away. Too often, this drifting away happens when youth leave high school after years of participating in church. They go off to college, only to drift away from church. Other things seem more interesting, more helpful. Without the familiarity of their home church they don't have the motivation to get involved. People sometimes drift away slowly, one turned-off alarm clock at a time. Sometimes one bad experience at church, one argument, or one incident of hurt feelings will cause people to drift away. A change in pastors at a congregation will cause some people to drift away.

Underlying these reasons may be the feeling that we don't see much happening. Rather than ushering the dominion of God, the church seems to fall into a routine. What Hebrews may be calling us to do is to see how God is working even in the routine, even in the ordinary, even when it seems like nothing much is happening.

If we find ourselves tempted to drift away, how exactly do we feed our faith? How does faith grow stronger? Where do we find the assurance of things hoped for? True faith is a matter of both head and heart. Faith is more than simply checking the "Yes" box for a set of doctrines. Nevertheless, Hebrews teaches us that what we believe can feed the faith of our hearts. Hebrews calls us to ask ourselves what exactly we believe about Christ. Do we believe, even if we do not fully understand how it is true, that Christ was the reflection of God's glory? Do we believe that Christ has entered our world and tasted both the joys and agonies of being human? When we look back at some moment of humanness that makes us wince, do we believe that Christ understands that moment, and became like us to redeem it? If we do believe those things, what should we do about it?

If we accept that Christ is somehow both divine and human, Hebrews then invites us to wrestle with these Old Testament stories of faith. Each of the stories has its own nuance. We can read them and ask which one of them fits our situation the best. Which one has the most to teach us in our particular circumstances? From Abraham we learn that faith grows best in a soil of risk. We also learn that we may not see results right away. We may not know until the resurrection how God was working to use and redeem our efforts. In spite of the uncertainty we keep going. Being willing to wait until God's time to see the results is the assurance of things hoped for. Faith is maintaining confidence in God, even when we are still hoping. When we wrestle in our heads with what we believe and step out in faith, our hearts will follow. The sense of trust can begin to grow.

If we hang in there and wrestle with our faith until we have strengthened our faith, until we trust in our hearts, we will find something that surprises us. We draw on the heroes of faith like Abraham. When we restore our faith, when we swim back to the shore, no longer drifting, we may find that we take Abraham's place. Much to our shock, we become a hero of faith to someone else. Amen.

Proper 15
Pentecost 13
Ordinary Time 20
Hebrews 11:29—12:2

Running With Perseverance

United Methodist Bishop, Robert Schnase, tells of his hobby as a "serious runner." He reports that people often ask him how to get started on a running program. He recounts the usual practice of people trying to become serious about running. The typical start date is January 1, as part of a New Year's resolution. The resolution holds fast for the first week, with an early rise and an eager first few jogs. The problems pop up "during the second week when the alarm screams them awake at six, they tell themselves, 'There's nothing wrong with running at seven rather than six,' and so they sleep another hour." Before long the running turns to walking and then fizzles out altogether by the second month at the latest. Bishop Schnase compares this fizzled running program to our attempts to become serious about reading the Bible.[1]

Vowing to read the Bible all the way through each year is only one way that we attempt to deepen our spiritual lives. We have to admit that, when it comes to our faith, most of us are like the runners that Schnase describes. We start well, but we fade over time. We may not completely drop out, but we don't push ourselves. We too easily become content with the level of spirituality, the Bible knowledge, the prayer life, the justice-seeking, the mission commitment that we have.

This passage from Hebrews specifically calls us to seek a deeper level for our faith, to push ourselves, to test our limits. Using specifically the language and imagery of running a race, the passage calls us to perseverance. Nurturing our faith is a distance run, and

Hebrews calls us to pace ourselves, not to give up, and to run with all that we have.

The problem for most of us is that we are not much up for a distance run. Let's face it, we live in a world of instant gratification. We can communicate across long distances in a flash. The cable channels practically report the news before it happens. Food pops out of our microwave in no time. Television conditions us to believe that every problem can be solved in an hour. We don't know much about endurance anymore. We know from other realms of life that perseverance pays off. If we want to speak a foreign language, we must keep at it. The pay off comes when we can converse with a native on our vacation. If we want to play an instrument, we must practice our scales. The pay off comes when beautiful music flows from within us, brought to life by the instrument we have mastered.

True faith needs perseverance. When we look at our own spiritual lives, we may be attracted to the high points. Maybe we can look back at a time when we felt God's presence in a strong, clear, unmistakable way. Maybe we experienced that when we first joined the church. Maybe it was a particular worship service. We remember a special Christmas program or a children's cantata. Perhaps, at some point an indescribable joy washed over us. We wish that feeling would last forever. Such feelings don't last. We look back and wish they would come again. When that feeling doesn't happen for us all over again, we need perseverance. We have to keep our faith going for the long haul.

Hebrews tells us that in this distance race, we need to lay aside every weight. Often that is our problem. No one would try to run a race carrying a weight. Yet, life weighs us down in our race to a strong faith. We could each name our own weights. Sometimes the joyful experiences of the past seem too long ago, with too much time in between. We may look at our past and see mostly times of hurt and brokenness, disappointments, rejections. Stress weighs us down. The craziness of the world weighs us down. We look out at the world and it seems as though things are not becoming any better. That can affect our faith. Arguments and disagreements in the church can weigh us down. At some point in the church, something or someone will hurt our feelings. It is hard to build our faith with all of these things weighing us down. We have trouble running with perseverance. We need a faith that sustains us. We need a faith that doesn't fade away in the middle of the race.

Hebrews assures us that we do not run this race only on our own power. We have help. Throughout chapter 11, the author of Hebrews recounts the stories of the heroes of the Old Testament. He includes the most obvious examples, Abraham and Moses. For these two prominent figures, the author gives brief descriptions over a few verses. At the point where our passage starts today, he picks up speed. In rapid-fire pace he tells of some of the lesser-known characters in scripture. Each incident receives only one verse. He condenses the entire exodus event into one verse about the people crossing the sea. The walls of Jericho fall; Rahab was obedient; then comes Gideon, Barak, Samson, Jephthah, David, and Samuel. After the names come the deeds: administered justice, obtained promises, shut the mouths of lions.... He goes so fast, we do not even know if the lion story refers to Samson or Daniel. He does not even bother with names after that. He simply recounts these wonderful faith stories. By the time he is finished, we are overwhelmed with what faith has done in these heroes. We don't have time to think about one deed before the next one flies at us. Just look at what faith can accomplish! Faith can quench fire, endure torture, hold up under mocking, and survive poverty. By the time he finishes in verse 38, we realize that faith can do anything!

These heroes of the faith are our inspiration. They hammer home the message that nothing the world can throw at us can get us down. Whatever we go through, these heroes have been through worse. Their faith held up; they persevered. We can persevere, too!

These heroes are more than just a distant inspiration for the author of Hebrews. They are with us now. The author presents a wonderful image beginning in chapter 12. We are in the stadium, about to begin our race, the long distance, grueling race that will require a persevering faith. We are at the starting line; the gun is about to go off. These heroes of the faith are there in the stadium with us! The author calls them a "great cloud of witnesses." Where are these heroes of the faith? They are not dead and gone. They are in the stands, cheering for us! We don't run this race alone. Abraham, Moses, David, Samuel, and even Rahab the redeemed prostitute, are rooting for us to keep going. I've talked to people who run the Susan Komen Race for the Cure every year. Cancer survivors will line the streets cheering for the runners. Those who run the race tell me that it really does help. So, if our faith is flagging, let us look up in the stands and see who is cheering for us.

Perhaps even these heroes of the Old Testament are not enough for us. We may need some modern day examples. One of these surely would be Patty Waterman, a United Methodist pastor from Illinois. In her mid-forties Waterman answered the call to ministry. Shortly after she began the process leading to ordination, she discovered that she had ovarian cancer. She undergoes chemotherapy once a month, sapping her strength. Nevertheless, she does not let the flu-like symptoms keep her down. She does her pastoral work with joy and grace, despite her cancer. That's perseverance. We cannot all be superwoman and maybe we shouldn't try. But, we can draw on the faith that doesn't let cancer win every battle.

If Old Testament heroes and modern day heroes are still not enough, Hebrews has one more example. Hebrews has many ways of describing who Christ is for us. He uses again one of those ways here. He calls Jesus the pioneer of our faith. Hebrews has been clear that Jesus has gone through the temptations and trials that we face. Jesus has run the race of perseverance. A pioneer is one who goes first, who cuts the trail, who hacks through the wilderness to make a path where there is no path. Jesus is the pioneer of our faith. If we go to a place we think no one has been before, Jesus has been there.

For what things do we need the perseverance of faith? Do we have intellectual doubts that nag us? Let us hang in there and have faith even without all of the answers. We can still trust God. Have our bodies begun to turn on us, causing us pain, leaving us weak? Let us persevere in faith, knowing that our spirits can transcend our bodies. Are we disappointed in ourselves, not seeing the spiritual growth that we wish we could see? Let us not despair. God is still at work in us. Are we weary of the hassles of the church, have our feelings been hurt, do we grow tired of committee work and bickering? Let us not give up. God still works through the church in spite of all of its problems. Let us persevere. Let us keep going. Are we ready to give up in the fight for justice? Does it seem as though we never get anywhere trying to help the poor and make our world fairer for all people? Let us not throw in the towel. Justice is God's will as well as ours. For the long run, nothing can thwart God's will.

We are running our faith race with a great cloud of witnesses cheering us on. We run with the inspiration of others who have faced the same problems we have. As we are running, we may find that our energy is low, and we want to drop out. If our feet are weary, our sides are aching, and we are gasping for breath, let us look up. Just ahead of us on the track is one who has run this race before. He is the pioneer of our faith. He is leading the way. If we look to him, we can keep putting one foot in front of the other. Amen.

---

1. Robert C. Schnase, *Five Practices of Fruitful Congregations* (Nashville: Abingdon, 2007), pp. 66-67.

**Proper 16
Pentecost 14
Ordinary Time 21
Hebrews 12:18-29**

God As A Consuming Fire

Every pastor sees the damage that is done to people by too heavy an emphasis on God's judgment. The damage often begins in childhood. Because children can be rambunctious, adults too often try to frighten them into obedience. The church is no exception to this practice. Parents sometimes report that their children have come home from Sunday school or vacation Bible school in tears and trembling because some misguided adult had tried to frighten them into faith with horrifying images of the punishment that awaited them after death. The adults behind such fear-mongering often claim that they have to do this in order for the children to understand.

Such tactics might get a quick walk down the aisle, but the damage shows up later. Some people in their seventies, eighties, and even nineties were introduced to the faith this way. They heard judgment without grace. They adjusted their behavior to meet the expectations of the adults, they joined the church, but weighed down by the fear, they never learned to love God. God remained someone to fear. Love had trouble breaking through the shell of the fear.

We cannot deny that the Bible consistently proclaims God's judgment. Throughout both testaments God judges sin, confronts our injuries and exploitation of others, calls us to faithfulness, and threatens punishment for disobedience.

If we look at the very earliest stories in the Bible, we see a remarkable portrayal of God. In the second of the two creation stories, the one that actually was written first, God is portrayed in a tender, attractive way (Genesis 2:4b-17). From the newly watered ground, God scoops up some mud and gently forms the first human, breathing life into his nostrils. God places the new person into a garden full of all that the human will need and delights for the senses. God cares about loneliness and so creates companions for the human, finally making another person for companionship. You cannot find a sweeter picture of God anywhere in scripture. Still, in the middle of the garden is the tree of the knowledge of good and evil. The fruit of that tree comes with a warning. If the human, loved and cherished by God, eats of the fruit of the tree, he will die. The threat of death hangs over this beautiful story.

When the Old Testament prophets proclaim judgment, they don't sugarcoat it like Genesis does. The prophets thunder about a God angry at the treatment of the poor, idolatry, greed, and soulless worship. If we want to choose a representative, maybe Amos is the most blistering of all. When the Lord roars, the pastures wither and the tops of mountains dry up (1:2). Amos compares God's punishment to being eaten by a lion; all that will be left over will be a few bits of flesh that the lion didn't bother with (3:12). We must admit that that is a fearsome image of God.

Church members will often say that the God of the Old Testament is judgmental, but the God of the New Testament is loving and forgiving. When we come to the New Testament, however, the images of judgment do not go away. Matthew repeats the phrase throughout his gospel that sinners will be thrust into the outer darkness, where there is weeping and gnashing of teeth (3:50; 22:13). We gnash our teeth when all is lost, when we feel helpless, when we have played all of our cards and still lost. Paul cautions that we are storing up wrath for ourselves on the day of wrath (Romans 2:5). We cannot oversimplify the portrayal of God in the New Testament.

Hebrews is no exception. The last verse of this passage describes God as a consuming fire. What a frightening image! We would be hard-pressed to decide which was more terrifying, the powerful jaws of a lion, or the scorching heat of a fire.

This verse from Hebrews is probably an allusion to the end of Moses' life. The people are about to cross from the wilderness wandering into the promised land. Moses knows he will not be allowed to go with them. Moses warns the people not to forget their covenant, because God is a devouring fire, a jealous God (Deuteronomy 4:21-24). Once more, the Bible portrays God's judgment as a means of controlling the behavior of the people.

We have here just a small sample: The threat of death, a snarling lion, the day of wrath, a consuming fire. We must take seriously these messages and images from scripture. While we are taking them seriously, we must be careful with them. We can make tragic mistakes with these images from scripture. We ignore them at our spiritual peril. If we use them wrongly, to frighten and control, we can crowd out the messages of God's love.

What we should never forget is that the messages of God's love come through the scriptures even more clearly and strongly than the messages of God's judgment. God threatens Adam and Eve with death if they eat the fruit, but they don't die. God drove them out of the garden and punished them, but God also made clothes for them. God continued to love and care for them, even after their disobedience. The prophets, for all of their thundering, teach God's love, also. Hosea could be almost as harsh as Amos, but he teaches about God's anguish over our sin. "My heart recoils within me; my compassion grows warm and tender. I will not execute my fierce anger; I will not again destroy Ephraim; for I am God and no mortal, the Holy One in your midst, and I will not come in wrath" (Hosea 11:8b-9). In Deuteronomy, right after the scary talk of God as a consuming fire, comes this heartening promise, "Because the Lord your God is a merciful God, he will neither abandon you nor destroy you" (Deuteronomy 4:31). Matthew talks of weeping and gnashing of teeth but also of a light burden and an easy yoke (Matthew 11:30) and of a risen Christ who will be with us always (28:20).

So, throughout the Bible messages of God's love and forgiveness, mercy and care are intertwined with messages of God's judgment and punishment. We cannot separate them out, keeping only what we want. In the movie *Wall-E*, the little robot finds a diamond engagement ring in its original box. He throws the ring away and keeps the box! We might wish we could throw the judgment passages away and keep the love, but that would not be the best thing for our souls, for our spiritual development. The passages about judgment are there for a reason.

To get at that reason, we can start with our own experience. In any attempt to master a craft or become an expert in a field, we must push ourselves. Often a coach or a teacher becomes the one who drives us to do our best. A music teacher prods a student to work on pieces the student thinks are too hard. A good coach will not let an athlete settle for a good enough effort. A good teacher will put just the right amount of pressure on a student to get the student to think more deeply. A wise teacher or coach with just the right amount of fear inducement can motivate the student/athlete to practice just hard enough, study just a few minutes longer, strain the muscles just a bit more to bring out the best. A mean, controlling bully will not work, but too soft a mentor will leave us just short of the mark. Much the same idea works in child-rearing. That is tricky business. Being too lenient can spoil a child, being too harsh does not give the child enough room to grow. Children need a healthy combination of love and respect for their parents.

The images of God's judgment serve another purpose as well. We have to face it. God needs to get our attention. We are too indulgent with ourselves. We buy our own excuses. We continue to do dumb things that we should know won't work. We buy gas-guzzlers, exceed the speed limit, and then wonder why the price of gas is so high. We continue on a self-destructive path, heedless of the consequences. If the images of God's judgment get our attention, then they are worth it.

The images of God's judgment remind us that our sin hurts people. When we exploit other people, when we neglect the poor, when we act selfishly, God cares about the damage we do. God cares about those who are stepped on in life, who are shoved out of the way. God's judgment is rooted in God's care for those we hurt. If these images of God's wrath motivate us to treat people better, they have done their job.

Now, maybe we are ready to read these words in Hebrews about God as a consuming fire. We must admit, this can seem to be a terrible image. Fire is a good thing, bringing heat, light, and protection. A *consuming* fire sounds different, though. Americans saw all we wanted to see of consuming fires on September 11, 2001. We have seen what fires do to people's homes and possessions. We have seen what fire has done to Iraq war veterans attacked with IEDs (Improvised Explosive Devices, used in Iraq). In some cases, their ears, hands, and even faces have been burned off. How can we see a loving God in such an image?

A young pastor, new to the country, once saw a fire raging on a neighbor's field near the parsonage. Rushing breathlessly to the fence the pastor called out desperately, trying to get the neighbor's attention. The old farmer who owned the land ambled out with a smirk on his face. "Relax, son," the farmer said, "it ain't hell yet!" The farmer had, of course, set the fire himself. He was burning the stubble from his field. It was the fastest, easiest, cheapest way to do it. Without the fire, the field would have no growth next season. God's consuming fire does not have to leave us scarred and disfigured. God's consuming fire can burn away the stubble in our souls, preparing us for new growth. That may not seem a pleasant image, but it may be what we need to hear.

Let us take seriously the images of God's judgment in scripture. Let us learn from them. Let us always balance these images with images of God's mercy. In Hebrews, the author passionately describes Jesus as one who became human to understand us, show us the way, and to redeem us. That is a God of love. A woman preparing for the ministry once wrote to her supervising pastor in the candidacy process. She exuberantly exclaimed that she was "head over heels in love with God."[1] In our teaching to other people, especially to children, let us remember that such an attitude is what we want. We cannot get there only on fear. A quaking fear of God is not right. We want people in church to learn to love God. We have a very good reason for doing that. From cover to cover, the Bible teaches that God is head over heels in love with us. Amen.

---

1. This quote comes from Mary Martin, a candidate for ministry in the North Texas Annual Conference. The quote is from an email sent to the author and used with permission.

Proper 17
Pentecost 15
Ordinary Time 22
Hebrews 13:1-8, 15-16

The Unchanging Christ In A Changing World

When we come to church, we usually do not come primarily to learn about doctrine. We come to find inspiration, to lay our hurts at the altar, and to draw strength from the fellowship. Doctrine can seem kind of dry. Doctrine causes arguments and who needs more of those? The book of Hebrews has been committed to the idea that a proper understanding of doctrine sustains our faith and keeps us from drifting away from it. Our passage for today has something important to say about how we understand Christ, and why it matters for our faith.

Hebrews is a puzzling book. We have no idea who wrote it. Even though the end of the book names some of Paul's associates, the author doesn't think or write anything like Paul. Father Origen, a second-century theologian and Bible scholar, famously said that only God knows who wrote Hebrews. We don't know for sure who first read it. It is not addressed to any particular group like Paul's letters, which are addressed to specific people or churches. We are not even sure what it is. We often call it a letter, but it doesn't start like a letter. Some people think it was a sermon, a rather long sermon at that.

If Hebrews is a sermon, the preacher is winding up by chapter 13. We are almost to the closing hymn and then racing to get in line at the restaurant. Experts at communication tell us preachers that people remember the beginning of a sermon and the end of a sermon. What's in the middle kind of fuzzes out. At the end of this sermon, the preacher announces how the gospel he has proclaimed affects the way Christians should live. That is a typical pattern for some of the books of the New Testament. Most of Paul's letters follow such a structure. First Paul describes our situation, the trap of sin we are caught in. Then he announces what Christ has done for us, how Christ has set us free. Finally, Paul declares the great "therefore." Therefore, live your lives this way. Hebrews has repeated a certain pattern throughout the book. He announces who Christ is and then exhorts the readers to do something about it. Now he has come to the end of the sermon. He has marshaled every argument to try to keep his readers from drifting away from the faith. Now he is finished, and he closes with a series of admonitions about what a Christian life should look like.

He starts with what Jesus called one of the two greatest commandments: that we love one another. We can never hear that too often in the church! Love sustains us. How many times has a hug or a kind word lifted our spirits? In how many ways has the love of a congregation kept a grieving person from collapsing? Love smoothes over differences, love brings reconciliation, love causes us to go the extra mile, and love creates friendships between people who have nothing in common. "Let mutual love continue" the preacher says. How much we need that!

He exhorts them to show hospitality. Hospitality is sort of a branch office of love. Hospitality is love for someone you don't know. Hospitality blazes a new trail of love, creating a relationship that wasn't there before. Let us never underestimate the power of hospitality. A young Hispanic boy, the son of immigrants, became a street child. He did what he had to do to survive. Living on the street, with no one to look after him, he became addicted to drugs. His life was headed nowhere. In an act of pure hospitality, a Presbyterian pastor took in the young street child, nurtured him, and put him back on the right path. That young street child grew up to be Reverend Harold Recinos, Ph.D. He is a United Methodist pastor and a professor at Perkins School of Theology in Dallas, Texas. Hospitality saved a boy's life, created a new person, and gave a gift to the church through Recinos' teaching and writing.

The preacher narrows hospitality down even further. He admonishes us to visit those in prison. The church is called to go into prisons. We are called to visit places of despair and seeming hopelessness. We are called to bring light to darkness. He tells us how we are to go into the prisons. We are not to go in judgment or in condescension. We are to go as those who are in prison ourselves. We are to look into the hearts of those we visit and imagine ourselves in their shoes.

The author of Hebrews could never have known how relevant his next message might be to American Christians in the twenty-first century. He tells us to minister to those who have been tortured. How can our country, which has claimed such a legacy of Christian influence, have allowed itself to get caught in the web of torture? What Hebrews calls us to is so necessary for us, in case we ever are tempted again. He says that we should see ourselves in those being tortured. If we see a fellow child of God in our enemy, we will know not to torture. We will also know that if we torture another person, our leaders open that door and pay for it with our money, then we will be the ones who are changed. The danger of torture is not so much what it does to the one being tortured, but what it does to the one committing the torture. Let us open our ears and hear these words.

He follows these exhortations with teaching about sex and money, two important ways that we are called to be faithful. We all know how much hurt is caused by sexual infidelity. We see the pain splashed across our television screens, as celebrity marriages crumble from unfaithfulness. Let the church demonstrate to the world that we can practice self-discipline and build committed relationships.

What we do with our money is a reflection of our faith. Do we give to God in gratitude? Do we give to our neighbor in love? Do we center our lives around Christ or on money? Hebrews calls us to show the world our faith by how we live.

In the midst of these ethical teachings, verse 8 stands out. Sort of out of nowhere, verse 8 announces a deep statement of theology. In this case, it announces something important about who Christ is. "Jesus Christ is the same yesterday, today, and forever." We could chew on that statement for several sermons, but let us reflect on it for this one sermon.

I want to suggest that, based on the book of Hebrews itself and our own life experience, we should have a two-handed response to this statement from Hebrews. We hate two-handed responses! They sound wishy-washy, as though we can't make up our minds. One of our presidents said that he wished he could find a one-handed economist. Every time he tried to get information about fiscal policy from economists, they always answered, "Well, on the one hand the economy might pick up; on the other hand, the economy might go soft." He wanted an economist with one hand.

I have a two-handed response to Hebrews' assertion that Jesus Christ is the same yesterday, today, and forever. On the one hand, we rejoice in what that statement affirms. We need a sense of stability in our lives. We Christians need something to unify us. We need something we can count on. The world seems as if it changes overnight. Technology, world events, oil prices, and a host of other things all seem to want to pull the rug out from under us.

In the midst of all that change, Christ gives us an anchor, something to keep us from being tossed about by all of the change. No matter how modern we become, or how sophisticated, we still look back to a man who lived 2,000 years ago as the pioneer of our faith. Jesus the Christ never drove a car; never used a land line, much less a cell phone; never turned on a computer; or sent a text message. Yet this man defines who we are, what it means that we exist at all, teaches us about God, and reconnects us to God.

When we worship, we draw on traditions that go back centuries. We read scripture written as much as 3,000 years ago or more. We recite prayers from ancient cultures that still speak to our hearts. We unite ourselves with Christians through the ages. Some version of the Lord's Prayer came from Jesus' lips. Taking the bread and cup go back to the upper room. The Apostles' Creed goes back to the second century. All of these things give us roots and stability in a changing world. We can look back and see how the risen Christ has guided the church over the centuries. We see the mistakes and the obstacles the church has overcome. Other Christians have shared our experiences; they have been through what we have been through. The risen Christ has been there for them. That assures us that Christ is here for us. So, on the one hand we celebrate and rejoice in the statement from Hebrews that Christ is the same yesterday, today, and forever.

On the other hand, the book of Hebrews itself pushes us to find new ways to interpret, understand, and explain who Christ is. Hebrews is as clear as any book in the New Testament that Christ is divine and human. Every way that we understand Jesus the Christ has to include those aspects of Christ's nature. So, in that way, the book of Hebrews is traditional in the way it presents Jesus. Hebrews also ventures out into new territory in explaining who Jesus was for the particular people who first read the letter. Hebrews names Jesus Christ as the great high priest in the order of Melchizedek. This is a complex idea in Hebrews, but at its essence, the presentation of Jesus in this book asserts that Jesus as the great high priest was without sin and made himself the sacrifice for our sins. Melchizedek was an obscure figure in Genesis 14 and Psalm 110. He was a priest, but was not from the right family to be a priest. Psalm 110 calls the king of Israel a high priest in the order of Melchizedek. If Jesus is prophet, priest, and king, then he, too, is a priest in the order of Melchizedek. Why might the author of Hebrews go through all of this explanation for his readers? Perhaps they missed something about the old priesthood. Perhaps they felt a sense of assurance about the daily sacrifice of the priests or the Day of Atonement every year. The regularity of that may have provided them a sense of assurance. Perhaps, they found a sense of security in Judaism, which was a more established religion in Greco-Roman society and provided more authenticity.[1] Whatever the reasons, the author of Hebrews explains Jesus to his readers in a way that meets their needs, that helps them understand their lives. If the priesthood is important to you, then Jesus is the great high priest. He is sinless and has atoned once and for all for your sins. Hebrews interprets Jesus in ways the congregation can understand.

That is what we in the church must do. If we go to the average person on the street today and say that Jesus is the Messiah, that person will not understand. It will not resonate. Holding on to Jesus as both God and human, we must explain Jesus in ways the world can understand, and in ways that meets the world's needs.

One theologian who helps us to do this is Luis Pedraja. Writing from the Hispanic perspective, Pedraja says that those in Hispanic culture understand that Jesus knew the pain of poverty and oppression and so can identify with the suffering they experience. On a deeper level, Pedraja writes that Hispanic culture is a mixed culture. Most Hispanics in the United States blend languages, ethnic identity, cultural roots, and genetic makeup. He calls Hispanics *mulato* and *mestizo* people. Then, he declares that in the incarnation, where Jesus combines divine and human natures, Jesus is a *mulato* and *mestizo*. "In this sense, the Incarnation incorporates divinity and humanity into each other, creating a new reality. Just like *mestizaje* and *mulatez* combine in Hispanics different traits, cultures, and races without dissolving their differences into sameness, the Incarnation joins human and divine natures without dissolving their differences."[2]

This is why doctrine matters. We need to understand Christ rightly. Hebrews teaches us of a Christ who is the same yesterday, today, and forever. We rejoice in that stability. Jesus still reveals God to us, still takes away our sins. Hebrews also teaches us of a Christ who speaks to us in ways we can hear. Let us open ourselves to the ways Christ speaks to us now. What need do we have? What pain are we carrying? In what ways do we need to grow? That is where we will find Christ. Hebrews teaches of a Christ who is always the same, but who will meet us where we need to be met. Amen.

---

1. Victor C. Pfitzner, *Hebrews* (Nashville: Abingdon Press, 1997), p. 29.

2. Luis G. Pedraja, *Jesus Is My Uncle: Christology from a Hispanic Perspective* (Nashville: Abingdon, 1999), pp. 82-83.

Proper 18
Pentecost 16
Ordinary Time 23
Philemon 1-21

From Slave To Brother

We often shortchange love. We think of it as sweet and sentimental, something that is good for children and family members. We think of love as sort of soft and cuddly, nice in its place, but not very useful in the things that really matter. Do we think of love as tough, transforming, powerful? This little book of Philemon, tucked into the back of the New Testament at the tail end of Paul's letters, teaches us about the potential of love.

Thomas Long, who teaches preaching at Emory University in Atlanta, reminds us that when we read from Paul in the New Testament, we are reading someone else's mail. Paul never intended his letters to be read in the twenty-first century in the United States of America. If we went into our neighbor's mailbox and took out personal letters, we would not be able to make much sense of some of the contents. The letters would presuppose that the reader knew some background. Much the same situation occurs when we read Paul's letters to his churches. If we are to see the ways in which we are somehow similar to the Corinthians, the Galatians, and the Thessalonians, we have to try to imagine their situation behind the actual words on the page. We aren't exactly like them, but what's the connection? All of that is especially difficult when we read this letter to Philemon. It is difficult for us to identify with Philemon, because his situation is so different from ours. More importantly, we are not quite sure what went on behind the scenes of this letter. This was a personal letter from Paul to one man, about one matter. That makes it different from Paul's other letters. Yet, the ones who compiled the New Testament thought it should be considered sacred scripture. What did they see in it?

Let us give our best effort to reconstructing the events behind this letter. Paul is in prison, but we are not sure where. Perhaps he is in Philippi or Caesarea. As we know, Paul spent much time in prison. Paul used this time to write, a fact for which we should be grateful. We have benefited from his suffering, because he might not have worked out some of his best ideas had he not been imprisoned. We might not have Philippians with its inspiring words about Jesus taking on the form of a slave. Imprisonment seems to have deepened Paul's commitment and his identification with Christ. At some point in his imprisonment, Paul encounters a runaway slave named Onesimus, a name that means "useful." Paul leads Onesimus to convert to Christ. Then comes the big question: What should Onesimus do now that he has become a Christian? Paul is tempted to keep Onesimus with him, so that he can help Paul in his ministry. Paul decides, though, to send Onesimus back to Philemon, his "owner," and one who received ministry from Paul. We don't know how much Paul agonized over this decision, or how he explained the decision to Onesimus, who surely did not want to go back.

If Paul sends Onesimus back, the slave's fate is up to the master. We can probably assume that Philemon is angry that his slave ran away. Paul even suggests in verse 18 that Onesimus might have done some harm or stolen something from Philemon. Paul sends a powerless slave back to an angry master. Almost no limits existed to what the master could do with a runaway slave. The master could torture a slave, send him to work in the salt mines, or even have him crucified. Why would Paul send Onesimus back to such a possibility? Paul calls Onesimus his "heart," so he loved Onesimus. Why take such a risk with one you love?

For Paul, sending Onesimus back to Philemon was an act of faith. Paul saw an opportunity for reconciliation, for Philemon to grow in his understanding of what it means to be a Christian. As Paul says in verse 14, "I preferred to do nothing without your consent, in order that your good deed might be voluntary and not something forced." Paul asked Onesimus to go back to his master, to step out in faith for who knows what? Oh, and by the way, take this letter with you!

Paul, who has led Onesimus to Christ, wants to lead Philemon to a deeper understanding of Christ. Now that Onesimus has become a Christian, everything has changed. To the world, a master was a master and a slave was a slave, and that was that. In the church, looking through Christian eyes, a slave and a master were brothers in the Lord. That kind of upsets the applecart! The person of lowest rank, with no status, no power, and no rights is now your brother. Remarkably, Paul does not tell Philemon exactly what to do with Onesimus. Paul doesn't say, "Now be sure not to punish him," or, "You know, you could set him free." All Paul says is that because of Christ, he is now your brother. Paul seems simply to have wanted that new idea to get under Philemon's skin.

When Paul sent the letter, he was acting in faith on three levels. First, he trusted Onesimus, who had already run away once, to carry the letter to his master without running away again. Second, he trusted Philemon, who might have punished Onesimus without even reading the letter, to understand what it means to be a Christian. Third, he trusted God that somehow this would all work out to some good end.

It is remarkable that Paul wrote the letter, given the risk he was taking. It is even more remarkable that the letter was preserved for us to read. What might well have happened is that Onesimus might have gone in the opposite direction from where Paul sent him. He might have used the letter to start a campfire to keep himself warm. He might have wanted nothing to do with Philemon, doubting Paul's confidence that it would turn out well. He might have thought that whatever caused him to run off the first time had not really changed. We might have expected that Philemon would read the letter, wad it up, and toss it in file thirteen. Even if Philemon had done just what Paul asked, why did he preserve the letter, and how did it begin to circulate along with Paul's other letters? We have to speculate a bit here, but it seems to be a justified speculation. We have to assume that everything worked out. We have to assume that Onesimus made it back to Philemon. We have to assume that Philemon took Paul's advice and began to see Onesimus in a new light, as a brother and not just a slave. If anything else had happened — if Onesimus had run off, or if Philemon had snarled, "Brother my hind foot, I'll show this worthless slave a thing or two," then this letter would never have been preserved.

This powerful, important letter raises the question of what it means to call one another brother and sister in the Lord. To call one another brother and sister in the Lord sounds easy, but as we see from this letter, that simple act can have far-reaching consequences. Simply calling one another brother and sister in Christ changes everything.

Malcolm Muggeridge found this truth out when he worked with Mother Teresa. Writing about his trips to leper colonies and working with unwanted children gave him new insights into what it means to show Christian love. "I found that I went through three phases. The first was horror mixed with pity, the second compassion pure and simple, and the third, reaching far beyond compassion, something I have never experienced before — an awareness that these dying and derelict men and women, these lepers with stumps instead of hands, these unwanted children, were not pitiable, repulsive or forlorn, but rather dear and delightful; as it might be, friends of long standing, brothers and sisters."[1]

We rejoice in such beautiful insight about the meaning of love and the act of calling another person a brother or sister in Christ. Let us begin to see other people, even people we might not be inclined to love in this way. Let us allow this insight to change the way we do mission work and charity. We are not just givers in mission work, we receive as well. We gain new brothers and sisters in the process. We can push the idea of seeing other people as our brothers and sisters even deeper, however.

What would it mean for our nation's immigration policy to call those from another country brothers and sisters in Christ? We may not think such a political question is appropriate in the pulpit, but the relationship between master and slave in the first century was a political question as well. Paul taught that love transformed the way we see all of life, even politics. We may say that immigrants should obey the law, but if Philemon had obeyed only the laws of the state, what would have happened? Paul does not advocate a specific policy; he just says that Philemon should love Onesimus as a brother and take it from there. Maybe we can't put forth a specific policy for immigration, but we can call the church to love immigrants as brothers and sisters and take it from there.

Let us talk of one other way in which we might read this letter about the importance of using the terms "brother" and "sister" in the church. In every mainline denomination, the arguments continue to rage over social and theological issues. These arguments over doctrine, human sexuality, reproductive policy, and other issues, cause much bitterness. How can we hear this call to love one another as brothers and sisters in Christ? Being a brother to Onesimus pushed Philemon to places he didn't want to go. For us, listening to people with whom we strenuously disagree, even over the most volatile of issues is part of being brother and sister. We may not come to an agreement, but maybe we can keep the dialogue open and keep the church intact. Liberals and conservatives are brother and sister to each other. Let us hear that and see where it will take us.

When Paul made his decision about Onesimus, and wrote this letter, he stepped out in faith, not knowing exactly what would happen. We don't know where showing real, Christian love will take us. Let us give love a chance to surprise us. Let us allow love to unleash its real power. Love can change things. Love can transform. God can take a small thing, like a letter, or the choice to call another person a brother or sister, and use it for things we could never imagine. Amen.

---

1. Malcolm Muggeridge, from *Something Beautiful for God*, quoted in Reuben P. Job and Norman Shawchuck, *A Guide to Prayer for Ministers and Other Servants* (Nashville: The Upper Room, 1983), p. 233.

**Proper 19
Pentecost 17
Ordinary Time 24
1 Timothy 1:12-17**

The Utmost Patience For The Foremost Sinner

We usually don't spend too much time thinking about our own sinfulness. On occasion, of course, our feelings of guilt overwhelm us. We can't stop thinking about our sinfulness. If we are in that situation, we may need to talk that out with someone. Apart from times like that, we don't think much about our own sinfulness. We have ways of getting around that.

We don't think about our sins because we are too appalled at the sins of others. The news media throws in our faces the outrageous sins of other people. We overdose on the spectacular murders, war crimes, cruelty, child abuse, and depravity of others. We know more than we want to know about parents who torture their children, sometimes in horrific ways, like cooking them in a microwave. We see such things and become too complacent about our own sins. As long as we are not as bad as some people, we must be doing okay.

Our emotional needs keep us from thinking about our sins. Most of the time we need all of our emotional energy just to get by. Life seems to throw everything at us that it can. We don't have time or energy left to think about our sins. We come to church to gain the emotional strength to survive the coming week, not to hear someone pound the pulpit about what sinners we are.

What is front and center for us is not our sins, but the ways others have sinned against us. We carry the memory of grudges big and small around inside of us. The sins against us that hurt the most are the ones that someone got away with or that no one ever noticed. How dare anyone bring up our sinfulness when we have been so sinned against!

Besides, our sins aren't that bad! We're not perfect by any means, but what we do is piddly stuff, right? A psychologist conducted an experiment in which he asked people to describe a time they had hurt someone. Then, they were to describe a time when they were hurt. When the subjects described a time they had hurt someone, they invariably thought the hurt they caused wasn't too bad and didn't last long. The other person got over it. What they had done was justifiable, unpreventable. But, when they described their own hurts, the pain was intense and long-lasting; they had trouble putting it behind them. The perpetrator acted out of bad motives. No excuse was good enough for what the other person had done. In many cases, both the hurt they caused, and the hurt they endured were about the same kind of thing.[1]

No matter how much we don't want to hear about our sinfulness, we need to hear about it. We fool ourselves. We let ourselves off the hook. We buy our own excuses. There's a danger to that.

Our passage today in 1 Timothy is an honest reflection on sinfulness. First Timothy is one of those books that New Testament scholars have trouble with. We are not sure if 1 Timothy was actually written by Paul. The ideas in the letter do not sound like Paul. The writing style is different. Some scholars think that one of Paul's students may have written it in Paul's name. Why would someone do that? We see a kind of modern-day parallel in the practice of United Methodist Bishop Woodie White, who writes an open letter every year to Martin Luther King Jr. Dr. King has been dead for over forty years. Nevertheless, Bishop White writes these letters to keep King's memory and influence alive and to discuss racial issues in an indirect way. Something like that may have been going on here in 1 Timothy. When the readers of the letter are reminded about Paul, they may pay closer attention. The question of authorship matters here because this passage talks in a very personal way about Paul's sins. Is this a first-person confession or a reflection on sin prompted by Paul's life? We can learn from it either way.

As the passage reminds us, Paul never hid from his sinfulness. In Romans 7, he speaks for people of all ages who have grappled with temptation.

> *For I know that nothing good dwells within me, that is, in my flesh. I can will what is right, but I cannot do it. For I do not do the good I want, but the evil I do not want is what I do.* — Romans 7:18-19

The book of Acts depicts barbaric things Paul did. He persecuted members of the early church. He held everybody's jackets when they stoned Stephen. He hauled off men and women to prison. In Acts, Paul was an angry control freak.

This passage uses three terms to describe Paul: blasphemer, persecutor, man of violence. These three terms reveal the comprehensive nature of Paul's sinfulness and teach us something about our own. If we examine these three terms carefully, we see what our sin does to us. Blasphemy is an insult to God. Persecution is cruelty to someone else. Violence is an attempt to control, arising out of the anger and hate within us. These three terms summarize our sinfulness. A blasphemer is alienated from God. A persecutor is alienated from other people. A person of violence, full of anger and hate, is alienated from him or herself. Our sinfulness wrecks all three relationships. We are isolated and estranged from everyone.

Many things cause this isolation and estrangement. Part of it, but not all of it, is our own rebellion against God. In our pride, we reject God's offer of grace and healing. We stubbornly refuse to submit ourselves to God's will. That rebellion is not the whole story, however. We live in a fallen world, a creation that is not what God intends. As Paul himself says, the creation is subjected to futility and in bondage to decay (Romans 8:20-21). The sin that holds the creation in bondage holds us in bondage as well. We are influenced by social, economic, and spiritual forces beyond our control. We cannot just excuse our bad behavior, but we are part of a larger problem. Alienation is part of the human experience. The Bible gives numerous examples of people who experienced God as far away. It is true that sometimes we separate ourselves from

God, but it is also true that sometimes God seems far away and we don't know why. We feel like the psalmist who cried out, "How long, O Lord? Will you forget me forever? How long will you hide your face from me?" (Psalm 13:1). Our sinfulness is something we do, we cause, and also something that is part of the whole creation, something we are trapped in.

This passage calls us to be honest about our part in our sinfulness, to own it, to face it, to admit it. If we feel blocked from God, what is our part in that? If we are cut off from other people, how much of that is our fault? If we are not at peace within ourselves, how are we to blame? If we deny our part, we can never feel the cleansing, the release, or the joy of being forgiven. We can never move past where we are. We can never feel reconnected to God. We can never sop up the bitterness of our broken relationships.

If we do not confess our sins, if we continue to deny them, we may dupe ourselves into thinking we have gotten away with them. Eventually, though, our sins leak out. Our well-guarded secret is put on display for the world to see. We certainly remember the embarrassment of former New York governor Eliot Spitzer when he was caught engaging in prostitution. His hypocrisy is compounded by a speech he gave before the incident. In 2007, alluding to theologian Reinhold Niebuhr, Spitzer spoke words that proved to be almost prophetic, "Driven by hubris, we become blind to our own fallibility and make terrible mistakes."[2] How ironic that he could not heed his own words. We cannot sweep our sins under the carpet forever.

The author of this passage, reflecting on Paul's life, called Paul a "man of violence." We have said that violence is a sign of unresolved anger within us. That anger can come out against other people, or we can turn in inward against ourselves. Sheron Patterson, a United Methodist pastor in Dallas, Texas, survived breast cancer. Heroically, she shared her journey with others through a series of articles in the *Dallas Morning News*. In one of the articles, she told of how unresolved anger may have played a part in the growth of her cancer. She named an oppressive situation that caused her to internalize her anger. She found forgiveness difficult. Nevertheless, she wrote the following, "The missing link in my healing process is confronting my anger and getting on with forgiveness."[3]

This passage calls us to confront our sin. Perhaps we can do that with soul-searching. Perhaps we need the guidance of another person. Perhaps we need to quit hiding from ourselves.

As much as this passage pushes us to be honest about our sins, it is even more confident about God's grace and forgiveness. The author of this passage reflected on Paul's guilt, but only to show the depth of God's forgiveness. As angry and mean as Paul was, God never gave up on him. This passage shows that God understands the reasons behind our sins: our ignorance, our hurts, our fear. God heals as well as forgives. We as Christians have to marvel at what God did with Paul. Paul was angry, mean, remorseless, and the control freak of all control freaks. God turned him into the man who could write the tender, beautiful words of 1 Corinthians 13. In the words of the passage, "in me, as the foremost, Jesus Christ might display the utmost patience" (v. 16).

Where are we with our sinfulness today? Are we denying it, bottling it up? Are we only too aware of some sin and the guilt won't let us go? God is patient with us. God can give us the courage to face what is inside of us. God is stronger than our sin and the causes behind it. God can release us, cleanse us, strengthen us, and enable us to move forward. God can get us over the hump if we are held back by our sins. Let us accept God's mercy; let us celebrate God's patience. Amen.

---

1. Shankar Vedantum, "Bush: Naturally, Never Wrong," *Washington Post*, July 9, 2007, A3.

2. Quoted in "Century Marks," *Christian Century*, April 8, 2008, p. 8.

3. Sheron Patterson, "Reaching Inside to Forgive," *The Dallas Morning News*, April 1, 2008, 12G.

**Proper 20
Pentecost 18
Ordinary Time 25
1 Timothy 2:1-7**

A Peaceful Life
In An Unpeaceful World

I'm tempted to ask for a show of hands. How many people here have passed on an email making fun of a politician or political leader? It can be fun to do that. Passing on a cartoon about a politician helps us vent our frustrations at the foibles of our government. We sometimes feel helpless in the face of all of the corruption, bickering, pandering, false promises, and just general buffoonery that go on in our government. We feel a bit better if we can poke fun at our leaders. If we are not careful, however, we can slide into cynicism. We can give up and stop caring.

We read today of an antidote for cynicism. First Timothy calls us to pray for kings and all who are in high positions. In the United States, we don't have kings to pray for, so we pray for the president and our elected officials. The first thing we can say to this call is that they need our prayers. The world is a scary place. If our prayers have any influence on their decisions, if it grants them any additional wisdom, if it moves their character up even one notch, then our prayers have done some good. Even if we do not see any immediate benefit from our prayers, let us continue to pray for them. They may continue to make mistakes, even big mistakes, but let us pray for them. Even if they act in despicable ways, let us pray for them. Let us pray for them because we believe in prayer. Let us pray for them because we never know what our prayers accomplish. It may be that our prayers keep things from becoming even worse. Let us pray for our leaders because of what it does for us if we pray for them. If we pray for them, we might be less cynical. If we pray for our president and our leaders, we will remain engaged in current events. If we pray, we may be less likely to throw up our hands and give up. If Christians everywhere pray for the president and our elected officials, maybe we can keep the animosity and bickering to a minimum. Above all, it is hard entirely to dislike and trash someone you pray for.

The author of 1 Timothy wanted his first readers to pray for kings and leaders for a specific reason. He says that his Christian community should pray for leaders so that church can lead a quiet and peaceable life. At the time that 1 Timothy was written, the church was a tiny minority in a vast pagan empire. People outside the church were suspicious of new religions. They were as suspicious of the church as we are of a celebrity who joins a new cult. The author of 1 Timothy wants the church to pray for political leaders so that everyone will see that the church is no threat to anyone. The author is asking everyone to pray for a pagan king, who, even though he is not a Christian, might still be God's instrument for order in society. If Christians pray for the king, then maybe the state will leave the church alone so that it can go about its ministry. The church would be free to bear witness to God, to Christ, to the resurrection, and the coming dominion of God. That reason for praying for the king joins the other reasons for doing so, the wisdom, the guidance, and the sense of duty of a Christian to the world.

As we ponder the phrase that the author uses — a quiet and peaceable life — we might hear many things in it. We might long for a quiet and peaceable life. When we hear quiet and peaceable, we might long for an end to the turmoil in our family. We might wish for fewer slammed doors and shouting matches. When we hear quiet and peaceable, we might wish that all of the bickering in our country would calm down. We might long for some things we can agree on. When we hear quiet and peaceable, we might wish that our own emotions would settle down within us. Sometimes, it seems as if a full-scale war rages inside us. We would give anything for some peace and quiet inside our own skins.

Before we talk about the ways this passage offers us quiet and peace, we need to clarify what quiet and peace do not mean. We are not offered a peace and quiet that detaches from the world. We can't go off on our own, ignoring the suffering of the world, just because we want a quiet and peaceful life. We cannot look at starving children and go off by ourselves to be peaceful. We can't look at war, torture, or poverty and seal ourselves off so that we can be quiet and peaceful. We cannot look at all of the sexual exploitation of children and turn a blind eye, because seeing such things disturbs our peacefulness. We must be engaged in the world, opening ourselves to the world's suffering, doing what we can to bring relief.

The quiet and peaceable life 1 Timothy promises us does not mean that the church should never be a place of controversy. From its earliest days, the church has had to think through and even argue about theology and ethical issues. We should love each other as we are arguing, but argue we must. A peaceable life for the church does not mean we will never face controversy. If we look at the ministry of the Old Testament prophets, they did not appear on the surface to live quiet and peaceable lives. Amos was told to go back where he came from (Amos 7:12). Jeremiah was accused of being unpatriotic (Jeremiah 37:13) and of demoralizing the troops (38:4). Elijah was called a "troubler of Israel" (1 Kings 18:17). The Old Testament prophets made outrageous statements. If you don't believe me, read Isaiah 1:21, and see what the prophet called Jerusalem said. I won't quote it; I'll let you read it for yourself. The Old Testament prophets did their ministry on the edge. They came just this close to going too far. On the surface, their ministry did not appear to be quiet and peaceable.

Being in ministry is not what we usually think of as quiet and peaceable. If we speak out against injustice, the result might not seem at first like quiet and peace. If we expose corruption in business or unfairness in the court system, the result might not be quiet and peace. Yet, how can we not speak out? It may seem more peaceful to look the other way, but the end result is not true peace. Even our work within the church on various committees is not outwardly peaceful. It can lead to long meetings and even some disagreements. If we are to be in ministry, we must understand peace and quiet in another way.

On a deeper level, we can claim the promise from this passage about quiet and peace. We cannot turn away from the world's suffering, but we take comfort in the assurance that God is at work in our world. However dangerous the world seems, however violent, however hopeless it all appears, God is at work in the world. God holds the future. We draw peace from that assurance. The more involved we become in the world's suffering, the more we stand up against injustice, the more we will experience true peace. The kind of peace that such ministry grants is the peace of knowing we did something, we made a difference. The kind of peace that such ministry gives is the kind of peace that depends on God to see us through. If we are involved in real ministry, we must depend on the kind of peace that only God can provide.

That kind of peace rests in the assurance that God will win the victory in the end. Our peace comes from the trust, faith, and hope that God will heal the creation and usher in the true peace of a world existing in harmony and justice. That kind of peace is the calm in the midst of a storm. It is the peace that allows inner city pastors to work in the midst of violence but trust in God. It is the kind of peace that enables the church to keep going even if the world considers it irrelevant. It is the kind of peace that continues to trust even in the face of setbacks and seeming defeats. It is the kind of peace that transcends disagreements and differences. Let us claim that peace for the church.

For our family squabbles and even shouting matches, God offers us peace. For our swirling emotions, God offers us peace. For our anxiety over the troubles of the world, God offers us peace. God does not offer the peace of being protected from the world's danger, but peace as God's strength and assurance in the midst of the craziness, violence, and turmoil of the world. No matter what political troubles our president faces, no matter how frightening our problems, no matter how hopeless it may seem, God is still at work. We should not minimize the problems of the world. Life can hurt. If we trust in God, we can find peace in a world that seems bereft of peace. Amen.

Proper 21
Pentecost 19
Ordinary Time 26
1 Timothy 6:6-19

How Rich Is Rich?

We can simply stay away from some of the things that are bad for us. A person who is addicted to drugs or alcohol will be counseled by those with experience to abstain totally from alcohol: no social drinking, no wine every now and then. Just leave it alone. Never touch it. The same principle applies if the addiction is to gambling or pornography and many other kinds of addiction. Overcoming an addiction is hard work. It takes courage, willpower, the support of others, and the grace of God at a minimum. But, at least you know what you have to do. You have to stay away from whatever it is you are addicted to. We can completely cut ourselves off from some things that are bad for us.

First Timothy proclaims that money is bad for us, or at least that coveting money, loving money, chasing after money is bad for us. If the passage is right, we are in trouble. We cannot get by without money. We don't have the option of living the way an alcoholic must live, never touching the stuff. We need money to survive. Dealing with money is a constant battle for all of us. We have to figure out what money means for our Christian faith.

As many people point out, the passage does not say that money itself is bad for us. The real trouble comes from inside us, in our greed, our lust for money. The way the passage puts it is that "the love of money is the root of all kinds of evil." This is a well-known phrase from this passage, but some of the other things it says about greed may actually be more interesting and instructive. It says that greed can be a trap and that the eagerness to be rich can cause us to pierce ourselves. A trap limits our freedom and piercing ourselves causes us pain.

We can see the wisdom of this passage in the headlines: the savings and loan crisis of the '80s, the collapse of Enron, the subprime mortgage debacle of a couple of years ago. They all arose out of greed. In order to make big bucks people took risks. Then they tried to cover their mistakes and hoped for the best. In all three cases, things did not work out well. Innocent people were hurt in the wake of the scandals. Taxpayers had to bail out the greedy. Employees lost their pensions. People lost their homes. It has always been the case that we are interconnected. What we do affects not just ourselves but many others. With the global economy, our decisions can have far-reaching consequences. Things can start small, but then the effects ripple through the economy, ruining lives and inflicting pain. When we trap ourselves, we catch other people. When we pierce ourselves, the lance cuts not just our own flesh.

How much more evidence do we need that money alone does not buy wholeness or happiness? We have seen — sometimes more than we want to see — how celebrities with everything still cannot get their lives together. Even though we seem fascinated by the lives of the young starlets, their troubles are sad. Despite the fact that they have all that money can buy, they must have a deep emptiness inside them that their lavish spending and partying cannot fill.

We can easily see the passage's point about the evils of pure greed. Greed can consume us, distort us, and twist our souls around. We have all the evidence we need of that. The question for us may not be about pure greed. The question for us is about our relationship to money. How does our faith affect our money? We must have money. We cannot completely banish it from our lives. We have to deal with money. How do we use our money? In the abstract, it is easy to preach against greed, against craving money. Money problems do not come to us in the abstract. Money problems are quite concrete. A bill that arrives in the mail is quite concrete. The price of gas is very concrete (and rising!).

We have to make certain decisions about money. We can do only three things with our money: spend it, invest it, or give it away. Sometimes the decision is made for us. We don't have the option of investing our money. Our only decision may be which bill to pay and which to hold off for later. Other times we do have a decision to make. What do we do with our money? We do not have time for a lesson in economics, but what Christians should do with their money is not always clear. The church is usually in favor of giving money away, but the other two can be a good way to deal with our money. Spending money creates jobs. Investing money creates capital for business. It seems selfish to spend money on ourselves. It seems selfish to invest money, even for retirement, when children are starving. Yet, economists tell us that consumer spending is good for the economy, and venture capital creates new small businesses. Money is complicated!

Even if we can do only three things with our money, sometimes it is not clear what to do. How much money should Christians have? If we claim that we are spending money to stimulate the economy, how do we know we are not fooling ourselves into indulgence? One way to ask the question is, "How rich is rich?" If we are comfortably middle class, is that rich? Perhaps one way out of the dilemma is to begin to ask ourselves some questions. What is the loving thing to do? How is a particular use of money an act of love for God and neighbor? If we invest in a certain way, if we spend in a certain way, if we give away, how does that act show love? That question can have far-reaching consequences. It affects the house we live in, the car we drive, the clothes we wear, and the mutual funds we choose. Our use of money, in response to what God has done for us, is not just dropping a few bucks in the collection plate and then moving on. How we use our money is a sign of how deep our faith is. We cannot solve every issue about money in this worship service, but if we can ask ourselves how our use of money shows love to God and neighbor, that is a start.

This passage is wise when it teaches us that our attitude toward money can become a trap. It is true that we can feel trapped if we do not have enough money, but we can feel trapped by the pursuit of money. Some people find that more money simply means more stress. Often, the more money a couple has, the more they argue about money. Such arguments show the wisdom of the passage that we pierce ourselves, we inflict our own pain. The more money we have invested, the more we fret when the stock market takes a downturn. Pursuing money can become a kind of trap.

We never completely escape from that trap. As we have said, we have to have money. Nevertheless, the passage offers us some relief. It shows us some ways to think that give us room to move within that trap. The problem with looking at money in a worship service is that we are in such different places. What works to move around in the trap for one person might not work well for another person. If our problem is that we don't have enough money, we experience the trap in one way. If our problem is deciding whether to invest, spend, or give away our money, we experience the trap another way. The advice of 1 Timothy can sound condescending to one person, but be just the right thing to say to someone else.

One of the ways the passage suggests that we move around in the trap is to be content with what we have. That is easier for some to hear than others. Some of us may be genuinely frightened by our financial situation. When 1 Timothy tells us to be content with what we have, it may sound like a slap in the face, as though the author just doesn't understand. Nevertheless, some people, faced with a shortage of money have found that, trusting in God, they can create ways to be content with just the necessities. They can move around inside the trap. Rebecca Frank, a pastor at University Park United Methodist Church in Texas, preached a sermon about a time when her life was disrupted. She was forced by circumstances to move into an efficiency apartment, with only the barest of essentials. She said in the sermon that she came to call her home her "sufficiency" apartment. It may not have looked like much to some, but it met her needs. She learned that abundant life is not all about things.

That is the essence of what the passage teaches us. It counsels us to concentrate less on what we have and more on who we are. It says to shun things like greed and to pursue righteousness, godliness, faith, love, endurance, and gentleness. It tells us to fight the good fight of the faith. We can pursue those things no matter what our financial situation might be. Those things come from within. Even if we are struggling financially, that struggle cannot keep us from developing righteousness, from seeking a deeper faith, from calling up endurance from inside us, and from loving one another.

    Talking about money from the pulpit can end up sounding like scolding or begging. In reality, though, the passage offers us contentment. This isn't the contentment of counting our own money but not caring about the needs of others. For those who have decisions to make about money, this passage offers contentment as well. People who give are happier than those who do not. This passage offers the contentment of living with less, of spending wisely, and of investing in ways that don't trouble our conscience. It is the contentment of trusting God for our needs and not judging ourselves by our possessions. Only a financial advisor should give advice about investing money. This passage tells us that investing in our faith will always pay off. Amen.

**Proper 22
Pentecost 20
Ordinary Time 27
2 Timothy 1:1-14**

Guarding The Treasure

Most of us have a long list of passwords, PINs, and usernames to type into our cell phones, our computers, our ATMs, and a host of other gadgets. We need these to protect ourselves. Identity theft has become a serious problem. We have all seen the commercials on television of the person bragging about a dream vacation, but the voice coming out of the character's mouth is another person's voice. The character in the commercial is portraying an identity thief. In real life, identity theft is not as funny as the commercials. People's lives have been ruined; some have seen their credit rating destroyed or their bank accounts wiped out. Some viruses are simply for meanness' sake. The perpetrator doesn't gain anything from it, just the perverse pleasure of hurting another. We use shredders, virus protection, and spy-catching software to guard against identity theft and to keep others from accessing our bank accounts and credit cards. We need all of these things because people wish to steal from us and to harm us.

Do we ever understand our participation in church as acting like a virus filter? That's part of the way 2 Timothy sees us. Our passage for today covers a lot of territory. It talks about faith, suffering, the work of Christ. It is all over the map. The last line, verse 14, ties all of this disparate material together. "Guard the good treasure entrusted to you, with the help of the Holy Spirit living in us." We are the virus software, guarding the treasure of the gospel.

The first place we guard that treasure is within ourselves. The passage calls us to "rekindle the gift of God that is within you." This verse may refer to Timothy's ordination. The image behind the term, "rekindle" is fanning something into flame. At some of their meetings, Boy Scouts have a contest on building a fire. Teams of scouts will be stationed at a campfire with a frame over the fire. The frame holds a pot of water. The goal is to start a fire, then build the fire up to the point that the water boils over the sides of the pot. The team that causes the water to spill over the side first wins. Watching such a contest can be exciting. The scouts fan with whatever they find handy as fast and furiously as they can. The flames of the fire leap up, the water in the pot begins to stir until finally a bubble leaks to the top. The water rolls with more energy until at last some of it splashes over the side. That's fanning into flame!

Where is the energy level in our faith? Is the water in the pot cold and still? Sometimes our faith needs to be rekindled. Stress, work, fatigue, disappointment, and heartache can all cause our flame to die down. We poke around in the embers, but we don't find much spark. Prayer, worship, and opening ourselves to the Holy Spirit can give us that energy. We should not mistake fanning the flame for mere emotionalism. Some leaders in the church try to whip us into pure emotion. We may not need to be like the water in the pot boiling over the sides. A good, strong flame that gives us energy is more what we need. Let us draw from the Holy Spirit as we fan the flame of our faith.

The passage mentions three specific gifts of the Spirit: power, love, and self-discipline. Each of the three is important, and all three reinforce each other. When we feel weak, we need God's power. We need power to overcome temptation. We need power to break free from the things that control us. We need power to grow in grace. We need power to keep the world from defining us. Love is the second gift mentioned. Love is healing and transforming. Perhaps love comes after power in the verse for a reason. We need power in order to love properly. Love needs strength. Love needs the strength of forgiveness and commitment. Love is not easy, but we should never underestimate what it can do. Self-discipline seems to be a lost art in our country. We eat too much, we spend too much, we exercise too little, we read too little, and we pray too little. As we said, the three things reinforce each other. We need power to love. We need self-discipline in order to have power.

If we practice the discipline of keeping in shape, we have physical power. If we practice the self-discipline of feeding our faith, we will have spiritual power. The first way we guard the treasure is within ourselves.

When we guard the treasure in ourselves, when we fan the flames of our faith, we do so for a larger purpose. The church guards the treasure for the world. The passage mentions Timothy's grandmother, Lois, and mother, Eunice. Timothy is third generation. The letter of 2 Timothy reflects a situation that confronted the church by the third generation. What happens when all of the disciples who had been with Jesus are gone? What happens when Paul is gone? Who will continue the mission work? Who will make sure the teaching of the church is sound?

This passage gives a brief thumbnail sketch of some of the essentials of Christian doctrine. We are saved by grace not works. We are called according to God's purposes. Jesus abolished death and brought life. From very early times in the church, good teaching has been twisted out of shape and turned inside out. The essence of heresy is to take a complex doctrine and oversimplify it. The church must guard the treasure of its teaching against heresy. Heresy and false teaching pose the genuine risk of the church losing its identity.

As examples of the heresies that the early church faced and that the church today still faces, we can look at the understanding of Christ, sin, and resurrection. When the church teaches about the nature of Jesus the Christ, we must always affirm that Christ was fully divine and fully human. We cannot adequately explain how that is so, we can only bear witness to it. Heresy oversimplifies the doctrine of Christ by teaching that Christ is only partly divine or partly human. In some cases, people in the early church completely dissolved either the human or divine nature of Christ. Teaching that Jesus is not fully divine or fully human makes the understanding of Christ easier to grasp, and so it is attractive. If we deny either part of Jesus' nature, we diminish Christ's act of salvation. That is the danger of heresy. It sounds good, but it is not really Christian teaching. Concerning sin, the church teaches that we are forgiven sinners. Some in the early church taught that once we became Christian we no longer sinned. Others taught that if we sinned, we could not be forgiven. Once again, we have to hold two ideas in our head that seem not to fit. To emphasize only one side of the doctrine of sin and forgiveness is to make it easier to understand. Misunderstanding the doctrine of sin can have two dangers. First, we might not take our sin seriously enough and not seek forgiveness. Secondly, we might not take forgiveness seriously enough and be trapped in our guilt. Even if sin and forgiveness are hard to explain and understand, the church must proclaim that we are forgiven sinners. When the church teaches about resurrection, it says that we will be fully raised in the afterlife, but that the joy of resurrection begins now. Some in the early church taught that the joy we experience now is all that we will have (see 2 Timothy 2:18). That is easier to understand, but it shortchanges the indescribable joy of the coming resurrection and the dominion of God. One of the ways the church guards the treasure is to uphold sound teaching, holding in balance the complexity of our understandings of such doctrines as Christ, sin, and resurrection. The temptation is to twist doctrine around so that people are not so confused by it. Another temptation is to forget doctrine and just try to make people in church feel good. Sound teaching gives responsible witness to what God is doing in the world.

Part of the reason we are in church today is to prepare ourselves to guard the treasure. We have a gift to offer the world. We sometimes do not fully appreciate the gift we have. A few years ago, some archivists discovered that pictures stored in the Library of Congress were more than they first appeared to be. The pictures had been mislabeled. They were really pictures of President Lincoln's second inaugural address. They were a treasure for historians. For years, the archivists had not known what they had. That is often the danger of the church. We don't realize the treasure we have to give the world. Sometimes we fall into a pattern in church. We pay our bills, we have our meetings, we chair our committees, we set our budgets, but we don't appreciate how valuable our work, our very presence in the world is. God has entrusted us with the message of the gospel. God has placed a treasure into our hands and called us to guard it. We guard hope in a world bent on self-destruction. We guard love in a world seething with hate. We guard God's affirmation of life in a world fascinated with death.

We may do our ministry in an increasingly secular and even pagan culture. We may feel as though we are losing ground or that our influence is diminishing. Nevertheless, let us continue our ministry. Let us continue to sing, to preach, to teach, to take care of each other, and to reach out. Let us fan the flames of our faith into a transforming energy. Let us share our treasure with the world. Amen.

Sermons On The Second Readings

For Sundays After Pentecost (Last Third)

A New Resolve

Scott Suskovic

**Proper 23
Pentecost 21
Ordinary Time 28
2 Timothy 2:8-15**

Living In Chains

"... suffer as I do" (2 Timothy 1:12).

It was in 1965 that the Rolling Stones recorded the song, "I Can't Get No Satisfaction." Even today, over forty years later, we are still saying the same words and feeling the same emptiness of trying and trying, but getting no satisfaction. Commercials promise it with whiter teeth and fresher breath. Wall Street promises it with higher returns. Soap operas promise it with a dynamic love life. Yet those who have conquered each of those summits come up with the same cry, "I can't get no satisfaction." Can you?

Contentment is a rare gift that comes through a deep, personal relationship with Jesus that transcends circumstances. It flows from a sure and certain hope that because Jesus lives, I will, too. Neither death nor life nor things present nor things to come will separate me from the love of God in Christ Jesus. In that promise, we find that rare gift of contentment, peace, and patience.

Whenever I read Paul's prison letter, I marvel at the peace and patience in his tone.

> *And because I preach this good news, I am suffering and have been chained like a criminal. But the word of God cannot be chained. I am willing to endure anything if it will bring salvation and eternal glory in Christ Jesus....* — 2 Timothy 2:9-10 (NLT)

Why isn't Paul lashing out against his unjust imprisonment? Why isn't he condemning those who arrested him? Why isn't he furiously scribbling out threats of revenge? I've always marveled at the peace and patience found in Paul's prison letters probably because I would have been far less graceful. There is truly a peace that passes all human understanding in these words, even while Paul was living in chains. It flows from a rare gift of peace and contentment.

In the 1730s and 1740s, Jonathan Edwards nearly single-handedly led the spiritual awakening in America. He is known best for his sermon, "Sinners in the Hands of an Angry God." However, there was one jealous pastor in town who took displeasure to Edwards' popularity and spread nasty rumors about this preacher. At first, no one took the rumors seriously. After all, this was Jonathan Edwards we were talking about. And then, as the rumors persisted, some asked Edwards about their validity. He refused to comment, which created even more gossip. His silence created even more controversy until finally the townspeople confronted Edwards and asked him to either confirm or deny the charges. Edwards still refused to comment saying that he would rather trust God to vindicate him than to rely on his own eloquence in defense.

Edwards displayed the same kind of peace and patience that Paul had while living in chains. While many of us would have sought revenge or at least cried out, "I can't get no satisfaction!" Edwards echoed the patience and peace of Paul when taking the higher ground. Paul wrote, "If we die with him, we will also live with him. If we endure hardship, we will reign with him" (2 Timothy 2:11-12).

When it comes to this kind of peace and patience, the Bible refers to two different kinds. The first is dealing with circumstances.

> *Be patient, therefore, beloved, until the coming of the Lord ... you have heard of the endurance of Job, and you have seen the purpose of the Lord, how the Lord is compassionate and merciful.* — James 5:7a, 11b

You've heard of the patience of Job. This was a patience of circumstance. Job wasn't angry at anyone in particular. His family was killed. His herds were lost. His home was destroyed and he was covered with sores. There was no one to get mad at, per se. He needed patience with the circumstance. This kind of patience is inspired by hope. Brighter days lay ahead because God is God and I am his. Job said, "I know that my redeemer lives and at the last when my flesh has been destroyed, then from my flesh I shall see God." Paul and Edwards shared that same hope in the midst of horrendous circumstances.

The second kind of peace and patience is with people. It is a patience not inspired by hope but rather with mercy. Let me explain. When I go to the hospital to be with someone whose loved one has died tragically, there is sadness, there is anger, there are questions, and sometimes it is all directed at me — "Why did this happen, pastor?" I know that they are not angry with me. I don't respond harshly and take offense. I respond as you would — with patience inspired by mercy. When you talk to a friend or a family member and it feels like you are being attacked, sometimes you just have to ask, "Is this really about me or is there something going on in her life ... and right now, I just need to take it. I'm not going to get upset or walk away but right now, I'm going to be patient because right now she needs mercy."

Sitting in prison, living in chains, Paul shows patience with his captors. They were not to blame. They were following orders. Edwards, on the other hand, showed patience with his accuser who was not following orders. In fact, he had malicious intent! But as Paul Harvey would say, here is the rest of the story of Jonathan Edwards. Unfortunately, the crowd eventually believed the rumors concerning Edwards, defrocked him, and kicked him out of town. He remained in exile for eight years until the other pastor, humbled by Edwards' example of mercy, stepped forward, and confessed that it was all a lie.

Now what? I understand that I, as a mature Christian, am not to seek revenge. *Vengeance is mine, says the Lord.* Why am I banned from seeking revenge? Because with my dark, sinful heart, I will never be content on just evening the score with my enemy. I'll go overboard. I'll get one up on him. I'll ... I'll.... You get the picture. You see why revenge is forbidden — because I can't be trusted with a tied game.

But what about vindication? What about being exonerated? What about correcting a lie? Martin Luther stood before the trial of his life, the Diet of Worms in 1521, and said, "Show me by reason and by scripture that I am a heretic and I'll be the first to throw my books on the fire." He wasn't silent. He took a stand. Where do we draw that line from patience to being a doormat in which you become walked upon, disregarded, and abused?

I don't know. I confess, I don't know. It is a razor-thin line at times. But let me share with you an image that came to me this past week. My ten-year-old son, Nathan, and I do this thing periodically, in which I'll tell him to, for example, clean up his room.

If he is in one of those moods, he'll say, "No."

I'll say a bit more firmly, "Clean up your room."

And more defiantly he says, "NO."

Squaring off to him, I say, "Now."

Facing me he says, "Nope." (Now you need to picture this with the two of us barely keeping a straight face.)

I'll take off my jacket, roll up my sleeves and say, "You know I can make you, don't you?"

He'll face me, drop his baseball, take off his jacket, and with a barely concealed smirk says, "No you can't."

Then I wrestle him to the carpet, pin him to the ground, get a couple of playful jabs in his belly, put him in a half nelson and when he says, "Uncle!" I say again, "Now, clean up your room. Please."

And he says, "Okay."

I have the power. Until he turns sixteen anyway, I have the power. I can choose to use it or I can choose patience. Can you image what would have happened if Jesus had argued at his trial? Can you imagine Jesus talking theology with the high priest or ethics with the temple guards or the essence of the messianic prophecies with the council? Who would you have put your money on? Who would have "won"? But he didn't. He had the power but he chose patience. He also had the power to call down legions of angels to defend him, restore him, and punish those false accusers. But he didn't. He had the power. He chose patience.

Where is that line drawn between patience and becoming a doormat that is walked upon, taken advantage of, and abused? I don't know. It's there, somewhere, I just not sure where. I do know that the answer is found in the extraordinary patience that God has shown me.

His conversation with me goes something like this. "Clean up your life."

"No."

"Stop doubting me."

"Can't."

"No more questions, and I mean it."

"Sorry, nope"

"I can make you."

"No you can't."

And sometimes, *sometimes* God has to get a little rough with me to make his point but always with patience and not with power.

If I am filled with his Spirit, then it is his peace in me that I work for in others and it is his patience with me that I extend to others, much like Paul living in chains or Edwards living with false accusations. How can I dare hold back from others the love, the forgiveness, the peace, and the patience that I have received from God? Amen.

Proper 24
Pentecost 22
Ordinary Time 29
2 Timothy 3:14—4:5

The Word Alone

"All scripture is inspired by God" (2 Timothy 3:16).

There was a woman who called her pastor late one night in a panic and said, "Pastor, quickly, tell me what I believe." Another believer from a different church who challenged her about her beliefs had cornered her. She quickly found that she could not articulate the basic teachings of her church. "Pastor, quickly, tell me what I believe."

There may be more than one person gathering in worship this morning who, if hard pressed, may be less than clear about what they believe. Are you one?

Where does one start in establishing a baseline for belief? Church doctrine? Parental teaching? The local pastor? Inner instinct?

For those coming from the Protestant Reformation, that baseline can only be scripture. From this sixteenth-century movement came the battle cry, "the word alone." Our baseline for what we believe must flow from the word alone. One of the many texts used to support this teaching and belief of the centrality of scripture is 2 Timothy 3. Let's look at that text again.

> *But as for you, continue in what you have learned and firmly believed, knowing from whom you learned it, and how from childhood you have known the sacred writings that are able to instruct you for salvation through faith in Christ Jesus. All scripture is inspired by God*

> *and useful for teaching, for reproof, for correction, and for training in righteousness, so that everyone who belongs to God may be proficient, equipped for every good work.* — 2 Timothy 3:14-17

Let's take that apart. The word "inspired" is a unique word. This is the only time it occurs in the New Testament. It refers to wisdom that comes from God, or quite literally, God's Spirit has been infused or breathed upon it. Therefore, more than just the creative thoughts or opinion of some authors writing on papyrus, scripture has a unique divine authority unlike any other writing.

That authority, that power, is shown in what God's word accomplishes. It inspired faith with a wisdom that transcends human knowledge. It teaches, reproofs, and corrects. It trains people in righteousness, equipping them for every good work. The power and the authority of scripture are found in what it does.

Luther knew this to be true. He knew and firmly believed that all theories, all theologies, all teachings are to be tested against the teachings of the Bible. If they contradict the teachings of the Bible, they are to be refused. If they are in agreement with the teachings of the Bible, they are to be followed ... come what may.

This firm belief and stance on the authority and inspiration of the Bible came to the ultimate test in 1521 when Luther was called on the carpet to denounce his books and his teachings. For months, Luther's books were being burned in Rome until finally the Pope ordered Luther to appear before a council in the city of Worms, Germany.

Make no mistake. This was a serious offense. If found guilty of heresy, Luther, a 38-year-old German monk, could not only be kicked out of the church but also be put to death. There was a lot on the line not only in Luther's life but also for the future of the Reformation.

For hours they went round and round, each side selecting their words carefully until, at the end, the interrogator looked at Luther and said, "Martin Luther, the teachings found in your book have been declared to be in error with the church. I ask you for the last time, do you recant your teachings or are you willing to bear the consequences?"

This is where the Hollywood version of things makes the reality fuzzy. The image that prevails is one of a tall Luther, defying the wicked and corrupt Roman structure, pounding his fist on the table, clutching a Bible and yelling, "Here I stand!" Then he mounts a white horse and begins the Reformation. That is the image you may have seen of Luther looking far off with a large Bible in his hands — defiant, confident, strong.

That's not what happened.

When he was asked for the last time to recant, Luther said in a voice that was barely audible, "Give me 24 hours." The magnitude of the moment as this 38-year-old German monk was telling the church that it had been wrong for centuries and that he alone bore the flame of truth almost came crashing down on him.

That night, in the solitude of his room, Luther wrote one of the most moving prayers ever written. It was his own time in the Garden of Gethsemane.

> *O God, Almighty God everlasting! How dreadful is the world! Behold how its mouth opens to swallow me up, and how small is my faith in Thee! ... Oh! the weakness of the flesh, and the power of Satan! If I am to depend upon any strength of this world — all is over ... Help me against all the wisdom of this world ... The work is not mine, but Thine. I have no business here ... I have nothing to contend for with these great men of the world! I would gladly pass my days in happiness and peace. But the cause is Thine ... And it is righteous and everlasting! O Lord! Help me! O faithful and unchangeable God! Do you not hear? My God. Are you no longer living? You have chosen me for this work. I know it ... Therefore, O God, accomplish your own will!*
>
> *Lord — where are you? Come, I pray. Behold, I am prepared to lay down my life for your truth. For the cause is holy. It is your own. I will not let you go. Though the world should be thronged with devils and this body should be cast forth, trodden under foot, cut in pieces, consumed to ashes, my soul is thine. O God, help me.... Amen.*[1]

The next morning, Luther returned to the courtroom to resume testimony. The prosecutor continued. "I ask you, Martin, for the last time — answer candidly and without horns — do you or do you not repudiate your books and the errors which they contain?"

In words of desperation, knowing there was no way to escape the inevitable, a tired and worn Luther replied not with defiance but with a sense of exhaustion, "Since then your Majesty and your lordships desire a simply reply, I will answer without horns and without teeth. Unless I am convinced by scripture and plain reason — I do not accept the authority of popes and councils, for they have contradicted each other — my conscience is captive to the word of God. I cannot and I will not recant anything, for to go against conscience is neither right nor safe. Here I stand, I cannot do otherwise. God help me."

It wasn't a matter of being stubborn. It wasn't an issue of having a grand vision of a Reformation. It wasn't the goal of having a church named after him. This was not movement fueled by an out-of-control ego.

It's about believing and trusting God's word — not a part of it — not selected sections that are to my advantage. It's about not dismissing those parts that make you squirm — the whole ball of wax — the entire package. It's about trusting and believing that God's word alone has the power and authority it claims.

- The word alone is the final authority for teaching, reproof, correcting, and training. It is the lamp unto our feet. It is inspired by God.
- It claims that I am saved not by my works or how much I give or how much I do or how often I attend. I am saved by my faith alone in Jesus Christ as my Lord.
- It claims that this salvation is never earned. Indeed everyone has fallen short of the glory of God. All deserve God's wrath. But instead, we receive not what we deserve but what God in his mercy wants to give ... his grace alone.
- It claims that everyone has been gifted by God with different talents, and God calls each as individuals to identify those

gifts, develop those gifts, and use those gifts in the body of Christ as a part of the priesthood of all believers.
- It claims that that Word of God became flesh in Jesus and dwelt among us full of grace and truth.

Following his interrogation at Worms, Luther translated the Bible into German and put it into the hands of all the German peasants. He did this under penalty of death because he was convinced that one German peasant armed with scripture is more powerful than 1,000 cardinals and bishops and popes without it. Clergy do not have a corner on the market because they are clergy. That truth comes from the word alone in the hands of any believer.

Here I stand. Amen.

---

1. Martin Luther, *Luther's Prayers* (Minneapolis, Augsburg, 1994).

**Proper 25
Pentecost 23
Ordinary Time 30
2 Timothy 4:6-8, 16-18**

Endurance

I have fought the good fight, I have finished the race, I have kept the faith. — 2 Timothy 4:7

When my daughter, Hannah, was five years old we lived in Minnesota. Before she entered kindergarten, she had to take an entrance exam. Being the non-competitive but responsible parent that I am, I decided to help Hannah prepare for this test. I taught her how to count to ten — in four languages. I taught her the colors by buying a box of crayons — 64 count, including turquoise, magenta, and chartreuse. We worked on a puzzle of the United States with each individual state cut out so we could learn the names, location, and capital of all fifty. After six months of cramming, I felt she was ready for her entrance exam. My wife took her to the test and then phoned me with the results. Do you know what? They didn't ask her to count to ten in Japanese. She wasn't asked the capital of Wyoming. But she was asked, "What's this?" And they pointed to her shoulder. "What's this?" And they pointed to her hand. "What this?" And they pointed to a part of her body that she had never seen, had no idea what it was, and had to shrug her shoulders. It was her elbow. I had forgotten to teach her what an elbow was. Thankfully, she was still allowed into kindergarten.

I'm still doing this cramming today as Hannah is preparing for graduation from high school and getting ready for college. Can you do laundry? Can you manage finances? Do you know how to make grandma's special sauce? You want them to do well and be ready. These are things they should know. There are things we should all know whether it is entering kindergarten or college. On the top of that list is endurance.

What do you wish you hadn't quit? College? Do you wish you would have finished that degree? How about the piano? Do you wish you had not stopped those lessons? What about exercise? Did you give up too early? What about a job that would have led to something or a hobby that once brought you great pleasure? What do you wish you hadn't quit? A marriage? Do you wish you would have tried harder? What about God? Maybe you gave up on God long ago — stopped praying, stopped believing, and now you are just going through the motions. What do you wish you hadn't quit?

Why did you quit? We all know the answer. It's the same reason we all quit. Because it was easy to quit. You didn't like taking tests so you quit college and got a job. You would rather go out and play with your friends than practice the piano. It was easier to walk out on the marriage than to sit down with that person and work it out. It was easier to sleep in on Sunday, read the paper, and drink a cup of coffee than to get the children up, fight the parking, and come to church. Come on, let's be honest. It's a whole lot easier to be a quitter.

I bet if you were to ask successful people about the secret to their success, one quality that would be consistent among them all would be endurance. In many cases, instead of taking the easy way, looking for shortcuts, or wanting instant success, they didn't quit. They were willing to delay gratification by making a conscious decision to endure the pain now in order to receive a greater reward later.

Many people, however, are wired differently. I'm told that there is a small box at Bell Laboratories. The box has one switch. When you turn the switch on, a skeleton hand comes out, reaches over, and turns itself off. That's all it does. It's wired to turn itself off. A lot of people are that way — wired to quit. At the first sight of hardship, at the first hint that this will take time, I'll just turn myself off. No endurance. It's just easier to quit

How do you find endurance? When you are at that quitting point, how do you move forward? When you are running the marathon and your body is screaming to quit; when your boss is a tyrant and you hate your job; when you've got one more exam, one more paper, and you are just spent; when you are having the same argument with your spouse for the twentieth time and you are getting nowhere; or when you've been praying for so long and haven't received so much as a whisper from God. How do you break through those quitting points when it would be a whole lot easier just to cash in, walk away, and quit?

For that, I want to turn to a favorite passage of mine in 2 Timothy 4:7. Paul is in prison awaiting his execution. He knows that the time of his death is soon. He has time to reflect on his life and writes with the deep contentment of one who has had endurance: "I have fought the good fight, I have finished the race, I have kept the faith."

Do you hear the contentment? Do you sense words of accomplishment? At the end of his life, Paul has no regrets. That would be great, wouldn't it? But you know that there were times Paul thought about quitting.

> *Five different times the Jewish leaders gave me thirty-nine lashes. Three times I was beaten with rods. Once I was stoned. Three times I was shipwrecked. Once I spent a whole night and a day adrift at sea. I have traveled on many long journeys. I have faced danger from rivers and from robbers. I have faced danger from my own people, the Jews, as well as from the Gentiles. I have faced danger in the cities, in the deserts, and on the seas. And I have faced danger from men who claim to be believers but are not. I have worked hard and long, enduring many sleepless nights. I have been hungry and thirsty and have often gone without food. I have shivered in the cold, without enough clothing to keep me warm.*
> — 2 Corinthians 11:24-27 (NLT)

How many times do you have to be tied to a pole and beaten to within an inch of your life until you call it quits? How many times do you have to be shipwrecked before you think, "There has to be an easier way"? How many times do you have to go hungry, be thirsty or cold, and say, "I am so out of here"? You know Paul thought about quitting often. But he didn't. He endured. Before he died, he left us with three keys to his endurance.

Fight The Good Fight

It wasn't just any fight. It was the good fight. It was a fight worth fighting. There are a lot of things we fight for, most of it is for pride and ego and greed. Those are not good fights. What is?

I'm thinking about an alcoholic I know who struggles each day wanting a drink but has not taken one for the past nineteen years — he fights the good fight. I'm thinking about the lawyer in our church who adopted some children. To give them the time they need, she gave up her practice — she fights the good fight. I know a couple who have reasons to go their separate ways but choose to do the hard job of making it work, every day — they fight the good fight. I'm thinking about the person who has lost a child, one of the greatest fears of a parent, yet comes here every Sunday to praise, thank, and worship God — he fights the good fight. I'm thinking about the college students with many opportunities to wander, many opportunities to slack off, and many opportunities to make bad choices when others around them seem to major in trouble — but they don't. They fight the good fight. Paul says here, decide right now what is good, what is important, what is worth having, and then choose to fight the good fight.

Finish The Race

There are plenty of people willing to start something — start a relationship, start a job, start an exercise program, or start a program. Starting is not the problem. It's finishing the race that takes endurance.

Problem is, Hollywood glamorizes quitters. Have you ever noticed how often on television or in the movies, the boss demands one more project, the tension builds, the music crescendos until finally the worker explodes, yells, "I quit," and slams the door and the crowd cheers? Wouldn't that be great? I want to have that moment with the drama, the music, with that flare. Or the marriage that explodes with nasty words, clothes thrown out the window, and a dagger in the back — that's the way I would like to leave, with a scene. Or the college student who is overwhelmed so he blows it off, parties, and we think that looks a whole lot more fun than the library. Hollywood glamorizes the quitter who has no endurance. They focus on that exhilarating moment — "I quit." They don't show the worker now in the third month of being unemployed and staring at an eviction notice. They don't show the fallout and pain from a broken home. They don't show the college student kicked out of school and now flipping burgers and drinking his way through the weekend.

Paul begins by saying that this is a good fight, something worth the hardship. Now finish it. Finish the race. Finish strong. How? By being a person of faith.

Keep The Faith

This one is hard, isn't it? Keeping the faith in the midst of the storm. Keeping your trust even when you think you are walking this path alone. Keep the faith. Let me be honest with you, this is difficult. I think of my ministry when the demands are so high and I think, "Am I the right person for this job?" It would be easier to not to finish. It would be easy to lose faith.

How many times did Jesus think about quitting? — when they pulled his beard, sunk thorns into his scalp, beat him, and nailed spikes through his hands and feet. How many times did he think, "I can't do this. I want to quit. Surely there has to be an easier way, God, than this."

But he didn't. He endured. He fought the good fight — and what made it good and worthwhile was you. You were worth the fight. He finished the race — the last words he breathed on this earth were, "It is finished." And he kept the faith — "Father, into your hands I commit my soul."

Endurance is something even more important than knowing that this is an elbow. It means to fight the good fight, finish the race, keep the faith. Why? For the prize; delaying gratification now for even greater pleasure in the future. Paul always had the end in mind. He wanted the prize. He wrote, "The crown of righteousness that the Lord, the righteous judge will give me on that great day of his return." Then he looks right at you and adds, "And the prize is not just for me, but for all who eagerly look forward to his glorious return." Endurance is more than just sticking to it — it's keeping your eye on the prize. Amen.

**Reformation Day
Romans 3:19-28**

Saint And Sinner

"Since all have sinned and fall short of the glory of God" (Romans 3:23).

In the mid-1920s there was a successful, young, stockbroker who made it big on Wall Street. Really big! He had it all, materially speaking; money, country club membership, wealthy friends. He also drank. A lot! When the crash hit in 1929 and lasted for several years, he lost everything ... except his bottle of gin. His wife had to go to work only to come home day after day exhausted to find her husband drunk on the couch again.

He tried many times to stop drinking but couldn't until, with the help of a friend who had himself overcome the bottle with strong spiritual guidance, this young stockbroker, Bill W., began a process known today as the 12-step approach. Today, millions have found sobriety through this organization co-founded by Bill W. known as Alcoholics Anonymous.

Though it is not a blatantly religious movement, AA is grounded in some very basic spiritual or religious tenets beginning with a strong belief that God is the only help to achieve sobriety.

Step one begins the process by admitting that you are powerless over alcohol and that God is your only strength. This first step is critical and one of the most difficult. What you are saying is that alcohol has taken control of your life, and you cannot fix this problem yourself. After this, additional steps include making an honest inventory of your life and confessing these sins to another person.

I have had the opportunity to attend a few AA meetings as I have accompanied parishioners to meetings for the first time for support and encouragement. You will never find a more honest group of people because, as they told me, an alcoholic is a great liar but one drunk cannot lie to another. They know all the lies, all the excuses, all the lines. Honesty is the only alternative.

The meetings begin with introductions. First names only, like Bill W., and with the same lines. "Hello, I'm Susan and I'm an alcoholic. I have been sober since May 3, 1988."

Did you catch that? She hasn't had a drink in over twenty years — dry, sober, alcohol-free. And yet, what did she say? "I'm Susan, I *used* to be an alcoholic? I'm a *recovering* or *recovered* alcoholic?" No, the reality is, "I'm Susan and I am an alcoholic."

Is Susan free from alcohol or is she still in its grips? On the one hand, Susan is 100% free from the grips of alcohol. She is sober, dry, and alcohol-free. By the grace of God and the power of the Holy Spirit, she has been transformed. On the other hand, she is still in bondage to the condition of alcoholism because one drink will start the downward spiral all over again.

The answer is both. She is free and she is enslaved.

Our modern-day understanding of alcoholism is the best example I know to explain an important teaching that flowed from the Reformation called, "Saint and Sinner." Indeed, this teaching is a cornerstone on which is built our entire teaching of grace and faith. Basically, the question is this: Are we free from sin, released from its grips by the power of Christ's death and resurrection, or are we still in bondage to sin and under its demise?

Like the struggle with alcoholism, the answer is both. We are, at the same time, saints and sinners.

Luther spoke and wrote often about this paradoxical condition of the believer. On the one hand, we are 100% saints — the shackles of death have been destroyed by the blood of Jesus. Paul writes in Galatians, "For freedom Christ has set you free; stand fast, therefore, and do not submit again to a yoke of slavery." In Romans, Paul writes, "... you have been set free from sin" (6:22). "For the law of the Spirit of life in Christ Jesus has set you free from the law of sin and of death" (8:2). We are born again through faith. Death has no power over us. The law no longer rules us. We are 100% saints through our faith in Jesus.

Yet, at the same time, we are 100% sinners in bondage to this condition called sin. Look closely at the reading for today, "For there is no distinction, since all have sinned and fall short of the glory of God" (Romans 3:22b-23). In Romans 3:9-10, "All people ... are under the power of sin. None is righteous — not even one." Unable to completely cast off our sinful nature, we are, in our heart of hearts, a rebel, fleeing from God, spitting apple into his face and declaring, "I am the captain of my own vessel. I am accountable to no one. Just let me be."

When it comes to the condition of sin, we all are addicted. We are all rebels in our hearts. Luther said that it was like the birds of winter. Those that do not fly south try to gather up morsels here and there to survive until spring. Luther went out to feed the birds in his backyard once and instead of coming to him and receive the food, what did they do? They flew away. Pointing at the birds, Luther said, "That's me! God comes to me with goodness, life, and blessings to give and instead of eagerly accepting what God has, I fly away. I'll die without God's help but I am filled with doubt, overcome with fear and wickedly stubborn. God only wants to help and save and I flutter away."

In the *Lutheran Book of Worship*, the confession has these striking words that capture our addiction to sin. *I confess that I am in bondage to sin and cannot free myself.* Bondage — that word refers to that rebellious side that joins Adam and Eve in taking that bite of apple and wanting desperately to become like God. Though we are a saint through our faith in Jesus, that sinner inside keeps us in bondage to sin and we cannot free ourselves.

Is there any hope for us? Any hope at all? I think our best hope is to follow the steps laid out by Alcoholics Anonymous. It has saved millions of people. It works. But do you know what? Just between you and me, it's not new. Even in 1935 when it was founded, they actually stole the idea. It's from the Bible. It is the simple plan of salvation reduced to some easy-to-follow steps. It works for alcohol and, more importantly, it works for this bondage we call sin.

Step One: Admit that you are powerless over sin. Let's take off the mask. Let's stop playing games. Let's no longer pretend we are actually nice people and God is going to grade on a curve. I may not be perfect, I may not be a Mother Teresa, but compared to the other people I know, I am pretty decent. Nonsense! Stop the lies. Each one of us silently jingles in our pockets the nails from the cross. I put him there. I nailed him there. I crucified Jesus. I am powerless over sin.

Step Two: Turn your life over to God. For if there is any hope for me, any hope at all beyond the grave, it will not come from me. I cannot get myself out of this box, this hole, this hell — I need to be lifted out from a power outside of me. Turn your life over to God.

Step Three: Come clean. In your own heart, in your own quiet time, make an honest inventory of your life — who you've wronged, what you've done, how you've messed up — everything. List it all. Don't edit it. Leave in the swear words. After it is completed, add some more.

There is a great story about how Luther dealt with this long list of sins. Evidently, one night he had a nightmare in which the devil took out this huge book full of Luther's sins. They were itemized, numbered, and dated. The sheer size and numbers were overwhelming. The weight of the sins drove Luther to his knees in despair. As the devil completed his evidence against a nervous and contrite Luther, Luther suddenly realized something and said, "You forgot a few." With that he added more and more to the list provided by the devil and then wrote on the bottom, "Paid in full by Jesus Christ."

Step Three is to come clean. Make a list. A long list. Add a couple of more things and then nail it to the cross and walk away. Your debt has been paid in full through the blood of Jesus.

In my last church there was a very active member named Tom. Since he was a member of the council, I made it a point to visit with him in his home. During the course of our talk, he pulled out a coin from his pocket and showed me it. In the center was a big number twenty. He said, "I took my last drink twenty years ago. I'm an alcoholic."

"How did you manage to stay sober?" I asked.

"AA, and by the grace of God," he said.

"Twenty years. That's a long time," I said.

Tom replied, "I don't think of it as twenty years. It is one day at a time. My goal each morning when I get up is to make it through that day without a drink. One day at a time."

That's not only good AA talk but is also good Reformation theology. For Luther knew that this struggle between being a saint and a sinner is a daily battle. He called believers to wage war every morning. Wake up each day with a prayer and the sign of the cross as a means of confessing that sinful nature before God and then, at the same time, receive that forgiveness and recommit yourself that day to walking as a saint in the freedom of the gospel. One day at a time.

When Paul laid out the reality that all have sinned and fall short of the glory of God, it was not meant to be the final word. These words are only the vehicle that moves us forward to hear what we celebrate on this Reformation Day:

> *[We] are now justified by his grace as a gift, through the redemption that is in Christ Jesus ... because in his divine forbearance he had passed over the sins ... for we hold that a person is justified by faith apart from the works prescribed by the law.*
> — Romans 3:24, 25, 28

It all begins today with the very first step. Hello, my name is Scott, and I am a sinner who is in bondage to sin and cannot free myself. But thanks be to God who has called me through the gospel, enlightened me by the Spirit, and who has set me free as a saint through the cross of Jesus Christ.

Thanks be to God! Amen.

All Saints
Ephesians 1:11-23

The Final Word

... we, who were the first to set our hope on Christ, might live for the praise of his glory.
— Ephesians 1:12

Several years ago, I was asked to perform a funeral for a brother of a member of our church. I'll call him Jason. When I don't know the person, I usually gather the family together and ask them about their most vivid memories of the person. Most of the time, the next hour is filled with laughter and tears and fond memories.

When I asked Jason's family about their memories, there was this awkward pause. It was as if they knew what they were supposed to say, but they couldn't say it. They knew they were supposed to say that Jason would have given the shirt off his back to a stranger. They knew they were supposed to say that Jason never said a bad word about anyone. They knew they were supposed to say that Jason had love for his family and loyalty to his friends. Only they couldn't say it. It didn't fit. It wasn't true.

Finally one of the family members broke the awkward silence said, "Jason had made many bad choices, burned a lot of bridges, and hurt a lot of feelings. The stories, images, and memories that we have just couldn't be shared at a funeral sermon."

Funerals bring with them a myriad of emotions — sadness, loneliness, anger, hurt feelings, and unresolved guilt. Most of it remains unspoken.

What do you say at a funeral? It's often awkward, isn't it? The soft smiles and hushed tones. The repetitive phrases, "I'm so sorry for your loss. He was a good man. Good to see you. I wish it were under better circumstances." It's awkward, so you kick the ground, adjust the tie, hold a cup of coffee, or don't say anything at all.

I've been to many funerals. Sometimes the preacher feels as if he must entertain us with off-color stories and funny events. At other times, the words are so flattering that you are sure that the deceased is on the fast track to canonization next to Mother Teresa. Sometimes, they don't know what to say and so they just talk ... just talk and fill the void with words. What do you say at a funeral?

In John 11, Jesus attended a funeral. He got there late — four days late. Didn't matter, though. They were waiting for him. They wanted him there, desperately. They wanted him to say something comforting, something meaningful. Surely Jesus will have something to say at this funeral. After all, Lazarus was a friend of Jesus — as well as his sisters, Mary and Martha. If anyone would have just the right words to say to take away the pain, bring comfort, and get life back on track, it would be Jesus. When he arrives, there is a sigh of relief.

Before Jesus could speak, Martha's the first to break the silence with words of accusation, "Lord, if you had been here, my brother would not have died" (John 11:21). Do you hear all the questions in this accusation?

"I don't understand. Help me make sense of this one, Jesus. You were two miles away. Why weren't you here? Why did my brother have to die?"

At every funeral there is a Martha who is seeking answers to difficult questions.

Jesus replied by reminding her that her brother would live again. But Martha seems to pass off those words as meaningless, pie-in-the-sky, sweet nothing, church talk better left for a Hallmark™ card, and says, "Oh, I know that he will rise on the last day ... but that doesn't help me here, right now. I want him alive. And you weren't here. Jesus, if you'd a been here, my brother would not have died." Do you hear the anger?

Jesus then shares some words. It isn't a cute story about when he and Lazarus went fishing one day. It wasn't flowery words about how everyone loved Lazarus. He didn't mention what a good

Christian Lazarus was nor did he give Martha one of those, "There, there. It'll be okay." He said the only thing to say at a funeral. "I am the resurrection and the life. Anyone who believes in me will live, even after dying" (John 11:25, NLT). Then came the punch line, "Do you believe this, Martha?" (John 11:26, NLT).

"I am the resurrection and the life." Those are the words that need to be said at a funeral. Those are the words that need to be heard on All Saints because they are the final word. The last remaining question is, "Do you believe this?"

There are so many other words and voices vying for our attention at a funeral. The Hallmark™ card wants to summarize our grief in a two-line limerick. The back of the mortuary card tells us the person is not gone but somehow present in the sunrise and the morning breeze. Our neighbor consults the stars, the spiritualist wants to meditate, the palm reader wants to look at your hand, and the atheist has nothing to say. People look and listen in all sorts of places, desperate to hear some answers and so they consult New Age to witchcraft to aroma therapy to a stiff drink. What do you say at a funeral?

The answer is: nothing. At least nothing from us. This is a time for God's word to be heard. Listen to the power and authority and hope and faith that Paul uses to describe the sure and certain hope that is ours in Jesus.

> *I pray that your hearts will be flooded with light so that you can understand the wonderful future he has promised to those he called. I want you to realize what a rich and glorious inheritance he has given to his people. I pray that you will begin to understand the incredible greatness of his power for us who believe in him....*
> — Ephesians 1:18-19

Our voice is the last thing that needs to be heard at a funeral. Our voice cannot lift the fog. Our voice cannot restore the hope. Our voice cannot raise the dead. There is only one voice that can do all of that. The voice that told his followers not just to hear his words but to follow him. The voice that did not correct Thomas when he cried out, "My Lord and my God." The voice who said if you have seen me, you have seen God. The voice that made it clear that he gave his life for the forgiveness of sins. The voice that says even through tears, "I am the resurrection and the life; he who believes in me, though he die, yet shall he live" (John 11:25 RSV).

That voice alone has the final word particularly on All Saints when we remember those who have died when each one of us feels this pain, this emptiness, this sadness, and even this anger and guilt from missing that person. Particularly on this day, more than any other day, we need to sift through all the noise, all the voices, all the garbage, and long to hear that one voice of truth and authority that alone can raise the dead.

What is that final word? What is that hope to which we've been called? That word is grace. Jesus came not to make bad people good through his example of purity but to make dead people live through his cross of forgiveness.

We did go through with Jason's funeral — the brother who made all those bad choices, burned bridges, and hurt feelings. We had his funeral. But we didn't list his Eagle Scout badge or mention the little old ladies he helped across the street or recall his generous heart and his deep love, because frankly, it wasn't true. Everyone in that room knew it wasn't true. No one dared say that they wished God would judge him on all the good that he did, because there wasn't much.

On that day, there was only one voice to be heard. The voice that spoke at Jason's funeral was the same that spoke at Lazarus' funeral and the same that spoke through the hope found in Paul's words to the Ephesians. It will be the same voice, the only voice that needs to be heard at your funeral. The voice of forgiveness. The only voice that can raise the dead. The voice of Jesus.

The family needed to hear forgiveness. All those hurt feelings and broken promises and bad choices — it was time to let them go. With death taking away the possibility of reconciling with Jason, they had a choice. They could harbor resentment and let it eat at their heart, or they could hear the voice of forgiveness and let it go.

Jason needed forgiveness. He was not a saint, but Jesus did not come for the saints. He came for the sick, the outcast, and the sinner. Jesus came for the likes of Jason because the playing field is level before the holy throne of God — knee level. We all approach not with a resume of good works, kind acts, and strong intentions but on our knees by faith right next to Jason.

There is only one voice I want to hear at my funeral. It is not a family member reciting how much we loved each other. It's not a friend retelling an embarrassing story about me. It's not a pastor reciting my accomplishments. There is only one voice, one final word that I want spoken at my funeral — the sure and certain hope that comes through the forgiveness of sins.

I pray that your hearts will be flooded with light so that you can understand the wonderful future he has promised to those he called. I want you to realize what a rich and glorious inheritance he has given to his people. I pray that you will begin to understand the incredible greatness of his power for us who believe in him. Amen.

**Proper 26
Pentecost 24
Ordinary Time 31
2 Thessalonians 1:1-4, 11-12**

Worthy Of Your Call

> ... *we always pray for you, that our God may make you worthy of his call....*
> — 2 Thessalonians 1:11 (RSV)

Worthy of your call. That is Paul's prayer for the Thessalonians; that they would be worthy of God's call (1:11). It is one thing to have low expectations, something that would take little effort to achieve. But in chapter 1 of 2 Thessalonians, we have a sense that God has larger aspirations for these young Christians — and so does Paul. You have a sense that through all the persecution and affliction that they have suffered (1:4), Paul envisions a God-sized dream for them.

What are your God-sized dreams? These are the dreams that you cannot achieve alone with just more education, more hours, more determination, and more contacts. These are dreams that only God can achieve by working through the likes of you, a flawed, cracked vessel. These are dreams that have nothing to do with your quick wit and winning smile. It may be a dream to grow a church that reaches thousands. It may be a program that will help transform a neighborhood. It may even be dreams of running for public office and truly serving the people. If all obstacles were taken away, what are your God-sized dreams?

Fulfilling that God-sized dream would be "worthy of your call."

What happens when the path leading to that dream is marked with the kind of persecution, affliction, and suffering these people from Thessalonica have suffered? What happens when what seemed to be the right path is suddenly blocked with obstacles beyond your control? How do you prove to be worthy of your call when your life is no longer energized by God-sized dreams but rather with nightmares that plunge you further in the pit?

I want to share with you a powerful testimony I heard Phil Vischer give while speaking at a conference at Willow Creek in Chicago. Have you heard of Phil Vischer? I had not, at least by name. But I certainly knew about his product. He is the creator of *VeggieTales*. Have you heard of *VeggieTales*? If you haven't, *VeggieTales* are animated, short videos for children featuring limbless vegetables acting out Bible stories and moral truths. When you put it that way, it doesn't sound very impressive, does it? However, consider this:

- *VeggieTales* has sold 40 million videos.
- In 1999 and 2000, *VeggieTales* outsold Barney, Scooby Doo, and Pokémon combined.
- Those same years, CNN announced that *VeggieTales* was listed in the top ten videos watched on college campuses.
- In 2000, Vischer was named as one of the top ten religious leaders in America with write ups in *Newsweek*, *Time*, and *People* magazines.

VeggieTales was an incredible, nearly overnight success story headed up a guy who, as he describes himself, was kicked out of Bible college after three semesters for failing chapel. He left school to pursue his God-sized dream. This was a man of faith who wanted to make a deep impact for the kingdom, not just sell videos and retire early in southern Florida. He caught the attention of Disney who surrounded him with a staff of over 200 people who whispered around the water cooler, "Phil Vischer is the next Walt Disney." Unbelievable!

In a sense, this was like the young church in Thessalonica. They had heard the gospel from Paul. He filled them with God-sized dreams coupled with the power of the Holy Spirit. They were on fire for their faith, ready to move mountains and transform the world, until persecution knocked the wind out of them.

In the case of Vischer, it was a former distributor who took him to court. Vischer knew that he was in the right but it doesn't matter when you are presented with a lawsuit. You go to court, you spend lots of money on lawyers, and in the end you are at the mercy of the court who decided against Vischer and gave the distributor everything they asked for ... and much more. Vischer had to close down the studio, lay off the staff, and sell *VeggieTales* in order to pay off the enormous debt. As quickly as this God-sized dream had grown, it disappeared. For Vischer, *VeggieTales* was finished.

How can you be worthy of your call with affliction like that?

Stunned, Vischer wondered, "How could you, God? How could you give me this incredible gift and then sit back and do nothing as I watched it die? How could you? How could you promise me this dream, deliver this dream, and then pop this dream?"

After a long time in prayer and reading his Bible, Vischer was drawn to Genesis 22 — Abraham's sacrifice of Isaac. Remember how Abraham was given a promise that his descendants would be more numerous than grains of sand? They would outnumber the stars. Sure, he had to wait a long time for the dream to actualize — 25 years of waiting. But now, the God-sized dream came true with Isaac. The God-sized dreams of descendants numbering more than grains of sands and stars in the sky could begin. Now Abraham could be worthy of his call.

Except, in Genesis 22, God says to Abraham, "Take your son, your only son, the one whom you love (and just so there is no misunderstanding), the one named Isaac and sacrifice him to me." God did not want Isaac's death. It was a test with only one question. "What is more important to you — the dream or God?" As Abraham raised his knife to Isaac, God knew that Abraham was willing to surrender and let go of everything, even his God-sized dream. He was willing to put it all on the altar and watch it die — everything, except for knowing and trusting God.

Through that experience of Abraham, Phil Vischer realized that he had confused doing the work of God with knowing God. His goal was to make a great impact, to reach more people, to do more wonderful things for God. All great and wonderful things. However, it was not to know God. Phil understood what had happened with *VeggieTales* as God was asking him to sacrifice his dream on the altar for the sake of keeping his eyes on Jesus. He had gotten ahead of God. He was asking God to catch up to him and bless what he had done. Bottom line: He had taken his eyes off Jesus.

Then Vischer asked a question to the congregation, "What do you dream that you can do for God? Expand your ministry? Increase membership? Impact more people? Build a bigger church? What do you dream that you can do for God?"

It is not a question to be taken lightly or answered flippantly. For a deeper affect, Vischer let the question hang in the air for several minutes until he concluded, "When you are ready to put that dream on the altar and kill it for the sake of knowing God, then you are ready."

Then you are ready. Or, in Paul's words, then you are worthy of your call.

Make no doubt here. Paul is not encouraging the Thessalonians to continue in their food pantry ministry. Paul is not advising them on how to plant another church. Paul is not asking them for more money. For Paul, to be worthy of your call is found in 1:3-4.

> ... *your faith is growing abundantly, and the love of everyone of you for one another is increasing. Therefore we ourselves boast of you among the churches of God for your steadfastness and faith during all your persecutions and the afflictions that you are enduring.*
> — 2 Thessalonians 1:3-4

To be worthy of your call is to keep your eyes fixed on Jesus. Everything else needs to be put on the altar and, at a moment's notice, be plunged with a knife. For the first commandment is clear; you shall have no other gods before me. This includes even your God-sized dreams. Amen.

**Proper 27
Pentecost 25
Ordinary Time 32
2 Thessalonians 2:1-5, 13-17**

Sarah

Don't be so easily shaken or alarmed by those who say that the day of the Lord has already begun.
— 2 Thessalonians 2:2 (NLT)

Max Lucado, in his book, *In the Eye of the Storm*, writes about a woman named Sarah who was rich.[1] Really rich! She inherited twenty million dollars plus had an additional income of $1,000 a day. That's a lot of money today. But in the late 1800s when Sarah lived, it was downright staggering.

You can imagine that she was well-known, having come from the elite, upper crust of the New England coast. Well-known and powerful. Her name and money opened doors closed to most of us. Colleges wanted her scholarships. Politicians wanted her support. Organizations wanted her donations.

Did I mention that she was rich? And powerful? And well-known? She was also miserable. Her only daughter died when she was five weeks old and her husband died shortly afterward, following their daughter to the grave. This left Sarah alone with her money, her memories, her misery, and enough guilt to max out even *her* credit cards.

It was primarily this last burden of her guilt that made her leave the luxury of her mansion in Connecticut and ride the train until its very last whistle stop in San Jose, California. It's amazing the distance we will travel to escape the reminders, silence the voices, and avoid the reality. She did escape — right into a prison of her own making.

She bought an eight-room farmhouse and 160 acres of land. She hired sixteen carpenters and put them to work — for 38 years. Every day. Twenty-four hours. She hired them to build, what? A mansion or was it a castle? Better yet, it was more like a prison.

Sarah oversaw the entire project all the way down to the eerie, macabre details like thirteen panes on each window, thirteen panels on each wall, thirteen hooks in each closet, and thirteen globes in each chandelier.

The floor plan was just as creepy. There were corridors snaking around the complex, some going nowhere. One door opened to a blank wall, another to a fifty-foot drop. One set of stairs led to a ceiling that had no door. Trapdoors, secret passageways, tunnels — think of the latest Stephen King horror movie and you get the picture.

The construction didn't end until Sarah finally died. In those 38 years, the estate sprawled over six acres with six kitchens, thirteen bathrooms, forty stairways, 47 fireplaces, 52 skylights, 467 inside doors, 10,000 windows, 160 rooms, and a bell tower.

Why? Why would you build such a place? Because you could afford it? That's too easy. There had to be something more to it than extravagance or opulence. Those acquainted with her said it was because she had so many visitors ... each night.

Legend has it that every evening at midnight a servant would pass through the secret labyrinth of tunnels to the bell tower. He would then ring the bell to summon the ghosts who would convene nightly in the blue room with Sarah. Together, they would linger until 2 a.m. when the bell would ring again. The spirits would return to their graves, and Sarah would return to her room.

Who were these spirits that haunted the mansion and would not let Sarah sleep? The legend says that they are all the Indians and soldiers and cowboys killed on the US frontier. Men, women, and children who were killed by bullets from the most popular and effective rifle and killing machine known in America — The Winchester. The same thing that brought death to these people brought millions of dollars to Sarah ... Sarah Winchester.

And now, as Paul Harvey would say, you know the rest of the story.

Sarah spent the last 38 years of her life trapped in a castle of memories, providing a home for the restless dead, and learning how to cope with her guilt ... according to legend, at least.

You don't have to build a Winchester mansion to deal with unresolved guilt or fear of the future. I suppose we all figure out different ways, more creative ways, less expensive ways to assuage a heart that just can't seem forget or ignore a page from our past or a lie in our present or the unknown of the future.

Some of us, like Sarah, are doomed to wander the halls and entertain those poltergeists in the dead of the night when they rise to haunt us, robbing us of sleep, and preventing peace.

Maybe you know a Sarah? Maybe Sarah's story is your story. Different portfolio, different floor plan, but same insatiable quest for forgiveness and resolution.

The answers to guilt's questions are not found in a new house. The answers are not found in a distracted life. The answers are not found in simply learning how to live with the restlessness. The answers are found in the one who has the power to forgive and forget. The answers are found in the one who promises to return to those who await him and give what they have waited a lifetime to hear.

Scholars say that 2 Thessalonians was written shortly after 1 Thessalonians as a way for Paul to clarify the widespread misunderstanding of Paul's teachings concerning the return of Jesus. Many who read the first letter thought that the end time had already begun. Judging from the content of 2 Thessalonians, many had quit work, fallen into despair, and lived with a constant fear.

> *And now, brothers and sisters, let us tell you about the coming again of our Lord Jesus Christ and how we will be gathered together to meet him. Please don't be so easily shaken and troubled by those who say that the day of the Lord has already begun.*
> — 2 Thessalonians 2:1-2 (NLT)

Paul wrote this follow-up letter to reprimand them sharply, to remind them of the true teaching, and to encourage them to live lives that would prepare them for Jesus' return. It is not a letter filled with fear and horrible images of damnation. Instead, Paul reminds them of the hope that is theirs to come.

> *As for us, we always thank God for you, dear brothers and sisters loved by the Lord. We are thankful that God chose you to be among the first to experience salvation, a salvation that came through the Spirit who makes you holy and by your belief in the truth.*
> — 2 Thessalonians 2:13 (NLT)

Paul needs to remind these young Christians who have either fallen into despair or tremble with fear about Jesus' authority to forgive sins. To have the power to forgive a person's sins is reserved only for the one who has the power, who has the authority, who sits on the right side of God as judge over the living and the dead and who promised to return one day for the cleansing of those who believe in him.

That's what the Son of Man does. That's what he came to do. That's what he has the power to perform. He forgives and then goes one step further. He forgets. He erases the board, shreds the evidence, destroys the chip, and deletes the screen. For all the things that the Son of Man promises to do for us, the one thing that he refuses to do is to remember.

> *... as far as the east is from the west, so far he removes our transgressions from us.* — Psalm 103:12

> *Even if you are stained as red as crimson, I can make you white as wool.* — Isaiah 1:18 (NLT)

> *I will be their God, and they shall be my people ... and I will remember their sins no more.*
> — Hebrews 8:10, 12

Do you believe that?

Jesus gives us a double promise; to forgive and forget. But we don't, do we? Not as easily, anyway. We have a good memory.

We are more like Sarah who entertains the ghosts of our past that still linger, robbing us of sleep and peace. What these demons that go bump in the night are doing, really, is trying to get you to forget whose you are. They are giving your spiritual journey a limp from some irritable stone in your sandal. They fill us with doubts whether or not God could actually do what he promises — forgive and forget. That's the gift that Jesus, the Son of Man, judge of the world gives to us — a terrible memory. He doesn't keep record of those past sins on his clipboard to check it next time you get on your knees and say you're sorry. Instead, his gift is a grace filled, mercy driven, terrible memory so you don't drive yourself crazy hanging out with the ghosts of the past.

You don't have to learn to live with your past and cope with your guilt like Sarah Winchester. You don't have to tremble and be shaken like those young Thessalonians. Jesus offers a cure.

My wife and I recently saw *A Beautiful Mind*. It has been a long time since a movie has made such an impact on me. It's about a lot of things — friendship, marriage, commitment, and love. It is also about mental illness. The movie suggests what I have always thought was most often the case with mental illness. That is, most people suffering from mental illness are not "cured" like some physical diseases through treatment, drugs, or surgery. Most often those with mental illness learn how to cope or live with or even ignore their illness — but it is still always there. Those with depression, anxiety, or, as in the case of this movie, schizophrenia, it doesn't actually go away but you learn how to deal with it, learn how to live with it, even learn how to ignore it. This movie depicts mental illness more like a bad back or diabetes or alcoholism. It never goes away but you learn ways to cope with it.

That might work with diabetes or depression. We might have wonderful drugs to mask the problems of anxiety or support groups to deal with addiction or exercises to ease lower back trouble. But when it comes to my guilt, I don't want a drug or a coping mechanism. I don't want to have to learn how to live with unresolved guilt, or cope with, live, or figure out how to ignore it. When it comes to sins, I'm not looking for a distraction or a class on how to live with it. There are too many Sarahs who are plagued with spirits of their past who rise when the sun goes down to make us doubt the very words of Jesus. I'm looking for someone who can bring a cure, wipe away all traces of it. I'm looking for a savior that Paul describes — one who forgives and forgets.

Maybe that is why when others refer to Jesus, they use Lord, Messiah, or Christ, and he is. But when Jesus refers to himself, by far the most common title he uses is Son of Man — the one who has the power and authority and might to heal us at our deepest level; at the level of our guilt with the power of his word, "Not guilty, for Jesus' sake."

Now you know the rest of the story. Amen.

---

1. Max Lucado, *In The Eye of the Storm* (Nashville: Thomas Nelson, 2001), p. 191.

**Proper 28
Pentecost 26
Ordinary Time 33
2 Thessalonians 3:6-13**

No Work, No Food!

Whoever does not work should not eat!
— 2 Thessalonians 3:10 (NLT)

Wow! Kind of takes your breath away, doesn't it? Not a lot of ambiguity in that rule. "You don't work, you don't eat." For a religion based on grace, it seems a bit unyielding.

You would expect that rule in our ever-productive society. After all, it seems that our worth is determined by how much we can produce. Therefore, we judge others on how much (or how little) they are contributing. But is this really the way we ought to proceed in our faith? Should productivity be the measure by which we decide whether or not a person is deserving of food?

I grew up in a family that could not stand idle time. They originated the saying, "Don't just sit there — do something!" It was most apparent when one of us got the flu. When one of us got sick, we were handed a sleeve of saltine crackers and a liter of Seven-Up® and sent to our rooms until we could become a productive member of society once again! (Okay, that is a bit of an exaggeration but you get the point. Thankfully, they still fed us during bed rest even if we did not work.) I understand a high work ethic.

When I read these strong words from Paul in 2 Thessalonians, I contrast it to the parable told by Jesus in Matthew 20:1-15 where day laborers went into the marketplace at dawn and the owners of the vineyards would go and hire as many workers as they needed. The going wage for one day of work was one denarius.

However, in the parable, one owner miscalculated the number of workers he needed. He returned to the marketplace four times: 9 a.m., noon, 3 p.m., and again at 5 p.m. just one hour before the whistle blew. Those who were hired at 9 a.m. expected the one denarius as payment. However, for those hired later in the day, all the owner said was, "I will pay you whatever is right." No contract. Just a promise.

Of course, you know how the story ends. They all line up after work for their paychecks. Beginning with the 5 p.m. workers, the owner pays everyone the same amount — one denarius. When those who were hired at the crack of dawn made it to the front of the line, they expected something more in their paychecks, but were disappointed to find out that their full-day work amounted to the same paycheck as those Johnny-come-latelys who only worked for one hour.

Jesus' parable reminds us that in the kingdom of God, all are seen as equals. From those who were baptized as infants to the thief on the cross who made it through the gates at the eleventh hour, all are treated equally. Does that mean that we can sleep in late, grab a late brunch with a Belgian waffle topped with whipped cream and fresh strawberries, catch the afternoon show of *Oprah*, and then around 5 p.m. show up for an hour of work?

You can hear from those who bore the heat of the full day cry out, "Unfair!" You can't give everyone the same pay. You can't give everyone the same grade. The whole class cannot be valedictorians. The entire team cannot be the captain. The entire business cannot be owners. Life is full of comparisons, some are higher, some are lower. It just goes against everything we do and believe to make all the workers equal. They grumble, "He made the ones who worked only for a few hours equal to those who bore the burden of the entire day."

Here is where the confusion lies — equality.

In the parable, Jesus is talking about our justification. Between the long time believer and the eleventh-hour-thief-on-the-cross, there is no distinction. There is no gradation in heaven. There is nothing extra in your paycheck when you pass through the pearly gates at the end of the day. Jesus is talking about how we are saved.

In the end, it doesn't matter if we believed our whole lives or had a deathbed conversion. We are all beggars in need of God's grace. None is deserving of more. Ironically, Jesus puts the gospel in the words of the grumblers when they say, "He made the ones who worked for only a few hours equal to those who bore the burden of the entire day." Exactly! That is the grace found in the kingdom of God.

But in 2 Thessalonians, Paul is talking about how we ought to live. In theological jargon, Jesus spoke about justification and Paul spoke about sanctification. Just like we cannot read Paul to defend works righteousness, we cannot read Jesus to defend laziness.

However, underlining both of their teachings is the same point — entitlement. Once we cross over that line from humility and gratitude to entitlement and demands, we miss seeing the surprise of the gospel at work in our lives.

To the longtime believer who approaches the throne of heaven with a laundry list of accomplishments from regular worship attendance to generous donations to volunteering at the soup kitchen, they are in for a surprise to find that many will cry out, "Lord, Lord" but he will not know them. Tradition has it that on his deathbed, after a lifetime of faithful service, Luther continued to preach grace by saying, "We are all beggars. This is most certainly true."

No one ought to have the arrogance of entitlement coming before the throne of God, demanding that to get exactly what you deserve — nothing more or nothing less. Such a demand for justice would only bring with it exactly that — damnation, judgment, and death. What Jesus taught in Matthew 20 was that entitlement does not enter into our ability to stand before God's throne.

Neither does entitlement factor into Paul's teaching in 2 Thessalonians.

Our church like many other congregations volunteers often at the local soup kitchen or homeless shelter. We don't turn away people due to gender or race or religion. We don't even turn away people because of a sense of entitlement. But there are certainly those guests who come with gratitude in their heart, thankful for what can be provided. And there are others who come with a sense of entitlement, demanding more than we have and ungrateful for what we can offer. We haven't come to the point of enforcing Paul's command, but we certainly understand Paul's point — if you don't work, you don't eat.

It comes down to entitlement. God does not have to forgive our sins, grant us mercy, and receive us into the kingdom. None of us are entitled. He does so out of love. In the same way, it is difficult to imagine that same entitlement thinking being appropriate at the soup kitchen or homeless shelter.

Rudyard Kipling, author of the *Jungle Book*, at the height of his career received large payments for even the shortest articles. Some struggling literature majors in England resented his success. After reading a report that Kipling had received a large sum for a short story, these students divided up the payment by the number of words in the essay and calculated that Kipling was paid fifty cents per word. With dripping sarcasm, the students mailed Kipling fifty cents and asked him to give them his best word. In a brief time, the students receive a letter from the author with only one word, "Thanks."

It is with such humility and gratitude that we approach both the throne of God as well as receive help from others — thanks. Amen.

Christ The King
Proper 29
Colossians 1:11-20

This Is A King?

> *He is the image of the invisible God, the firstborn of all creation; for in him all things in heaven and on earth were created ... in him all the fullness of God was pleased to dwell...* — Colossians 1:15-16, 19

I grew up during all those *Godfather* movies, and I never saw a single one. I don't know why. I was busy. It was a three-hour movie. I had to study. So when I heard jokes about a horse's head or making an offer that he couldn't refuse, I didn't get it. The same is true today, right? There are those who have not watched or read a single *Harry Potter* story or a single *Star Wars* movie. When they hear, "The Force be with you," some only think, "And also with you." They don't get it. That's true with many things. There are those who have never been on a golf course, never went sailing, and never had children. Their understanding of these things is limited.

There are even those who haven't heard much about Jesus except how to curse using his name. They've never cracked open a Bible. They've never darkened the door of a church. They've never attended Sunday school. Now, put yourself into their world and you hear that this Jesus

> *He is the image of the invisible God, the firstborn of all creation; for in him all things in heaven and on earth were created ... in him all the fullness of God was pleased to dwell...* — Colossians 1:15-16, 19

You would expect someone like Jesus to stand out. You would expect someone like this to have words of wisdom. You would expect someone in whom the fullness of God dwelt to take your breath away. What you don't expect is the Jesus of the New Testament who says ...

> *Fortunate are those who are poor, Lucky are those who are hungry, Blessed are those who weep. If you are being persecuted, abused, beaten — rejoice.*
> — Matthew 5:3, 6, 11 (paraphrased)

> *Don't hate your enemies, love them. Do good things for them. If they hit you on one cheek, turn and let them strike you on the other. If they demand your coat, give them your shirt also.*
> — Matthew 5:40, 43-44

> *Also, you know that it is wrong to murder, but I tell you that even if you think angry thoughts about someone it is the same as murder. And you know that you should not commit adultery. But I tell you even looking at another person and having lustful fantasies, you are as guilty as the one who crawls into bed with him or her.*
> — Matthew 5:21, 27-28 (paraphrased)

Can you hear these words for the first time? Remember, you don't know that these words are from Jesus. You have heard nothing about the Sermon on the Mount. Lucky are the poor. Rejoice that you are beaten. Love your enemies. You think there's nothing wrong with cursing someone under your breath? You think there's no harm in just looking? Think again, you murderer. Reconsider, you adulterer. Now, what is your reaction? Honestly? It's got to be one of four.

First, *that's just stupid!* Philip Yancey in his book, *The Jesus I Never Knew*, quotes a professor at Texas A&M who had her English comp class read these words from the Beatitudes from Jesus and asked them to write an essay. She expected them to have some basic biblical knowledge but soon found out they had very little. She grew up in a church with a picture of Jesus teaching these words on a small mountain overseeing a green hillside surrounded by eager pink children.

She never heard these words with disgust or anger. But that is what her students wrote:

> *The stuff the churches preach is extremely strict and allows for almost no fun without thinking it is a sin or not.*
>
> *The things asked in this sermon are absurd. To look at a woman is adultery. That is the most extreme, stupid, unhuman statement that I have ever heard.*
>
> *There is an old saying that you shouldn't believe everything you read and it applies in this case.*

It never occurred to this professor that someone might call Jesus stupid. Yet what she heard from her students was a pure, unfiltered reaction to the words of Jesus that have not been spiritualized by the church. These words are offensive and when they were first uttered by Jesus, he didn't just puzzle the people, he infuriated them.

Second, *it isn't that nice!* It means you have no intention of taking it to heart. Jesus was just throwing out Hallmark™ card platitudes to the poor people, "God bless you." To those whose faces were wet with tears, Jesus comforted them, "Count your blessings." But we don't really believe it, do we?

Philip Yancey wrote that he and about a dozen evangelicals were invited to breakfast with President Clinton. Clinton was low in the polls with conservative Christians, and he wanted to hear from them. Each guest was given five minutes. What should he say? Yancey thought he should say what Jesus would have said:

> *Mr. President, first I want to advise you to stop worrying so much about the economy and jobs. A lower Gross National Product is actually good for the country because the more poor we have in America, the more blessed we are.*
>
> *And don't worry about health care. You see, Mr. President, the more people who weep and mourn, the more fortunate that we are.*

> *And I know that you have heard from the "Religious Right" about prayer taken out of schools and protesters against abortion being arrested. Relax, sir. More government oppression actually gives Christians an opportunity to be persecuted and we want to thank you for those expanded opportunities.*

He didn't share those words with the president. Why? Because we really don't believe it. No one is striving to be more poor, more hungry, or more abused. This is America! Happy are the strong, the rich, the healthy, and the confident.

Even the church thinks this way. The theologian, Soren Kierkegaard, once attended a large cathedral in Europe that took decades to build and cost millions of dollars. The priest stood before an ivory altar in his silver threaded chasuble, lifted up the gold chalice of fine wine and read, "Blessed are the poor, blessed are the hungry ..." and Kierkegaard looked around and realized no one laughed. If they took Jesus' words seriously, there should be laughter because even the church isn't living it. Blessed are the poor? Isn't that nice? Bless his heart.

There is a third response from those who hear these words and think, *if that is what Jesus said, then I'll do it.* Let me tell you about Linda. Linda's not right. Linda's from New York where she had a home and a job and family. She said that God put it on her heart to leave it all and do ministry in Romania. She contacted "Smiles," an organization in Great Britain that works with the poor of Romania and told them of her intentions. The director, Kevin Hoy, said, "That's fine but have you been to Romania before?"

"No," she replied.

"Do you think you should come once before you quit your job and sell everything?"

She did, but only to appease the director. Her mind was made up. If Jesus called us to serve the poor, then Linda needed to roll up her sleeves and begin the work.

In Romania, Linda lives alone and raises pigs and chickens for food that are slaughtered for the poor. She's a city girl who spends her time cleaning out the pig sty. She gets up about 5 a.m. to go out and water the many acres of cucumbers, tomatoes, corn, and peppers while singing, "How Great Thou Art." She says that the plants think that she is singing about them and they like it.

She gets no salary. She has to raise all of her living expenses; nothing is provided for her. Her one luxury is a bath twice a week. For the past couple of years, I've brought Linda a jar of peanut butter when I travel with a missionary team to Romania. From her reaction, you would think it was filet and lobster.

I look at Linda, I hear her love for the pigs and the vegetables and how they will feed the hungry children we work with there. I hear her joy about living with the poor of Romania. I hear her sacrifice of what she has given up to serve God. And I think, she's not right. Even if I were single and had few responsibilities, I still wouldn't do that. Linda's not right. But in my heart, I know Linda is right, more right with God than I am.

Which brings me to the fourth response to these strange words of Jesus. *How is it that Jesus made the law impossible for anyone to follow and then demands us to keep it?* If I am angry with someone, I'm a murderer? If I have a lustful thought, I'm an adulterer? Give away all that I have to the poor? If my hand causes me to sin, cut it off? Do not worry about tomorrow? What am I to do? Cash out my IRA and scatter it among the panhandlers? Cancel my insurance and trust God? Throw out my television and cancel the newspaper and magazines with the ads that tempt me to buy more?

If these words of Jesus are not stupid, if they are not some Hallmark™ card platitude (isn't that nice), if they are true then the bar is too high for me to reach. If these words are true, they drop me to my knees and reveal to me just how far short I fall of Jesus. Now what?

It is right there, at that fourth response, dropped to our knees that we grasp the very heart of Jesus' message on this Christ The King Sunday. You misunderstand this and you misunderstand the very core of Jesus' teachings. You miss this and you miss who he really is.

> *He is the image of the invisible God, the firstborn of all creation; for in him all things in heaven and on earth*

> *were created ... In him all the fullness of God was pleased to dwell...* — Colossians 1:15-16, 19

These words of Jesus are not so much telling us what we should be like but what God is like. Even Linda, who is trying to be obedient to these words of Jesus, knows how far short she falls from the glory of God. She's been dropped to her knees. She knows that the chasm that separates her from God is huge and that at the last trumpet sound, when Christ the King will stand upon the earth, we all will stand on level ground before the throne of God — murderers, temper-throwers, adulterers, lusters, thieves, coveters. We are all desperate and in need of a king who is first a Savior.

Jesus the king came to make self-absorbed, guilt-driven, dead people alive with the only words that make a difference, the only words that will drop you to your knees, the only words that matter when he returns — "Your sins are forgiven for Jesus' sake."

That's not crazy talk. That's not Hallmark™. That is the very heart of Jesus' promise to return as King of kings and Lord of lords; so that you might know, believe, confess, and walk daily in the shadow of the cross and in the grace of God. Amen.

Thanksgiving Day
Philippians 4:4-9

A New Resolve

"Stand firm in the Lord" (Philippians 4:1).

Last summer, my children rode a flight simulator. Basically, they strap you into a box in front of a screen and shake it upside down. It is supposed to feel more like flying an airplane than a Disney ride. They also had a camera on the people inside the simulator so that those waiting outside can see what was going on inside the cockpit. When my daughter had the controls, the plane was level, missed the trees, and landed smoothly. When my son took over the controls, the box spun with barrel rolls, shot straight up, and then dove nose first into a spectacular crash landing.

All fun and games but not to a real pilot. They spend hours in that little box not for amusement but to train themselves and to prepare for worst-case scenarios so that when lightning does hit or an engine goes out or a landing gear is stuck in real life, they will know what to do. Without that training and foundation, they would be lost.

Can you imagine going into battle without the foundation of basic training? Can you imagine going into a highly technical computer job without some basic training in computers? Can you imagine going through job loss, divorce, or death without the foundation of new hope?

The point is, you need some basic training, some foundation, before going into a cockpit, battle, or surgery. Paul uses that same logic when he talks about life. To introduce our lesson in Philippians 4:4-9, Paul begins in 4:1 with the imperative, "Stand firm in the Lord." The imagery that Paul is using with this phrase is that of a guard or a sentry who, with weapon in hand, stands firm. He is guarding something or someone. He makes sure that nothing will get through him, not on his watch.

Paul is telling us to do the same thing. Stand firm. Do not be caught off guard. As I look at 4:4-9, the word that comes to mind is "resolve." Stand firm with resolve. The time for the pilot to figure out how to land a plane with a blown engine is not mid-air. The time for a married couple to figure out how to fight fairly is not in the middle of the argument. The time for the young adult to figure out their sexuality is not in the moment of passion. Paul is saying that the time for the Christian to decide how to respond in crisis is not when you are overcome by pain, grief, and doubt. Resolve right now how you will act, respond, and speak while you are still in the simulator. To be sure, real life is far more intense and unpredictable than a simulator but start building that foundation now.

Paul knew what he wrote about. Remember, Paul wrote this letter while beaten and imprisoned in Rome, awaiting his execution. Yet he wrote, "Rejoice in the Lord always" (v. 4). How can Paul write that? Because long before he was thrown into prison, Paul decided how he would respond. He resolved in his own mind how to stand firm, how to guard his heart and mind. And now he shares three very specific things for us to guard.

First, *guard your relationship with God*. Paul begins by writing, "Do not worry about anything" (v. 6). Isn't that crazy? That must be the most difficult command to obey. If someone were to come to me saying that he lost his job, was going through bankruptcy, his wife was leaving him, his children were strung out on drugs, and now he wants to end it all, could you imagine simply saying, "Don't worry about anything"? That would be crazy. So how does Paul get away with it? Because it is not an emotion that Paul is commanding. It's a relationship with God. When that breaks down, worry increases because most worry is not trusting God. Most worry is unnecessary and destructive. A recent study discovered that:

- 40% of our worries never happen,
- 30% of our worries concern the past,

- 12% of our worries are needless about health,
- 10% of our worries are insignificant and petty, and
- 8% of our worries are legitimate, appropriate worries.

Even Jesus said in Matthew 6 not to worry about tomorrow because tomorrow will have its own worries. Let the day's own worries be sufficient for the day. So there are some things to worry about but they are few. The rest is highly destructive and reveals a lack of trust in God.

What's the answer? One church sign read, "Why pray when you can worry and take tranquilizers?" Paul would disagree. He says, "Don't panic, pray. Be a person of prayer." "In everything by prayer and supplication with thanksgiving let your requests be made known to God" (v. 6b).

Second, *guard your thoughts.* "Finally, beloved, whatever is true, whatever is honorable, whatever is just, whatever is pure, whatever is pleasing, whatever is commendable, if there is any excellence and if there is anything worthy of praise, think about these things" (v. 8). Guard your thoughts.

We become what we think. Did you know that? Proverbs 23:7 says, "As a man thinks in his heart, so is he." I read one quote that put it well: "Sow a thought, reap an action. Sow an action, reap a habit. Sow a habit, reap a character. Sow a character, reap a destiny." We become what we think. Therefore, Paul puts out eight filters for us to determine whether or not this guard, this sentry, is in our minds and hearts. Is it true, honorable, just, pure, and so on? Because there is a lot of stuff out there that is not.

We pay $10 a month for cable. Basic cable. It's not much, as my kids keep reminding me. I would like to get ESPN. I would like to get Discovery. But I can't get those two without letting in a whole lot of garbage into my house that's not true, just, pure, pleasing, and so on. We argue about what movies to see because I don't want some images to be in my children's hearts and minds. I'm concerned at some sleepovers that it will be different elsewhere. When we download iTunes, we check out the lyrics.

This has always been an issue. Nothing has changed. Polluting the mind must have been an issue in Philippi. It certainly was for

Luther. He said, "You can't stop a bird from flying overhead but you can stop it from nesting in your hair."

The mind and heart will be filled with images and thoughts. Paul is saying if you want to stand firm and live with resolve before the crisis hits, then guard your thoughts. Ask yourself, "Is it true, pure, just, acceptable?"

Third, *guard your examples. Keep on doing the things that you have learned and received and heard and seen in me.* Is that arrogant? A little bit earlier, Paul said, "Join in imitating me. Let me be your example." Is that conceited? I don't think so. I think it is mentoring. Christian mentoring. We all need examples.

When I'm confronted with a tough theological question, I think, "WWLD" "What would Luther do?" He would stand firm on justification by faith alone. When I'm confronted with a tough pastoral issue, I think, "WWCD" what would Charlie do? (Charlie was my first senior pastor who taught me about the ministry.) When I'm trying to figure out how to handle a delicate issue with another person, I think "WWGD" what would Gretchen do? (She's my wife who is a whole lot nicer than I am!) Surround yourselves with the best examples.

Paul is a mature Christian. He is writing to baby Christians. He has seen a lot more, experienced a lot more. He can say, "Learn from me, follow me, listen to me," not with arrogance but with some wisdom gained over the years. We can do the same.

My most successful counseling sessions happen when I get out of the way. When I talk with someone in the middle of crisis who needs advice, I say, "I want you to talk to so and so." I give them the name of a person in the church who has gone through the same ordeal and lived to tell about it. They have learned for their experience and can say what Paul said, "learn from me, follow me, listen to me," not out of arrogance but out of experience.

Paul says, "Guard those examples. Surround yourselves with those examples. Learn from those examples." And then, let's be bold. Go one step further. Be that example — to others. Be that example. Because others are watching. It's been said that children learn what they live. Look up the poem "Children Learn What They Live" by Dorothy Law Nolte online.

Guard your relationship with God. Guard your thoughts. Guard your examples.

And then Paul makes a promise. If you do this, "the peace of God will guard your hearts and your minds." You deliberately, consciously, faithfully guard relationships, those thoughts and those examples and you will find that God's peace will place a sentry inside of you and guard your heart and mind when crisis hits.

When will that be? Unfortunately, none of us knows. There are times, however, in which my mind wanders and I think — how would I hold up if a September 11 attack hit my family? How would I hold up if a Hurricane Katrina hit my home? How would I hold up if that drunk driver took my wife? How would I hold up if it were my child in that hospital bed? I don't think any of us know for sure but this much is certain. There will come a day in which you will walk out of that simulator and into real life. That's not the time to figure it out. Paul's saying, "Now. Now is the time."

Guard your relationship with God. Guard those thoughts that enter in. Guard those examples so that when you leave this room, this simulator, and enter the real world, you can stand firm with a new resolve. Amen.

Lectionary Preaching After Pentecost

The following index will aid the user of this book in matching the correct Sunday with the appropriate text during Pentecost. All texts in this book are from the series for the Second Readings, Revised Common Lectionary. (Note that the ELCA division of Lutheranism is now following the Revised Common Lectionary.) The Lutheran designations indicate days comparable to Sundays on which Revised Common Lectionary Propers or Ordinary Time designations are used.

(Fixed dates do not pertain to Lutheran Lectionary)

Fixed Date Lectionaries *Revised Common (including ELCA)* *and Roman Catholic*	Lutheran Lectionary *Lutheran*
The Day Of Pentecost	The Day Of Pentecost
The Holy Trinity	The Holy Trinity
May 29-June 4 — Proper 4, Ordinary Time 9	Pentecost 2
June 5-11 — Proper 5, Ordinary Time 10	Pentecost 3
June 12-18 — Proper 6, Ordinary Time 11	Pentecost 4
June 19-25 — Proper 7, Ordinary Time 12	Pentecost 5
June 26-July 2 — Proper 8, Ordinary Time 13	Pentecost 6
July 3-9 — Proper 9, Ordinary Time 14	Pentecost 7
July 10-16 — Proper 10, Ordinary Time 15	Pentecost 8
July 17-23 — Proper 11, Ordinary Time 16	Pentecost 9
July 24-30 — Proper 12, Ordinary Time 17	Pentecost 10
July 31-Aug. 6 — Proper 13, Ordinary Time 18	Pentecost 11
Aug. 7-13 — Proper 14, Ordinary Time 19	Pentecost 12
Aug. 14-20 — Proper 15, Ordinary Time 20	Pentecost 13
Aug. 21-27 — Proper 16, Ordinary Time 21	Pentecost 14
Aug. 28-Sept. 3 — Proper 17, Ordinary Time 22	Pentecost 15
Sept. 4-10 — Proper 18, Ordinary Time 23	Pentecost 16
Sept. 11-17 — Proper 19, Ordinary Time 24	Pentecost 17
Sept. 18-24 — Proper 20, Ordinary Time 25	Pentecost 18

Sept. 25-Oct. 1 — Proper 21, Ordinary Time 26	Pentecost 19
Oct. 2-8 — Proper 22, Ordinary Time 27	Pentecost 20
Oct. 9-15 — Proper 23, Ordinary Time 28	Pentecost 21
Oct. 16-22 — Proper 24, Ordinary Time 29	Pentecost 22
Oct. 23-29 — Proper 25, Ordinary Time 30	Pentecost 23
Oct. 30-Nov. 5 — Proper 26, Ordinary Time 31	Pentecost 24
Nov. 6-12 — Proper 27, Ordinary Time 32	Pentecost 25
Nov. 13-19 — Proper 28, Ordinary Time 33	Pentecost 26
	Pentecost 27
Nov. 20-26 — Christ The King	Christ The King

Reformation Day (or last Sunday in October) is October 31 (Revised Common, Lutheran)

All Saints (or first Sunday in November) is November 1 (Revised Common, Lutheran, Roman Catholic)

US/Canadian Lectionary Comparison

The following index shows the correlation between the Sundays and special days of the church year as they are titled or labeled in the Revised Common Lectionary published by the Consultation On Common Texts and used in the United States (the reference used for this book) and the Sundays and special days of the church year as they are titled or labeled in the Revised Common Lectionary used in Canada.

Revised Common Lectionary	Canadian Revised Common Lectionary
Advent 1	Advent 1
Advent 2	Advent 2
Advent 3	Advent 3
Advent 4	Advent 4
Christmas Eve	Christmas Eve
The Nativity Of Our Lord/ Christmas Day	The Nativity Of Our Lord
Christmas 1	Christmas 1
January 1/New Year's Day	January 1/The Name Of Jesus
Christmas 2	Christmas 2
The Epiphany Of Our Lord	The Epiphany Of Our Lord
The Baptism Of Our Lord/ Epiphany 1	The Baptism Of Our Lord/ Proper 1
Epiphany 2/Ordinary Time 2	Epiphany 2/Proper 2
Epiphany 3/Ordinary Time 3	Epiphany 3/Proper 3
Epiphany 4/Ordinary Time 4	Epiphany 4/Proper 4
Epiphany 5/Ordinary Time 5	Epiphany 5/Proper 5
Epiphany 6/Ordinary Time 6	Epiphany 6/Proper 6
Epiphany 7/Ordinary Time 7	Epiphany 7/Proper 7
Epiphany 8/Ordinary Time 8	Epiphany 8/Proper 8
The Transfiguration Of Our Lord/ Last Sunday After Epiphany	The Transfiguration Of Our Lord/ Last Sunday After Epiphany
Ash Wednesday	Ash Wednesday
Lent 1	Lent 1
Lent 2	Lent 2
Lent 3	Lent 3
Lent 4	Lent 4
Lent 5	Lent 5
Passion/Palm Sunday	Passion/Palm Sunday
Maundy Thursday	Holy/Maundy Thursday
Good Friday	Good Friday

Easter Day	The Resurrection Of Our Lord
Easter 2	Easter 2
Easter 3	Easter 3
Easter 4	Easter 4
Easter 5	Easter 5
Easter 6	Easter 6
The Ascension Of Our Lord	The Ascension Of Our Lord
Easter 7	Easter 7
The Day Of Pentecost	The Day Of Pentecost
The Holy Trinity	The Holy Trinity
Proper 4/Pentecost 2/O T 9*	Proper 9
Proper 5/Pent 3/O T 10	Proper 10
Proper 6/Pent 4/O T 11	Proper 11
Proper 7/Pent 5/O T 12	Proper 12
Proper 8/Pent 6/O T 13	Proper 13
Proper 9/Pent 7/O T 14	Proper 14
Proper 10/Pent 8/O T 15	Proper 15
Proper 11/Pent 9/O T 16	Proper 16
Proper 12/Pent 10/O T 17	Proper 17
Proper 13/Pent 11/O T 18	Proper 18
Proper 14/Pent 12/O T 19	Proper 19
Proper 15/Pent 13/O T 20	Proper 20
Proper 16/Pent 14/O T 21	Proper 21
Proper 17/Pent 15/O T 22	Proper 22
Proper 18/Pent 16/O T 23	Proper 23
Proper 19/Pent 17/O T 24	Proper 24
Proper 20/Pent 18/O T 25	Proper 25
Proper 21/Pent 19/O T 26	Proper 26
Proper 22/Pent 20/O T 27	Proper 27
Proper 23/Pent 21/O T 28	Proper 28
Proper 24/Pent 22/O T 29	Proper 29
Proper 25/Pent 23/O T 30	Proper 30
Proper 26/Pent 24/O T 31	Proper 31
Proper 27/Pent 25/O T 32	Proper 32
Proper 28/Pent 26/O T 33	Proper 33
Christ The King (Proper 29/O T 34)	Proper 34/Christ The King/ Reign Of Christ
Reformation Day (October 31)	Reformation Day (October 31)
All Saints (November 1 or 1st Sunday in November)	All Saints' Day (November 1)
Thanksgiving Day (4th Thursday of November)	Thanksgiving Day (2nd Monday of October)

*O T = Ordinary Time

About The Authors

Richard Gribble, CSC is a Catholic priest and associate professor of religious studies at Stonehill College in North Easton, Massachusetts. He is the author of 25 books, including a three-volume series on *The Parables of Jesus* (CSS), as well as more than 250 articles and reviews, and he has been the recipient of three Catholic Press Association of America awards. A member of the Congregation of Holy Cross, Father Gribble holds a Ph.D. from The Catholic University of America, and he is also a graduate of the United States Naval Academy, the University of Southern California, and the Jesuit School of Theology at Berkeley.

Steven E. Albertin is the pastor of Christ Lutheran Church of Zionsville, Indiana. He previously served parishes in Indianapolis and Fort Wayne, Indiana. Albertin is the author of *Against the Grain — Words for a Politically Incorrect Church*, and a co-author of *Sermons on the First Readings* (Series I, Cycle C) and *Sermons on the Second Readings* (Series II, Cycle A). He has received degrees from Concordia College (B.A.), Concordia Seminary in Exile, St. Louis (M.Div.), Christ Seminary — Seminex (S.T.M.), and the Lutheran School of Theology at Chicago (D.Min.).

April Yamasaki is the lead pastor of Emmanuel Mennonite Church in Abbotsford, British Columbia. She is a regular contributor to the devotional magazine *Rejoice!* a former columnist for *Canadian Mennonite*, and has written extensively for other publications. Yamasaki is the author of *Where Two Are Gathered*; *Remember Lot's Wife And Other Unnamed Women of the Bible*; *Living The Vision: Leadership and Community*; and *Making Disciples:*

Preparing People for Baptism, Christian Living, and Church Membership. She is a graduate of the University of British Columbia (B.A) and Regent College (M.C.S.).

Charles L. Aaron Jr. is the pastor of First United Methodist Church in Farmersville, Texas. In addition to serving in the parish ministry, Aaron has also taught at Perkins School of Theology, Austin Presbyterian Theological Seminary, and Duke University Divinity School. Aaron is a prolific writer whose articles, sermons, and book reviews have appeared in many publications, including *Lectionary Homiletics*, *Preaching Great Texts*, *Catholic Biblical Quarterly*, and *Preaching Word and Witness*. He is the author of *Preaching Hosea, Amos, and Micah* (Chalice Press) and *Your Faith Has Made You Well* (CSS), and a contributing author to *Sermons on the First Readings* (Series I, Cycle A) and *Sermons on the Gospel Readings* (Series II, Cycle A). Aaron is a graduate of Lambuth College (B.A.), Memphis State University (M.S.), Perkins School of Theology at Southern Methodist University (M.Div.), and Union Theological Seminary in Virginia (Ph.D. in Old Testament).

Scott Suskovic is the senior pastor of Christ Lutheran Church in Charlotte, North Carolina, a thriving congregation with an average worship attendance of more than 1,100 in both contemporary and traditional settings. He previously served churches in Florida and Minnesota, and he has been a contributor to several editions of Augsburg Fortress's *Sundays and Seasons* series. Suskovic is a co-author of *Sermons on the First Readings* (Series III, Cycle B), and he is a former member of the writing team for the online preaching resource *The Immediate Word* (www.sermonsuite.com). He is a graduate of St. Olaf College (B.A.), Luther Seminary (M.Div.), and Boston University (D.Min.).

www.ingramcontent.com/pod-product-compliance
Lightning Source LLC
Chambersburg PA
CBHW050133240426
43673CB00043B/1651